What's Wrong With My Plant?

What's Wrong With My Plant? (And How Do I Fix It?)

A Visual Guide to Easy Diagnosis and Organic Remedies

David Deardorff
and
Kathryn Wadsworth

TIMBER PRESS
Portland · London

To Eleanor Summy Deardorff, in memoriam
  and
To Ruth Olvey Murphy

We dedicate this book with great love to our mothers,
two wonderful women who taught us to plant seeds,
inspired us to celebrate nature,
encouraged us to explore the wild,
and urged us to follow our dreams.

Published in 2009 by Timber Press, Inc.

The Haseltine Building
133 S.W. Second Avenue, Suite 450
Portland, Oregon 97204-3527
www. timberpress.com

2 The Quadrant
135 Salusbury Road
London NW6 6RJ
www. timberpress. co. uk

Printed in China
Text designed by Susan Applegate
Illustrations produced by Marjorie C. Leggitt

ISBN-13: 978-0-88192-961-4
ISBN-13: 978-1-60469-098-9

Catalog records for this book are available from the Library of Congress
and the British Library.

Contents

Acknowledgments 6
Introduction 7

Part 1. What's Wrong?
Easy Diagnosis: The Flow Charts 9

Chapter 1. The Whole Plant 11
Chapter 2. Leaves and Leafy Vegetables 25
Chapter 3. Flowers, Flower Buds, and
Edible Flowers 61
Chapter 4. Fruits and Vegetables 93
Chapter 5. Stems, Trunks, and Branches
126
Chapter 6. Roots, Bulbs, and Root
Vegetables 159
Chapter 7. Seeds and Seedlings 192

Part 2. How Do I Fix It?
Natural Solutions and Organic Remedies 207

Chapter 8. Growing Conditions 212
Chapter 9. Fungi 241
Chapter 10. Insects 259
Chapter 11. Mites 286
Chapter 12. Bacteria 298
Chapter 13. Viruses 307
Chapter 14. Nematodes 313
Chapter 15. Other Pests 321

Part 3. What Does It Look Like?
A Photo Gallery of Common Problems 333

Problems on Whole Plants 334
Problems on Leaves and Leafy Vegetables
338
Problems on Flowers, Flower Buds, and
Edible Flowers 360
Problems on Fruits and Vegetables 376
Problems on Stems, Trunks, and Branches
389
Problems on Roots, Bulbs, and Root
Vegetables 404
Problems on Seeds and Seedlings 412

Appendix. What's Wrong With My Lawn? 417
Resources 423
Glossary 427
References 434
Index 435

Acknowledgments

We owe a debt of gratitude to many people for helping us bring this book to fruition. The debt is so great that all should really be at the top of the list. We are amazed by the dedication, diligence, and depth of our editor, Franni Farrell, and greatly appreciate all her help. We are indebted to Regina Ryan, whose professional guidance and patience lit up the path and showed us the way. To the greatest critique group on the planet, Kona Ink, whose members—Rebecca Cantrell, Judith Heath, and Karen Hollinger—went above and beyond the call of duty, time and again. Thanks to Elinor Gollay, Rex Brassell, Steve and Louise Carroll, and Meg Elaine Deardorff for providing us with a series of roofs above our heads while we worked. Thanks to Jeanne Huber for striking the match of inspiration in the first place. Many thanks to Mike and Michele Henery and the staff and customers at Henery's Garden Center for helping us refine the questions; and to the Master Gardeners of Washington state for helping us test the diagnostic flow charts. We also owe a great deal to all the loving friends and family members who watered the garden and gave us support every step of the way. We are especially grateful to Barbara Ansley-Vensas, Barbara Smith, Randy Deardorff, Shirley Otis, Michael and Teresa Forrest, and Dave and Anita Weakley. A special thanks to Jake and Annod Bickley for their weekly injection of perspective. Finally, we'd like to thank Tom Fischer, Neal Maillet, and everyone at Timber Press whose professionalism and expertise has made this journey joyful and worthwhile.

Introduction

Whether your garden consists of herbs on a kitchen window sill or a densely planted parking strip, a terraced half-acre in Maine or containers on a lanai in Hawaii, it contributes to the well-being of life on earth. Plants are the basic building material for the community of life. All the creatures in our gardens, backyards, balconies, or patios, including us, depend completely on plants because none of us can make energy, we can only consume it.

Those of us who love plants may eventually develop close relationships with them. They have subtle and intriguing ways to communicate with us. Healthy green leaves let us know that the plant is growing well, manufacturing food from the sun's energy. Yellowing leaves with dark lesions tell us the plant is in trouble. Flowers that are ragged and full of holes let us know something is eating them. All these symptoms, things you can easily observe with your own eyes without a microscope, are the ways in which a plant communicates its health, happiness, or distress.

"What's wrong with my plant?" is the question we hear most from plant owners in distress. This book will help you answer that question, as well as the second most frequently asked question, "How do I fix my plant—without using toxic chemicals?" *What's Wrong With My Plant?* provides a unique step-by-step method to diagnose and treat diseases, disorders, and pests of the plants entrusted to your care. Be your own plant doctor. No Ph.D. required.

In Part 1, organized by plant part, we present easy-to-follow, illustrated flow charts that lead to a diagnosis, the specific cause of the symptoms you are seeing. We developed the flow charts from years of working with distraught gardeners and plant owners who brought us samples of their problem plants. We found ourselves asking the same questions repeatedly—how much sun is the plant getting each day? how often do you water? have you seen pests? With David's background in plant pathology and botany, we soon realized we could arrange these questions in dichotomous pairs. In the flow charts, we present these questions, step by step, to filter all the many possibilities down to only one, the diagnosis (sooty mold, for example).

In Part 2, organized by general type of cause (fungi, in Chapter 9, to continue the example), we recommend safe, organic solutions and discuss both the destructive and benign aspects of the culprit. Sample photographs of common problems appear in Part 3.

Using the diagnostic flow charts, you can find out what ails sick plants by observing symptoms. No need to collect bugs or get lost in reference books trying to identify plant species or pathogens. All you need to do is look at the roots, stems, or leaves, note the symptom, and follow the illustrated flow charts to a solution.

To use this book successfully

Above all, do no harm. Before leaping to the conclusion that your plant is dying and then reaching for a toxic chemical to treat it, examine the plant. Whether it is potted up on the sill above your kitchen sink, in a container on the deck, or out in the garden, decide which part of your plant shows symptoms. Then turn to the flow charts in Part 1 for the plant part that exhibits symptoms. Follow the flow charts to identify the problem. Answer the questions. Whenever the answer is yes, follow that arrow or turn to the page listed under the question. When you encounter a diagnosis, turn to the page(s) indicated, for solutions in Part 2 and photographs in Part 3.

PART 1

What's Wrong?

Easy Diagnosis: The Flow Charts

Why use a diagnostic system?

Most resources on plant problems are difficult to use. Almost all require you to know the name of your plant before you can proceed. But what if you inherited the garden or received the plant as a gift, and you have no handy map or label? In some resources you can page through photographs hoping to find a picture that matches the problem you see. But, what if you can't find a match? What do you do now?

This book is different. It presents a diagnostic system with easy-to-use flow charts. The diagnostic flow charts consist of a series of simple questions, presented in pairs. Each pair is illustrated. Each question can be answered "yes" or "no." By observing symptoms on your plant and answering the questions, you can follow the flow charts to a diagnosis. The diagnosis gives you the cause of the problem.

How do I use the flow charts?

1. Whether your plant is indoors or outside, be sure to examine it carefully. If you find more than one symptom, even if you are beset with problems, concentrate on one. It is important to pursue just one symptom at a time. Turn to the table of contents to decide whether it is the whole plant or a specific plant part that exhibits a symptom.

2. Turn to the chapter about the plant part with the symptom. Look at each illustration and read the text beside it. Find the plant symptom that most closely matches yours and decide in which category of the flow charts your plant belongs.

3. Turn to the page indicated for that category of the flow charts—your tool for pinpointing the problem. WARNING: It is sometimes tempting to try to match your plant to an illustration without reading the accompanying text. However, it is important to consider the questions. Simply visually matching your plant to a drawing may lead to the wrong diagnosis.

4. Each flow chart poses a series of paired questions (couplets) about a symptom. Answer the questions yes or no. Only one member of each pair of questions can be answered yes.

5. When the answer is yes, follow that arrow or turn to the page listed under the question. Continue answering the questions and following the "yes" arrows through the chart.

6. For the most part, the questions on the left-hand side of the flow charts indicate several symptoms; therefore, they are often not illustrated.

7. When you reach a diagnosis, in red, turn to the page indicated for a solution. If there is a reference to a photo, turn to that page to see a plant with a similar problem.

1 The Whole Plant

What is a plant?

A plant is one of the evolutionary miracles that fuels life in our biosphere. A plant is a living organism that breathes in carbon dioxide and exhales oxygen. It absorbs water and minerals through its roots and makes food in its leaves using the magic of photosynthesis. Most plants are green because they contain a green pigment, chlorophyll, that harvests and converts solar energy, which the plant then stores as food. Like ours, a plant's body is made up of many cells organized into tissues and organs.

Plant organs—leaves, flowers, fruit, stems, roots, and seeds—are each the subject of a chapter in Part 1 of this book.

Plants vary tremendously and their evolutionary path is complex. They began as simple plants, like algae, with few types of organ systems. Without the ability to make seeds, these simple plants reproduce, instead, by means of spores.

The production of seeds moved plants to the next important rung on the evolutionary ladder. Two kinds of seed-producing plants, non-flowering and flowering, thrive on our green planet. Both are quite complex and highly organized.

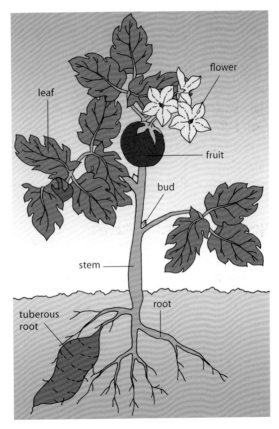

Compared to the major organ systems of an animal's body, those of a plant seem deceptively simple. Yet plant organs, too, actively engage in complex physiological functions.

The non-flowering plants—pine (*Pinus*), spruce (*Picea*), juniper (*Juniperus*), cedar (*Cedrus*), and fir (*Abies*), for example—produce seeds inside a cone (hence, conifer).

The other group, the flowering plants, are the most complex of all. The evolution of flowers as a reproductive organ gave plants the ability to expand into new ecosystems. This group includes lilies (*Lilium*), roses, oaks (*Quercus*), maples (*Acer*), orchids, palms, grasses, apples (*Malus*), and all other plants that have flowers and produce seeds inside a fruit. Flowering plants are further subdivided into two groups—the dicotyledons, also known as dicots, and the monocotyledons, or monocots.

Because of their variability and adaptability, plants have successfully colonized most of the earth's surface, and even thrive under the sea. The food they make and the oxygen they breathe makes life as we know it possible.

What does a plant do?

A plant takes on many jobs. In addition to producing the air we breathe, it makes much of the food we eat and the building materials we use. It can also enrich and stabilize soil, modify the climate, and provide food and shelter for other animals.

Each of a plant's organ systems has specific functions which contribute to the success of the whole plant. A leaf manufactures food from sunlight, water, and carbon dioxide, and all other plant systems are completely dependent on this ability. The flower or cone is the reproductive system. A fruit is a mature ovary containing seeds and develops from the flower of a flowering plant. Stems support the aerial portion of the plant's body. They also transport water and mineral nutrients up from the roots to the leaves, and carry food in the form of sug-

The dicots, such as the maples (*Acer*) and oaks (*Quercus*) in this forest, diversified into more species than any other group of plants. Dicots include familiar garden favorites like roses, delphiniums, rhododendrons, apple (*Malus*) trees, and edibles like beans (*Phaseolus*), squash (*Cucurbita*), tomatoes (*Lycopersicon esculentum*), and cabbage (*Brassica oleracea*).

This elegant fern reproduces from spores, not seeds, marking it as a member of one of the earliest groups of plants to colonize terrestrial ecosystems.

ars and starches, from the leaves down to the roots. From the soil, the root system absorbs water and mineral nutrients and delivers them to the other parts of the plant. Roots also anchor the plant firmly in its environment. A seed is a compact package that contains a baby plant and enough nutrients for the youngster to live on until it is able to make its own food. Seeds are also dispersal mechanisms that allow the off-spring to ride the wind, or the gut of an animal, to a new location.

Plants conquered dry land a very long time ago. Today they thrive in every ecosystem from tropical rainforests, deserts, and grasslands to high mountaintops. In nature, plants associate in natural plant communities according to the dictates of ecosystem requirements. In our gardens they thrive in constructed communities, connecting us to the community of life that surrounds and sustains us all.

What are plant symptoms?

You will find problems involving the entire plant striking and distressing. Symptoms are frequently dramatic. Follow these steps to find a diagnosis and a safe, appropriate solution.

1. Be sure to look at all sides of the plant. If you find more than one symptom, even if you are beset with problems, concentrate on one. It is important to pursue just one symptom at a time.
2. Look at each illustration on page 15 and read the text beside it. Find the plant symptom that most closely matches yours and decide in which category of the flow charts your plant belongs.
3. Turn to the page indicated for that category of the flow charts—your tool for pinpointing the problem.

This cone of *Pinus sylvestris* (Scots pine), a conifer, bears two winged seeds at the base of each woody scale. When mature, the cone scales open, and the seeds fly away on the wind.

The evolution of the flower provided significant advantages for plants. This lily, *Lilium columbianum*, represents the monocots, a large group that includes grasses, orchids, palms, and many ornamental bulbs.

Deserts are one of the newest eco-systems on earth. This harsh environment with limited water favors plants that evolve water conserving adaptations. This agave's leaves store water.

WARNING: It is sometimes tempting to try to match your plant to an illustration without reading the accompanying text. However, it is important to consider the questions. Simply visually matching your plant to a drawing may lead to the wrong diagnosis.

4. Each flow chart poses a series of paired questions (couplets) about a symptom. Answer the questions yes or no. Only one member of each pair of questions can be answered yes.

5. When the answer is yes, follow that arrow or turn to the page listed under the question. Continue answering the questions and following the "yes" arrows through the chart.

6. For the most part, the questions on the left-hand side of the flow charts indicate several symptoms; therefore, they are often not illustrated.

7. When you reach a diagnosis, in red, turn to the page indicated for a solution. If there is a reference to a photo, turn to that page to see a plant with a similar problem.

Categories of plant symptoms

The whole plant is wilted. Go to page 16.

The whole plant is not wilted, but some or all of the leaves are discolored. Go to page 21.

The whole plant is wilted

For other categories of plant symptoms, see page 15

Are some or all of the leaves discolored yellow, red, brown, or black?

OR Are the leaves normal in color? If yes, go to page 20.

YES

↓

Is the wilted plant stunted, that is, smaller than normal?

OR Is the wilted plant normal in size? If yes, go to page 17.

YES

↓

Do the roots have peculiar knobs or swellings on them? (Note: Do not confuse these with normal nitrogen-fixing nodules on legumes.) If yes, **root-knot nematodes**. For solution, see page 315.

OR Are peculiar swellings on the roots absent, but are branches dying one at a time? If yes, **bacteria**. For solution, see page 301; for photo, see page 335.

The whole plant is wilted

For other categories of plant symptoms, see page 15

The wilted plant is normal in size (from page 16)

Is the soil moist or is the temperature normal with calm winds?

YES

↓

OR Has the soil dried out or is it especially hot and windy? If yes, **drought**. For solution, see page 231; for photo, see page 334.

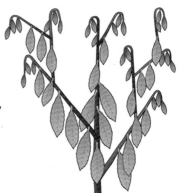

Is the plant well established in its current location?

YES

↓

OR Has the plant been recently transplanted? If yes, **transplant shock** For solution, see page 231; for photo, see page 334.

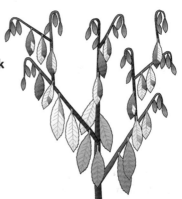

Has the plant not received fertilizer, and has no run-off from salt or deicing reached the plant? If yes, go to page 18.

OR Has the plant recently received fertilizer, or could run-off from salt or deicing reach the plant? If yes, **salt damage**. For solution, see page 238; for photo, see page 335.

The whole plant is wilted

For other categories of plant symptoms, see page 15

The plant has not received fertilizer recently, and run-off from salt or deicing is not reaching the plant (from page 17)

Has the root zone been disturbed or compacted? If yes, **mechanical damage**. For solution, see page 225; for photo, see page 334.

OR   Has there been no disturbance or compaction in the root zone?
YES
↓

If you cut into the stem, are no dark streaks visible in the wood?
YES
↓

OR   If you cut into the stem, are dark streaks visible in the wood? If yes, **fusarium**, **verticillium**. For solution, see page 252; for photo, see page 335.

Are fuzzy gray-brown patches absent? If yes, go to page 19.

OR   Are there fuzzy gray-brown patches on dead tissue (either stems or leaves)? If yes, **botrytis** aka **gray mold**. For solution, see page 252; for photo, see page 335.

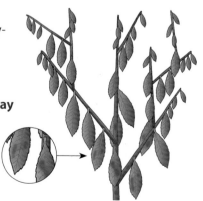

The whole plant is wilted

For other categories of plant symptoms, see page 15

Fuzzy gray-brown patches are absent (from page 18)

Are fluffy patches absent? (Note: White patches may be present, but they are not fluffy and there are no small, hard, black nodules.)

YES

OR

Are there fluffy, white patches with small, hard, black nodules developing on or inside the stem? If yes, **white mold**. For solution, see page 252.

If yes, **armillaria root rot**. For solution, see page 252; for illustration see both drawings below.

Clusters of honey-colored mushrooms grow around the base of the plant and if you cut the stem, white patches are present.

If you cut the stem, white patches are present, but clusters of honey-colored mushrooms around the base of the plant are absent.

The whole plant is wilted

For other categories of plant symptoms, see page 15

The leaves are normal in color (from page 16)

Is the plant growing in the ground, OR Is the plant growing in
not in a container?   a container? If yes,
  YES   **rootbound**. For solution,
  ↓   see page 227; for photo,
                                        see page 334.

Are no holes in the stem?   OR Are there holes in the
  YES   stem? If yes, **borers**.
  ↓   For solution, see page
                                     282; for photo,
                                     see page 335.

If you dig up the plant, do you find fat, white   OR   If you dig up the plant, are roots missing or
grubs eating the roots? If yes, **root weevil**   has bark at the stem base been chewed
larvae, Japanese beetle larvae. For solution,   away? If yes, **gophers, rabbits, other**
see page 284.   **mammals**. For solution, see page 329.

The whole plant is not wilted, but some or all of the leaves are discolored

For other categories of plant symptoms, see page 15

Has the plant experienced normal winter temperatures?

 YES

 ↓

OR Has the plant been subjected to severe winter cold? If yes, **freeze damage**. For solution, see page 232; for photo, see page 336.

Has the plant received the normal amount of water?

 YES

 ↓

OR Have the roots remained soaking wet? If yes, **overwatering**. For solution, see page 232; for photo, see page 336.

Is the plant mature, not a seedling? If yes, go to page 22.

OR Is the plant a seedling that has fallen over on its side? If yes, **damping off**. For solution, see page 252.

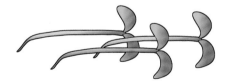

The whole plant is not wilted, but some or all of the leaves are discolored

For other categories of plant symptoms, see page 15

The plant is mature, not a seedling (from page 21)

Is the plant still in its normal position?

YES

↓

OR Has the plant fallen over on its side? If yes, **blow down**. For solution, see page 225; for photo, see page 336.

Are branches with discolored leaves free of small holes?

YES

↓

OR Are there small holes in branches with discolored leaves? If yes, **borers**, **bark beetles**. For solution, see page 282; for photo, see page 337.

Is the stem or trunk free of large galls at its base? If yes, go to page 23.

OR Is there a large gall at the base of the stem near the soil line? If yes, **crown gall**. For solution, see page 305; for photo, see page 337.

The whole plant is not wilted, but some or all of the leaves are discolored

For other categories of plant symptoms, see page 15

The stem or trunk is free of large galls at the base (from page 22)

Are the leaves normal in size and shape?

    YES

    ↓

OR Are the leaves distorted in size and shape? If yes, **herbicide damage**. For solution, see page 226; for photo, see page 336.

Are the leaves free of odd yellow markings, such as mottling, rings, or zigzags?

    YES

    ↓

OR Do the leaves have odd yellow markings, such as mottling, rings, or zigzags? If yes, **virus**. For solution, see page 309; for photo, see page 337.

Is the stem or trunk free of wire or rope wrapped tightly around it? If yes, go to page 24.

OR Does the stem or trunk have wire or rope wrapped tightly around it? If yes, **girdling**. For solution, see page 225.

The whole plant is not wilted, but some or all of the leaves are discolored

For other categories of plant symptoms, see page 15

The stem or trunk is free of wire or rope wrapped tightly around it (from page 23)

Are the young leaves at the tips of the branches normal in color, while the older leaves at the base of the branches are turning yellow? If yes, **nitrogen or magnesium deficiency**. For solution, see page 238; for photo, see page 337.

OR   Are the young leaves at the tips of branches turning yellow, while the older leaves at the base of the branches remain normal in color? If yes, **iron or manganese deficiency**. For solution, see page 238; for photo, see page 336.

2 Leaves and Leafy Vegetables

What is a leaf?

A leaf is one of the plant's organs. It is usually defined as that green appendage, borne on a stem, that presents itself to the sun and air.

The basic structure includes a petiole, the stalk that attaches the leaf to the stem; a midrib and veins that carry nutrients and water to the leaf cells, and food to the stem; and interveinal areas, where cells carry out photosynthesis.

Leaves seem simple, deceptively so, for they are elegantly complex. They come in a stupefying array of sizes, shapes, and colors. In fact, they are so varied, it is sometimes difficult to tell exactly which part of the plant is its leaf.

Commonly encountered leaves like those on houseplants such as African violets, philodendrons, or orchids, or those in the garden, like roses, maples, and tomatoes, are familiar and easily recognizable.

Plants also adapt to specific circumstances, and leaves evolve to meet new challenges, so other leaves are less recognizable. Many people are surprised to learn that each needle of a pine, spruce, heath, and heather is a leaf. So small it hardly seems like a leaf, each tiny scale of a juniper, cypress, and arborvitae is in fact a leaf.

Likewise, each prickly spine of a cactus is a leaf, highly modified to prevent losing too much moisture to dry desert air. The white "petals" of a dogwood flower are actually bracts, a type of leaf that has altered over time in order to attract pollinators to the insignificant true flowers.

Blades of grass and grass-like plants are simple leaves, long and narrow, that grow from the base of the plant, and so are not attached by a

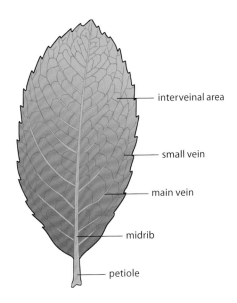

interveinal area

small vein

main vein

midrib

petiole

petiole to the stem. Fronds of ferns or palms are compound leaves, where the leaf is divided into numerous leaflets.

In any of its many forms, a leaf performs the magic of the plant kingdom. Like spinning straw into gold, it turns water, air, and light into food.

What does a leaf do?

The primary function of a leaf is photosynthesis, harvesting the energy of the sun and converting it to chemical energy. The plant uses the energy created by the leaf for growth and reproduction, storing the excess as sugar or starch.

Carbon dioxide gas (CO_2) enters the leaf from the air through the stoma in the lower epidermis. The energy of the sun breaks water (H_2O) down into hydrogen and oxygen. The carbon dioxide and hydrogen combine to make sugar, and the oxygen (O_2) is released into the air through the stoma.

Sugar is the food plants make for their own use, but leaves themselves are food for many animals, including us. Leaves we eat, such as let-

Pothos (*Epipremnum pinnatum* 'Aureum'), widely grown as a houseplant, is a straightforward example of a simple leaf.

Vine maple (*Acer circinatum*), another simple leaf, is palmately lobed, meaning it has a shape similar to the palm of a human hand.

The many simple leaves of annual bluegrass (*Poa annua*) grow directly from the base.

Each needle of a noble fir (*Abies procera*) is a leaf.

The white bracts of Pacific dogwood (*Cornus nuttallii*) are modified leaves.

Three leaflets of evergreen clematis (*Clematis armandii*) comprise a single compound leaf.

tuce, spinach, and cabbage, are full of vitamins and minerals to keep us healthy. We also use leaves for flavorings and spices, such as parsley, sage, rosemary, and thyme. Even the animals many of us eat depend on the leaves of alfalfa, grasses, and clover.

Leaves also clean the air of the carbon dioxide gas (exhaled from our bodies and emitted by factories and automobiles) while making oxygen for us to breathe. Because they actively absorb carbon dioxide, one of the major components of greenhouse gasses, plants are valuable partners in our efforts to curtail global warming. Planting trees can be a tremendous help to reduce the atmospheric carbon dioxide load of our blue planet.

What are leaf symptoms?

Symptoms on leaves are conspicuous. Often leaf problems are the first signal you have that something is wrong with your plant. Follow these steps to diagnose the problem, and find the right solution.

1. Examine the leaf carefully. Turn it over and look at both sides. If you find more than one symptom, pursue only one at a time. Even if you are beset with problems, it is important to select just one symptom.
2. Look at each illustration on page 29 and read the text beside it. Find the leaf

Each twig of western red cedar (*Thuja plicata*) has minute scale-like leaves.

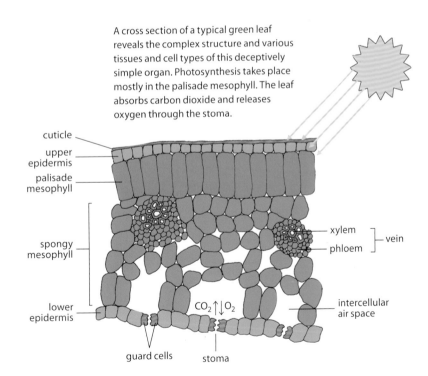

A cross section of a typical green leaf reveals the complex structure and various tissues and cell types of this deceptively simple organ. Photosynthesis takes place mostly in the palisade mesophyll. The leaf absorbs carbon dioxide and releases oxygen through the stoma.

cuticle
upper epidermis
palisade mesophyll
spongy mesophyll
lower epidermis
guard cells
stoma
$CO_2 \uparrow \downarrow O_2$
xylem
phloem
vein
intercellular air space

symptom that most closely matches yours and decide in which category of the flow charts your leaf belongs.

3. Turn to the page indicated for that category of the flow chart—your tool for pinpointing the problem.

   WARNING: It is sometimes tempting to try to match your leaf to an illustration without reading the accompanying text. However, it is important to consider the questions. Simply visually matching your leaf to a drawing may lead to the wrong diagnosis.

4. Each flow chart poses a series of paired questions (couplets) about a symptom. Answer the questions yes or no. Only one member of each pair of questions can be answered yes.

5. When the answer is yes, follow that arrow or turn to the page listed under the question. Continue answering the questions and following the "yes" arrows through the chart.

6. For the most part, the questions on the left-hand side of the flow charts indicate several possible symptoms; therefore, they are often not illustrated.

7. When you reach the diagnosis, in red, turn to the page indicated for a solution. If there is a reference to a photo, turn to that page to see a leaf with a similar problem.

   NOTE: In the following flow charts, the drawing of the leaf with the petiole on the right illustrates the upper surface of the leaf. When the petiole is on the left, the drawing shows the underside of the leaf.

petiole

Upper surface.

petiole

Underside.

Categories of leaf symptoms

The whole leaf is discolored. Go to page 30.

The leaf has discrete, rounded spots or speckles of any size. Go to page 34.

The leaf has very large, irregular spots or blotches. Go to page 40.

The leaf has stripes or diffuse mottling. Go to page 42.

The leaf is wilted, limp, and droopy. Go to page 44.

The leaf has holes or chewed edges, or you see pests. Go to page 47.

The leaf has raised bumps, warts, or weird growths. Go to page 55.

The leaf is distorted—that is, bubbled, cupped, curled, puckered, bulged, stunted, or twisted. Go to page 58.

The whole leaf is discolored

For other categories of leaf symptoms, see page 29

Is the leaf turning yellow, brown, or white, but not black?

YES

OR Is the entire leaf turning black?

YES

Can you rub off the black revealing green beneath? If yes, **sooty mold**. For solution, see page 254; for photo, see page 340.

OR Does the black discoloration not rub off? If yes, **sulfur phytotoxicity**. For solution, see page 233; for photo, see page 338.

Is the leaf turning yellow or brown, but not white?

YES

OR Is the entire leaf turning pale green to white? (Note: The leaf is often swollen.) If yes, **leaf gall**. For solution, see page 244; for photo, see page 340.

Are some of the leaves on all the branches yellow or brown? If yes, go to page 31.

OR Are all the leaves on some of the branches yellow or brown? If yes, go to page 33.

The whole leaf is discolored

For other categories of leaf symptoms, see page 29

Some of the leaves on all the branches are yellow or brown (from page 30)

Are some of the leaves turning brown?

YES

↓

OR   Are some of the leaves turning yellow? If yes, go to page 32.

Are the leaves at the base of the branches turning brown?

YES

↓

OR   Are the leaves at the tips of the branches turning brown? If yes, **leaf scorch**. For solution, see page 231; for photo, see page 338.

Is the soil under the plant always dry to very dry, even shortly after watering? And is excess fertilizer or salt not reaching the plant? If yes, **drought**. For solution, see page 231; for photo, see page 338.

OR   Is the soil not always dry? Is excess fertilizer or salt runoff reaching the plant? If yes, **salt burn**. For solution, see page 238; for photo, see page 338.

The whole leaf is discolored

For other categories of leaf symptoms, see page 29

Some of the leaves are turning yellow (from page 31)

Are the leaves at the base of the branches turning yellow?

YES

OR   Are the leaves at the tips of the branches turning yellow?

YES

Are the leaves at the tips of the branches completely yellow? If yes, **too much light**. For solution, see page 229; for photo, see page 339.

OR   Are the leaves at the tips of the branches yellow, but the main veins stay green? If yes, **iron or manganese deficiency**. For solution, see page 238; for photo, see page 339.

Are the leaves at the base of the branches completely yellow?

YES

OR   Are the leaves at the base of the branches yellow, but the main veins stay green? If yes, **nitrogen or magnesium deficiency**. For solution, see page 238; for photo, see page 339.

Is the soil soggy and always wet? If yes, **overwatering**. For solution, see page 232; for photo, see page 339.

OR   Is the soil not soggy? If yes, **old age**. For solution, see page 222; for photo, see page 340.

The whole leaf is discolored

For other categories of leaf symptoms, see page 29

All the leaves on some of the branches are yellow or brown (from page 30)

Are the affected branches all on one side of the plant?

YES

↓

OR   Are the affected branches randomly scattered through the canopy of the plant? If yes, **borers**. For solution, see page 282; for photo, see page 340.

Has the plant been subjected to extreme heat, or root zone disturbance, but not to severe cold?

YES

↓

OR   Has the plant been subjected to severe winter cold, usually combined with bright sunlight and high wind? If yes, **winter desiccation**. For solution, see page 232; for photo, see page 339.

Has the plant been subjected to extreme heat and high wind, but no construction or digging in the root zone? If yes, **scorch**. For solution, see page 231; for photo, see page 338.

OR   Has the plant been subjected to no heat and no wind, but there has been construction or digging in the root zone? If yes, **mechanical damage**. For solution, see page 225; for photo, see page 339.

The leaf has discrete, rounded spots or speckles of any size

For other categories of leaf symptoms, see page 29

Are the spots easy to see?
  YES

  ↓

OR   Are the spots difficult to see? Are they very tiny speckles, streaks, or stipples over the upper surface of the leaf? If yes, go to page 37.

Are the spots small to medium in size? (Note: Small to medium means less than half the distance between the midrib and the edge of the leaf.)
  YES

  ↓

OR   Are the spots very large? (Note: Very large means greater than half the distance between the midrib and the edge of the leaf.) If yes, go to page 40.

Are the spots raised up from the surface of the leaf, like bumps or blisters? If yes, go to page 38.

OR   Are the spots flat or sunken? If yes, go to page 35.

The leaf has discrete, rounded spots or speckles of any size

For other categories of leaf symptoms, see page 29

The spots are flat or sunken (from page 34)

Are the spots flat?
  YES

  ↓

OR Are the spots sunken with a lacy network of fibers? If yes, **skeletonizers**. For solution, see page 267, 282; for photo, see page 342.

Are the spots individual and discrete, and not formed of collections of tiny speckles? (Note: Tiny speckles may appear in these discrete spots.)
  YES

  ↓

OR Are the spots actually collections of tiny speckles? (Note: Larger spots do not surround the tiny speckles.) If yes, **leafhoppers**. For solution, see page 267; for photo, see page 343.

Are the spots opaque? Not translucent, like grease spots on paper? Are they rounded? Not angular because they are not confined by leaf veins?
  YES

  ↓

OR Are the spots at first translucent, like grease spots on paper, becoming angular because they are confined by the leaf veins? If yes, **bacterial leaf-spot**. For solution, see page 301; for photo, see page 343.

Do the spots never cross over veins and never have brown or black centers? If yes, **physiological leaf-spot**. For solution, see page 222; for photo, see page 341.

OR Do the spots cross over veins, and sometimes have brown or black centers? If yes, go to page 36.

The leaf has discrete, rounded spots or speckles of any size

For other categories of leaf symptoms, see page 29

The spots cross over veins and sometimes have brown or black centers; the spots can be white, yellow, orange, rust, brown, purple, or black (from page 35)

Are the spots any color but white?

YES

↓

OR Are the spots white? (Note: They are white, powdery areas on the surface of the leaf.) If yes, **powdery mildew**. For solution, see page 244; for photo, see page 341.

Are the spots any color but black with fringed edges?

YES

↓

OR Are the spots black with ragged, fringed edges? If yes, **black spot**. For solution, see page 244; for photo, see page 341.

Do the spots lack colorful powdery spores on the underside of the leaf? If yes, **leaf-spot**. For solution, see page 341.

OR Do the spots have colorful powdery spores on the underside of the leaf? If yes, **rust**. For solution, see page 244; for photo, see page 341.

The leaf has discrete, rounded spots or speckles of any size

For other categories of leaf symptoms, see page 29

The spots are difficult to see; they are very tiny speckles, streaks, or stipples over the upper surface of the leaf (from page 34)

Are the speckles or stipples separate and distinct and not aggregated into streaks?

YES

↓

OR   Are the speckles aggregated, that is, merged together into streaks? If yes, **thrips**. For solution, see page 267.

Are both fine webbing, like spider silk, and tiny bugs absent from the upper surface of the leaf?

YES

↓

OR   Is there fine webbing, like spider silk, on the leaves with tiny bugs rapidly crawling about? If yes, **spider mites**. For solution, see page 288; for photo, see page 343.

Are black specks present on the underside of the leaf? And are wedge-shaped bugs absent from the underside of the leaf? If yes, **lace bugs**. For solution, see page 267; for photo, see page 342.

OR   Are black specks absent from the underside of the leaf? And are wedge-shaped bugs present on the underside of the leaf? (Note: They often fly away immediately.) If yes, **leafhoppers**. For solution, see page 267; for photo, see page 343.

The leaf has discrete, rounded spots or speckles of any size

For other categories of leaf symptoms, see page 29

The spots are raised up from the surface of the leaf, like bumps or blisters

(from page 34)

Are the bumps neither shiny nor brown? They can be on either the upper surface or underside of the leaf.

YES

OR Are the bumps small, shiny, and brown, most of them appearing on the underside of the leaf? If yes, **scale**. For solution, see page 267; for photo, see page 342.

Are the bumps variously colored but not white?

YES

OR Are the bumps white and cottony, appearing on the underside of the leaf? If yes, **mealybugs**, **adelgids**, **cottony scale**. For solution, see page 267; for photo, see page 342.

Are the bumps on both sides of the leaf? And do the bumps lack colorful, powdery spores? If yes, go to page 39.

OR Are the bumps only on the underside of the leaf? And do the bumps have colorful, powdery spores? If yes, **rust**. For solution, see page 244; for photo, see page 341.

The leaf has discrete, rounded spots or speckles of any size

For other categories of leaf symptoms, see page 29

The bumps are on both sides of the leaf and lack colorful powdery spores

(from page 38)

Are there few bumps?

YES

↓

OR   Are there many bumps? If yes, **blister mites**. For solution, see page 295; for photo, see page 343.

Is the leaf without deformity, but with a concave bubble on the upper surface of the leaf and a yellow convex bubble on the underside? If yes, **fungus**. For solution, see page 244; for photo, see page 341.

The leaf has very large, irregular spots or blotches

For other categories of leaf symptoms, see page 29

The spots or blotches are very large (from page 34 or 29)

Are the blotches flat (not sunken) and without exposed veins?
    YES
    ↓

OR   Are the blotches sunken with exposed veins in the bottom of the depression? If yes, **skeletonizers**. For solution, see page 282; for photo, see page 345.

Are the blotches brown or black, and not silvery?
    YES
    ↓

OR   Are the blotches silvery trails? If yes, **leafminers**. For solution, see page 267, 282; for photo, see page 345.

If you pinch the blotch and rub your fingers together does the tissue stay put? It does not slide back and forth?
    YES
    ↓

OR   If you pinch the blotch and rub your fingers together does the tissue slide back and forth? If yes, **leafminers**. For solution, see page 267, 282; for photo, see page 345.

Are the blotches on the edge or tip of the leaf? If yes, go to page 41.

OR   Are the blotches in the middle of the leaf? If yes, **sunburn**. For solution, see page 344; for photo, see page 229.

The leaf has very large, irregular spots or blotches

For other categories of leaf symptoms, see page 29

The blotches are on the edge or the tip of the leaf (from page 40)

Do the blotches cross over main veins?

   YES

   ↓

OR Are the blotches initially confined by the main veins? If yes, **foliar nematodes**. For solution, see page 315; for photo, see page 345.

Are the blotches brown with black areas (dots or larger spots)? If yes, **leaf-spot**. For solution, see page 244; for photo, see page 344.

OR Are the blotches completely brown? If yes, **insufficient water**. For solution, see page 231; for photo, see page 344.

The illustrations below have brown blotches with black dots or spots, and each represents a leaf-spot fungus infection.

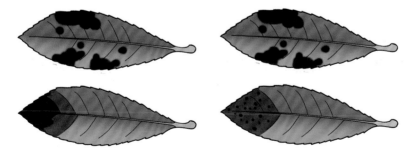

The leaf has stripes or diffuse mottling

For other categories of leaf symptoms, see page 29

Has the leaf remained normal in size and shape?

    YES

    ↓

OR Has the leaf changed size and/or shape in addition to having stripes or diffuse mottling? If yes, **herbicide damage**. For solution, see page 226; for photo, see page 346.

Does the leaf have no zigzag lines or circles of abnormal color?

    YES

    ↓

OR Does the leaf have zigzag lines or circles of abnormal color? If yes, **virus**. (Note: Virus symptoms are highly variable.) For solution, see page 309; for photo, see page 346.

Does the leaf have no brown, dead tissue around the edges and between the veins? If yes, go to page 43.

OR Does the leaf have brown, dead tissue around the edges and between the veins? If yes, **insufficient water**. For solution, see page 231; for photo, see page 346.

The leaf has stripes or diffuse mottling

For other categories of leaf symptoms, see page 29

The leaf has no brown, dead tissue around the edges and between the veins

(from page 42)

Does the leaf have no discolored spots on the underside?

YES

↓

OR Does the leaf have discolored spots on the underside? If yes, **fungus**. For solution, see page 244; for photo, see page 346.

Are the stripes or mottles on the leaves at the base of the branches? If yes, **nitrogen or magnesium deficiency**. For solution, see page 238; for photo, see page 346.

OR Are the stripes or mottles on the leaves at the tips of the branches? If yes, **iron or manganese deficiency**. For solution, see page 238; for photo, see page 346.

The leaf is wilted, limp, and droopy

For other categories of leaf symptoms, see page 29

Are some but not all of the leaves wilted?
   YES
     ↓

OR Are all the leaves on the plant wilted? If yes, go to page 16.

Are the wilted leaves mostly normal in color or do they have small areas of discoloration?
   YES
     ↓

OR Are the wilted leaves mostly brown, black, yellow, or gray? If yes, go to page 45.

Are the wilted leaves slightly discolored at their tips or edges?
   YES
     ↓

OR Are the wilted leaves normal in color? If yes, **insufficient water**. For solution, see page 231; for photo, see page 347.

Are the wilted leaves translucent at their tips? If yes, **insufficient water and tissue damage**. For solution, see page 231; for photo, see page 347.

OR Are the wilted leaves turning brown at their tips? If yes, **insufficient water and death of tissue**. For solution, see page 231; for photo, see page 347.

The leaf is wilted, limp, and droopy

For other categories of leaf symptoms, see page 29

The wilted leaves are mostly brown, black, yellow, or gray (from page 44)

Are the wilted leaves firm to the touch, and do they lack mold?

   YES

   ↓

OR

Are the wilted leaves soft and fuzzy to the touch and moldy? If yes, **brown rot**. For solution, see page 244; for photo, see page 349.

Are the wilted leaves crispy and crunchy? If yes, **fire blight**. For solution, see page 301, 306; for photo, see page 349.

OR

Are the leaves relatively normal in texture?

   YES

   ↓

Is there no gummy substance oozing from the bark near the wilted leaves? (Note: If gum and holes are present, see page 144.)

   YES

   ↓

OR

Is there a gummy substance oozing from the bark near the wilted leaves and are holes in the twig absent? If yes, **bacteria**. For solution, see page 301; for photo, see page 349.

Are there holes in the twig near the wilted leaves, along with little bits of sawdust? If yes, **borers**. For solution, see page 282; for photo, see page 348.

OR

Are there no holes in the twig near the wilted leaves? If yes, go to page 46.

The leaf is wilted, limp, and droopy

For other categories of leaf symptoms, see page 29

There are no holes in the twig near the wilted leaves (from page 45)

Is there no sunken discolored lesion on the twig?

   YES

   ↓

OR   Is there a sunken discolored lesion encircling the twig? If yes, **cankers**. For solution, see page 244; for photo, see page 348.

When you cut the twig with a knife, is the wood without dark streaks?

   YES

   ↓

OR   When you cut the twig with a knife, does the wood have dark streaks? If yes, **verticillium wilt**. For solution, see page 244, 252; for photo, see page 348.

Is the twig broken? If yes, **mechanical damage**. For solution, see page 225; for photo, see page 347.

OR   Is the twig intact, not broken?

   YES

   ↓

Are the leaves and twigs without gray-brown mold?

   YES

   ↓

OR   Does gray-brown mold grow on the leaves and twigs? If yes, **botrytis** aka **gray mold**. For solution, see page 244; for photo, see page 348.

Have the leaves and twigs at the tips of branches suddenly turned brown or black? If yes, **freeze damage**. For solution, see page 232; for photo, see page 347.

OR   Have the leaves at the base of branches in the interior of the plant turned brown? If yes, **flagging**. For solution, see page 222; for photo, see page 348.

The leaf has holes or chewed edges, or you see pests

For other categories of leaf symptoms, see page 29

Can you see no pests of any sort on the damaged leaf?

YES

↓

OR Can you see pests of some sort on the damaged leaf? If yes, go to page 48.

Are most of the holes in the middle of the leaf, with few on the edges?

YES

↓

OR Are the edges of the leaf chewed away, with few or no holes in the middle? If yes, go to page 51.

Do the holes have smooth edges, and does the leaf lack discolored spots? If yes, go to page 53.

OR Do the holes have ragged edges, and are discolored spots on the leaf? If yes, go to page 54.

The leaf has holes or chewed edges, or you see pests

For other categories of leaf symptoms, see page 29

You see pests of some sort on the damaged leaf (from page 47)

Do the pests look like worms, caterpillars, or slugs?

YES

OR   Do the pests look like insects? (Note: An insect has a jointed body, six legs, and a hard exoskeleton.) If yes, go to page 49.

Are the pests slimy and slug-like, but never hairy?

YES

OR   Are the pests worm-like, but not slimy? They might be hairy or smooth. If yes, **caterpillars**. For solution, see page 267; for photo, see page 352.

Are the pests large and wrinkled, with eyes on tentacles? If yes, **slugs or snails**. For solution, see page 325; for photo, see page 354.

OR   Are the pests small, without wrinkles or eyes on tentacles? If yes, **sawfly larvae**. For solution, see page 267; for photo, see page 350.

The leaf has holes or chewed edges, or you see pests

For other categories of leaf symptoms, see page 29

The pests look like insects (from page 48)

Do the pests have no long snout?

YES

↓

OR Do the pests have a long snout? If yes, **weevils**. For
solution, see page 267; for photo, see page 351.

Are the pests small to medium,
and do you see no very long hind
legs? (Note: The pests might have
long legs, but you cannot see the
legs because they are hidden
beneath the wings.)

YES

↓

OR Are the pests large, and do you see very long hind
legs? If yes, **grasshoppers**. For solution, see page 267;
for photo, see page 352.

Do the pests lack large pincers on
the rear?

YES

↓

OR Do the pests have large pincers on the rear? If yes,
earwigs. For solution, see page 267; for photo, see
page 351.

Are the pests usually on the
underside of the leaf? And do they
lack shiny, hard wing covers; in
other words, do they look like
something other than beetles? If
yes, go to page 50.

OR Are the pests usually on both surfaces of the leaf? And
do they have shiny, hard wing covers; in other words,
do they look like beetles? If yes, **beetles**. For solution,
see page 267; for photo, see page 353.

The leaf has holes or chewed edges, or you see pests

For other categories of leaf symptoms, see page 29

The pests are usually on the underside of the leaf, and they lack shiny, hard wing covers; in other words, they look like something other than beetles

(from page 49)

Are the pests any of several colors, except bright white?

YES

↓

OR Are the pests bright white and fly up when the plants are disturbed. If yes, **whiteflies**. (Note: White residue is often all you see.) For solution, see page 267; for photo, see page 351.

Are the pests some shape other than wedge-shaped?

YES

↓

OR Are the pests wedge-shaped? If yes, **leafhoppers**. For solution, see page 267; for photo, see page 350.

Do you see tiny, pear-shaped pests and ants? If yes, **aphids**. For solution, see page 267.

OR Do you see tiny, pear-shaped pests, but no ants? If yes, **aphids**. For solution, see page 267; for photo, see page 352.

The leaf has holes or chewed edges, or you see pests

For other categories of leaf symptoms, see page 29

The edges of the leaf are chewed away, with few or no holes in the middle

(from page 47)

Are the edges of the leaf chewed away?

YES

↓

OR Are large areas of the leaf, or is the whole leaf missing? If yes, **deer, other mammals.** For solution, see page 329; for photo, see page 354.

Are the holes in the leaf edges some shape other than circular?

YES

↓

OR Are the holes in the leaf edges circular? If yes, **leafcutter bees.** For solution, see page 267; for photo, see page 350.

Do the leaf edges have no narrow channels or notches, but holes of a different shape? If yes, go to page 52.

OR Do the leaf edges have narrow channels or notches chewed away? If yes, **weevils.** For solution, see page 267; for photo, see page 351.

The leaf has holes or chewed edges, or you see pests

For other categories of leaf symptoms, see page 29

The leaf edges have no narrow channels or notches, but holes of a different shape (from page 51)

Are there no triangular-shaped holes along the leaf edges?

YES

OR Are triangular-shaped holes along the leaf edges? If yes, **birds**. For solution, see page 328.

Are the leaf veins still present?

YES

OR Are the leaf veins eaten away? If yes, **caterpillars**, **grasshoppers**. For solution, see page 267; for photo, see page 352.

Are both the small veins and the main veins still present, leaving the leaves lace-like? If yes, **beetles**. For solution, see page 267; for photo, see page 353.

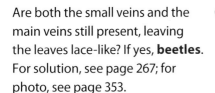

OR Are the small veins eaten away, leaving only the main veins? If yes, **beetles**. For solution, see page 267; for photo, see page 353.

The leaf has holes or chewed edges, or you see pests

For other categories of leaf symptoms, see page 29

The holes have smooth edges, and the leaf lacks discolored spots

(from page 47)

Are both older, tougher leaves and   OR   Are only new, tender leaves affected? If yes, **earwigs**.
new, tender leaves affected? For solution, see page 267; for photo, see page 351.

   YES

Are the holes small, and are there   OR   Are the holes large, and are slime trails on or near the
no slime trails on or near the leaf? leaf? If yes, **slugs or snails**. For solution, see page 325;

   YES for photo, see page 354.

Are the holes irregularly shaped?   OR   Are the holes round? If yes, **flea beetles**. For solution,
If yes, **caterpillars**. For solution, see page 267; for photo, see page 353.
see page 267; for photo, see
page 352.

The leaf has holes or chewed edges, or you see pests

For other categories of leaf symptoms, see page 29

The holes have ragged edges, and discolored spots are on the leaf

(from page 47)

Are there many small ragged holes?

YES

↓

OR Are there only a few large, ragged holes, sometimes accompanied by discolored patches on the same leaf? If yes, **fungus**. For solution, see page 244; for photo, see page 350.

In addition to the holes, are there flat, discolored spots that do not have a lace-like pattern?

YES

↓

OR Are there sunken, discolored spots with a lace-like pattern or uneaten veins in the bottom of the sunken patches? If yes, **skeletonizers**. For solution, see page 267, 282; for photo, see page 350.

Are some of the discolored spots angular in shape and confined by leaf veins? If yes, **bacteria**. For solution, see page 301; for photo, see page 353.

OR Are the discolored spots rounded, and do they cross over leaf veins? If yes, **leaf-spot**. For solution, see page 244; for photo, see page 350.

The leaf has raised bumps, warts, or weird growths

For other categories of leaf symptoms, see page 29

Are the growths easily removed by gently scraping with a fingernail?

YES

↓

OR Are the growths difficult or impossible to remove by scraping? If yes, go to page 56.

Are there white, cottony bumps on either side of the leaf?

YES

↓

OR Are small, shiny, brown bumps on the underside of the leaf? If yes, **scale**. For solution, see page 267; for photo, see page 355.

Are the white, cottony bumps on a plant that is not a conifer? If yes, **mealybugs**, **cottony scale**. For solution, see page 267; for photo, see page 355.

OR Are the white, cottony bumps on a conifer? If yes, **adelgids**. For solution, see page 267; for photo, see page 355.

The leaf has raised bumps, warts, or weird growths

For other categories of leaf symptoms, see page 29

The growths are difficult or impossible to remove by scraping (from page 55)

Are the growths neither lacy nor mossy?

YES

↓

OR   Are the growths lacy and/or mossy? If yes, **mossyrose gall**. For solution, see page 285; for photo, see page 356.

Are the growths smooth, not bristly?

YES

↓

OR   Are the growths bristly? If yes, **spiny rose gall**. For solution, see page 285; for photo, see page 356.

Has the leaf retained its normal shape?

YES

↓

OR   Has part of the leaf rolled up and become a bright red, swollen structure? If yes, **kinnikinnik leaf gall aphid**. For solution, see page 285; for photo, see page 356.

Are the growths soft to the touch and nipple-shaped? If yes, **bladder gall mites**. For solution, see page 295; for photo, see page 356.

OR   Are the growths firm to the touch and of any other shape and color? If yes, go to page 57.

The leaf has raised bumps, warts, or weird growths

For other categories of leaf symptoms, see page 29

The growths are firm to the touch and of any other shape and color

(from page 56)

Are the growths of any shape but round?

YES

↓

OR   Are the growths round, either small or large? If yes, **galls**. For solution, see page 285; for photo, see page 355.

Are the growths flattened, not pointy?

YES

↓

OR   Are the growths pointy? If yes, **galls**. For solution, see page 285.

Do the growths have no powdery spores on the underside of the leaf?

YES

↓

OR   Do the growths have colorful powdery spores on the underside of the leaf? If yes, **rust**. For solution, see page 244; for photo, see page 355.

Are the growths brown, corky tissue that is rough to the touch? If yes, **edema**. For solution, see page 232; for photo, see page 355.

OR   Are the growths smooth to the touch and of various shapes and colors? If yes, **blister mites**. For solution, see page 295; for photo, see page 356.

The leaf is distorted—that is, bubbled, cupped, curled, puckered, bulged, stunted, or twisted

For other categories of leaf symptoms, see page 29

Is the leaf nearly normal in size?
YES
↓

OR Is the leaf badly stunted, much smaller than normal, as well as distorted? If yes, go to page 60.

Are the leaf edges not cupped upward?
YES
↓

OR Are the leaf edges cupped upward? If yes, **psyllids**. For solution, see page 267; for photo, see page 358.

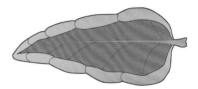

Is the leaf not pleated?
YES
↓

OR Is the leaf pleated, accordian-style? If yes, **lack of humidity**. For solution, see page 231; for photo, see page 357.

Is the leaf not rolled into a cylinder? If yes, go to page 59.

OR Is the leaf rolled into a cylinder and sewn together with silk? If yes, **leafrollers**. For solution, see page 267, 282; for photo, see page 359.

The leaf is distorted

For other categories of leaf symptoms, see page 29

The leaf is not rolled into a cylinder (from page 58)

Is the distorted leaf free of white mold?

YES

↓

OR Is the distorted leaf blotched with white mold? If yes, **powdery mildew**. For solution, see page 244; for photo, see page 357.

Is the distorted leaf not red and purple?

YES

↓

OR Is the distorted leaf red and purple? If yes, **peach leaf curl**. For solution, see page 244; for photo, see page 358.

Is the distorted leaf without dark spots?

YES

↓

OR Is the distorted leaf spotted with dark spots? If yes, **leaf-spot**. For solution, see page 244; for photo, see page 358.

Is the leaf puckered, with no insects present? If yes, **irregular watering**. For solution, see page 231; for photo, see page 357.

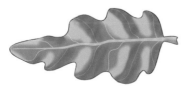

OR Is the leaf puckered and twisted and full of insects on the underside of the leaf? If yes, **aphids**. For solution, see page 267; for photo, see page 358.

The leaf is distorted

For other categories of leaf symptoms, see page 29

The leaf is badly stunted, much smaller than normal, as well as distorted

(from page 58)

Is the leaf not brownish-green to bronze, or purplish?

YES
↓

OR Is the leaf brownish-green to bronze or purplish? If yes, **mites**. For solution, see page 288; for photo, see page 359.

Are the leaf edges not curled down?

YES
↓

OR Are the leaf edges curled down? If yes, **midges**. For solution, see page 267.

Are the leaf edges not cupped upward? If yes, **virus**. (Note: Virus symptoms are highly variable.) For solution, see page 309; for photo, see page 359.

OR Are the leaf edges cupped upward? (Note: Leaves may also be long and narrow and/or discolored.) If yes, **herbicide damage**. For solution, see page 226; for photo, see page 357.

3 Flowers, Flower Buds, and Edible Flowers

What is a flower?

The flower is the joy, the poetry, and the song of the green world. To a botanist a flower is also the future. The flower is the reproductive organ of a seed-producing plant that flowers. This may sound obvious, but there are many plants that produce seeds, yet do not flower. Flowers contain either the female sexual organs (ovaries) or the male sexual organs (stamens) or both. Plant ovaries contain the seeds, which result from sexual reproduction.

Floral morphology, the study of flower form, describes the flower parts, including the sex parts, and is the primary way to identify a plant. Botanists use the reproductive structures of plants as the basis for plant classification systems.

Think of flowers. Do you conjure flamboyant petals enticing you with attractive scents? This is the reproductive strategy of many plants. Plants that do not flower have other reproductive strategies, but that's a whole different story. Flowers attract pollinators using color and fragrance. In doing so, plants entice animal assistants to act as sexual surrogates and move sperm to the egg. Even flowers that are not showy to the human eye are showy to their pollinators. If you were a tiny insect, a tiny flower could be far more attractive than a big one.

Other plants with flowers employ a different strategy. Ones that use wind for pollination produce naked flowers. These plants, including many trees, don't have to grow petals and sepals, thus saving energy for foliage, fruit, and seed growth.

Flowers vary tremendously, sometimes even disguising themselves as vegetables. An artichoke, for example, is an inflorescence of many very tiny flowers. The part of the broccoli (*Brassica*) that we eat is an inflorescence of flower buds.

While flowers beautify the world, their importance lies in the fact that the ovary becomes a fruit, providing food for wildlife and humans, and creating the next generation of plants.

What does a flower do?

A flower produces fruits and seeds, the potential for next year's plants, and often food for us. It also provides nutrition for pollinators in the form of sugar-rich nectar or protein-rich pollen. This cornucopia frequently invites wildlings into our lives. As they search for food, animals like birds, butterflies, bees, and beneficial insects venture from their niches in the natural ecosystem into the garden.

Pollination ecology, the study of the co-evolution of animals and plants, explains why flowers take on so many different forms. Hummingbirds, for example, are attracted to red, have long tongues that can reach deeply into the flower, and hover, so they don't need a landing platform. Thus, tubular red flowers lure hummingbirds to carry pollen on their foreheads and beaks from one flower to the next, pollinating them as they go. In exchange for this service, the birds get to feed on the rich nectar. A good deal all around.

Bees favor blue, yellow, or purple flowers, and appreciate structures like the nectar guides that many flowers provide. Pansies (*Viola*) and many orchids display lines of contrasting color that radiate from the throat of the flower. Bees and other pollinators use these as signposts to help them find nectar and pollen.

Brightly colored small flowers, aggregated into a head, attract butterflies who prefer to land and walk from flower to flower while feeding on nectar and transporting pollen.

Flowers deliver more than their biological functions. When we give them as gifts we use their beauty and variety to declare love, demonstrate friendship, and express compassion.

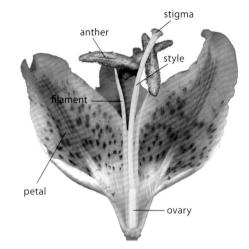

Cross-section of a lily flower. The female sex parts are the stigma, style, and ovary. The ovary produces seeds and becomes the ripe fruit. The male sex parts are stamens, consisting of an anther and a filament. Anthers produce pollen. The large and showy petals attract pollinators.

What are flower symptoms?

Flower problems are frequently as noticeable as leaf symptoms. Follow these steps to discover what ails your plant and find a solution.

1. Examine the flower carefully. If you find more than one symptom, even if you are beset with problems, concentrate on one. It is important to pursue just one symptom at a time.

2. Look at each illustration on page 65 and read the text beside it. Find the flower symptom that most closely matches yours and decide in which category of the flow charts your flower belongs.

3. Turn to the page indicated for that category of the flow charts—your tool for pinpointing the problem.
   WARNING: It is sometimes tempting to try to match your flower to an illustration without reading the

African violets (*Saintpaulia*) use their colorful flowers to attract the right pollinator.

Often powerfully fragrant, roses (*Rosa*) advertise their charms with both scent and color.

The tiny oblong nubbins at the base of the chokes on this artichoke (*Cynara*) are very small flowers.

Pansies (*Viola*) have guidelines to lead bees to nectar and pollen.

The yarrow (*Achillea*) cultivar 'Terracotta' guarantees many butterfly visits from the wild to your yard.

accompanying text. However, it is important to consider the questions. Simply visually matching your flower to a drawing may lead to the wrong diagnosis.

4. Each flow chart poses a series of paired questions (couplets) about a symptom. Answer the questions yes or no. Only one member of each pair of questions can be answered yes.

5. When the answer is yes, follow that arrow or turn to the page listed under the question. Continue answering the questions and following the "yes" arrows through the chart.

6. For the most part, the questions on the left-hand side of the flow charts indicate several symptoms; therefore, they are often not illustrated.

7. When you reach a diagnosis, in red, turn to the page indicated for a solution. If there is a reference to a photo, turn to that page to see a flower with a similar problem.

Categories of flower symptoms

NOTE: Symptoms in the flow charts that follow apply to both flowers and buds, unless otherwise specified.

The flower is discolored. Go to page 66.

The flower has holes or chewed edges, or you see pests. Go to page 72.

The flower is distorted or stunted. Go to page 77.

The flower is rotten, wilted, or decayed. Go to page 82.

The plant has flowered poorly, has failed to flower, or has dropped buds. Go to page 86.

The flower is discolored

For other categories of flower symptoms, see page 65

Is the flower not rotten, but has some other discoloration?

   YES

   ↓

OR   Is the flower rotten, wilted, and/or decayed? If yes, go to page 82.

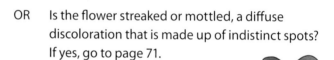

Is the flower spotted (rounded discolorations) or blotched (irregular discolorations)? If yes, go to page 67.

OR   Is the flower streaked or mottled, a diffuse discoloration that is made up of indistinct spots? If yes, go to page 71.

The flower is discolored

For other categories of flower symptoms, see page 65

The flower is spotted or blotched (from page 66)

Are the spots and/or blotches some color other than grayish-white?

YES

OR

Are the spots and/or blotches grayish-white?

YES

Are the grayish-white spots translucent and not powdery? If yes, **botrytis** aka **gray mold**. For solution, see page 244; for photo, see page 361.

OR

Are the grayish-white spots opaque and powdery? If yes, **powdery mildew**. For solution, see page 244; for photo, see page 361.

Are the spots and/or blotches brown, yellow, white, purple, or black? If yes, go to page 68.

OR

Are the spots and/or blotches a paler version of the normal flower color? If yes, **sunscald**. For solution, see page 229; for photo, see page 360.

The flower is discolored

For other categories of flower symptoms, see page 65

The spots and/or blotches are brown, yellow, white, purple, or black

(from page 67)

Are the spots and/or blotches some shade of brown, purple, or black?
   YES
   ↓

OR

Are the spots and/or blotches yellow or white? If yes, **virus**. For solution, see page 309.

Does the flower have small spots? (Note: Large blotches may also be present.)
   YES
   ↓

OR

Does the flower have large blotches, but no small spots? If yes, go to page 70.

Do the spots and/or blotches start small and grow larger?
   YES
   ↓

OR

Do the spots stay the same size? If yes, **herbicide or pesticide damage**. For solution, see page 226; for photo, see page 360.

Are the spots and/or blotches brown or black? If yes, go to page 69.

OR

Are the spots purple when small? (Note: The small purple spots may become large brown blotches.) If yes, **anthracnose**. For solution, see page 244; for photo, see page 361.

The flower is discolored

For other categories of flower symptoms, see page 65

The spots and/or blotches are brown or black (from page 68)

Do the spots and/or blotches become covered with grayish-brown mold during humid weather?

YES

↓

OR   Do the spots and/or blotches never get covered with grayish-brown mold? If yes, **camellia flower blight**. For solution, see page 244; for photo, see page 362.

Do the moldy flowers fall off the plant? If yes, **botrytis** aka **gray mold**. (Note: Botrytis does not occur on stonefruits [*Prunus*]— peach, nectarine, apricot, plum, cherry, and almond, for example.) For solution, see page 244; for photo, see page 361.

OR   Do the moldy flowers hang on to the plant? If yes, **brown rot**. (Note: Brown rot occurs mainly on stonefruits [*Prunus*] and infrequently on apples [*Malus*].) For solution, see page 244; for photo, see page 362.

The flower is discolored

For other categories of flower symptoms, see page 65

The flower has large blotches but no small spots (from page 68)

Does the plant appear as though it has received adequate water?

YES

↓

OR

Does the plant appear as though it has not received adequate water? (Note: As a result the flower cells have died and turned brown.) If yes, **insufficient water**. For solution, see page 231; for photo, see page 360.

Are the first flowers to open turning brown while the last flowers to open are still fresh? (Note: This refers to flowers only, not buds.) If yes, **old age**. For solution, see page 222; for photo, see page 361.

OR

Has the plant experienced a sudden cold snap or freezing weather? If yes, **frost damage**. For solution, see page 232; for photo, see page 361.

The flower is discolored

For other categories of flower symptoms, see page 65

The flower is streaked or mottled, a diffuse discoloration that is made up of indistinct spots (from page 66)

Are the streaks or mottles yellow, white, or brown, but not silvery-white?

YES

↓

OR Are the streaks or mottles silvery-white? If yes, **thrips**. For solution, see page 267; for photo, see page 362.

Are the streaks or mottles brown? If yes, **pesticide or herbicide damage**. For solution, see page 226; for photo, see page 360.

OR Are the streaks or mottles yellow or white? If yes, **virus**. For solution, see page 309.

The flower has holes or chewed edges, or you see pests

For other categories of flower symptoms, see page 65

Do you see no pests on or near the flower?

YES

OR Do you see pests on or near the flower? If yes, go to page 74.

Are slime trails absent from the damaged flower or plant? (Note: Rain may wash away slime trails, so check the flower and plant frequently.)

YES

OR Are slime trails on or nearby the damaged flower or plant? If yes, **slugs or snails**. For solution, see page 325; for photo, see page 366.

Are there holes on the edges of petals, or are petals almost completely eaten away? If yes, go to page 73.

OR Are there holes in the middle of soft tender petals and new leaves? If yes, **earwigs**. For solution, see page 267; for photo, see page 364.

The flower has holes or chewed edges, or you see pests

For other categories of flower symptoms, see page 65

There are holes on the edges of petals, or petals are almost completely eaten away (from page 72)

Can you find no pests hiding anywhere on the plant, even after a thorough examination?

   YES

OR   Can you find pests hiding somewhere on the plant? If yes, go to page 74.

Can you find no fat caterpillars hiding on or in the soil?

   YES

OR   Do you find fat caterpillars hiding on or in the soil? (Note: The caterpillars will be curled into a C-shape and usually hiding in the soil.) If yes, **climbing cutworms**. For solution, see page 267.

Do you see no small pellets of caterpillar poop scattered on the leaves? (Note: Sometimes leaves will also be gone or partially eaten.) If yes, **deer**. For solution, see page 329; for photo, see page 366.

OR   Do you see small green or black pellets of caterpillar poop scattered on the leaves? (Note: Leaves usually have holes as well. Sometimes you will find green caterpillars that move by looping themselves along like inchworms.) If yes, **caterpillars**. For solution, see page 267; for photo, see page 364.

The flower has holes or chewed edges, or you see pests

For other categories of flower symptoms, see page 65

You see pests on or near the flower (from page 72) **or you find pests hiding somewhere on the plant** (from page 73)

Are the pests any shape except small and pear-shaped with two tubes on the rear end?

> YES
> ↓

OR

Are the pests small and pear-shaped with two tubes on their rear ends? (Note: They are often clustered on the undersides of petals, sepals, or flower stems.) If yes, **aphids**. For solution, see page 267; for photo, see page 363.

Do you see no globs of foamy "spittle" on the plant?

> YES
> ↓

OR

Do you see globs of foamy "spittle" attached to flower stems and sometimes to sepals and petals? (Note: A small soft-bodied bug hides inside the foam.) If yes, **spittlebugs**. For solution, see page 267; for photo, see page 364.

Do you find no caterpillars anywhere on the plant? If yes, go to page 75.

OR

Do you find caterpillars somewhere on the plant? If yes, **caterpillars**. For solution, see page 267; for photo, see page 364.

The flower has holes or chewed edges, or you see pests

For other categories of flower symptoms, see page 65

You do not find caterpillars anywhere on the plant (from page 74)

Do you find no slugs or snails anywhere on the plant?
  YES
  ↓

OR Do you find slugs and snails somewhere on the plant? If yes, **slugs or snails**. For solution, see page 325; for photo, see page 366.

Do you find no beetles anywhere on the plant? (Note: Beetles are insects with colorful wing covers that shield the entire abdomen.)
  YES
  ↓

OR Do you find beetles somewhere on the plant? If yes, **beetles**. (Note: For a discussion of the many different kinds of beetles, see page 262.) For solution, see page 267; for photo, see page 363, 365.

Do you find no true bugs anywhere on the plant? (Note: True bugs, in the order Hemiptera, have wing covers that only partially shield the abdomen.) If yes, go to page 76.

OR Do you find true bugs somewhere on the plant? (Note: These bugs will have piercing/sucking mouthparts that leave marks where they've been feeding.) If yes, **squash bugs**, **stink bugs**, **spittlebugs**. For solution, see page 267; for photo, see page 363, 364.

The flower has holes or chewed edges, or you see pests

For other categories of flower symptoms, see page 65

You find no true bugs anywhere on the plant (from page 75)

Do you find no grasshoppers anywhere on the plant?

YES

↓

OR Do you find grasshoppers somewhere on the plant? If yes, **grasshoppers**. For solution, see page 267; for photo, see page 363.

Do you find no ants anywhere on the plant?

YES

↓

OR Do you find ants somewhere on the plant? If yes, **ants**. For solution, see page 267; for photo, see page 363.

Do you find earwigs somewhere on the plant? (Note: Earwigs have pincers at the rear end.) If yes, **earwigs**. For solution, see page 267; for photo, see page 364.

OR Do you find weevils or curculios somewhere on the plant? (Note: These pests have long snouts.) If yes, **weevils**, **curculios**. For solution, see page 267; for photo, see page 363.

The flower is distorted or stunted

For other categories of flower symptoms, see page 65

Is the flower distorted or deformed but normal size?

  YES

OR Is the flower stunted but normal in shape? If yes, go to page 80.

Does the deformed flower lack a powdery grayish-white coating?

  YES

OR Does the deformed flower have a powdery grayish-white coating? If yes, **powdery mildew**. For solution, see page 244.

Is the deformed flower not turning green, and are the leaf veins not turning yellow? If yes, go to page 78.

OR Is the deformed flower turning green while the leaf veins are turning yellow? If yes, **aster yellows**. For solution, see page 306.

The flower is distorted or stunted

For other categories of flower symptoms, see page 65

The deformed flower is not turning green, and the leaf veins are not turning yellow (from page 77)

Do no tiny, leafy branches grow in the center of the flower?

YES

↓

OR

Do tiny, leafy branches grow in the center of the flower? If yes, **aster yellows**. For solution, see page 306.

Is the deformed flower some color other than brown?

YES

↓

OR

Is the deformed flower brown? If yes, **flower thrips**. (Note: Tiny insects will fall out when you shake the flower over white paper.) For solution, see page 267; for photo, see page 368.

Is the flower not turning black? If yes, go to page 79.

OR

Is the flower turning black? (Note: New leaves will be crinkled and discolored.) If yes, **cyclamen mites**. For solution, see page 288.

The flower is distorted or stunted

For other categories of flower symptoms, see page 65

The flower is not turning black (from page 78)

If you pick apart the deformed flower are there no aphids living inside the distorted tissue? (Note: For a description of aphids, see at right.)

    YES

    ↓

OR   If you pick apart the deformed flower are small, pear-shaped insects with two tubes on their rear ends living inside the distorted tissue? If yes, **aphids**. For solution, see page 267; for photo, see page 368.

Does the flower have no dry brown spots?

    YES

    ↓

OR   Does the flower have dry brown spots? If yes, **herbicide damage**. For solution, see page 226; for photo, see page 367.

Is the flower a blackberry, and are the petals twisted and reddish in color? If yes, **double blossom**. For solution, see page 309.

OR   Do flower buds form in the center of an existing flower? If yes, **proliferation**. For solution, see page 232; for photo, see page 367.

The flower is distorted or stunted

For other categories of flower symptoms, see page 65

The flower is stunted but normal in shape (from page 77)

Is the stunted flower not faded in color, and are the leaves not yellowing, curling, and dying?
YES
↓

OR Is the stunted flower faded in color, and are the leaves yellowing, curling, and dying? If yes, **fusarium yellows**. For solution, see page 252.

Are the leaves without shiny black or brown dots on the undersides?
YES
↓

OR Do the leaves have shiny black or brown dots on the undersides? If yes, **lace bugs**. For solution, see page 267; for photo, see page 368.

Are the leaves normal in shape and color, and are stems not twisted and distorted? If yes, go to page 81.

OR Are the leaves long, skinny, and discolored, and are stems twisted and distorted? If yes, **herbicide damage**. For solution, see page 226; for photo, see page 367.

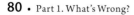

The flower is distorted or stunted

For other categories of flower symptoms, see page 65

The leaves and stems are normal in shape and color (from page 80)

In addition to stunted flowers, is the plant itself smaller than it should be? (Note: The leaves will be wilted.) If yes, go to page 16.

OR Is the plant normal in size but the flowers smaller than they should be? If yes, **lack of disbudding**. For solution, see page 227; for photo, see page 367.

The flower is rotten, wilted, or decayed

For other categories of flower symptoms, see page 65

Has the flower turned brown or black?

YES

↓

OR Has the flower wilted without turning brown or black? If yes, go to page 85.

Has the flower turned brown?

YES

↓

OR Has the flower turned black? If yes, go to page 84.

Does the rotten brown flower hang onto the plant? If yes, go to page 83.

OR Does the rotten brown flower drop off the plant and is it a camellia? If yes, **camellia flower blight**. For solution, see page 244; for photo, see page 370.

The flower is rotten, wilted, or decayed

For other categories of flower symptoms, see page 65

The rotten brown flower hangs onto the plant (from page 82)

Does grayish-brown mold grow on the rotten tissue?

    YES

OR

Does the brown flower lack grayish-brown mold? If yes, **balling**. For solution, see page 232; for photo, see page 369.

Is the plant something other than a stonefruit tree? (Note: Stonefruits [*Prunus*] include peach, nectarine, apricot, plum, cherry, and almond.) If yes, **botrytis** aka **gray mold**. For solution, see page 244; for photo, see page 370.

OR

Is the plant a stonefruit tree? If yes, **brown rot**. (Note: Brown rot infects mainly stonefruits [*Prunus*]; see examples, left.) For solution, see page 244; for photo, see page 370.

The flower is rotten, wilted, or decayed

For other categories of flower symptoms, see page 65

The flower has turned black (from page 82)

Is only the flower bud affected, and is it a rose (*Rosa*) bud? (Note: Small white maggots are feeding inside the bud.) If yes, **rose midge**. For solution, see page 267; for photo, see page 370.

OR Are both flowers and buds affected? If yes, **fire blight**. (Note: This bacterial disease infects only members of the rose family.) For solution, see page 301, 306; for photo, see page 370.

The flower is rotten, wilted, or decayed

For other categories of flower symptoms, see page 65

The flower has wilted without turning brown or black (from page 82)

Are only the flowers wilted, not the whole plant?

YES

↓

OR Is the whole plant wilted along with the flowers? If yes, go to page 16.

Is the flower an orchid?

YES

↓

OR Is the flower on a plant other than an orchid? If yes, **insufficient water**. For solution, see page 231; for photo, see page 369.

Has the orchid been exposed to a source of ethylene gas? (Note: Ethylene is generated naturally by ripening apples, bananas, and other fruit. It is also present in natural gas.) If yes, **ethylene**. For solution, see page 222; for photo, see page 369.

OR Has the orchid been pollinated by you or an insect such as a bee? (Note: This is a normal reaction to pollination in orchids.) If yes, **pollination**. For solution, see page 222; for photo, see page 369.

The plant has flowered poorly, has failed to flower, or has dropped buds

For other categories of flower symptoms, see page 65

Has the plant flowered but the buds dropped off or the flowers were too few and/or too small?

YES

OR Has the plant failed to flower? (Note: If you cannot tell, look for dried up flowers, buds, or flower stalks on the ground or the plant. If there are none, then the plant has failed to flower.) If yes, go to page 89.

Are the flowers too few and/or too small, but most of the buds remain on the plant?

YES

OR Have most of the buds dropped off the plant? If yes, go to page 91.

Has the plant not been recently transplanted, planted out, or up-potted?

YES

OR Has the plant been recently transplanted, planted out, or up-potted? If yes, **transplant shock**. For solution, see page 231; for photo, see page 371.

Is the plant growing normally or poorly, but not with wild abandon? If yes, go to page 87.

OR Is the plant growing with wild abandon, with abundant new succulent vegetative growth but few flowers? If yes, **excess nitrogen**. For solution, see page 238; for photo, see page 372.

The plant has flowered poorly, has failed to flower, or has dropped buds

For other categories of flower symptoms, see page 65

The plant is growing normally or poorly, but not with wild abandon

(from page 86)

Is the plant growing poorly?

   YES

    ↓

OR   Is the plant growing normally? If yes, go to page 88.

Are leaves not becoming yellow between the veins?

   YES

    ↓

OR   Are leaves becoming yellow between the veins? If yes, **poor nutrition**. For solution, see page 238; for photo, see page 372.

Is the plant thin, weak, and pale green? If yes, **too much shade**. For solution, see page 229; for photo, see page 373.

OR   Are leaves turning brown at the tips? If yes, **insufficient water**. For solution, see page 231; for photo, see page 375.

The plant has flowered poorly, has failed to flower, or has dropped buds

For other categories of flower symptoms, see page 65

The plant is growing normally (from page 87)

Does the plant flower every year, and has it not stopped flowering in mid-season?

YES

↓

OR Does the plant flower in alternate years and/or has it stopped flowering in mid-season? If yes, **lack of deadheading**. (Note: Deadheading prevents the flower from making seeds. Many plants will stop flowering once they make seeds.) For solution, see page 227; for photo, see page 371.

Is the plant not flowering too early, but has very few flowers? If yes, **wrong temperature regime**. (Note: This means the plant's temperature needs have not been met. It has been too hot, too cold, not hot enough, or not cold enough.) For solution, see page 233; for photo, see page 373.

OR Is the plant flowering too early? If yes, **bolting**. (Note: This is primarily a problem of certain vegetables, such as spinach [*Spinacia*] and lettuce [*Lactuca*].) For solution, see page 233; for photo, see page 371.

The plant has flowered poorly, has failed to flower, or has dropped buds

For other categories of flower symptoms, see page 65

The plant has failed to flower (from page 86)

Did no one prune the plant within the last year, or if someone did, did the pruner follow the plant's pruning requirements?

OR

Did someone prune the plant within the last year and forget to follow the plant's pruning requirements? If yes, **poor pruning timing**. For solution, see page 227; for photo, see page 371.

YES

↓

Was there no freezing cold snap after the buds began to open in the spring?

OR

Was there a freezing cold snap after the buds began to open in the spring? If yes, **freezing**. For solution, see page 232.

YES

↓

Is the plant something other than a bulb? If yes, go to page 90.

OR

Is the plant a bulb?

YES

↓

Did you plant the bulb at the proper time of year? If yes, go to page 90.

OR

Did you plant the bulb at the wrong time of year? If yes, **poor planting timing**. For solution, see page 233; for photo, see page 371.

The plant has flowered poorly, has failed to flower, or has dropped buds

For other categories of flower symptoms, see page 65

The plant is not a bulb; or, if it is a bulb, it was planted at the right time of year

(from page 89)

Is the plant growing poorly or normally, but not with wild abandon?
    YES
    ↓

OR   Is the plant growing with wild abandon, with abundant new succulent vegetative growth? If yes, **excess nitrogen**. For solution, see page 238; for photo, see page 372.

Is the plant growing poorly?
    YES
    ↓

OR   Is the plant growing normally? If yes, **lack of winter chill**. For solution, see page 233; for photo, see page 373.

Is the plant stunted, but not weak, spindly, and pale green?
    YES
    ↓

OR   Is the plant thin, weak, spindly, and pale green, but not stunted? If yes, **too much shade**. For solution, see page 229; for photo, see page 373.

Are leaves turning brown at the tips or around the edges? If yes, **lack of water**. For solution, see page 231; for photo, see page 375.

OR   Are leaves turning yellow between the veins? If yes, **poor nutrition**. For solution, see page 238; for photo, see page 372.

The plant has flowered poorly, has failed to flower, or has dropped buds

For other categories of flower symptoms, see page 65

Most of the flower buds have dropped off the plant (from page 86)

Were the flower buds not dried out and not shriveled prior to dropping?

   YES

   ↓

OR Were the flower buds dried out and shriveled prior to dropping? If yes, **insufficient water**. (Note: Many factors can result in an inadequate water supply to developing buds, such as wind, root rot, bark beetles, borers, or heat.) For solution, see page 231; for photo, see page 374.

Is the soil around the plant not too wet, and are older leaves green or brown?

   YES

   ↓

OR Is the soil around the plant too wet, and are older leaves turning yellow? If yes, **excess water**. For solution, see page 232; for photo, see page 374.

Is the plant not spindly, weak, and pale green? If yes, go to page 92.

OR Is the plant spindly, weak, and pale green? If yes, **too much shade**. For solution, see page 229; for photo, see page 374.

The plant has flowered poorly, has failed to flower, or has dropped buds

For other categories of flower symptoms, see page 65

The plant is not spindly, weak, and pale green (from page 91)

Was there no period of abnormal freezing weather during the past winter or spring?

   YES

   ↓

OR   Was there a period of abnormal freezing weather during the past winter or spring? If yes, **frost damage**. For solution, see page 232; for photo, see page 373.

Were the buds not nicked, gouged, or eaten prior to falling off the plant?

   YES

   ↓

OR   Were the buds nicked, gouged, or eaten prior to falling off the plant? If yes, **plum curculios**. (Note: This is primarily a problem for apples [*Malus*], stonefruits [*Prunus*], and their relatives.) For solution, see page 267; for photo, see page 375.

Are the buds of roses (*Rosa*)? (Note: Riddled with holes, the bud dries up, turns brown, and eventually drops to the ground.) If yes, **rose curculios**. For solution, see page 267; for photo, see page 375.

OR   Are the buds of strawberry (*Fragaria*), blackberry (*Rubus*), or raspberry (*R. idaeus*)? If yes, **strawberry bud weevil**. (Note: The weevil drills a hole in the flower bud to lay an egg. She then cuts part way through the stem below the bud, which droops, dries out, turns brown, and eventually drops to the ground.) For solution, see page 267; for photo, see page 375.

4 Fruits and Vegetables

What is a fruit?

A fruit embodies the future. A fruit is a mature, ripened ovary that contains a seed or seeds. Only plants that have flowers can make fruit, because it all begins with pollination. The paternal plant's sperm fertilizes the maternal plant's egg cells. The ovules, containing the eggs, begin to grow and develop into seeds. The ovules are inside the ovary, which becomes the fruit, protecting and nourishing the seeds.

A placenta connects the mother plant with her offspring and supplies rich nutrients for the developing seed to fill its cotyledons. The seed lives on this stored food from the time it germinates until it can begin making its own food from sunlight.

Mostly we think of fruit as that delectable food, juicy and sweet, that we love to eat.

Yet the term for that ripened ovary, a fruit, also includes almost everything we call a vegetable. Green beans (*Phaseolus vulgaris*), tomatoes (*Lycopersicon esculentum*), and zucchini (*Cucurbita pepo*), along with oranges (*Citrus sinensis*), apples (*Malus*), and blueberries (*Vaccinium*), are all fruit.

There are even more surprises in the world of fruit. A dry poppy (*Papaver*) capsule is also a fruit. In fact, all flowering plants in your garden produce fruit, only some of which are edible. Ornamental grasses, maple (*Acer*) trees, and dandelions (*Taraxacum officinale*) all produce flowers that contain ovaries; therefore, they

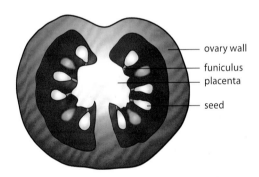

The fruit of a tomato (*Lycopersicon esculentum*), a berry, demonstrates three important functions. The ovary protects the developing seeds and provides nourishment to the embryo through the placenta and the funiculus, an umbilical-cord-like structure. When mature and ripe, the ovary, now a fruit, is attractive to animals like birds and humans who eat the fruit and carry the seeds away from the mother plant inside their digestive systems.

also produce fruit. Even a grain of rice (*Oryza sativa*) is a fruit, the ripened ovary of a grass that grows throughout the world.

What does a fruit do?

Fruit is the supernanny of the plant world. Its major task is to protect and feed the plant's babies, and it has very specific functions that contribute to the reproductive success of the plant. The fruit's first task is to nurture and protect the seed. When the seed is mature and the fruit is ripe, this task has been completed. The fruit's second task is to disperse seeds to new locations so that the plant's babies will not compete with their mother for essential nutrients, water, or sunlight. In the case of dry fruits, many split open at maturity to release seeds. In fact, some fruits explode when ripe, forcibly ejecting the seeds.

Other fruits split open more gently to allow seeds equipped with wings or parachutes to fly on the wind to a new location, rather than drop to the ground nearby.

In dandelions (*Taraxacum officinale*), the fruit itself takes wing and is borne aloft until it can come to rest and germinate in the middle of your perfect lawn.

Fruits that are fleshy and juicy, however, utilize animals to move their seeds around. Fruits of apples (*Malus*), peaches (*Prunus persica*), cherries (*P. avium*), and berries are designed for an animal to eat and poop out the seed somewhere else. This system provides the seedling with a dollop of fertilizer, scarification to enhance germination, and a free ride to a new home. The animal gets a caloric reward in the form of food, and the plant gets its babies distributed. All in all a good symbiotic arrangement, benefitting each partner.

Easily recognized as a fruit by most people, the mature ovary of a flowering plant like the cantaloupe (*Cucumis melo*) guarantees that the seeds it contains will be dispersed because it is sweet and attracts animals.

When fully mature, the ovary of the green bean (*Phaseolus vulgaris*), one of the fruits called a vegetable, dries up and splits open, releasing its seeds.

The berries of the tomato (*Lycopersicon esculentum*) are sometimes known as vegetables and sometimes as fruit.

What are fruit symptoms?

Problems on fruit can be perplexing. Follow these steps to diagnose the problem, so you can find a safe, appropriate solution.

1. Turn the fruit over and look at all sides. If you find more than one symptom, even if you are beset with problems, concentrate on one. It is important to pursue just one symptom at a time.

2. Look at each illustration on page 96 and read the text beside it. Find the fruit symptom that most closely matches yours and decide in which category of the flow charts your fruit belongs.

3. Turn to the page indicated for that category of the flow charts—your tool for pinpointing the problem. WARNING: It is sometimes tempting to try to match your fruit to an illustration without reading the accompanying text. However, it is important to consider the questions. Simply visually matching your fruit to a drawing may lead to the wrong diagnosis.

4. Each flow chart poses a series of paired questions (couplets) about a symptom. Answer the questions yes or no. Only one member of each pair of questions can be answered yes.

5. When the answer is yes, follow that arrow or turn to the page listed under the question. Continue answering the questions and following the "yes" arrows through the chart.

6. For the most part, the questions on the left-hand side of the flow charts indicate several symptoms; therefore, they are often not illustrated.

7. When you reach the diagnosis, in red, turn to the page indicated for a solution. If there is a reference to a photo, turn to that page to see a fruit with a similar problem.

The fruit of a milkweed (*Asclepias*) splits open to release its seeds to float away on the wind.

The fruit of cat's ear (*Hypochaeris radicata*), like its close relative the dandelion (*Taraxacum officinale*), has a parachute that allows it to float on the wind, carrying its seed far from the parent plant.

The winged fruit of maples (*Acer*), called a samara, spins like a helicopter as it drops from the tree, safely carrying the seed it contains to a new location away from its parent.

Like the green bean, the fruit of the perennial sweet pea (*Lathyrus latifolius*) splits open at maturity, often with enough force to cast the seeds over a large area.

Categories of fruit symptoms

The whole fruit is discolored.
Go to page 97.

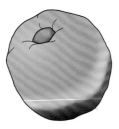

The fruit has spots of any size.
Go to page 99.

The fruit has holes, or is missing, partly
eaten, or cracked. Go to page 110.

The fruit is distorted, stunted,
or shriveled. Go to page 115.

The fruit is mushy, wormy, moldy,
or rotten. Go to page 121.

The whole fruit is discolored

For other categories of fruit symptoms, see page 96

Is the fruit mature? (Note: It may be a mature citrus fruit or any other kind of mature fruit.)
  YES
  ↓

OR Is the fruit an immature citrus fruitlet? (Note: The fruitlet has silvery streaks or scabs.) If yes, **citrus thrips**. For solution, see page 267.

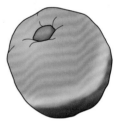

Is the fruit ripe?
  YES
  ↓

OR Has the fruit failed to ripen and remained green, especially at the stem end? If yes, **greenback**. For solution, see page 232; for photo, see page 376.

Does the fruit have no white, pale green, and dark green patches? If yes, go to page 98.

OR Does the fruit have white, pale green, and dark green patches? If yes, **mosaic virus**. For solution, see page 309; for photo, see page 380.

The whole fruit is discolored

For other categories of fruit symptoms, see page 96

The fruit does not have white, pale green, and dark green patches (from page 97)

Is the fruit something other than a mature citrus?

YES

↓

OR

Is the fruit a mature citrus? (Note: It has brown lesions and the flesh is dry and pulpy.) If yes, **citrus freeze damage**. For solution, see page 232; for photo, see page 376.

Is the fruit covered with black "soot" that rubs off? If yes, **sooty mold**. For solution, see page 254.

OR

Is the fruit covered with grayish-white powder? If yes, **powdery mildew**. For solution, see page 244.

The fruit has spots of any size

For other categories of fruit symptoms, see page 96

Are the spots some color other than white, grayish-white, or silvery?

YES

↓

OR Are the spots white, grayish-white, or silvery? If yes, go to page 102.

Are the spots a color other than black or dark brown? (Note: The spots may be light brown, like a brown paper bag, or chestnut brown, but not as dark as roasted coffee beans.)

YES

↓

OR Are the spots black or dark brown, like the color of roasted coffee beans? If yes, go to page 104.

Are the spots smooth and not corky? (Note: Corky tissue is dry, rough, and orange-brown.) If yes, go to page 100.

OR Are the spots corky? If yes, go to page 106.

The fruit has spots of any size

For other categories of fruit symptoms, see page 96

The spots are smooth and not corky (from page 99)

Are the spots some color other than light brown, like a brown paper bag, to chestnut brown?
YES
↓

OR Are the spots light brown, like a brown paper bag, to chestnut brown? If yes, go to page 107.

Are the spots some shape other than long, narrow, and curving?
YES
↓

OR Are the spots long, narrow, and curving under the skin of the fruit? If yes, **European apple sawfly**. (Note: These occur only on apples [*Malus*] and pears [*Pyrus*].) For solution, see page 282.

Are the spots some color other than purple? If yes, go to page 101.

OR Are the spots purple and scattered over the surface of the fruit? If yes, **shot hole fungus**. (Note: This occurs only on apples [*Malus*] and stonefruits [*Prunus*].) For solution, see page 244.

The fruit has spots of any size

For other categories of fruit symptoms, see page 96

The spots are some color other than purple (from page 100)

Are the spots yellow or orange?   OR   Are the spots red?
YES   YES

Do the spots start out yellow but later become orange? If yes, **cedar-apple rust**. (Note: This occurs only on apples and crab apples [*Malus*].) For solution, see page 244; for photo, see page 379.

OR   Are the spots yellow and do they remain yellow? (Note: The spots are scattered over the surface of the fruit.) If yes, **stink bugs**. For solution, see page 267.

Is there a patch of red unripened tissue on an otherwise ripe blackberry (*Rubus*)? If yes, **redberry mites**. (Note: These occur only on blackberries.) For solution, see page 295; for photo, see page 379.

OR   Are the spots red with white centers? If yes, **San Jose scale**. For solution, see page 267.

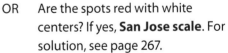

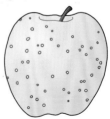

The fruit has spots of any size

For other categories of fruit symptoms, see page 96

The spots are white, grayish-white, or silvery (from page 99)

Do the spots lack grayish white powder?

YES

   ↓

OR

Do the spots have a grayish white powder on them? If yes, **powdery mildew**. For solution, see page 244.

Is the fruit something other than an immature citrus fruitlet? (Note: The fruit could be a mature citrus.)

YES

   ↓

OR

Is the fruit an immature citrus fruitlet? (Note: The spots are silvery.) If yes, **citrus thrips**. For solution, see page 267.

Does the fruit have no white, pale green, and dark green patches? If yes, go to page 103.

OR

Does the fruit have white, pale green, and dark green patches? If yes, **mosaic virus**. For solution, see page 309; for photo, see page 380.

The fruit has spots of any size

For other categories of fruit symptoms, see page 96

The fruit has no white, pale green, and dark green patches (from page 102)

Does the fruit lack smooth white patches that become dry and papery?

  YES

  ↓

OR

Does the fruit have smooth white patches that become dry and papery? If yes, **sunscald**. For solution, see page 229; for photo, see page 377.

Does the fruit have soft watery spots that later develop gray-brown mold? If yes, **botrytis** aka **gray mold**. For solution, see page 244; for photo, see page 378.

OR

Does the fruit have soft watery spots that later develop white mold? (Note: Sometimes hard, black, "seed-like" nodules grow within the mold.) If yes, **white mold**. For solution, see page 244, 252; for photo, see page 378.

The fruit has spots of any size

For other categories of fruit symptoms, see page 96

The spots are black or dark brown, like the color of roasted coffee beans

(from page 99)

Do the spots remain on the fruit even when rubbed?

YES

↓

OR Do the spots rub off the fruit? If yes, **sooty mold**. For solution, see page 254.

Are the spots not confined to the blossom end?

YES

↓

OR Are the spots only on the blossom end? If yes, **blossom end rot**. For solution, see page 238; for photo, see page 378.

Are the spots on the shady side as well as the sunny side of the fruit? If yes, go to page 105.

OR Are the spots only on the sunny side of the fruit? If yes, **sunburn**. For solution, see page 229.

The fruit has spots of any size

For other categories of fruit symptoms, see page 96

The spots are on the shady side as well as the sunny side of the fruit

(from page 104)

Are the spots dull and scattered across the surface of the fruit?

YES

OR Are the spots shiny and clustered into a patch on the surface of the fruit? If yes, **fly speck**. For solution, see page 244; for photo, see page 379.

Are the spots flat or sunken?

YES

OR Are the spots very small, raised, black bumps, like scabs? If yes, **bacterial spots**. For solution, see page 301; for photo, see page 380.

Do the spots start as small brown specks that become sunken circular black spots? If yes, **anthracnose**. For solution, see p age 244.

OR Do the spots start out dark brown and become large black blotches that rot the fruit? If yes, **black rot**. For solution, see page 244; for photo, see page 378.

The fruit has spots of any size

For other categories of fruit symptoms, see page 96

The spots are corky (from page 99)

Are the corky spots discrete and do not spread over the surface of the fruit?
    YES

  ↓

OR   Do the corky spots spread over the surface of the fruit? If yes, **russeting**. For solution, see page 224; for photo, see page 377.

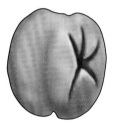

Does the fruit remain undistorted as it matures?
    YES

  ↓

OR   As it matures, does the fruit become distorted around the corky tissue? (Note: Most references call this distortion "cat face.") If yes, **tarnished plant bugs**. For solution, see page 267; for photo, see page 379.

Does the fruit have small scab-like spots that drop off, leaving corky lesions? If yes, **shot hole fungus**. (Note: This occurs only on apples [*Malus*] and stonefruits [*Prunus*].) For solution, see page 244.

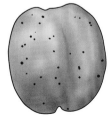

OR   Does the fruit have large spots of corky tissue on the surface? If yes, **scab**. For solution, see page 244; for photo, see page 379.

The fruit has spots of any size

For other categories of fruit symptoms, see page 96

The spots are light brown, like a brown paper bag, to chestnut brown

(from page 100)

Are the spots flat or raised?
  YES

   ↓

OR   Are the spots sunken? If yes, go to page 109.

Is there no grub in the center of the fruit? (Note: A grub has a brown head and three pairs of jointed legs.)
YES

   ↓

OR   Is there a worm-like grub in the center of the fruit? If yes, **raspberry fruitworm**. (Note: This insect larva, which occurs only on raspberries and blackberries [*Rubus*], causes the stem end of fruit to turn brown.) For solution, see page 282.

Is the fruit something other than a mature citrus? If yes, go to page 108.

OR   Is the fruit a mature citrus? (Note: The fruit is scarred with brown lesions and the flesh is dry and pulpy.) If yes, **citrus freeze damage**. For solution, see page 232; for photo, see page 377.

The fruit has spots of any size

For other categories of fruit symptoms, see page 96

The fruit is something other than a mature citrus (from page 107)

Do the spots get larger?
  YES
  ↓

OR Do the spots remain the same size? If yes, **mechanical damage**. (Note: Hail storms, bird pecks, or other wounds can result in small brown spots on fruit.) For solution, see page 225.

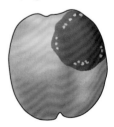

Are there no translucent spots? (Note: Translucent spots look like grease spots on paper.)
  YES
  ↓

OR Are there translucent spots that become dry, brown patches? If yes, **bacterial blight**. For solution, see page 301; for photo, see page 380.

Are large brown areas under the fruit's skin soft and wet? If yes, **late blight**. For solution, see page 244; for photo, see page 379.

OR Are large brown areas under the fruit's skin firm and dry? If yes, **brown rot**. (Note: This occurs mainly on stonefruits [*Prunus*] and infrequently on apples [*Malus*].) For solution, see page 244; for photo, see page 378.

The fruit has spots of any size

For other categories of fruit symptoms, see page 96

The spots are sunken (from page 107)

Do the spots stay small?

YES

↓

OR Do small spots enlarge rapidly? If yes, **bitter rot**. (Note: This affects only apples [*Malus*] and pears [*Pyrus*]. Spots 1 inch, 2.5 cm, or more in diameter develop concentric rings in their centers.) For solution, see page 244.

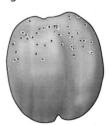

Does the flesh of the fruit have numerous pale brown corky spots or speckles? If yes, **bitter pit**. (Note: This occurs only on apples [*Malus*].) For solution, see page 238.

OR Are the spots surrounded by yellow haloes? If yes, **bacterial leaf-spot**. For solution, see page 301; for photo, see page 380.

The fruit has holes or is missing, partly eaten, or cracked

For other categories of fruit symptoms, see page 96

Does the fruit have holes?

   YES

OR Is the fruit missing, partly eaten, or cracked? If yes, go to page 113.

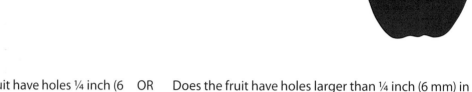

Does the fruit have holes ¼ inch (6 mm) or less in diameter, and are there no slime trails?

   YES

OR Does the fruit have holes larger than ¼ inch (6 mm) in diameter, and are slime trails present? If yes, **slugs or snails**. For solution, see page 325; for photo, see page 383.

Are the holes round and deeper than ⅛ inch (3 mm)? If yes, go to page 111.

OR Are the holes crescent-shaped and shallow, about ⅛ inch (3 mm) deep or less? If yes, **plum curculios**. For solution, see page 267; for photo, see page 381.

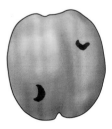

The fruit has holes or is missing, partly eaten, or cracked

For other categories of fruit symptoms, see page 96

The holes are round and deeper than ⅛ inch (3 mm) (from page 110)

Is the fruit something other than a grape?
   YES

OR   Is the fruit a grape (*Vitis*)? (Note: The grapes are webbed together and filled with sawdust-like material.) If yes, **grape berry moth**. For solution, see page 282.

Is the fruit of a fruit tree, and are worms inside the fruit? If yes, go to page 112.

OR   Is the fruit of a non-woody plant, and are worms inside the fruit? If yes, **tomato fruitworm, corn earworm, European corn borer, army worm**. For solution, see page 267, 282; for photo, see page 381, 382.

The fruit has holes or is missing, partly eaten, or cracked

For other categories of fruit symptoms, see page 96

The fruit is of a fruit tree, and worms are inside the fruit (from page 111)

Does the fruit have worms some color other than orange, and are there no webs inside the fruit?

YES

OR

Does the fruit have orange worms that spin webs inside the fruit? If yes, **navel orange worm**. (Note: This insect primarily attacks nuts, citrus, and figs [*Ficus*].) For solution, see page 282.

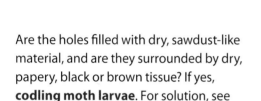

Are the holes filled with dry, sawdust-like material, and are they surrounded by dry, papery, black or brown tissue? If yes, **codling moth larvae**. For solution, see page 282; for photo, see page 382.

OR

Are the holes filled with moist, gummy material, and are they surrounded by dry, papery, black or brown tissue? If yes, **oriental fruit worm**. (Note: This insect attacks fruit trees.) For solution, see page 282.

The fruit has holes or is missing, partly eaten, or cracked

For other categories of fruit symptoms, see page 96

The fruit is missing, partly eaten, or cracked (from page 110)

Is the fruit present, but partly eaten or cracked?
   YES
   ↓

OR   Is the fruit missing? If yes, **birds**, or **bears, coyotes, raccoons, deer, children**. For solution, see page 328 or 329, respectively.

Is the fruit partly eaten?
   YES
   ↓

OR   Is the fruit cracked? If yes, go to page 114.

Does the partly eaten fruit have no pointed holes poked into the flesh?
   YES
   ↓

OR   Does the fruit have pointed holes poked into the flesh? If yes, **birds**. For solution, see page 328; for photo, see page 382.

Are wasps and/or yellowjackets eating the fruit? (Note: If they are not currently present, check again at a different time of day.) If yes, **wasps, yellowjackets**. For solution, see page 267; for photo, see page 381.

OR   Is the fruit marked with parallel grooves where it has been eaten? If yes, **rodents**. For solution, see page 329; for photo, see page 382.

The fruit has holes or is missing, partly eaten, or cracked

For other categories of fruit symptoms, see page 96

The fruit is cracked (from page 113)

Is the crack dry?
   YES

OR   Is the crack moist? If yes, **excess water**. For solution, see page 232; for photo, see page 381.

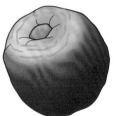

Is the crack filled with brown corky tissue, and does it run lengthwise along the fruit? If yes, **scab**. For solution, see page 244; for photo, see page 381.

OR   Is the crack dry and scabbed over, and does it encircle the stem end of the fruit? If yes, **growth cracks**. For solution, see page 231; for photo, see page 381.

The fruit is distorted, stunted, or shriveled

For other categories of fruit symptoms, see page 96

Is the fruit distorted or shriveled?
   YES

OR   Is the fruit stunted, but not distorted or shriveled? If yes, go to page 119.

Is the fruit distorted, but not shriveled?
   YES

OR   Is the fruit shriveled? If yes, go to page 120.

Are there no insect larvae (maggots, grubs, caterpillars) inside the fruit? If yes, go to page 116.

OR   Are insect larvae inside the fruit? If yes, go to page 118.

The fruit is distorted, stunted, or shriveled

For other categories of fruit symptoms, see page 96

There are no insect larvae inside the fruit (from page 115)

Is the fruit not knobby and pitted?   OR
  YES

↓

Is the fruit knobby and pitted? If yes, **pear stony pit virus**. (Note: This affects only pears [*Pyrus*]. The fruit has hard patches throughout the flesh.) For solution, see page 309.

Does the fruit have no corky scabs on the surface? (Note: Corky tissue is dry, rough, and orange-brown.)   OR
  YES

↓

Does the fruit have corky scabs on the surface? (Note: The fruit may also be cracked.) If yes, **scab**. For solution, see page 244; for photo, see page 385.

Is the mature fruit not pinched in at the blossom end? If yes, go to page 117.   OR

Is the mature fruit pinched in at the blossom end? If yes, **rosy apple aphid**. (Note: This insect attacks only apples [*Malus*].) For solution, see page 267; for photo, see page 386.

The fruit is distorted, stunted, or shriveled

For other categories of fruit symptoms, see page 96

The fruit is not pinched in at the blossom end (from page 116)

Does the fruit have no pale yellow spots?
  YES

  ↓

OR Does the fruit have pale yellow spots? If yes, **cedar-apple rust**. (Note: The spots enlarge, turn orange, and develop tiny black dots. This occurs only on apples [*Malus*].) For solution, see page 244; for photo, see page 385.

Is one end or side of the fruit stunted and misshapen, while the other end appears to be normal? If yes, **poor pollination**. For solution, see page 227; for photo, see page 384.

OR Does the fruit have rough skin, like sandpaper, that is faded and mottled? If yes, **mosaic virus**. For solution, see page 309.

The fruit is distorted, stunted, or shriveled

For other categories of fruit symptoms, see page 96

Insect larvae are inside the fruit (from page 115)

Is there no webbing that binds the fruit together?

YES

↓

OR

Does webbing bind the fruit together? (Note: Caterpillars are inside the fruit.) If yes, **cherry or cranberry fruitworm**. For solution, see page 267, 282.

Does the fruit have maggots inside, but no grubs? (Note: A maggot has no obvious head and no legs.)

YES

↓

OR

Does the fruit have grubs inside, but no maggots? (Note: A grub has a brown head and three pairs of jointed legs.) If yes, **plum curculios**. For solution, see page 267.

Is the fruit mature and ripening? (Note: The fruit is distorted and pulpy.) If yes, **fruit fly**. For solution, see page 267, 282; for photo, see page 386.

OR

Is the fruit an immature fruitlet? If yes, **pear midge**. (Note: The fruitlet turns black, swells up, and drops from the plant. This occurs only on pears.) For solution, see page 267, 282.

The fruit is distorted, stunted, or shriveled

For other categories of fruit symptoms, see page 96

The fruit is stunted (from page 115)

Is the fruit something other than a raspberry (*Rubus idaeus*)?

    YES

    ↓

OR Is the fruit a raspberry? If yes, **crumbly berry virus**. (Note: The fruit is small and crumbly. This virus affects only red raspberries.) For solution, see page 309.

Is the plant sickly and growing slowly, but you find no pests or symptoms of disease?

    YES

    ↓

OR Is the plant healthy? If yes, **too much fruit**. For solution, see page 227; for photo, see page 384.

Does the fruit fail to ripen properly, and is it dry and pulpy? If yes, **environmental stress**. For solution, see page 224; for photo, see page 384.

OR Is the plant producing small crops of fruit that don't taste very good? If yes, **insufficient nutrients**. For solution, see page 238; for photo, see page 384.

The fruit is distorted, stunted, or shriveled

For other categories of fruit symptoms, see page 96

The fruit is shriveled (from page 115)

Does the fruit fall from the plant?

   YES

   ↓

OR Does the fruit remain on the plant, but turns black and dries out? If yes, **black rot of grape**, **blueberry mummy berry**, **brown rot**. For solution, see page 244; for photo, see page 385.

Is the fruit a cucumber (*Cucumis sativus*)? (Note: If you cut the stems, the sap is milky and sticky.) If yes, **cucurbit bacterial wilt**. For solution, see page 306; for photo, see page 386.

OR Is the fruit an immature tomato, pepper, melon, or other fleshy fruit? If yes, **anthracnose**. For solution, see page 244; for photo, see page 385.

The fruit is mushy, wormy, moldy, or rotten

For other categories of fruit symptoms, see page 96

Do you see no insect larvae and no signs of larvae inside the fruit? (Note: Insect larvae include maggots, grubs, and caterpillars; for definitions, see glossary.)

YES

OR Do you see insect larvae or signs of larvae inside the fruit? (Note: Signs include exit holes, larva excrement, and tunnels.) If yes, go to page 124.

Is the fruit rotten, but there is no mold?

YES

OR Is there mold on the fruit? If yes, go to page 123.

Does the fruit have brown spots, but they do not turn black? If yes, go to page 122.

OR Does the fruit have brown spots that turn black? If yes, **black rot**. For solution, see page 244; for photo, see page 387.

The fruit is mushy, wormy, moldy, or rotten

For other categories of fruit symptoms, see page 96

The fruit has brown spots that do not turn black (from page 121)

Is the rotten fruit moist and soft? (Note: The rotten fruit has sunken pits with yellow haloes.) If yes, **bacterial leaf-spot**. For solution, see page 301; for photo, see page 388.

OR Is the rotten fruit dry and firm? (Note: The rotten fruit may shrivel and mummify, hanging on the tree through winter.) If yes, **brown rot**. For solution, see page 244; for photo, see page 387.

The fruit is mushy, wormy, moldy, or rotten

For other categories of fruit symptoms, see page 96

There is mold on the fruit (from page 121)

Is the mold cream-colored? (Note: The rotten fruit may shrivel and mummify, hanging on the tree through winter.) If yes, **brown rot**. For solution, see page 244; for photo, see page 387.

OR Is the mold gray-brown? If yes, **botrytis** aka **gray mold**. For solution, see page 244; for photo, see page 387.

The fruit is mushy, wormy, moldy, or rotten

For other categories of fruit symptoms, see page 96

You see insect larvae or signs of larvae inside the fruit (from page 121)

Is there no large black decayed area in the core of the fruit?

YES

↓

OR Is there a large black decayed area in the core of the fruit? (Note: A tunnel leads to the surface.) If yes, **codling moth larvae**. For solution, see page 282; for photo, see page 388.

Is there no caterpillar inside the fruit?

YES

↓

OR Do you see a pink or tan caterpillar with any color stripes inside the fruit? If yes, **European corn borer**. For solution, see page 282.

Is the fruit mushy, and is there a maggot inside? (Note: A maggot has no obvious head and no legs.) If yes, go to page 125.

OR Is the fruit mushy, and is there a grub inside? (Note: A grub has a brown head and three pairs of jointed legs.) If yes, **plum curculios**. For solution, see page 267.

The fruit is mushy, wormy, moldy, or rotten

For other categories of fruit symptoms, see page 96

The fruit is mushy, and there is a maggot inside (from page 124)

Is the fruit an immature fruitlet? (Note: The fruitlet drops from the plant.) If yes, **European apple sawfly**. For solution, see page 282; for photo, see page 388.

OR Is the fruit a mature fruit? If yes, **apple maggot**, **blueberry maggot**, **currant fruit fly**, **cherry fruitworm**. For solution, see page 267, 282; for photo, see page 388.

5 Stems, Trunks, and Branches

What is a stem?

A stem is the plant organ that supports all the above-ground plant parts—the leaves, flowers, and fruits. In trees we commonly call this a trunk, branch, or twig, while in other plants we might call it a stalk. The stem also transports water and nutrients from the roots to the other parts, and food from the leaves down to the roots. At its tip, stems grow new living tissue.

Inside, the stem's cells are organized into various tissues. Just as we do, plants have veins. Vascular tissue is composed of xylem and phloem. Thick-walled, sturdy, and hollow like a straw, xylem carries water and mineral nutrients from the roots to the leaves. Phloem carries sugar produced by the leaves through the stem to the rest of the plant.

Stems can be modified in various ways. The simple stem, or trunk, of the coconut palm is a perfect example of a normal, non-specialized stem.

Some plants, however, have highly modified stems. Stems of vines, for example, are extremely long with widely separated nodes and buds.

Strawberry (*Fragaria*) runners, or stolons, are modified stems. Like all stems, stolons have nodes with buds that can grow out into new plants. Strawberry stems are also modified into

crowns, extremely short stems with congested internodes.

Stems may also undergo extreme specialization for storage of food and water. Many orchids (Orchidaceae), for example, have stems modified into pseudobulbs.

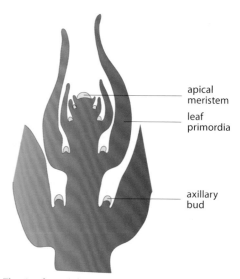

apical meristem

leaf primordia

axillary bud

The tip of a stem has microscopic leaf primordia which develop into full-sized leaves as the stem matures. Axillary buds, which can generate new stems, occur at the node where the leaf joins the stem. All stems have nodes and buds.

The cactus family (Cactaceae) has modified its leaves into spines and its stems into green, photosynthetic organs that have taken over the function of leaves.

Rhizomes, tubers, and corms are underground stems so highly modified as to be nearly unrecognizable as stems. All of them, along with root vegetables such as bulbs and tuberous roots, occur in the soil environment and are subject to many of the same pests and diseases as roots. Therefore, we treat underground stems and root vegetables in the next chapter.

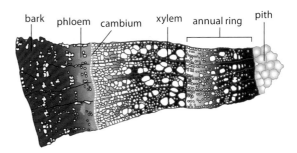

This sector from a cross section of a two-year-old woody dicot stem exhibits the cell types and tissues normally found in stems. Xylem cells are dead at maturity and extremely strong, providing support for all the aboveground structures. The wood we use for construction is composed of xylem. Non-woody stems and monocot stems lack annual rings.

What does a stem do?

A healthy stem is crucial to the well-being of a plant. A stem provides water, nutrients, and structural support, holding leaves and flowers up to the sun. In many cases it also stores food in specialized cells called parenchyma, which forms pith in the center of the stem. Sugar cane (*Saccharum officinarum*) is a good example of this specialization. The bark or skin of the stem provides protection against disease-causing bacteria and fungi and protects against water loss.

The stem is also able to grow roots and, since it has buds which can grow new stems, a small section can generate a whole new plant. Stems are widely used for asexual propagation, or cloning, of selected individual plants using sections of stems called cuttings. New plants can also be obtained from stems by layering, grafting, budding, and tissue culture micropropagation.

We use stems for so many things that our well-being might also be due to healthy plant stems. Stems of trees provide us with shelter as wood for building structures. Used as firewood they keep us warm. They give us clothing in the form of linen made from the stems of flax, and, of course, provide us with food.

What are stem symptoms?

Because the stem is vital for plant health, problems here can be life threatening. If the stem is compromised, follow these steps to diagnose the cause and find a safe, appropriate remedy.

1. Be sure to look at all sides of the stem. If you find more than one symptom, even if you are beset with problems, concentrate on one. It is important to pursue just one symptom at a time.

2. Look at each illustration on page 129 and read the text beside it. Find the stem symptom that most closely matches yours and decide in which category of the flow charts your stem belongs.

3. Turn to the page indicated for that category of the flow charts—your tool for pinpointing the problem.
   WARNING: It is sometimes tempting to try to match your stem to an illustration without reading the accompanying text. However, it is important to consider the questions. Simply visually matching your stem to a drawing may lead to the wrong diagnosis.

4. Each flow chart poses a series of paired questions (couplets) about a symptom. Answer the questions yes or no. Only one member of each pair of questions can be answered yes.

5. When the answer is yes, follow that arrow or turn to the page listed under the question. Continue answering the questions and following the "yes" arrows through the chart.

6. For the most part, the questions on the left-hand side of the flow charts indicate several symptoms; therefore, they are often not illustrated.

7. When you reach a diagnosis, in red, turn to the page indicated for the recommended treatment. In addition, if there is a reference to a photo, turn to that page to see a stem with a similar problem.

Stems can also serve as food or water storage organs, such as the pseudobulbs of this oncidium orchid. Many orchids are epiphytes that live on the branches of trees and have access to water only when it rains.

Extreme specialization of stems characterizes cacti. This prickly pear (*Opuntia*) has green, photosynthetic stems with leaves modified into spines. Food is manufactured and stored in the stem along with enough water to survive the harsh conditions of desert habitats.

The number of stems can be quite high, as in this maple/oak (*Acer/Quercus*) deciduous forest. The wood obtained from forest trees provides us with numerous products, from paper to construction timbers.

Categories of stem symptoms

The whole stem is discolored, dying, or dead. Go to page 130.

The stem is distorted or stunted. Go to page 148.

The stem is moldy, mushy, rotten, or slimy. Go to page 151.

The stem has spots of any size. Go to page 136.

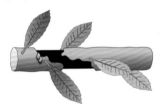

The stem has lumps or foreign growths, or you see pests. Go to page 153.

The stem has holes or is chewed, split, cracked, or broken. Go to page 143.

The whole stem is discolored, dying, or dead

For other categories of stem symptoms, see page 129

Are cankers absent? (Note: Cankers are patches of sunken tissue that may encircle the stem.)
  YES
  ↓

OR   Do you see cankers? If yes, go to page 132.

Is the stem without holes?
  YES
  ↓

OR   Do you see holes in the stem? If yes, go to page 134.

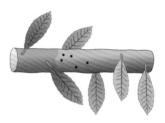

Is no bark missing, and is it not peeling off? If yes, go to page 131.

OR   Is bark missing or peeling off? If yes, go to page 133.

The whole stem is discolored, dying, or dead

For other categories of stem symptoms, see page 129

No bark is missing and it is not peeling off (from page 130)

Are knots, knobs, bumps, or warts absent?

YES

↓

OR Do you see knots, knobs, bumps, or warts? If yes, go to page 135.

Do stems (branches and twigs) turn yellow in a random pattern on the plant?

YES

↓

OR Do stems (branches and twigs) turn yellow and drop from only one side of the plant? (Note: The stem tissue at the soil line has dark brown streaks when cut open.) If yes, **fusarium wilt**. For solution, see page 244; for photo, see page 389.

Do twigs wilt and die and remain on the plant?

YES

↓

OR Do twigs wilt and die and drop to the ground? If yes, **twig girdler**, **twig pruner**. For solution, see page 282.

Is the plant a raspberry (*Rubus idaeus*), and do canes have two rows of punctures. If yes, **raspberry cane borer**. For solution, see page 282; for photo, see page 391.

OR Is the plant something other than a raspberry, and are worms present inside the twigs? If yes, **peachtwig borer**, **oriental fruit moth**. For solution, see page 282; for photo, see page 391.

The whole stem is discolored, dying, or dead

For other categories of stem symptoms, see page 129

You see cankers, patches of sunken tissue that may encircle the stem (from page 130)

Is fluffy gray mold absent?
YES

↓

OR Does fluffy gray mold grow on the affected area? If yes, **botrytis** aka **gray mold**. For solution, see page 244; for photo, see page 389.

Is the affected plant something other than a rose (*Rosa*)?
YES

↓

OR Is the affected plant a rose? (Note: Rose canes discolor and die back.) If yes, **rose canker and dieback**. For solution, see page 244; for photo, see page 389.

Have no raised, hard, red-orange or coral, pinhead-sized balls formed on the affected stem?
YES

↓

OR Have raised, hard, red-orange or coral, pinhead-sized balls formed on the affected stem? If yes, **coral spot**, **European canker**. For solution, see page 244; for photo, see page 390.

Do the cankers ooze sticky gum? If yes, **brown rot**, **cankers**, **eutypa dieback**. For solution, see page 244; for photo, see page 390.

OR Do new shoots wilt, blacken, and die? If yes, **lilac blight**, **fire blight**. For solution, see page 301; for photo, see page 392.

The whole stem is discolored, dying, or dead

For other categories of stem symptoms, see page 129

The bark is missing or peeling off (from page 130)

Is the bark peeling off in thin papery strips? (Note: The bark of some trees, such as certain birches [*Betula*] and maples [*Acer*], peels away naturally.) If yes, **papery bark**. For solution, see page 244; for photo, see page 390.

OR Are patches of bark missing from trunk, stem, or branches? If yes, **rodents**, **deer**, or **lawnmowers**, **weed-eaters**. For solution, see page 329 or 225, 331; for photo, see page 392.

The whole stem is discolored, dying, or dead

For other categories of stem symptoms, see page 129

You see holes in the stem (from page 130)

Does new growth have a caterpillar inside the middle of the stem? (Note: A round hole also appears in the bark.) If yes, **Nantucket pine tip moth**, **oriental fruit moth**, **peachtwig borer**. For solution, see page 282; for photo, see page 391.

OR Do D-shaped holes occur in the bark? (Note: Branches have zigzag tunnels under the bark.) If yes, **two-lined chestnut borer**. For solution, see page 282.

The whole stem is discolored, dying, or dead

For other categories of stem symptoms, see page 129

You see knots, knobs, bumps, or warts (from page 131)

Are blister-like areas that erupt in powdery black spores absent?

    YES

    ↓

OR

Do raised blister-like areas erupt in masses of black powdery spores? If yes, **smut**. For solution, see page 244.

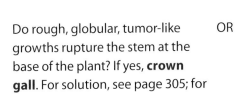

Do no small, hard bumps encrust the stem?

    YES

    ↓

OR

Is the stem encrusted with small, hard bumps? If yes, **lecanium scale**, **San Jose scale**, **juniper scale**, **oyster scale**. For solution, see page 267; for photo, see page 391.

Do rough, globular, tumor-like growths rupture the stem at the base of the plant? If yes, **crown gall**. For solution, see page 305; for photo, see page 392.

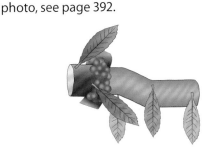

OR

Do rough, long, tumor-like growths encase the stem? If yes, **black knot**. For solution, see page 244; for photo, see page 390.

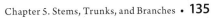

The stem has spots of any size

For other categories of stem symptoms, see page 129

Is the stem without small holes, cracks, or splits? (Note: This applies to both non-woody and woody plants.)

YES

↓

OR Is the plant a woody tree or shrub and does the stem have small holes, cracks, or splits? If yes, go to page 139.

Is the stem without knots, knobs, or bumps?

YES

↓

OR Does the stem have knots, knobs, or bumps? If yes, go to page 140.

Is the stem free of distortion?

YES

↓

OR Is the stem distorted? If yes, go to page 141.

Is the stem or trunk free of rot or mold? If yes, go to page 137.

OR Is the stem or trunk rotten or moldy? If yes, go to page 142.

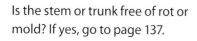

The stem has spots of any size

For other categories of stem symptoms, see page 129

The stem or trunk is free of rot or mold (from page 136)

Are cankers absent? (Note: Cankers are patches of sunken tissue that may encircle the stem.)

YES

↓

OR Are cankers present? (Note: Cankers may also ooze sticky gum.) If yes, **brown rot**, **cankers**, **eutypa dieback**. For solution, see page 244; for photo, see page 393, 394.

Are there no purple spots with buff or gray centers?

YES

↓

OR Do purple spots have buff or gray centers? If yes, **raspberry cane spot**. (Note: These spots enlarge rapidly and are found only on raspberries [*Rubus idaeus*].) For solution, see page 244.

Is this a mature stem, or if it is a new shoot, does it never wilt, turn brown-black, and die? If yes, go to page 138.

OR Is this a new shoot that wilts, turns brown-black, and dies? (Note: The leaves of infected plants may have angular dark spots.) If yes, **bacterial blight**. For solution, see page 301; for photo, see page 394.

The stem has spots of any size

For other categories of stem symptoms, see page 129

The stem is mature, or it is a new shoot that never wilts, turns brown-black, and dies (from page 137)

Does the stem have patches of some color other than dark brown?

YES

↓

OR

Does the stem have dark brown patches? (Note: The leaves above the affected area dry up, turn yellow-brown, and die.) If yes, **rose canker and dieback**. For solution, see page 244; for photo, see page 394.

Does the stem lack olive-brown spots?

YES

↓

OR

Does the stem have olive-brown spots? (Note: The leaves have velvety, olive-brown spots and are distorted.) If yes, **scab**. For solution, see page 244; for photo, see page 394.

Does the stem have a green to yellow stain under the bark with masses of black spores? If yes, **sycamore maple sooty bark disease**. (Note: This fungus attacks only maples [*Acer*].) For solution, see page 244.

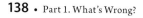

OR

Does the stem have a grayish green patch with small orange to brown spots? If yes, **endothia canker**. (Note: This fungus attacks chestnuts, oaks, and beeches.) For solution, see page 244.

The stem has spots of any size

For other categories of stem symptoms, see page 129

The plant is a woody tree or shrub and has small holes, cracks, or splits

(from page 136)

Does the stem have cracks or splits?

YES

↓

OR Does the stem have holes in the bark? (Note: Tunnels under the bark are filled with sawdust.) If yes, **borers**. For solution, see page 282; for photo, see page 395.

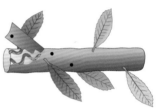

Do cracks appear anywhere on the stem?

YES

↓

OR Do sunken, dark cracks appear only on the sunny side of the stem? If yes, **sunscald**. For solution, see page 229.

Is the crack filled with a bright orange powder? If yes, **rust**. For solution, see page 245.

OR Do concentric rings of black tissue appear inside the crack? (Note: Small, hard, round white or red fungi grow on the rings.) If yes, **apple canker**, **pear canker**. For solution, see page 245; for photo, see page 394.

The stem has spots of any size

For other categories of stem symptoms, see page 129

The stem has knots, knobs, or bumps (from page 136)

Does the bump produce no shoots?
   YES

↓

OR Does the bump produce yellow-brown or olive-colored short, leafless shoots? If yes, **dwarf mistletoe** (*Arceuthobium*). (Note: This parasite is found only on conifers.) For solution, see page 331.

Do white cottony bumps and/or white fluffy patches appear on the stem? If yes, **cottony scale**, **woolly aphids**, **adelgids**, **mealybugs**. For solution, see page 267; for photo, see page 395.

OR Do white, fan-shaped fungal knobs grow beneath the bark at the base of stems and trunks? (Note: The fungal mats smell strongly of mushrooms.) If yes, **armillaria root rot**. For solution, see page 252.

The stem has spots of any size

For other categories of stem symptoms, see page 129

The stem is distorted (from page 136)

Are galls absent? (Note: A gall is an abnormal growth attached to the stem.)

YES

↓

OR Are pineapple-shaped, dry, brown galls attached to the stem? If yes, **Cooley spruce gall adelgid**. (Note: These galls form only on spruces [*Picea*] and are distorted new shoots.) For solution, see page 285; for photo, see page 395.

Is the plant a Douglas fir (*Pseudotsuga menziesii*) with cottony white spots on the stem? If yes, **Cooley spruce gall adelgid**. (Note: Twigs and leaves are bent and twisted only on Douglas fir.) For solution, see page 267.

OR Is the plant other than a Douglas fir, and are bright yellow and black aphids visible? (Note: Aphids are small, pear-shaped, soft-bodied insects.) If yes, **oleander aphid** aka **milkweed aphid**. For solution, see page 267.

The stem has spots of any size

For other categories of stem symptoms, see page 129

The stem or trunk is rotten or moldy (from page 136)

Is fluffy gray mold absent?
   YES

   ↓

OR Does fluffy gray mold grow on the spots? If yes, **botrytis** aka **gray mold**. For solution, see page 244; for photo, see page 393.

Is the plant of any type, and does the stem have dense, white, fluffy mold on it? (Note: Hard, black, "seed-like" nodules may be embedded in the mold.) If yes, **white mold**. For solution, see page 252.

OR Is the plant a woody tree or shrub with a cinnamon-brown rotten area at the base? (Note: The roots will also be brown and decayed.) If yes, **phytophthora root rot, crown rot**. For solution, see page 252; for photo, see page 393.

The stem has holes or is chewed, split, cracked, or broken

For other categories of stem symptoms, see page 129

Does the stem have no holes?
  YES
   ↓

OR Does the stem have holes?
If yes, go to page 144.

Does the stem have no splits or cracks, but patches of stem tissue are missing?
  YES
   ↓

OR Is the stem split, cracked, or broken? If yes, go to page 146.

Is the plant something other than an asparagus?
  YES
   ↓

OR Is the plant an asparagus, and are patches of surface tissue missing? (Note: The stem bends, dries up, and turns yellow-brown.) If yes, **asparagus beetle**. For solution, see page 267; for photo, see page 397.

Does the stem have random scrapings that have removed surface tissue? (Note: These injuries are found only at the base of the plant.) If yes, **lawnmowers**, **weed-eaters**. For solution, see page 225, 331; for photo, see page 398.

OR Does the stem have tooth marks where the surface tissue is missing? If yes, **rodents**. (Note: Rodent tooth marks are parallel grooves.) For solution, see page 329; for photo, see page 398.

The stem has holes or is chewed, split, cracked, or broken

For other categories of stem symptoms, see page 129

The stem has holes (from page 143)

Are the holes less than 1 inch (2.5.cm) in diameter?

YES

↓

OR   Are the holes larger than 1 inch (2.5 cm) in diameter? If yes, **woodpeckers**. For solution, see page 328; for photo, see page 398.

Does no sawdust spill out of the holes?

YES

↓

OR   Does sawdust (or sawdust look-alike) or gum spill out of the holes? If yes, **flatheaded borer, dogwood borer, carpenter ants, pecan borer, European corn borer, rhododendron borer, squash vine borer, shot hole borer**. For solution, see page 282; for photo, see page 397.

Are zigzag tunnels and D-shaped holes absent? If yes, go to page 145.

OR   Are there zigzag tunnels under the bark and D-shaped holes in the stem? If yes, **two-lined chestnut borer**. For solution, see page 282.

The stem has holes or is chewed, split, cracked, or broken

For other categories of stem symptoms, see page 129

Zigzag tunnels and D-shaped holes are absent (from page 144)

Are parallel rows of shallow holes absent?

YES

↓

OR   Does the stem have a grid pattern of parallel rows of shallow holes? If yes, **sapsuckers**. For solution, see page 328; for photo, see page 398.

Is the plant a woody tree or shrub?

YES

↓

OR   Is the plant a corn (*Zea mays*) stalk? (Note: The corn fails to produce ears and may be wilting and dying.) If yes, **common stalk borer**. For solution, see page 282.

Are there holes in the bases of needles, buds, and shoots of a pine (*Pinus*) tree? (Note: Pine needles at the branch tips turn yellow, brown, and die.) If yes, **Nantucket pine tip moth**. For solution, see page 282.

OR   If you peel away the bark, do you find tunnels radiating out from a central line? (Note: This is usually found on dying or recently dead trees or shrubs.) If yes, **bark beetles**. For solution, see page 282; for photo, see page 397.

The stem has holes or is chewed, split, cracked, or broken

For other categories of stem symptoms, see page 129

The stem is split, cracked, or broken (from page 143)

Are there no bright orange spore masses rupturing out of the stem?
YES
↓

OR Have bright orange spore masses ruptured out of the stem leaving fissures behind? If yes, **rust**. For solution, see page 245.

Is the plant a woody tree or shrub with no broken branches?
YES
↓

OR Are branches broken where they join the main stem or trunk? If yes, **heavy fruit crop**, **heavy snow**, **strong wind**, **weak forks**, **bears**, **children**. For solution, see page 227; for photo, see page 396.

Are concentric rings of flaky bark absent? If yes, go to page 147.

OR Have cankers split and cracked, forming concentric rings of flaky bark? (Note: Cankers are patches of sunken tissue that may encircle the stem.) If yes, **cankers**. For solution, see page 245; for photo, see page 396.

The stem has holes or is chewed, split, cracked, or broken

For other categories of stem symptoms, see page 129

Concentric rings of flaky bark are absent (from page 146)

Are the splits and cracks found in locations other than the sunny side?

YES

↓

OR Are the splits and cracks found only on the sunny side of a tree? If yes, **sunscald**. For solution, see page 229.

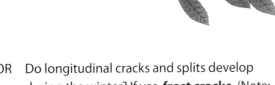

Do longitudinal cracks and splits develop during the growing season? If yes, **irregular watering**. For solution, see page 231; for photo, see page 396.

summer

OR Do longitudinal cracks and splits develop during the winter? If yes, **frost cracks**. (Note: These usually close in summer.) For solution, see page 232; for photo, see page 396.

winter

The stem is distorted or stunted

For other categories of stem symptoms, see page 129

Are small holes absent and are no insects visible?

    YES

    ↓

OR   Are small holes present or are insects visible? If yes, go to page 150.

Are pineapple-shaped, dry, brown galls absent?

    YES

    ↓

OR   Are pineapple-shaped, dry, brown galls attached to the branches? If yes, **Cooley spruce gall adelgid**. (Note: These galls form only on spruces [*Picea*] and are distorted new shoots.) For solution, see page 285; for photo, see page 399.

Is the stem other than wide, flat, and ribbon-like? If yes, go to page 149.

OR   Is the stem wide, flat, and ribbon-like at the tip? (Note: Flowers and bracts may be numerous, congested, and stunted.) If yes, **fasciation**. For solution, see page 306; for photo, see page 399.

The stem is distorted or stunted

For other categories of stem symptoms, see page 129

The stem is not flat, wide, and ribbon-like (from page 148)

Is there no looping or twisting of the stem?

YES

↓

OR Is the stem spirally twisted or looping crazily? (Note: Leaves may be narrowed, discolored, and/or cupped. Abnormal roots may form on the stem.) If yes, **herbicide damage**. For solution, see page 226; for photo, see page 399.

Is stunting and swelling absent from the stem base?

YES

↓

OR Is the stem stunted and swollen at the base? (Note: Upper leaves will be strongly narrowed, becoming stringy.) If yes, **phlox nematode**. For solution, see page 315.

Are there closely packed, dense clusters of stunted twigs that persist year after year? If yes, **witches' broom**. For solution, see page 309; for photo, see page 399.

OR Are there closely packed dense clusters of stunted twigs for only a season or two? If yes, **herbicide damage**. For solution, see page 226; for photo, see page 399.

The stem is distorted or stunted

For other categories of stem symptoms, see page 129

Small holes are present or insects are visible (from page 148)

Is the plant something other than corn (*Zea mays*)?

   YES

   ↓

OR

Is the plant corn? If yes, **common stalk borer**. (Note: This insect attacks only corn.) For solution, see page 282.

Do you see no bright yellow and black aphids? (Note: For a description of aphids, see at right.)

   YES

   ↓

OR

Do you see bright yellow and black aphids? (Note: Aphids are small, pear-shaped, soft-bodied insects with two tubes on their rear ends.) If yes, **oleander aphid** aka **milkweed aphid**. For solution, see page 267.

Does the main shoot at the top of the stem droop, curl, yellow, and die? If yes, **white pine weevil**. (Note: This affects only white pine [*Pinus*] trees.) For solution, see page 282.

OR

Do you see cottony white dots on the stem? If yes, **Cooley spruce gall adelgid**. (Note: Twigs and leaves are bent and twisted only on Douglas fir [*Pseudotsuga menziesii*].) For solution, see page 267.

The stem is moldy, mushy, rotten, or slimy

For other categories of stem symptoms, see page 129

Is the base of the stem some color other than brown?

YES

⌄

OR

Is the base of the stem brown? (Note: The roots are brown and rotten.) If yes, **phytophthora root rot, crown rot**. For solution, see page 252; for photo, see page 400.

Is the stem moldy or leaking fluid, or are mushrooms or other fungal organisms present?

YES

⌄

OR

Is the stem slimy and decayed, and do you see tiny black pellets at the base of the plant? If yes, **stem rot**. For solution, see page 252; for photo, see page 400.

Are no stringy, white fungal strands growing at the base of the stem? If yes, go to page 152.

OR

Are stringy, white fungal strands growing around the base of the stem? (Note: This occurs in waterlogged heavy soil, and the stem is soft and rotten.) If yes, **stem rot**. For solution, see page 252.

The stem is moldy, mushy, rotten, or slimy

For other categories of stem symptoms, see page 129

There are no stringy, white fungal strands growing at the base of the stem

(from page 151)

Does no fluffy white mold grow on the stem?

YES

↓

OR Does dense, white, fluffy mold grow on the stem? (Note: Hard, black, "seed-like" nodules may be embedded in the mold.) If yes, **white mold**. For solution, see page 252.

Do you see shelf-like growths, mushrooms, or other fungi growing out of the side or base of a tree? (Note: The wood is discolored and spongy.) If yes, **heart rot**. For solution, see page 257; for photo, see page 400.

OR Does smelly fluid ooze out of the side of a tree? If yes, **slime flux**. For solution, see page 305, 306; for photo, see page 400.

The stem has lumps or foreign growths, or you see pests

For other categories of stem symptoms, see page 129

Do no obviously foreign plant-like growths grow on the stem?

YES

↓

OR

Do obviously foreign, plant-like growths, such as mushrooms, a different kind of plant, like mistletoe, or some crusty or leaf-like things grow on the stem? If yes, go to page 156.

Are the lumps larger than ½ inch (1.25 cm), and are no insects present?

YES

↓

OR

Do you see small (less than ½ inch, 1.25 cm) bumps or insects on the stem? If yes, go to page 158.

Are no slimy orange horns produced in wet weather? If yes, go to page 154.

OR

Do hard, knobby growths produce weird slimy orange horns in moist weather? If yes, **cedar-apple rust**. For solution, see page 245.

The stem has lumps or foreign growths, or you see pests

For other categories of stem symptoms, see page 129

No slimy orange horns are produced in wet weather (from page 153)

Are swollen, blister-like areas that produce powdery black spores absent?

YES

↓

OR

Do swollen, blister-like areas erupt in masses of powdery black spores? If yes, **smut**. For solution, see page 244.

Do you see no black cylindrical growths on the stem?

YES

↓

OR

Do you see black, cylindrical, corky growths to 12 inches (30 cm) long and 1 inch (2.5 cm) in diameter on the stem? If yes, **black knot**. For solution, see page 244; for photo, see page 401.

Are growths that burst out of the stem absent? If yes, go to page 155.

OR

Do rough, rounded growths burst out of the stem, rupturing it? If yes, **aerial crown gall**. For solution, see page 305; for photo, see page 403.

The stem has lumps or foreign growths, or you see pests

For other categories of stem symptoms, see page 129

Growths that burst out of the stem are absent (from page 154)

Are globs of frothy white "spittle" stuck to the stem? If yes, **spittlebugs**. For solution, see page 267; for photo, see page 402.

OR Do round, swollen growths turn orange or yellow in spring? If yes, **gall rust of pines** (*Pinus*). For solution, see page 245.

The stem has lumps or foreign growths, or you see pests

For other categories of stem symptoms, see page 129

Obviously foreign, plant-like growths, such as mushrooms, a different kind of plant, like mistletoe, or some crusty or leaf-like things grow on the stem

(from page 153)

Does no green, leafy, branched plant grow directly out of the stem?

    YES

OR Does a green, leafy, branched plant grow directly out of the stem? If yes, **leafy mistletoe** (*Phoradendron*). (Note: This evergreen parasite is easily seen when the host tree is deciduous.) For solution, see page 331; for photo, see page 403.

Does no yellow-brown, branched plant without leaves grow on the stem?

    YES

OR Does a yellow-brown, branched plant without leaves grow directly out of the stem? If yes, **dwarf mistletoe** (*Arceuthobium*). (Note: This parasite is found only on conifers.) For solution, see page 331.

Do no organisms that are dry and firm or leafy grow on the stem? If yes, go to page 157.

OR Do green, gray, brown, orange, or chartreuse organisms that are dry and firm or leafy grow on the stem? If yes, **lichens**, **algae**. (Note: These organisms are not parasites; they do not harm your plants.) For photo, see page 403.

The stem has lumps or foreign growths, or you see pests

For other categories of stem symptoms, see page 129

No organisms that are dry and firm or leafy (lichens or algae) grow on the stem

(from page 156)

Does no soft, mossy, green ball grow on the stem?

   YES

OR Do you see a soft, mossy, green ball growing on the stem? If yes, **mossyrose gall**. For solution, see page 285; for photo, see page 402.

Do honey-colored mushrooms grow out of the base of the stem? If yes, **armillaria root rot**. For solution, see page 252.

OR Do shelf-like, mushroom-like organisms grow out of a tree trunk? If yes, **bracket fungus**. For solution, see page 257; for photo, see page 401.

The stem has lumps or foreign growths, or you see pests

For other categories of stem symptoms, see page 129

You see small (less than ½ inch, 1.25 cm across) bumps or insects on the stem

(from page 153)

Do you see lumps and bumps that are smaller than ¼ inch (6 mm) in diameter on the stem, or do you see insects? (Note: This category includes many insects that look nothing like insects.)

   YES

OR Do you see brown lumps about ¼ inch (6 mm) in diameter clustered on the stem? If yes, **lecanium scale**. (Note: These are insects, but they do not look like insects.) For solution, see page 267; for photo, see page 402.

Are small, pear-shaped insects absent?

   YES

OR Do you see small, pear-shaped insects with two tubes on their rear ends? If yes, **aphids**. For solution, see page 267; for photo, see page 401.

Do hard, circular or oval bumps encrust the stem? If yes, **San Jose scale, oyster scale, juniper scale**. For solution, see page 267; for photo, see page 401.

OR Does white, fluffy wax that looks like cotton or mold cover various insects? If yes, **cottony scale, mealybugs, adelgids, woolly aphids**. For solution, see page 267; for photo, see page 402.

6 Roots, Bulbs, and Root Vegetables

What is a root?

A root is the organ that mines the soil for water and nutrients to nourish the rest of the plant. The root normally grows below ground, where it anchors the plant to the earth. However, sometimes a root fastens the plant to a tree limb high above the forest floor.

A root cap protects the sensitive tip of the root as it pushes its way through the soil, or rhizosphere. This complex living ecosystem teems with millions of bacteria, fungi, insects, and other animals. This zone is critical to the cycling of nutrients and to preventing disease. The root feeds this community by secreting carbohydrates, manufactured by the leaves. In exchange the community gathers the water and mineral nutrients that the root then feeds to the plant.

Roots surprise us with their ability to adapt to their environment and take on many shapes and sizes. Most plants have a fibrous root system, an extensive network of small roots that occupies a large volume of soil.

Prop roots, found on corn (*Zea mays*), extend from the side of a stem to the ground and help stabilize the tall stem. A clever technique of engineering.

The roots of some plants grow from their own branches or stems. For example, philodendrons, banyan (*Ficus*) trees, and some orchids

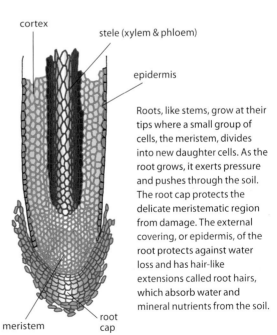

cortex

stele (xylem & phloem)

epidermis

meristem

root cap

Roots, like stems, grow at their tips where a small group of cells, the meristem, divides into new daughter cells. As the root grows, it exerts pressure and pushes through the soil. The root cap protects the delicate meristematic region from damage. The external covering, or epidermis, of the root protects against water loss and has hair-like extensions called root hairs, which absorb water and mineral nutrients from the soil.

(Orchidaceae) have aerial roots that develop from stem tissue and grow above ground.

What does a root do?

Whether the plant is rooted in the ground or in the crown of a rainforest tree, anchoring the plant firmly in its environment is one primary task of the root system. All above-ground plant parts require a constant supply of moisture, and it is the root's job to supply it. The root's third fundamental task is to store food, and some highly specialized food storage roots, such as carrots (*Daucus*), beets (*Beta*), sweet potatoes (*Ipomoea*), are important and nourishing food crops called root vegetables. Next time you enjoy some candied yams at Thanksgiving, think of the incredibly complex series of processes that must take place before you can indulge in this delectable treat.

All these functions are vital for the overall health of the plant. Should the integrity of the root system's anchoring capacity be weakened by disease, disorders, or pests, the plant might

The fibrous roots of a cabbage (*Brassica oleracea*) exemplify the unspecialized root systems of the majority of plants.

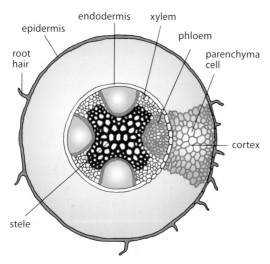

In cross section, the internal structure of the root shows a central core, or stele, bounded by the endodermis, where the vascular elements of xylem and phloem are located. The large undifferentiated parenchyma cells of the cortex are often used for food storage.

This tropical epiphytic orchid, *Vanda coerulea*, lives in treetops with aerial roots that capture rainfall and never touch the ground.

collapse. If the demand for water exceeds the root's ability to provide it, then the leaves will begin to scorch, that is, to die at the tips and edges. In fact, this could be your first clue that something might be amiss with the roots. Without the food storage capability of roots, some plants would not survive.

Organs other than roots can also serve as underground food storage structures. White potatoes (*Solanum tuberosum*) and iris rhizomes, for example, are modified stems. Onion (*Allium cepa*), tulip (*Tulipa*), and daffodil (*Narcissus*) bulbs are modified leaves. Because all underground plant parts—roots, modified stems, and leaves—grow in soil, they are exposed to soil-borne pests and pathogens. For this reason all these organs are included in this chapter.

Roots anchor and nourish the rest of the plant and are critical to its survival. We acknowledge these important functions in our own lives by expressing our connection to community as "putting down roots," and by thinking of our family "tree" as our roots.

What are root symptoms?

Because the absorption of water and mineral nutrients from the soil are vital for plant health, problems of the roots can be life threatening. If the root system of your plant is compromised, follow these steps to diagnose the cause and find a safe, appropriate remedy.

1. Turn the root over and look at all sides. If more than one symptom occurs, even if you are beset with problems, concentrate on one. It is important to pursue just one symptom at a time.
2. Look at each illustration on page 163 and read the text beside it. Find the root symptom that most closely matches yours and decide in which category of the flow charts your root belongs.
3. Turn to the page indicated for that category of the flow charts—your tool for pinpointing the problem.
   WARNING: It is sometimes tempting to try to match your root to an illustration

The sweet potato (actually a morning glory relative, *Ipomoea batatas*, and not a potato at all) does not have eyes like a white potato. This means it lacks nodes and buds, good evidence that it is, in fact, a root modified to serve as a food storage organ.

A white potato (*Solanum tuberosum*) has eyes, which are nodes and buds; these provide solid evidence that it is a modified stem, not a root at all.

An onion (*Allium cepa*) bulb, often called a root vegetable, has roots only at its base.

without reading the accompanying text. However, it is important to consider the questions. Simply visually matching your root to a drawing may lead to the wrong diagnosis.

4. Each flow chart poses a series of paired questions (couplets) about a symptom. Answer the questions yes or no. Only one member of each pair of questions can be answered yes.

5. When the answer is yes, follow that arrow or turn to the page listed under the question. Continue answering the questions and following the "yes" arrows through the chart.

6. For the most part, the questions on the left-hand side of the flow charts indicate several symptoms; therefore, they are often not illustrated.

7. When you reach the diagnosis, in red, turn to the page indicated for a solution. If there is a reference to a photo, turn to that page to see a root with a similar problem.

Categories of root symptoms

The whole root is discolored. Go to page 164.

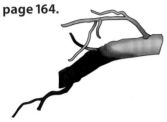

The root has discolored areas of any size. Go to page 167.

The root has holes; is chewed, cracked, or split; is partially or entirely missing; or you see pests. Go to page 177.

The root is distorted, stunted, or shriveled. Go to page 183.

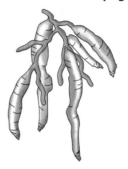

The root is moldy or rotten. Go to page 188.

The root has bumps, warts, or nodules. Go to page 191.

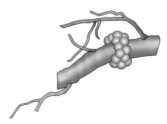

The whole root is discolored

For other categories of root symptoms, see page 163

Is the root a large, fleshy storage structure? (Note: This includes fleshy roots, bulbs, rhizomes, corms, tuberous roots, and tubers; for definitions, see glossary.)
    YES
    ↓

OR Is the root something other than a large, fleshy storage structure, and is it brown or black? If yes, **root rot**. For solution, see page 252; for photo, see page 404.

Is the discoloration some color other than brown?
    YES
    ↓

OR Is the discoloration brown? If yes, go to page 165.

Is the discoloration some color other than gray?
    YES
    ↓

OR Is the discoloration gray? (Note: This applies only to onions.) If yes, **heat or cold injury**. For solution, see page 233; for photo, see page 404.

Is the root a beet (*Beta*) that is unusually pale? (Note: Cut it open to find prominent light and dark rings within.) If yes, **excessive heat and uneven moisture**. For solution, see page 233.

OR Is the root a beet that is unusually dark? If yes, **potassium deficiency**. For solution, see page 238.

The whole root is discolored

For other categories of root symptoms, see page 163

The discoloration is brown (from page 164)

Is the large, fleshy storage root something other than a potato (*Solanum tuberosum*)?

YES

↓

OR Is the root a potato? If yes, **potato bacterial ring rot**. (Note: Cut it in half to find a light brown ring of crumbly, decayed flesh.) For solution, see page 305; for photo, see page 404.

Is the root something other than an onion (*Allium cepa*)?

YES

↓

OR Is the root an onion? If yes, go to page 166.

Is the root a dahlia tuber and does pink and yellow mold grow on dark brown, sunken lesions? If yes, **dahlia tuber rot**. For solution, see page 258.

OR Is the root a gladiolus corm and is it shriveled, with dark brown ridges? If yes, **gladiolus corm rot**. For solution, see page 258.

The whole root is discolored

For other categories of root symptoms, see page 163

The root is an onion (*Allium cepa*) (from page 165)

Is the onion bulb soft and brown inside, and does white mold grow on the surface? If yes, **onion fusarium basal rot**. For solution, see page 252.

OR   Is the onion bulb healthy, but have the small feeder roots turned pinkish brown and shriveled up? If yes, **onion pink root**. For solution, see page 252.

The root has discolored areas of any size

For other categories of root symptoms, see page 163

Are discolored areas only on the surface of the root?

YES

↓

OR   If you cut the root in half, do you find discolored areas inside? (Note: Discolored areas may also be on the surface.) If yes, go to page 173.

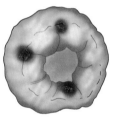

Are the discolored areas free of mold?

YES

↓

OR   Are the discolored areas moldy? If yes, go to page 172.

Are the discolored areas flat or raised?

YES

↓

OR   Are the discolored areas sunken? If yes, go to page 170.

Are the discolored areas flat? If yes, go to page 168.

OR   Are the discolored areas raised? If yes, go to page 171.

The root has discolored areas of any size

For other categories of root symptoms, see page 163

The discolored areas are flat (from page 167)

Are the discolored areas some color other than black or brown? (Note: The discolored areas may be green, dark green, silvery, or gray.)

YES

OR   Are the discolored areas black or brown?

YES

↓

Is the root a fibrous feeder root? If yes, **root rot**. For solution, see page 252; for photo, see page 405.

OR   Is the root a fleshy storage root? If yes, **scurf**. For solution, see page 252.

Are the discolored areas some color other than pale silvery-gray with brown edges? If yes, go to page 169.

OR   Are the discolored areas pale, silvery-gray with brown edges? (Note: This affects only potatoes.) If yes, **potato silver scurf**. For solution, see page 252.

The root has discolored areas of any size

For other categories of root symptoms, see page 163

The discolored areas are some color other than pale silvery-gray with brown edges (from page 168)

Are discolored areas some color other than light green?

YES

↓

OR Are the discolored areas light green? If yes, **exposure to sunlight**. For solution, see page 229; for photo, see page 406.

Are the discolored areas pale, as if bleached, and soft? If yes, **sunscald**. For solution, see page 229.

OR Are the discolored areas dark green, with very dark concentric rings? If yes, **onion smudge**. For solution, see page 245.

The root has discolored areas of any size

For other categories of root symptoms, see page 163

The discolored areas are sunken (from page 167)

Are the discolored areas firm and dry?
  YES

OR Are the discolored areas soft and mushy? If yes, **soft rot**. For solution, see page 305.

Are the discolored areas black or brown, but not purplish? If yes, **fungus**. For solution, see page 258; for photo, see page 405.

OR Are the discolored areas purple-brown? If yes, **late blight of potato**. (Note: Cut it in half to find dry red-brown areas near the surface.) For solution, see page 245; for photo, see page 406.

The root has discolored areas of any size

For other categories of root symptoms, see page 163

The discolored areas are raised (from page 167)

Are the discolored areas round?

YES

OR Are the discolored areas raised ridges? If yes, **bulb fungus**. For solution, see page 258.

Are tiny, hard, black bumps embedded in the discolored area? If yes, **tulip fire**. (Note: This fungus attacks only tulips [*Tulipa*].) For solution, see page 245.

OR Are the discolored areas rough and corky? If yes, **scab**. For solution, see page 252; for photo, see page 405.

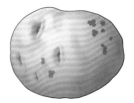

The root has discolored areas of any size

For other categories of root symptoms, see page 163

The discolored areas are moldy (from page 167)

Is the root something other than an onion (*Allium cepa*)?

> YES

OR Is the root an onion bulb, soft and brown inside with fluffy white mold on the outside? If yes, **onion fusarium basal rot**. For solution, see page 252.

Are the discolored areas red-brown lesions? If yes, **bulb blue mold**. For solution, see page 258; for photo, see page 406.

OR Do tufts of pink, white, or blue-green mold grow on shrunken, brown areas? If yes, **bulb rot**. For solution, see page 252; for photo, see page 405.

The root has discolored areas of any size

For other categories of root symptoms, see page 163

The discolored areas are inside (from page 167)

Is the root something other than a potato (*Solanum tuberosum*)?

YES

↓

OR Is the root a potato? If yes, go to page 175.

Are the discolored areas some color other than brown?

YES

↓

OR Are the discolored areas brown? If yes, go to page 174.

Are the discolored areas black or gray?

YES

↓

OR Are there concentric rings of light and dark red, like a bull's eye? (Note: This applies to beets [*Beta*]. Cut one in half, from side to side, not top to bottom, to find the bull's eye effect.) If yes, **excessive heat and uneven moisture**. For solution, see page 233.

Is the root black, mushy, and rotten? If yes, **mechanical injury followed by disease**. For solution, see page 225.

OR Are there hard, dark patches inside the flesh? If yes, **boron deficiency of beet**. For solution, see page 238.

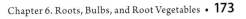

The root has discolored areas of any size

For other categories of root symptoms, see page 163

The discolored areas are brown (from page 173)

Is the root a bulb, and is it soft and brown inside with fluffy white mold on the outside? If yes, **onion fusarium basal rot**. For solution, see page 252.

OR

Is the root a bulb, and do you find brown concentric rings inside? (Note: Cut the bulb in half from side to side, not top to bottom, to see the concentric rings.) If yes, **nematodes**. For solution, see page 315; for photo, see page 406.

The root has discolored areas of any size

For other categories of root symptoms, see page 163

The root is a potato (*Solanum tuberosum*) (from page 173)

Is there no light yellowish-brown ring inside?

YES

↓

OR   Is there a light yellowish-brown ring inside? If yes, **potato bacterial ring rot**. For solution, see page 305.

Are there no tan, curved lines (arcs) inside?

YES

↓

OR   Are there tan curved lines (arcs) inside? If yes, **potato spraing**. For solution, see page 252.

Are the discolored areas some color other than pink? If yes, go to page 176.

OR   Are the discolored areas pink? If yes, **potato gangrene**. For solution, see page 258.

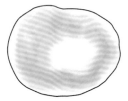

The root has discolored areas of any size

For other categories of root symptoms, see page 163

The discolored areas are some color other than pink (from page 175)

Are there gray to black areas inside? (Note: The center may be hollow.) If yes, **poor growing conditions**. For solution, see page 224.

OR Is there a black, rotted ring at the stem end? If yes, **bacterial ring rot**. For solution, see page 305; for photo, see page 406.

The root has holes; is chewed, cracked, or split; is partially or entirely missing; or you see pests

For other categories of root symptoms, see page 163

Is the root without cracks or splits?   OR   Is the root cracked or split open? If yes, **irregular**

YES   **watering**. For solution, see page 231; for photo, see

↓   page 407.

Are insects or their larvae absent?   OR   Are insects or their larvae (maggots, grubs,
(Note: Insect larvae include   caterpillars) present on or inside the root or in the soil?
maggots, grubs, and caterpillars;   If yes, go to page 179.
for definitions, see glossary.)

YES

↓

Does the root have a cavity or a   OR   Does the root have holes, or is it chewed, or partially
hollowed-out space? If yes, go to   or entirely missing? If yes, go to page 181.
page 178.

The root has holes; is chewed, cracked, or split; is partially or entirely missing; or you see pests

For other categories of root symptoms, see page 163

The root has a cavity or a hollowed-out space (from page 177)

Does the root have a small hole leading to a larger hollowed-out chamber? If yes, **slugs or snails**. For solution, see page 325; for photo, see page 408.

OR   Does the root have a hollow space inside but lack a small hole leading to the exterior? If yes, **cavity spot**. For solution, see page 238.

The root has holes; is chewed, cracked, or split; is partially or entirely missing; or you see pests

For other categories of root symptoms, see page 163

Insects or their larvae (maggots, grubs, caterpillars) are present on or inside the root or in the soil (from page 177)

Are insect larvae (maggots, grubs, caterpillars) present, but adult insects absent?

    YES

    ↓

OR Are adult insects (for example, aphids, mealybugs) present, but insect larvae absent? If yes, go to page 182.

Are the larvae white, pink, or tan?

    YES

    ↓

OR Are the larvae long and yellowish-orange or gray? If yes, **wireworms**. (Note: These are grubs, living in tunnels in the root tissue. A grub has a brown head and three pairs of jointed legs.) For solution, see page 284; for photo, see page 407.

Are the larvae white or tan? If yes, go to page 180.

OR Are the larvae pinkish? If yes, **iris borers**, **potato tuberworms**. For solution, see page 284; for photo, see page 408.

The root has holes; is chewed, cracked, or split; is partially or entirely missing; or you see pests

For other categories of root symptoms, see page 163

The larvae are white or tan (from page 179)

Are the larvae white?

YES

OR   Is there a single larva and is it tan? (Note: A single large tan maggot dwells in the middle of a bulb filled with muddy excrement.) If yes, **narcissus bulb fly**. For solution, see page 284.

Does the root have dry tunnels and channels, and are maggots absent? (Note: A maggot has no obvious head and no legs; see the drawing to the right.)

YES

OR   Does the root have slimy tunnels and channels, and are white maggots present? (Note: The tunnels are scarred with brown lesions.) If yes, **root maggots**, **cabbage maggots**, **onion maggots**, **rust flies**. For solution, see page 284; for photo, see page 407.

Does the root have dry tunnels and channels, and do you see white grubs with brown heads? If yes, **carrot weevil**, **flea beetle larvae**, **sweet potato weevil**. For solution, see page 284.

OR   Does the root have large, shallow scars, and do you see white grubs with brown heads? If yes, **white-fringed beetle larvae**, **cucumber beetles**, **Japanese beetle larvae**. For solution, see page 284.

The root has holes; is chewed, cracked, or split; is partially or entirely missing; or you see pests

For other categories of root symptoms, see page 163

The root is chewed, or partially or entirely missing (from page 177)

Is the root entirely missing, or if partially eaten, do you see tooth marks that are parallel grooves? If yes, **rodents**. For solution, see page 329; for photo, see page 408.

OR Does the root have holes, or is it ragged from being chewed, but you see no tooth marks? (Note: You may find C-shaped white grubs in the soil.) If yes, **wireworms**, **corn rootworm**, **strawberry root weevil**, **black vine weevil**, **Japanese beetle larvae**. For solution, see page 284.

The root has holes; is chewed, cracked, or split; is partially or entirely missing; or you see pests

For other categories of root symptoms, see page 163

Adult insects are present on the root (from page 179)

Are globular, creamy-brown aphids (small, pear-shaped insects with two tubes on their rear ends) feeding on the roots? If yes, **root aphids**. (Note: These aphids secrete a white waxy powder.) For solution, see page 284.

OR   Are oval, white insects feeding on the roots? If yes, **root mealybugs**. (Note: These insects also secrete a white waxy powder.) For solution, see page 284.

The root is distorted, stunted, or shriveled

For other categories of root symptoms, see page 163

Is the root distorted or shriveled, but not stunted?

YES

↓

OR   Is the root stunted? If yes, go to page 186.

Is the root distorted?

YES

↓

OR   Is the root shriveled? If yes, go to page 187.

Is the root distorted in a way that is not club-like? If yes, go to page 184.

OR   Is the root swollen, thickened, and distorted, resembling a club? (Note: This applies to cabbage and its relatives [Brassicaceae], such as kale, broccoli, cauliflower, radish, and mustard.) If yes, **clubroot**. For solution, see page 252.

The root is distorted, stunted, or shriveled

For other categories of root symptoms, see page 163

The root is distorted in a way that is not club-like (from page 183)

Is the root without small wart-like bumps?

YES

↓

OR   Does the root have any small wart-like bumps? If yes, **nematodes**. For solution, see page 315.

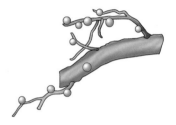

Is the root knobby, bent, or otherwise distorted, but not forked?

YES

↓

OR   Is the root forked? If yes, **rocky, lumpy, or compacted soil**. For solution, see page 238; for photo, see page 409.

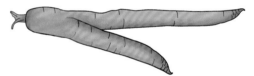

If you cut the root open, are light brown curved lines or arcs absent? If yes, go to page 185.

OR   Is the root a potato (*Solanum tuberosum*), and if you cut it open do you find light brown curved lines or arcs inside? If yes, **potato spraing**. For solution, see page 252.

The root is distorted, stunted, or shriveled

For other categories of root symptoms, see page 163

If you cut the root open, light brown curved lines or arcs are absent

(from page 184)

Is the root a potato (*Solanum tuberosum*) that is knobby, bent, and deformed? If yes, **uneven moisture**. For solution, see page 231; for photo, see page 409.

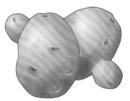

OR Is the root an onion (*Allium cepa*) bulb that is abnormally thick at the top? (Note: The onion takes on the shape of a teardrop.) If yes, **seedstalk formation**. For solution, see page 229.

The root is distorted, stunted, or shriveled

For other categories of root symptoms, see page 163

The root is stunted (from page 183)

Is the root a fleshy storage structure like a carrot (*Daucus*), beet (*Beta*), or onion (*Allium cepa*)?

YES

OR Is the root a small feeder root, not a fleshy storage structure? If yes, **nematodes**. For solution, see page 315.

Are the small side roots of normal size and number (not tiny and hairy), and is the main root normal in texture (not woody)?

YES

OR Is the root covered with tiny, hairy side roots, and is it woody? If yes, **aster yellows**, **curly top virus**. For solution, see page 306 or 309, respectively.

Is the root small, poorly developed, and pale in color? If yes, **poor growing conditions**, **overcrowding**, **nutrient deficiency**. For solution, see page 224.

OR Is the root an onion (*Allium cepa*) that is small or has failed to develop even though the plant has adequate nutrients, space, light, and water? (Note: Onion varieties form bulbs depending on daylength. Long-day varieties cannot make bulbs if planted in winter when days are short. Short-day varieties cannot make bulbs under the long days of summer.) If yes, **daylength**. For solution, see page 229.

The root is distorted, stunted, or shriveled

For other categories of root symptoms, see page 163

The root is shriveled (from page 183)

Is the root something other than an onion (*Allium cepa*)? If yes, **drought**. For solution, see page 231.

OR Is the root an onion? (Note: The roots of the onion, not the bulb, shrivel and turn pink.) If yes, **onion pink root**. For solution, see page 252.

The root is moldy or rotten

For other categories of root symptoms, see page 163

Is part or all of the root rotten?   OR   Is the root moldy? If yes, go to page 190.

YES

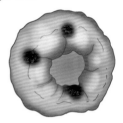

If you break the root open, are tiny white mites absent? (Note: Mites are very tiny spider relatives that look like grains of white sand.)

YES

OR   Is the root a bulb, and if you break it open, do you find tiny white mites inside? If yes, **bulb mites**. For solution, see page 296; for photo, see page 411.

Is all of the root rotten? If yes, go to page 189.

OR   Is the root a potato (*Solanum tuberosum*), and does it have a rotten black ring inside at the stem end? If yes, **bacterial ring rot**. For solution, see page 305; for photo, see page 411.

The root is moldy or rotten

For other categories of root symptoms, see page 163

All of the root is rotten (from page 188)

Is thick, foul-smelling ooze absent?

YES

↓

OR   Is the rotten root filled with thick, foul-smelling ooze? (Note: The ooze may be white or yellowish and turn dark on exposure to air.) If yes, **bacterial rot**. For solution, see page 305; for photo, see page 411.

Is the root soft and slimy and are small brown pellets absent? If yes, **bulb rot**, **soft rot**, **root rot**. For solution, see page 252; for photo, see page 410.

OR   Is the root soft and crumbly and are small brown pellets the size of mustard seeds on the root and in the soil? If yes, **crown rot**. For solution, see page 252; for photo, see page 410.

The root is moldy or rotten

For other categories of root symptoms, see page 163

The root is moldy (from page 188)

Is the root something other than an onion (*Allium cepa*)?

YES

↓

OR Is the root an onion, soft and brown inside with fluffy white mold on the outside? If yes, **onion fusarium basal rot**. For solution, see page 252.

Is the root a dahlia tuber with tufts of pink and yellow mold? If yes, **dahlia tuber rot**. For solution, see page 258.

OR Is the root a bulb (narcissus, for example), and does it have sunken, reddish brown lesions with blue-green or white mold growing on them? If yes, **bulb blue mold**. For solution, see page 258; for photo, see page 410.

The root has bumps, warts, or nodules

For other categories of root symptoms, see page 163

Are large tumor-like growths absent?

YES

↓

OR Are there large tumor-like growths on the root? If yes, **crown gall**, **root gall**. For solution, see page 305.

Are small, knot-like swellings absent?

YES

↓

OR Does the root have small knot-like swellings? (Note: Small swellings on the roots of nitrogen-fixing legumes [Fabaceae] are normal and are not knot-like.) If yes, **root-knot nematodes**. For solution, see page 315.

Are globular, creamy brown aphids (small, pear-shaped soft-bodied insects with two tubes on their rears) feeding on the root? If yes, **root aphids**. (Note: These aphids secrete a white waxy powder.) For solution, see page 284.

OR Are oval, white insects feeding on the roots? If yes, **root mealybugs**. (Note: These insects also secrete a white waxy powder.) For solution, see page 284.

7 Seeds and Seedlings

What is a seed?

A seed is a miraculous invention that helped plants conquer all terrestrial environments. A seed is a small, easily dispersed package containing a dormant baby plant with enough food reserves for the little plant to survive until it is capable of making its own food from sunlight, carbon dioxide, and water. Like an astronaut asleep in his space capsule, the dormant little plant travels far while awaiting a safe landing. Some seeds fly on wings, some float on parachutes, and some ride in the gut of a bird or mammal. Seeds can lie in wait, for years if necessary, until environmental conditions of rainfall and temperature are favorable for germination and growth.

Seeds, as used in this chapter, include various kinds of fruits that are commonly referred to in popular language as seeds or nuts. A fruit like an unshelled sunflower "seed," for example, is a fruit type called an achene. The dry black and white striped hull is the ovary wall, which you break open to eat the actual seed it contains.

Corn (*Zea mays*), like other cereal grasses, has a special fruit type called a caryopsis, but which popular language names a kernel, grain, or "seed." Each kernel of corn is in reality a fruit that contains the actual seed.

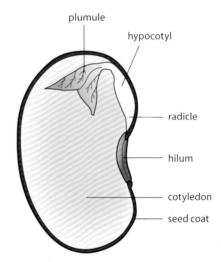

This cross section of a dicot seed, a bean, illustrates what a beautifully compact unit of dispersal a seed really is. The seed coat is the external covering that protects the seed. The baby plant, the plumule, is safely tucked in between two huge cotyledons stuffed with food reserves. The plant uses the food to grow until it can function on its own. The hilum is just like our belly button. Germination begins when water is absorbed through this scar left by the seed's attachment to the mother plant. The radicle grows first and becomes the root system. When the seedling is well anchored by the root system, the hypocotyl flexes, lifting the seedling out of the soil and up into the sunlight.

Some of the delicacies that are commonly called nuts, such as coconuts (*Cocos*), are actually seeds contained in a fruit type called a drupe, just like a peach or plum (*Prunus*). Other fruits that are called nuts—hazelnuts (*Corylus*) and acorns from oaks (*Quercus*), for example—really are nuts.

Edible seeds that are actually seeds include all the legumes (dry beans, shelled peas, and shelled peanuts), shelled sunflower seeds, and pumpkin seeds. Seeds commonly used in planting our gardens include those of the cabbage and its kin (Brassicaceae), tomatoes (*Lycopersicon esculentum*), eggplant (*Solanum melongena*), peppers (*Capsicum*), and members of the squash family (Cucurbitaceae).

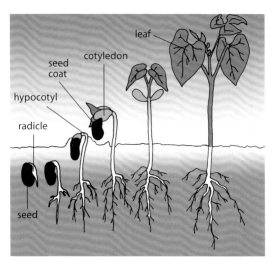

Germination of a seed is an orderly process that begins when water is absorbed and the embryonic plant mobilizes enzymes to utilize the stored fuel in the cotyledons. The first external evidence of germination is the extension of the radicle, the primary root, which quickly anchors the little plant. When the hypocotyl begins to flex and the root is anchored, the cotyledons turn green and raise up out of the ground. Then the seed coat is shed. Now, standing erect, the cotyledons spread wide and the first pair of leaves begins to expand. When the first pair of true leaves forms, the cotyledons shrivel and drop off.

What does a seed do?

The prime directive for the seed is to find the right location in the right environment where it is safe to germinate and grow into a new plant, the next generation of its species.

In order to find the right location and environment, seeds often travel long distances. They travel by a myriad of means, either by themselves or inside the fruit in which they formed. Some stick to clothing, fur, or feathers, and hitchhike a ride to new territory. Others get eaten by birds or mammals when the fruit is gobbled down. The seed is pooped out much later, after the animal has moved on. And some seeds ride the wind.

Of course, this shotgun approach to dispersal results in many failures. Of the billions of seeds produced annually and sent out randomly into the environment, most will fall on stony ground, rain gutters, pavement, or some other inappropriate place where successful germination and establishment is impossible. For the lucky few that settle in a place that provides the proper environmental conditions, a sequence of events is initiated when the seed absorbs water.

Once water is absorbed through the hilum, the dormant seed "awakens" and begins to sprout. Sprouting involves the production of enzymes that break down food such as starch, stored in the cotyledons, into simple energy-rich compounds like sugar to fuel growth. By burning its stored fuel, the little seedling mobilizes all its resources and bursts into rapid growth. It sends out a root which immediately begins to grow down into the soil, anchoring the seedling and providing leverage to pull its stem and cotyledons free. Standing erect, the seedling's cotyledons are now bright green, providing energy through photosynthesis. The seedling produces its first true leaves shortly thereafter, the cotyledons wither and drop off, and the seedling is self-sufficient from this time forward.

What are seed symptoms?

Problems of the seed may be subtle, but symptoms on seedlings are usually obvious. Follow these steps to discover the cause of the problem and find a safe, appropriate remedy.

1. Be sure to look at all sides of your seed or seedling. If more than one symptom occurs, even if you are beset with problems, concentrate on one. It is important to pursue just one symptom at a time.
2. Look at each illustration on page 195 and read the text beside it. Find the seed symptom that most closely matches yours and decide in which category of the flow charts your seed or seedling belongs.
3. Turn to the page indicated for that category of the flow charts—your tool for pinpointing the problem.

WARNING: It is sometimes tempting to try to match your seed or seedling to an illustration without reading the accompanying text. However, it is important to consider the questions. Simply visually matching your seed to a drawing may lead to the wrong diagnosis.

4. Each flow chart poses a series of paired questions (couplets) about a symptom. Answer the questions yes or no. Only one member of each pair of questions can be answered yes.
5. When the answer is yes, follow that arrow or turn to the page listed under the question. Continue answering the questions and following the "yes" arrows through the chart.
6. For the most part, the questions on the left-hand side of the flow charts indicate several symptoms; therefore, they are often not illustrated.
7. When you reach the diagnosis, in red, turn to the page indicated for a solution. If there is a reference to a photo, turn to that page to see a seed or seedling with a similar problem.

In corn (*Zea mays*) and other cereal grasses, the kernel, grain of rice (*Oryza*), or wheat (*Triticum*) berry is both the ovary and the seed.

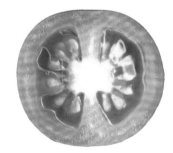

True seeds are borne inside a fruit, which is itself the ripened ovary of a flower as shown in this cross section of a tomato (*Lycopersicon esculentum*).

Categories of root symptoms

Seeds or seedlings are discolored, distorted, or shriveled. Go to page 196.

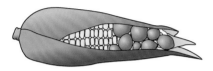

Seeds or seedlings have holes of any size, or fail to emerge after planting. Go to page 197.

Seeds or seedlings are chewed or missing. Go to page 200.

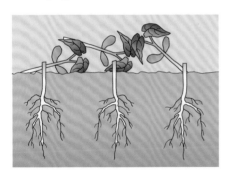

Seedlings grow poorly. Go to page 204.

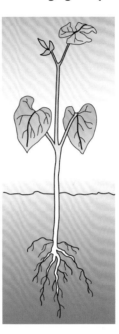

Seeds or seedlings are discolored, distorted, or shriveled

For other categories of seed or seedling symptoms, see page 195

Are seeds never swollen, distorted, and blue-gray in color?

YES

OR Are seeds grotesquely swollen, distorted, and blue-gray in color? If yes, **smut**. (Note: This affects only corn [*Zea mays*], sometimes whole ears; kernels rupture to release masses of powdery black spores.) For solution, see page 245.

Do seeds lack brown spots and cavities?

YES

OR Do seeds have brown spots and cavities inside? If yes, **manganese deficiency**. For solution, see page 238; for photo, see page 412.

Are the seeds nuts, and do the husks have soft, black, rotten blotches? (Note: Creamy to yellowish maggots feed inside.) If yes, **husk flies**. For solution, see page 267, 282; for photo, see page 412.

OR Are the seeds walnuts (*Juglans*), and do the husks have hard, black, sunken blotches? If yes, **walnut blight**. For solution, see page 301; for photo, see page 412.

Seeds or seedlings have holes of any size, or fail to emerge after planting

For other categories of seed or seedling symptoms, see page 195

Do seeds or seedlings have no holes?

YES

OR Do seeds or seedlings have holes? If yes, go to page 198.

Has no rotting of seeds occurred?

YES

OR Have seeds rotted in the soil? If yes, **damping off**. For solution, see page 252; for photo, see page 413.

Are soft-bodied, white grubs with brown heads eating seeds in the soil? (Note: A grub has a brown head and three pairs of jointed legs.) If yes, **corn rootworms**, **seedcorn beetles**, **white grubs**. For solution, see page 284.

OR Are worm-like, hard-shelled, yellow-brown to reddish-brown grubs eating seeds in the soil? If yes, **wireworms**. For solution, see page 284.

Seeds or seedlings have holes of any size, or fail to emerge after planting

For other categories of seed or seedling symptoms, see page 195

Seeds or seedlings have holes (from page 197)

Do seedlings have holes?

YES

OR Do seeds have holes? If yes, go to page 199.

Do germinating seedlings get holes after they emerge from the soil?

YES

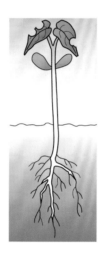

OR Do germinating seedlings get holes before they emerge from the soil? If yes, **white maggots**. (Note: Maggots are insect larvae with no legs and no obvious head.) For solution, see page 282.

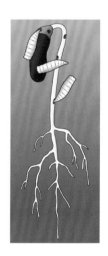

Are slime trails absent? If yes, **earwigs**. For solution, see page 267.

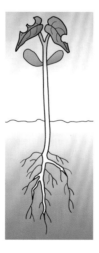

OR Are slime trails present? (Note: Leaves of seedlings may be missing entirely.) If yes, **slugs or snails**. For solution, see page 325.

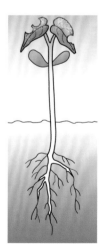

Seeds or seedlings have holes of any size, or fail to emerge after planting

For other categories of seed or seedling symptoms, see page 195

Seeds have holes (from page 198)

Are the seeds nuts, and do they drop early from the tree? If yes, **codling moth larvae**, **pecan shuckworm**, **hickory shuckworm**. (Note: This affects walnuts [*Juglans*], pecans [*Carya illinoinensis*], and hickory nuts [*C. ovata*]. A fat pinkish or white caterpillar has eaten the insides of the nut.) For solution, see page 282.

OR Do seeds have circular holes? If yes, **seed weevils**, **nut weevils**. (Note: This affects many seeds and nuts; white grubs with brown heads have eaten the seeds.) For solution, see page 283; for photo, see page 413.

Seeds or seedlings are chewed or missing

For other categories of seed or seedling symptoms, see page 195

Are seedlings chewed or missing?   OR   Are seeds chewed or missing? If yes, go to page 201.

YES

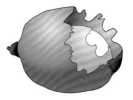

Are seedlings partially or entirely missing?

YES

OR   Are roots missing, but the seedlings are lying on the ground? If yes, **burrowing mice**. For solution, see page 329.

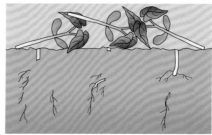

Are seedlings missing entirely, leaving no stubs behind? If yes, **grasshoppers**, **birds**. (Note: Look for grasshoppers in your garden; if these are absent, suspect birds.) For solution, see page 267 or 328, respectively.

OR   Are seedlings chewed off just above the soil line leaving stubs behind? If yes, **cutworms**, **rabbits**. (Note: Look for fat, green or brown caterpillars that curl into a C-shape and hide in the soil around your plants; if these are absent, suspect rabbits.) For solution, see page 267 or 329, respectively.

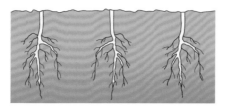

Seeds or seedlings are chewed or missing

For other categories of seed or seedling symptoms, see page 195

Seeds are chewed or missing (from page 200)

Are seeds or nuts chewed, but have not been removed from the plant?
>   YES
>   ↓

OR   Are seeds or nuts missing? (Note: They may be lying on the ground under the plant.) If yes, go to page 203.

Are olive-green caterpillars with yellow-brown heads absent?
>   YES
>   ↓

OR   Are the seeds nuts of a pecan (*Carya illinoinensis*) tree, and are olive-green caterpillars with yellow-brown heads eating the nuts? If yes, **pecan nut casebearer**. (Note: Clusters of nuts may be webbed together with silk.) For solution, see page 283.

Are small cream-colored caterpillars with dark spots absent? (Note: Other caterpillars may be present.) If yes, go to page 202.

OR   Are the seeds peas, and are small cream-colored caterpillars with dark spots feeding on them inside the pods? If yes, **pea moth larvae**. (Note: Little piles of excrement inside the pods show where they have been dining.) For solution, see page 283.

Seeds or seedlings are chewed or missing

For other categories of seed or seedling symptoms, see page 195

Small cream-colored caterpillars with dark spots are absent, though other caterpillars may be present (from page 201)

Are small black beetles with yellow spots absent?

   YES

   ↓

OR   Are the seeds corn kernels, and are small black beetles with yellow spots hollowing them out in the upper half or tips of the ears? If yes, **sap beetles**. For solution, see page 283.

Are the seeds corn (*Zea mays*) kernels, and are large numbers of brown caterpillars with yellow, orange, or dark brown stripes devouring foliage and boring into ears of corn? If yes, **army worms**. (Note: These caterpillars move about en masse and are quite active.) For solution, see page 283.

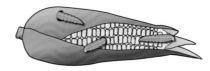

OR   Are the seeds corn kernels, and are ears infested with yellow-, brown-, or green-striped caterpillars, feeding at the tip of the ear inside the husk? If yes, **corn earworms**. For solution, see page 283; for photo, see page 414.

Seeds or seedlings are chewed or missing

For other categories of seed or seedling symptoms, see page 195

Seeds or nuts are missing, though they may be lying on the ground (from page 201)

Are there no cracked nut shells littering the ground? (Note: Uneaten nuts or seeds may be on the ground.)

YES

OR Is the ground littered with cracked nut shells? (Note: Seed or nut meat is gone.) If yes, **squirrels**. For solution, see page 329; for photo, see page 414.

Are there uneaten nuts lying on the ground? If yes, **raccoons**, **bears**, **humans**. For solution, see page 329.

OR Are no uneaten nuts lying on the ground? If yes, **birds**. For solution, see page 328; for photo, see page 414.

The seedlings grow poorly

For other categories of seed or seedling symptoms, see page 195

Are seedlings other than tall, spindly, and pale green?

YES

↓

OR Are seedlings tall, spindly, and pale green? If yes, **insufficient light**. For solution, see page 229; for photo, see page 415.

Are seedling leaves never dark purple with purple veins?

YES

↓

OR Are seedling leaves tinted dark purple with purple veins? If yes, **phosphorus deficiency**. For solution, see page 238.

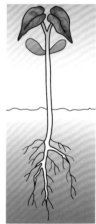

Do seedlings have adequate roots? If yes, go to page 205.

OR Are the seedlings' deep roots dying or dead, while only the shallow roots remain? If yes, **excess water**. For solution, see page 232; for photo, see page 415.

The seedlings grow poorly

For other categories of seed or seedling symptoms, see page 195

Seedlings have adequate roots (from page 204)

Is the pH too high or too low? (Note: Use a simple test kit.) If yes, **pH imbalance**. For solution, see page 238.

OR Are the seedlings warm season plants (tomatoes [*Lycopersicon esculentum*], green beens [*Phaseolus vulgaris*], corn [*Zea mays*]) and has the weather been cool? If yes, **cool weather**. For solution, see page 232.

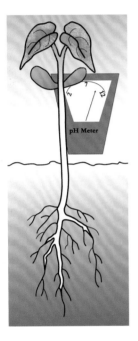

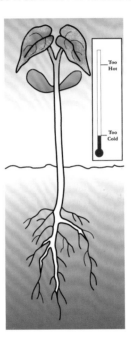

PART 2

How Do I Fix It?

Natural Solutions and Organic Remedies

Prevention is the best medicine

Prevention is always the easiest, cheapest, and most effective solution to any plant problem. The disease triangle is the best guideline for understanding the concept of prevention.

In order for disease to occur on your plant it must be a susceptible host, prone to infection; resistant varieties are less likely to get sick. There must also be a favorable environment; 80 percent of plant problems may be attributed to less-than-ideal growing conditions. And finally, a pest or pathogen (a disease-causing agent) must be present. Fungal spores drift in the air, bacteria are borne by wind-driven rain and water splash, and insects fly in from the neighborhood. There is no shortage of pathogens and pests. They are ever-present.

Best lines of defense

When diseases or pests attack your plants, first check the conditions under which you are growing them. A major weapon in the battle against disease is matching the plant to its best environment. Every plant has an optimum environment. When you create a suitable microclimate for your plant, it experiences much less stress. Just like people, plants under stress can become ill.

1. Put the right plant in the right place. This lets the plant you choose thrive in its own niche: with proper soil conditions and the right amount of light, water, and temperature to enjoy robust good health. If you do all you can to provide a stress-free environment, you will have planted for success.
2. As you plan your garden, or decide which plants to keep in your home, choose varieties that are genetically resistant to diseases or pests.
3. Manage the planting site to permit free air flow and adequate light.
4. Utilize the right amount of water.
5. Protect your plants from extremes of temperature—freezing cold or baking heat.
6. Amend the soil correctly and add the right nutrients.

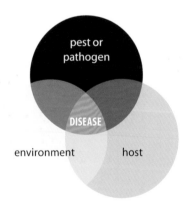

The disease triangle. For disease or pests to occur, all three elements in the large circles must be present.

Resort to chemicals only when necessary

Your second line of defense against plant problems is an arsenal of safe, organic chemicals with very low toxicity. You may wish to use these on your houseplants, outdoor container plants, vegetables, or landscape plants. Various chemicals are certified for use in organic gardening. Many of these organic treatments are relatively safe for you and the environment. Some have been in use for hundreds of years, others are quite new. Look for OMRI (Organic Materials Review Institute) certification on the label.

Remedies acceptable in organic gardening are those derived from naturally occurring substances that come directly from the earth or from plants. They are generally less toxic to humans and to the biosphere than modern, synthetic, designer remedies. They also break down quickly to harmless products. Nevertheless, all chemicals should be stored in a safe place where inquisitive children and pets cannot get at them.

Your personal safety and the safety of your family, pets, and neighborhood are important issues when using remedies of any kind, especially on houseplants. Avoid using chemicals, even organic ones, near bodies of water because many fish and shellfish can be harmed by them. Also, remember that many families of organisms have a "bright side" and a "dark side." Some, such as mycorrhizal fungi or beneficial insects, are the ones that help us grow better plants; others, such as fungal pathogens or insect pests, are the ones that harm our plants. Use organic remedies wisely and protect the good fungi and insects while saving your plants from the bad guys.

Read the label, follow directions, and use products only on the plants specified on the label. Wait for calm weather so that the wind doesn't carry spray drift to places you don't want it to go. If ripe fruit is available for harvest, pick it before you spray. Dress properly for the job at hand and wear long pants, long-sleeved shirts, gloves, goggles, and respiratory protection. Check your equipment to make sure the nozzle is not clogged and the tank is clean before

Roses (*Rosa*) need full sun, regular moisture, and air movement. If they get what they need, they'll get fewer diseases.

Rose (*Rosa*) cultivars that are resistant to disease, such as this climber, 'Dortmund', avoid the devastating impact of the major fungal diseases of roses: black spot, powdery mildew, and rust.

Here's a rose (*Rosa*) with a fighting chance. 'Tournament of Roses', a mildly fragrant, disease-resistant grandiflora, is an All-America Rose Selection, a good indication of quality.

EQUIPMENT

For small tasks in the house or the garden, use an ordinary hand held sprayer with a trigger mechanism.

For larger jobs out in the yard, use a pump-up sprayer with a 1- or 2-gallon capacity.

On even larger outdoor projects, you may want a large capacity backpack sprayer or a hose-attached sprayer.

you mix your solution. Only mix as much as you need. Measure the proper amount of chemical and follow directions. More is not better. Measure accurately. Follow the directions on the label to learn how to dispose of any leftover chemical.

Apply sprays in the early morning to give foliage a chance to dry out unless the instructions on the label advise otherwise. This also helps to protect beneficial insects, which are more active later in the day, after it warms up. Apply thoroughly to both sides of leaves, stems, and trunks. When you're finished, take a shower and put on fresh clothes.

We highly recommend that you stroll through your garden or "visit" your houseplants at least once a week and really look at your plants. This gives you the opportunity to observe the health and beauty of your plants. You will also find that life is more enjoyable.

SAFETY FIRST

1. Always keep all these products **out of the reach of children and pets.**

2. **Read the label.** Use only chemicals that list the plants or type of plant you wish to protect on their labels. For example, a label may say "For use on ornamentals." Do not use this on a food plant.

3. **Follow the directions on the label.** Remember that more is not better. Many chemicals can actually damage some plants. This kind of damage is called a phytotoxic reaction. It is important to read the label and follow the manufacturer's instructions. If you put too much of the active ingredient on your plant, or if you put it on the wrong plant, you may do more harm than good.

   Every package or bottle of a garden remedy product has a label on the back that peels open. Unfold it and read the tiny print inside to learn what the product is used for, which plants to use it on, when to use it, and how much to use. Some of these labels unfold into long pages of instructions. Be patient, get out your magnifying glass, and read them carefully. Follow those directions.

4. **Always use the least toxic product first.** Look for a signal word on the label. These signal words are required by federal law under the Federal Insecticide, Fungicide and Rodenticide Act (FIFRA). All commercially sold pesticides must be registered with the Environmental Protection Agency (EPA), the registration authority for pesticides, and tested for modes of transmission into the body: inhalation, ingestion, dermal contact, primary eye, and primary skin. Toxicity Category IV requires no signal word because tests have shown the product to be non-toxic; these products, such as baking soda spray and insecticidal soap, are the safest, least toxic products you can use. Any pesticide determined to be in Toxicity Category III must be labeled **CAUTION**. Any in Toxicity Category II must carry the label **WARNING**. Those in Category I must be labeled either **DANGER** (the most toxic product available to the home gardener) or **DANGER— POISON**, with an image of a skull and crossbones. The last is most toxic of all. It is available only to licensed pesticide applicators.

5. **Wear protective gear and clothing.** Wear goggles, a respiratory face mask, a long-sleeved shirt, long pants, and shoes. Wash your clothes when you are finished using any product with a signal word.

8 Growing Conditions

What are growing conditions?

Growing conditions are environmental factors that affect the well-being of your plants. Light, water, temperature, and soil nutrients are the factors we look at in this chapter.

Sunlight is, of course, vital. All green plants manufacture food from sunlight through photosynthesis. Fertilizer and mineral nutrients are sometimes called "plant food," but that is an erroneous concept. Sugar is actually "plant food," and plants create sugar out of solar energy, water, and carbon dioxide. Obviously, if a plant does not get enough sunlight it becomes malnourished and could even starve to death.

Water, like sunlight, is also absolutely vital to a plant's well-being. It moves through the plant's veins like blood in our own bodies. Water transports food and mineral nutrients to every cell. Roots absorb water, which moves up through the stem and is lost to the air through the leaves. Losing water through the leaves is the pump that drives water movement through the plant's body. If the pump stops, the plant can get into serious, life-threatening trouble very quickly.

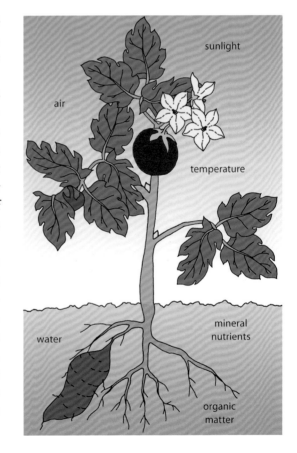

212

Many people pay attention to a plant's temperature needs, because they are aware of the danger of winter cold. In the United States, the Department of Agriculture (USDA) created a winter hardiness zone map, and almost all plant labels in U.S. nurseries list the USDA zones to which the plant is adapted. For example, a plant label may list appropriate zones as 9 through 11. This means that the plant will freeze to death in zones 1 through 8. This zone system does not reflect other temperature factors, such as heat tolerance, or whether a plant needs winter chilling to flower and set fruit.

Healthy soil is a microcosmic ecosystem, filled with millions of bacteria and fungi, and with organic matter. This teeming micro-flora and -fauna maintains mineral nutrients, outcompetes pests and disease-causing pathogens, and conserves water. If your soil is healthy and rich, you have met the most fundamental requirement for happy, healthy plants.

Freezing winter cold constitutes poor growing conditions for this avocado (*Persea*) in California.

What do growing conditions affect?

Good growing conditions are the foundation for plant health. Eighty percent of plant problems are due to poor growing conditions.

Plant problems caused by inadequate growing conditions are called disorders, not diseases or pests. A disorder is caused by too much or too little of some critical factor: light, water, temperature, or nutrients. Disorders can also be caused by poor management, such as failure to thin a heavy crop of fruit, lack of deadheading (removing the spent flower clusters before they make seeds), or pruning at the wrong time of year. By contrast, a disease is caused by a patho-

Heavy fruit on this peach (*Prunus persica*) tree caused an overloaded branch to break. The grower should have thinned the crop.

gen, such as a fungus, bacterium, or virus. A pest is a destructive organism, such as an insect, mite, nematode, rodent, or deer.

Sometimes it can be difficult to determine whether you are dealing with a disorder, a disease, or a pest. Yellowing leaves, for example, can be caused by many things, such as lack of nitrogen (disorder), root rot (a fungal disease), or aphids (pests). Accurate diagnosis requires detective work, which is exactly what you do when you work your way through the questions in the flow charts of Part 1 of this book. The questions are designed to detect information that eliminates, one by one, all alternative causes and results in an accurate diagnosis.

Types of solutions

For prevention, solutions begin on page 215.

Prevention is the best long-term solution for problems due to disorders, pests, and diseases. There are a host of pro-active things you can do to prevent problems from arising in the first place. They work equally well to keep problems from coming back. Incorporate prevention measures into your garden or container plantings during the planning stage. Implement them as a matter of routine in your management and maintenance program.

For cultural conditions, solutions begin on page 222.

Common cultural problems are things that affect the performance of your plant. Your plant may fail to flower because you cut off all the flower buds by pruning at the wrong time of year. Branches of your apple tree may break off due to the weight of too many apples because you did not thin the crop. Perhaps your plant produces lots of small flowers instead of a few big ones because you did not disbud it at the appropriate time. These are all management issues. They are not due to pests or diseases, and they are very common in many gardens.

For light conditions, solutions begin on page 229.

Every plant has an optimum range of light that it needs. There are several things you can do to limit or increase the amount of light your plant is getting.

For managing water, solutions begin on page 229.

Too much or too little water also has a major impact on plant performance. Both conditions are life threatening to your plant. Managing water properly to meet the needs of your plant is very important.

For temperature conditions, solutions begin on page 232.

Temperature requirements are also critical for plant health. Plants can freeze because it is too cold. This is clearly a serious problem, but there are less dire temperature disorders as well.

For managing soil and nutrients, solutions begin on page 234.

Nutrient deficiencies are very common disorders that many plant owners eventually encounter. Encouraging healthy soil is key to plant health.

Solutions for prevention

We begin with prevention because by using these techniques as soon as possible, pests and disease will not spread to your healthy plants. Using preventive measures also makes less work and lower costs for you. Even better, prevention lessens environmental impacts on our precious natural resources.

▶ **Put the right plant in the right place.** A good plant in the wrong location is a plant under stress, which increases susceptibility to pests and diseases. Water, sunlight, temperature, and soil nutrient imbalances all contribute to plant problems.

Consult plant labels and packaging, and reliable books, magazines, and Internet sites to determine a plant's requirements for water, sunlight, temperature, and soils. Use this information to better meet plants' needs or to move unhappy plants. Then:

- Put plants with similar needs in the same bed or area.
- Transplant an ailing plant to a more appropriate location if you can do so without damaging the plant or its root system.
- Move plants in containers, whether on your deck or in your house, to the appropriate microclimate.

▶ **Choose resistant cultivars.** Many new varieties of popular vegetables and ornamental plants are genetically resistant to pests or diseases, which helps prevent diseases and pests from getting a toehold. Certain cultivars of roses (*Rosa*), for example, are resistant to leaf fungus diseases like black spot, powdery mildew, or rust. Some cultivars of corn (*Zea mays*) are more resistant to corn earworms than others because their husks are tighter and keep insects out. Some cultivars of tomato (*Lycopersicon esculentum*) are more resistant to aphids than others. Pest and disease organisms often have host plant preferences, and you can use this knowledge to your advantage. Whiteflies, for example, love hibiscus but do not like pepper plants (*Capsicum*) nearly so much.

To find pest- or disease-resistant varieties, check with your Cooperative Extension Service and your local Master Gardener organization. Local knowledge is invaluable. Look in catalogs from suppliers, or do an Internet search. Read labels on plants, bulbs, tubers, or seed packets:

- A package of green bean (*Phaseolus vulgaris*) seeds may read, "An extra bonus is the proven disease resistance of 'Slenderette' to bean mosaic and curly top virus." 'Slenderette' is the cultivar name.
- Other packaging might read, "Green bean 'Slenderette', BCMV." BCMV signifies resistance to bean common mosaic virus.
- Packaging of vegetables might have the letters N for nematode resistance, TMV for tobacco mosaic virus resistance, F for fusarium fungus resistance, and V for verticillium fungus resistance.

Many resources also list deer-resistant plants. If a catalog description does not say a plant or seed is disease- or pest-resistant, then it probably isn't. Internet searches will yield vast amounts of information, and you will quickly find appropriate varieties, and locations where you can purchase them.

If you need to remove a dead or dying plant due to a pest infestation or a lethal infection, replace your dead plant with one that is resistant to the problem. Do not put the same kind of plant back in the infected planting hole. Select a completely different kind of plant, one that is resistant to the pest or disease.

▶ **Start with disease-free seeds, plants, and bulbs.** Inspect bulbs, tubers, corms, and rhizomes. Look for brown spots, moldy patches, or shriveled tissue. Buy only those that are firm and free of spots or mold. Examine the leaves, stems, and flowers of plants you want to purchase and check for discolored spots, distorted tissues, wilting, or other problems. Buy only plants that are healthy and free of obvious defects.

You may find the cheap 59-cent specials at the supermarket very attractive because of the

Check flowers, stems, leaves, and roots for problems before you buy. These pansies (*Viola*) are in good condition.

extremely low price. But beware, supermarkets rarely have the personnel or the knowledge to maintain healthy plants. These bargain basement plants can easily have serious problems that make them far more trouble than they are worth.

▶ **Quarantine and isolate.** You cannot see some pests and diseases. Two-spotted spider mites, cyclamen mites, and some bacterial diseases are examples. In addition, a sick plant may be symptomless in the early stages of infection. Whenever you buy a new plant or receive a gift plant, if you have any doubts about its health, keep your new plant in quarantine. Isolate it from existing plants until you are sure it is free of pests or disease.

Be sure to move the quarantined plant far away from all your other plants even if those plants are not related to the sick plant. Insect-borne plant viruses can frequently cross genetic barriers and infect many different kinds of plants. Be sure to clean your tools and wash your hands after working with any plant in quarantine.

▶ **Plant polycultures, not monocultures.** Putting the same plant, or closely related plants, next to each other allows rapid spread of diseases. Imagine a field of corn (*Zea mays*), or an apple (*Malus*) orchard, or a lawn. These are monocultures, situations where a large number of plants, all of the same kind, are growing in close proximity to each other, and all are susceptible to the same pests and diseases. Containers placed close to each other, all planted with the same plant, effectively create monocultures. As with people crowded onto an airplane, one sick individual can infect many.

By contrast, a polyculture helps to inhibit the spread of pests and diseases. Distributing flowers, herbs, and vegetables throughout garden beds, so each plant's closest neighbor is different, greatly reduces the incidence of diseases (fungal, bacterial, and viral) and pests (insects, mites, and nematodes).

Incorporating flowers and herbs into the vegetable garden provides multiple benefits in the form of effective pest and disease management. Herbs such as fennel (*Foeniculum*) and dill (*Anethum*) attract beneficial insects to help control insect pests. Flowers like yarrow (*Achillea*), cosmos, and rudbeckia also attract beneficial insects, and marigolds repel root-knot nematodes. Lavender (*Lavandula*), rosemary (*Rosmarinus*), thyme (*Thymus*), and sage (*Salvia*) repel deer.

Container gardening also benefits from the polyculture concept. Plant different kinds of plants in your containers in a harmonious combination of color, texture, and form. Then arrange your containers so that unrelated plants are near each other.

▶ **Rotate plants.** Do not put the same plants or the same kinds of plants in the same location year after year. For annuals, vegetables, and bulbs, this is an effective way to avoid soil-borne diseases caused by fungi and bacteria, and pests such as insects and nematodes.

Vegetables. Many experienced vegetable gardeners have well-thought-out plans for rotating their crops. For example, they may grow tomatoes every year, but each year, for three

years, they put them in a different location. In the fourth year, they go back to the first tomato plot. This planting sequence, known as a three-year crop rotation, can be repeated indefinitely.

Suggested three-year crop rotation.

	YEAR 1	YEAR 2	YEAR 3	YEAR 4
Bed A	Group 1	Group 2	Group 3	Repeat Year 1
Bed B	Group 3	Group 1	Group 2	Repeat Year 1
Bed C	Group 2	Group 3	Group 1	Repeat Year 1

Group 1	Nightshades: tomato, potato, bell pepper, chili pepper, eggplant, tomatillo
Group 2	Root vegetables: carrot, onion, sweet potato, beet
Group 3	Cole crops: cabbage, broccoli, cauliflower, Brussels sprouts, kohlrabi, kale

As you plan your crop rotation scheme, keep in mind that you want polycultures. When you plant each bed or container, be sure to interplant with different kinds of plants. For example, include marigolds (*Tagetes*) between your tomatoes (*Lycopersicon esculentum*), and when you move your tomato planting bed each year, move your marigolds along with it.

Annuals. Flowers such as petunias, marigolds, or impatiens that live for a single season are called annuals. Like vegetables, you should not plant the same kind of plant in the same location every year. Make a plan that allows you to follow a rotation schedule similar to the one you use for vegetables.

Spring and summer bulbs. Some bulbs must be dug up each season and stored until replanted. Rotate their planting sites just as you would for vegetables or annuals. Spring bulbs, like tulips (*Tulipa*), daffodils (*Narcissus*), or crocus, are lifted in summer, after the foliage dies down, when they have become crowded and no longer flower well. Summer bulbs or tubers, like gladiolus, dahlias, or begonias, are lifted (dug up) in fall to protect them from freezing. In either case, replant in new locations.

Perennials, trees, and shrubs. Plants such as perennials, trees, and shrubs, which are permanently planted in the landscape, clearly cannot be rotated in the same way as annual vegetables can. But should you lose a tree or shrub to a root-destroying fungus, nematodes, or insect pests, do not replace it with the same species in the same planting hole. Some fungi and nematodes can live in the soil for years. If you really must have the same plant in that hole, wait five years. It is better to find an acceptable substitute that is resistant to the pest or disease that killed your original tree.

Dying branches of this juniper (*Juniperus*) indicate *Fusarium*, a serious fungus infection that jeopardizes the plant's life. Replace this shrub with a *Fusarium*-resistant plant.

▶ **Plant at the right time.** Insects are major vectors for transmitting viral and bacterial diseases, but insect populations fluctuate according to the seasons. For many insects, their numbers generally increase as spring progresses into summer and decrease as summer yields to fall. Therefore, it is sometimes possible to time your planting to lessen the insects' effect on the health of your plant. For example, plant peas (*Pisum*) in early spring so that the peas mature before the weather gets warm enough for the pea aphid population to build up. This avoids virus diseases that aphids transmit to your pea crop.

Exact timing depends on the climate in your specific geographic location, the kinds of pest insects present in your area, and which kinds of plants you want to grow. Search the Internet, or check with your Cooperative Extension Service and your local Master Gardener organization. These are all sources of information specific to your particular location and pest species.

▶ **Encourage beneficial organisms.** To attract beneficial organisms to your garden, grow species of plants these animals prefer as sources of food or shelter. Also provide water in very shallow containers, such as a bird bath or plant saucer. Some examples of plants to grow:

- The carrot family (Apiaceae): coriander, dill, fennel, parsley
- The mint family (Lamiaceae): catnip, thyme, rosemary, hyssop, lemon balm
- The daisy family (Asteraceae): cosmos, yarrow, coneflower

Spiders and birds are also efficient predators of insects and other pests. A spider's web may be a nuisance if its location is inconvenient for you, but it's better not to kill the spider. She's just doing her job—to catch and eat as many insects as she can. Many birds eat insects exclusively, while some are part-time insect eaters. Other birds relish snails and slugs. Attract birds of all kinds to your garden with water and shelter. They are valuable allies.

To increase your chances of controlling pests with beneficial organisms, purchase them at your local garden center or through mail-order suppliers. Check with the supplier to determine which species is the best choice for your particular problem, host plants, and environmental conditions.

- Green lacewings, ladybird beetles, praying mantises, mealybug destroyers, and minute pirate bugs all hunt, kill, and eat many pests.
- Parasitoids—such as *Trichogramma* wasps for caterpillars, *Encarsia formosa* for whitefly, and several aphid parasites—lay their eggs inside other insects.
- Beneficial nematodes control insects that dwell in the soil for all or a portion of their life cycle.
- Predatory mites attack and kill spider mites and cyclamen mites. Species of *Phytoseiulus*, *Amblyseius*, or *Metaseiulus* are available.

At garden centers, purchase a packet that contains a card that you mail to a supply company. The company then sends you 200 or more eggs or pupae. Put many of the eggs or pupae where the pests are most abundant, but be sure to distribute the rest throughout your plants.

You can also buy praying mantis eggs at many garden centers; keep the eggs indoors until they hatch (four to six weeks), then release the babies outdoors. Adult ladybird beetles (lady bugs) are also available. Be sure to release these in the early evening only, so that they turn to settling in instead of flying off to your neighbor's yard.

▶ **Provide air movement.** Whether they're on your windowsill, on your deck, or out in the garden, plants crowded together and plants with dense foliage are more susceptible to pests and diseases. Give each plant room enough for the air to move freely between them. Prune individual plants to open them up to light and air. Both these tactics allow the foliage to dry quickly after rain and reduce the number and kind of fungus infections on your plants. Both tactics also expose insect pests to predators, allowing the predators to help you control these pests.

Space plants well apart. Allow plenty of air flow between the plants. Plants in containers, indoors or out, need adequate air movement in order to avoid fungus diseases and insect pests. For houseplants, use a fan on a low setting to keep air moving around foliage and flowers.

Prune woody plants to open the center. Allow more air and sunlight to reach foliage by pruning roses, fruit trees, and ornamental shrubs and trees to allow better air circulation and rapid drying. In general, prune woody plants like fruit trees and roses (*Rosa*) to a scaffold of branches that resembles an inside-out umbrella or a martini glass. The center is kept completely open.

Plants like rhododendrons, azaleas, and other woody ornamentals where a rounded crown is desired may be better served by thinning excess stems out of the center while leaving enough foliage to close the canopy for a full look.

Prune surrounding plants. Add sunlight and air to a plant's microclimate by pruning the surrounding plants to give your plant more space. This decreases shade, increases air circulation, and exposes pests to predators.

Prune roses (*Rosa*) and fruit trees to open the center to light and air. Keep the main branches in the shape of a cone.

▶ **Mulch and top-dress.** Mulch is material used to cover the surface of the soil around plants. Mulch for container plants, called topdressing, is usually more decorative than outdoor mulch.

Mulch and topdressing help prevent weeds, conserve moisture, and control pests and diseases. These materials also prevent water-splash. Plant parts close to the ground or growing media are most susceptible to infection from fungus spores, bacteria, and nematodes splashing up from the ground in water. Mulch and topdressing also help control insect pests that hide in the soil during the day and come out at night to devour your plants. Many materials can be used for mulch:

- Biodegradable materials, such as sustainably harvested bark mulch, crushed coconut and other nut husks, pine needles, straw, newspaper, and cardboard. These break down and add nutrients to the soil

A woody plant in need of pruning can be handled in one of two ways: by thinning or clipping. Thinning appears in image A; and clipping appears in image B.

A. The best way to prune a woody plant is to thin out (remove) excess branches selectively. All blue branches in the image above are being removed.

B. Another, but less desirable, pruning method, is clipping. All branches on the plant are clipped back. Clipping can remove flower buds and alters the natural shape of the plant.

over time. Cardboard should be top-dressed with a more attractive material. Do not use "Beauty Bark," since it may be treated with herbicides.

- Fine gravel, decorative stone, or sand. Use as a topdressing on container plants to control fungus gnats or as a mulch around lavender (*Lavandula*) or other plants to control root rot.
- Grass clippings. But be careful: You must be certain no weed killer was used on the grass, and you must also be sure that the clippings contain no weed seeds.

▶ **Remove weeds.** Getting rid of weeds is a big help in managing diseases, insect populations, and other pests like slugs and snails in your garden. Weeds compete with your plants for water, nutrients, and sunlight. In addition, many weeds harbor plant diseases, harmful insects, and other pests. Some viral, bacterial, and mollicute diseases, for example, that infect weeds are brought into your garden by insects that first feed on the infected weeds and then feed on your plants. Weeds also provide hiding places for slugs and snails. Some techniques to control weeds:

- Sheet mulch. An excellent way to eliminate pernicious perennial weeds. First, mow or cut the weeds to ground level. Cover the area with flattened cardboard boxes or several thicknesses of newspaper. Do not allow any sunlight to penetrate through to the ground. Cover the cardboard with a layer of organic mulch. Within a few months to a year, so long as the weeds cannot get any sunlight, they

will die. The cardboard will decompose to fertilizer.

- Hoe or pull weeds. This works well in established areas where you leave the plants you want to keep. Some weeds such as Canada thistle (*Cirsium*), field bindweed (*Convolvulus*), or horsetail (*Equisetum*) regenerate from tiny pieces of root that you leave behind. This can be absolutely maddening, but diligence is rewarded with eventual success.
- Use a pre-emergent herbicide (germination inhibitor). Corn gluten prevents weed seeds (and any other seeds) from germinating. It has no effect on established plants. It is an organic product that feeds the soil as it degrades and provides nitrogen to enrich the soil. Non-GMO corn gluten is available for those concerned about using genetically modified corn products in gardens. Search for it on the Internet.
- Flame with a weed burner. It goes without saying that you need to be extremely careful not to burn down the neighborhood. Wait for a calm day and do not use it near any area with an extensive fuel load of dead grass, weeds, or brush.

▶ **Sterilize tools.** Any time you wound a plant with any tool you can inadvertently spread viruses, bacterial diseases, or nematodes. If you cut any plant for any reason, sterilize your tools before you use them on another plant. Be especially vigilant if you suspect a plant is sick but have not yet removed and destroyed it.

Pests and diseases can also travel from one

location to another on a dirty shovel. After you dig up an infected plant, clean your shovel.

- Soap and water. At a minimum, wash your tools with soap and water, then rinse them off with rubbing alcohol. This may not be 100 percent effective.
- Bleach. Soak pruners, saws, knives, and other tools in a 10 percent solution of household bleach (1 cup of bleach to 9 cups of water) for five minutes. Rinse the bleach off and wipe the tool with a good quality oil. This method will eventually corrode metal tools.
- Heat. Using a blowtorch, heat your tools until they are very, very hot. Let them cool before using them again. This method will not corrode metal tools.

▶ **Learn proper pruning techniques.** Pruning is a very complex subject, and, in fact, arborists go to school for years to become genuine experts. Consult a good reference book that describes the pruning needs of each plant you are thinking of pruning. The timing of your pruning can be critical to flower or fruit production. Nevertheless, you can use the general guidelines that we call the Four-D Rule and the Three-Protection Regulations (with a wink and a nod to the EPA).

▶ **Change the place to suit the plant.** If you are managing an existing garden it may be difficult to put an ailing plant in a more appropriate location. Nevertheless, when you have a plant in trouble, look it up in a garden book to determine its needs. If a plant cannot be moved, try modifying the local microclimate to better suit the needs of your plant. Be creative. Here are some tips:

- If the plant receives too much sunlight and is getting sunburned, create shade. Build a small individual trellis overhead or plant a tree to cast dappled light on it on hot afternoons.
- For more light and air, decrease shade and increase air flow by pruning surrounding plants.
- For too much water, improve the drainage or reroute runoff away from the plant.
- For too little water, reroute runoff toward the plant or increase watering time or amount.
- If the plant requires acid soil (like blueberries, rhododendrons, or gardenias) acidify the soil with sulfur, coffee grounds, or an acid fertilizer specifically made for these plants.

Solutions for cultural conditions

Normal processes

Diagnoses from Part 1.

CHAPTER	PAGE	DIAGNOSIS
2 Leaves	32	old age
2 Leaves	35	physiological leaf-spot
2 Leaves	46	flagging
3 Flowers	70	old age
3 Flowers	85	ethylene
3 Flowers	85	pollination (wilting)

Old age of leaves (from page 32) and **flagging** (page 46). Most people know that when autumn leaves turn color and fall, the leaves have reached the end of their time, the end of the growing season. This is normal. People new

THE FOUR-D RULE

Always prune woody plants in the following order:

1. **Dead.** Prune away any branches or twigs that are already dead or clearly dying.

2. **Damaged.** Look for damaged and broken branches and remove them.

3. **Diseased.** Remove branches and other stem tissue that have diseases or pests, such as cankers, galls, bacterial or fungal infections, or insect infestations.

4. **Deranged.** Look over your plant carefully and prune away branches that cross into the middle of the plant or that take off in weird directions.

After you have removed material in this order, then look at your plant to decide if it needs further pruning for shape, size, fruit production, or aesthetic appeal.

THREE-PROTECTION REGULATIONS

These three "regulations" protect your plant from the dangers of wanton pruning.

1. **Always prune just above a node.** Never leave a stub. The node is where buds are located. If you prune just below a node or in between two nodes, you leave a stub. This section of stem (the internode) cannot grow new stems. All it can do is sit there and become infected and rot. A stub is an open invitation to diseases that can kill your plant.

2. **Prune to nodes with buds that face away from the center of the plant.** New branches that grow from these buds will grow out and away from the center of the plant, leaving the center open to fresh air and sunshine. This helps to avoid diseases and pests.

3. **Never cut a branch off flush with the trunk.** The place where a branch joins the main trunk or larger branch is usually slightly swollen and is called a collar. The collar is special tissue that can quickly grow over and seal the wound when you prune off the branch. Always protect the collar.

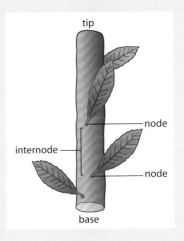

to the world of plants may not know that all leaves, even evergreen leaves, have a finite life span. Plants discard old leaves. Old pine (*Pinus*) needles, arborvitae (*Thuja*) twiglets, rhododendron leaves, and other evergreen foliage fall at certain times of the year. This is also normal.

Physiological leaf-spot (from page 35). Leaves of some plants develop spots that look like leaf-spot fungus infections at certain times of the year. The leaves of photinias, cherry laurel (*Prunus laurocerasus*), and some *Rhododendron* cultivars commonly develop dark reddish-purple to purple-black spots in the fall and winter. It is an environmental disorder, not a disease, and is primarily induced by cold weather. No corrective action needs to be taken.

Old age of flowers (from page 70), **ethylene** (page 85), and **pollination** (page 85). Most flowers have a much shorter life span than leaves. The petals normally wilt and drop to the ground as they age, especially after they have been successfully pollinated. The ageing process can mimic fungal or bacterial disease, however, especially in flowers with thick petals that turn brown and blotchy in old age. Make sure that young flowers that have recently opened are unaffected (if they are affected, consult Chapter 9). If older flowers only are affected, this is a normal ageing process, not a disease, and you need take no action.

Phalaenopsis and many other orchid flowers wilt slowly after they have been successfully pollinated but do not drop off the plant. Ethylene gas, generated by ripening apples, also causes orchid flowers to wilt. If wilt is caused by pollination, only one or two flowers in an inflorescence wilt. With ethylene gas, all the flowers on the whole inflorescence wilt. To control unwanted pollination, screen windows and vents to keep pollinators, such as bees, out. To control ethylene gas wilt, keep ripening fruit away from orchids.

Poor growing conditions

Diagnoses from Part 1.

CHAPTER	PAGE	DIAGNOSIS
4 Fruit	106	russeting
4 Fruit	119	environmental stress
6 Roots	176	poor growing conditions
6 Roots	186	poor growing conditions, overcrowding, nutrient deficiency

Russeting (from page 106). Patches of corky tissue on the surface of fruit is called russeting. It is commonly caused by environmental factors,

Brown corky tissue developing on this apple is called russeting.

such as water remaining on the surface of the fruit for long periods. Prevent this condition by watering the soil, not the plant, so that the fruit does not get wet (see page 229). Also, prune the plant to expose the fruit to light and air so that it dries quickly after rain (see page 219).

Environmental stress (from page 119). Insufficient water causes dry, pulpy fruit. When your plant is not getting enough water, it looks sickly and grows slowly, and the fruit quality is very poor. To avoid this problem make sure your plant is adequately hydrated.

Poor growing conditions (from page 176, 186) including **overcrowding** and **nutrient deficiency**. Root vegetables, such as potatoes, may develop gray/black hollow cavities when the soil environment is too cold and too wet for long periods during the growing season. Improve drainage and allow the soil to dry out (see page 230). Small, poorly developed roots

Failure to thin carrots adequately has resulted in stunted, misshapen roots due to overcrowding.

that are pale in color signal a variety of environmental issues. Make sure your plants are spaced or thinned properly to avoid overcrowding. Also, make sure your mineral nutrition is adequate (see page 234).

Mechanical damage

Diagnoses from Part 1.

CHAPTER	PAGE	DIAGNOSIS
1 Whole Plant	18	mechanical damage
1 Whole Plant	22	blow down
1 Whole Plant	23	girdling
2 Leaves	33	mechanical damage (to root system)
2 Leaves	46	mechanical damage (broken branches)
4 Fruit	108	mechanical damage (hail)
5 Stems	133, 143	lawnmowers, weed-eaters
6 Roots	173	mechanical injury followed by disease

Mechanical damage (from page 18, 33) to the root system of your plant can result from disturbance to the root zone, or compaction of the soil during construction projects, or digging around your plants. The plant may die many months after the project is completed. If only a portion of the root system has been damaged, however, the plant may recover and grow a new root system to replace the damaged portion. If you have recently completed a construction project and your plant is looking sickly but isn't dead yet, give it extra fertilizer and water to help it grow new roots.

Blow down (from page 22) can result from several factors. The tree may be shallow-rooted because the water table is too high. It may have been severely rootbound in its container when it was planted, and the roots have continued to grow in a spiral, failing to anchor the tree securely. The roots may have been killed by root rot fungi or rodents. Whatever the cause, you cannot save the tree. When you plant a new tree, however, make sure you correct whatever condition caused the failure of your first tree so that the second attempt has a better chance of success.

Girdling (from page 23). When a rope, wire, clothesline, or string is wrapped so tightly around the trunk of a tree or shrub that it cuts off the supply of nutrients or water, girdling results. Leaves and branches above the constriction will be stunted, off-color, and sickly. Below the obstruction, growth will be normal. The remedy? Remove the obstruction, and the plant should recover nicely.

Broken branches (from page 46) will cause the leaves above the break to wilt, discolor, and die. Below the break, the plant will be normal. You cannot heal the break, just prune the broken branch away.

Hail storms (from page 108) can leave permanent marks on developing fruit. The tissue is damaged by the impact of the hail stones and does not recover. No pests or diseases are involved in this problem; it is strictly an environmental issue. If you live in an area where hail storms are a regular occurrence, plant after the hail season is over for the year.

Trees and shrubs can be damaged by **lawnmowers, weed-eaters, and other equipment** (from page 133, 143) resulting in missing patches of bark on trunks or exposed roots at or near the soil line. These wounds are an open invitation to pathogenic fungi and bacteria. Protect your plants by creating barriers to keep equipment away from them.

Roots and root vegetables can turn black, mushy, and rotten after **mechanical injury** (from page 173) by shovels, hoes, or other tools. The wounds provide an entry point for pathogenic fungi or bacteria to invade and ruin the plant. The solution here is to be careful when using tools in the ground and avoid injuring your plants.

Herbicide or pesticide damage

Diagnoses from Part 1.

CHAPTER	PAGE	DIAGNOSIS
1 Whole Plant	23	herbicide damage
2 Leaves	42, 60	herbicide damage
3 Flowers	68, 71	herbicide or pesticide damage
3 Flowers	79, 80	herbicide damage
5 Stems	149	herbicide damage

Herbicide or pesticide damage can occur on the whole plant, leaves, flowers, or stems. The damage causes a variety of symptoms. Once the damage has occurred, the affected tissue will not recover. The plant may grow out of it, however, and be back to normal the next growing season. We do not recommend the use of herbicides (weed killers). If you decide you need to use one of these products anyway, do so on a day that is not windy in order to avoid spray drift onto your plants. If your neighbor uses her-

Brown, dead tissue on the leaves of this dandelion (*Tarax-acum*) will never recover from the effects of an herbicide. However, the plant may recover and grow new leaves.

bicides, ask them not to apply them on a windy day. Some pesticides like sulfur and copper can also harm your plants, causing a phytotoxic reaction. Read the label and follow directions in order to avoid harm to your plants.

Improper management

Diagnoses from Part 1.

CHAPTER	PAGE	DIAGNOSIS
1 Whole Plant	20	rootbound
3 Flowers	81	lack of disbudding
3 Flowers	88	lack of deadheading
3 Flowers	89	poor pruning timing
4 Fruit	117	poor pollination
4 Fruit	119	too much fruit
5 Stems	146	heavy fruit crop, heavy snow, wind, weak forks, bears, children

Rootbound (from page 20) plants in containers frequently wilt and need to be watered regularly because the plant has outgrown its pot. One remedy is to up-pot the plant to a larger container to give it a larger volume of soil to plumb for water. Another remedy is to pull the plant out of its pot, shave off 1 inch (2.5 cm) of roots and soil around all the sides and bottom of the root ball, then put the plant back in its pot and pack it with fresh potting soil; this technique will keep a woody plant like a tree or shrub in the same container for many years.

Lack of disbudding, lack of deadheading, poor pruning timing (from page 81, 88, 89). The point of **disbudding** (removing all but one flower bud from each inflorescence) is to force the plant to put all its energy into one really big flower instead of lots of small flowers. If you are disappointed in the size of your roses or dahlias, try disbudding while the flower buds are still very tiny. **Deadheading** (removing spent flowers before they make seeds) prevents the plant from putting all its energy into making seeds. Once seed production begins, many plants will stop flowering completely. Some shrubs, such as lilacs (*Syringa*), flower only in alternate years if they are not deadheaded. **Pruning at the wrong time** of the year can cut off all the flowers so that your plant never gets a chance to bloom. Some plants, such as lilacs, forsythia, and mock orange (*Philadelphus*) need to be pruned in early summer, as soon as they have finished their spring bloom. Other plants, such as fruit trees and grapes (*Vitis*), need to be pruned in winter when they are dormant. Still others, such as ever-blooming roses should be pruned throughout the growing season, every time you cut a flower. Consult a good garden reference book for specific instructions on when to prune specific plants. Do not prune every plant in your garden at the same time; rather, prune according to each plant's specific needs.

Poor pollination (from page 117) means few seeds, which can result in misshapen fruit. No pollination means no seeds, and that means no fruit. If only a few seeds develop because pollination was inadequate, the ovary does not get

The blue orchard mason bee is a very effective pollinator of fruit trees. This solitary bee is native to North America. It does not live in colonies or hives.

Nesting houses for blue orchard mason bees are readily available at many garden centers, and easily placed in the garden.

sufficient stimulation, and the fruit can be distorted. It may be shaped normally at one end (where seeds are developing) and be shriveled at the other end (where no seeds are developing). This problem is usually weather related; bees are most active on sunny, warm days and less active on cold, wet days.

Aside from bad weather, too few bees can also cause this problem. Honey bee colonies are dying due to colony collapse disorder (CCD). For insurance, create habitat for the blue orchard mason bee and other native solitary bees. They are extremely efficient pollinators of numerous crops. Nest boxes for these and other native bees are available at most garden centers and on the Internet.

For wind-pollinated crops like corn (*Zea mays*), inadequate pollination results in ears that are only partially filled. Lots of kernels are missing and ears may be small. Plant your corn in blocks (several short, parallel rows adjacent to each other) rather than one long row to ensure better pollination.

Too much fruit (from page 119) results in stunted fruit. Thin the fruit while the fruitlets are still quite small, about the size of the end of your finger. Pull most of the fruitlets off the plant, leaving only a few on each branch.

Heavy fruit crop, heavy snow, strong wind, weak forks, bears, children (from page 146)— all can result in broken branches on your trees. Fence your yard to keep the bears and neighborhood kids away from your apples. Prune your trees to a strong scaffold of main branches that can support the weight of a crop of fruit and also withstand the force of the wind and snow load (see page 220).

Solutions for light conditions

Diagnoses from Part 1.

CHAPTER	PAGE	DIAGNOSIS
2 Leaves	32	too much light
2 Leaves	40	sunburn
3 Flowers	67	sunscald
3 Flowers	87, 90, 91	too much shade
4 Fruit	103	sunscald
4 Fruit	104	sunburn
5 Stems	139, 147	sunscald
6 Roots	169	exposure to sunlight
6 Roots	169	sunscald
6 Roots	185	seedstalk formation
6 Roots	186	daylength
7 Seeds	204	insufficient light

Too much light, sunscald, sunburn, and **exposure to sunlight.** Provide shade for shade plants by planting a tree that will cast filtered shade onto your plant during the hottest part of the day. A structure such as an overhead trellis can also provide adequate protection from intense sunlight. For exposure to sunlight and sunscald specifically, bury the plant more deeply.

Too much shade (from page 87, 90, 91) and **insufficient light** (page 204). If you cannot move a sun plant to a more appropriate location, you can sometimes modify existing conditions to provide more light for them, or remove any structures that block sunlight. Prune away overhanging limbs of nearby plants.

For all problems attributable to light conditions, prevention is the best remedy.

▶ **Put the right plant in the right place.** See page 215.

▶ **Plant at the right time.** For daylength and seedstalk formation, especially. See page 218.

Solutions for managing water

We begin with water management guidelines because effective water management often means the difference between gardening success or failure. Too much water, and the roots of your plant suffocate and die, or are subject to invasion by root rot fungi. Too little water, and your plant will die of drought. Even the method you choose to apply supplemental water can affect the incidence of disorders, pests, or diseases in your garden.

▶ **Water properly.** Apply water to the root zone of the plant, not the foliage. Fungi often, and bacteria and foliar nematodes always, need a film of moisture on the surface of the plant in order to infect the host. Some ways to water without getting the plant wet:

- Lay down soaker hoses. These hoses are permeable (leaky). They allow water to slowly drip out of their sides for the entire length of the hose. They are easily hidden from view under mulch.
- For hand watering, use any system that delivers water to the roots and not the leaves, such as hose-attached water wands, or watering cans with a long thin spout to deliver water under the foliage.
- In your vegetable garden, dig furrows between the rows. Lay a hose at one end of each furrow; turn the water on to a slow flow and fill the furrow with water.

- Install drip-trickle watering systems that do not use overhead spray nozzles. This solution works best if you are just installing your garden, doing a major renovation, or can install underground portions without destroying existing plants.
- For container plants, use a watering can or hose with a narrow tip and water directly on the growing media at the base of the plant.

▶ **Water wisely.** To determine the right amount of water for a particular plant, read the tag that came with your plant, or consult the Resources at the back of this book. Most good garden books list the water requirements of each plant they discuss.

▶ **Allow the soil to dry out.** Do not allow the soil to stay too wet for too long. This solution applies to plants in the ground as well as those in containers. Some root rot fungi, called water molds, thrive in soggy soil. *Phytophthora* and *Pythium* are the most frequently encountered genera of water molds. You do not need to identify the fungus to treat the problem, but overly wet soil stresses plants, making them susceptible to invasion by deadly pathogens. Most plants cannot tolerate these conditions, though aquatic plants (those that grow naturally in water, wetlands, or bogs) may do fine.

Water molds and other fungi live freely in soil. They do not have to infect a host plant in order to survive, thus they are not obligate pathogens. But, given the opportunity to infect a plant, they will do so. All root rot fungi can be lethal. They are well able to kill fully mature trees as well as tiny seedlings.

▶ **Check drainage.** Dig a hole near any area where the soil seems too wet for too long. This should be near any affected plant, but not so close that you will cut roots. Fill the hole with water and time how long it takes for the water to drain away. If it takes longer than an hour, then you need to improve drainage.

▶ **Improve drainage.** Several techniques can improve drainage, and you must determine which choice best fits your situation.

- Dig a hole in the wet area. Make sure you do not cut the roots of your plant. See if a layer of clay, rock, or other hard material prevents water from draining away. If so, dig through the layer to create a drainage hole. If that is not possible, choose another technique.
- Dig a drainage ditch to drain excess water away from the planting area. If you need a series of ditches, drains, or sump pumps, consult an engineer or landscape architect. Local and state governments regulate how you treat wetlands and water run-off. Be aware of any regulations that apply to this technique.
- Plant in raised beds. Berms, containers, constructed beds, and terraces stand above the natural soil level and all effectively constitute raised beds. Because raised beds are on top of the wet soil they are better drained and help to prevent the problems presented by saturated soil.
- For plants in containers: do not allow the pot to sit in a water-filled saucer. Put supports under the pot to lift it above standing water; and allow the soil to dry out between watering.

▶ **Do not work with wet plants.** Wet plants are most susceptible to invasion by bacteria, foliar nematodes, and some fungi. Most bacterial pathogens require moisture to stay alive. Many move from plant to plant in flowing water, driving rain, or splash-up from the soil. Bacteria, foliar nematodes, and many fungi need a film of moisture on the surface of the plant to infect the host. Do not walk through your garden while it is wet. Do not handle your houseplants after watering them, if the foliage is wet.

Too little water

Diagnoses from Part 1.

CHAPTER	PAGE	DIAGNOSIS
1 Whole Plant	17	drought
2 Leaves	31	drought
2 Leaves	31	leaf scorch
2 Leaves	33	scorch
2 Leaves	41, 42, 44	insufficient water
2 Leaves	44	insufficient water and death of tissue
2 Leaves	44	insufficient water and tissue damage
3 Flowers	70, 85, 87, 90, 91	insufficient water, lack of water
6 Roots	187	drought

▶ **Water properly.** See page 229.

▶ **Water wisely.** See page 230.

▶ **Increase the watering time or amount.** In addition, reroute runoff from your rain gutter downspouts and direct it toward plants that need supplemental water. Constructed dry stream beds are effective and aesthetically pleasing methods of re-routing water. Catch-ment devices such as rain barrels or garden ponds are useful to store water for later use.

Plants in containers are particularly susceptible to drought, especially if they are rootbound and have outgrown their pots. Up-pot them to larger containers with a greater volume of soil that will hold more water.

If you water your plant and it does not recover, drought is not the problem. Look at the roots and stems, and if you see a problem on either, go back to the flow charts in Part 1.

Transplant shock

Diagnoses from Part 1.

CHAPTER	PAGE	DIAGNOSIS
1 Whole Plant	17	transplant shock
3 Flowers	86	transplant shock

When you move or up-pot a plant, provide extra water and nutrients. See discussions on watering wisely and organic fertilizer, pages 230 and 237, respectively.

Irregular watering

Diagnoses from Part 1.

CHAPTER	PAGE	DIAGNOSIS
2 Leaves	58	lack of humidity
2 Leaves	59	irregular watering
4 Fruit	114	growth cracks
5 Stems	147	irregular watering
6 Roots	177	irregular watering
6 Roots	185	uneven moisture

See water management guidelines, page 229.

If a plant receives irregular watering, it wilts

from drought, then recovers when watered. This disrupts its ability to grow uniformly, and leaves buckle and pucker, fruit cracks, and roots become misshapen.

Organs in active growth are soft, and their cells are actively dividing and expanding. When subjected to drought, the cells harden. When watered again, new cells start to divide and expand but the hardened cells cannot. The hardened sectors are rigid, causing the whole organ to distort as the softer sectors expand. Fruits, such as tomatoes (*Lycopersicon esculentum*) or cherries (*Prunus avium*), split when a sudden rainstorm causes them to swell after they have matured and the skin has hardened.

Do not allow your plants to wilt. Provide adequate water during the growing season to avoid these problems. You cannot control rainstorms, but you may wish to harvest your fruit if you know a storm is coming.

Too much water

Diagnoses from Part 1.

CHAPTER	PAGE	DIAGNOSIS
1 Whole Plant	21	overwatering
2 Leaves	32	overwatering
2 Leaves	57	edema
3 Flowers	91	excess water
4 Fruit	114	excess water
7 Seeds	204	excess water

▶ **Allow the soil to dry out.** See page 230.

▶ **Water wisely.** See page 230.

▶ **Improve drainage.** See page 230.

Solutions for temperature conditions

Extremes of temperature affect plants in several ways. Obviously, plants can freeze in winter and sustain severe damage or be killed outright. For many plants, excessive heat—above 85°F (29.4°C)—causes photosynthesis to slow down or even cease altogether. Warm temperatures at night can cause plants to burn up more fuel (through respiration) than they make during the day (through photosynthesis), causing them to die from starvation. This is why temperate zone plants like miniature roses (*Rosa*) do not survive as houseplants.

Too cold

Diagnoses from Part 1.

CHAPTER	PAGE	DIAGNOSIS
1 Whole Plant	21	freeze damage
2 Leaves	33	winter desiccation
2 Leaves	46	freeze damage
3 Flowers	70, 92	frost damage
3 Flowers	79	proliferation
3 Flowers	83	balling
3 Flowers	89	freezing
4 Fruit	97	greenback
4 Fruit	98, 107	citrus freeze damage
5 Stems	147	frost cracks
7 Seeds	205	cool weather

Many common plant problems due to temperature are due to cold. Some plants withstand freezing (they are hardy); others are tender (they're not hardy). Hardiness refers strictly to a plant's ability to tolerate freezing winter temperatures; it does not refer to toughness under other adverse conditions, such as drought.

Freeze damage, frost damage, citrus freeze damage, freezing, frost cracks (from page 21, 70, 89, 92, 98, 107, 147). Provide winter protection for any plants too tender for your location by planting them up against a south-facing wall. Reflected, stored heat from the wall can get them through the winter.

Stop feeding your plants fertilizer in late summer so that they harden off before winter arrives. Soft, succulent new stems are subject to freeze damage and frost cracking in severe winter weather.

Be aware that cold winter air flows downhill like water. It pools in depressions and dams up against barriers, creating frost pockets. Avoid putting tender plants in frost pockets.

Winter desiccation (from page 33). Give coniferous and broadleaved evergreens supplemental water in winter. Plants that keep their leaves all winter long can become desiccated (dried out) if the soil is frozen and their roots cannot absorb water. This is especially dangerous if the sun is bright and it is windy. Wrapping your plants in a protective barrier against the wind and sun can help a great deal. The fabrics made for floating row covers work well for this purpose.

Greenback (from page 97). Greenback of tomatoes (*Lycopersicon esculentum*), where the stem end of the fruit remains green, occurs when temperatures are too cool. Early in the growing season, after winter has passed, warm up the soil with a layer of black plastic that traps the heat of the sun.

Proliferation (from page 79). Temperatures that are cold, but not freezing, in the spring can cause proliferation in some plants. In prolifer-ation, the flower develops an anomalous, sterile, green button in the center and becomes distorted. Subsequent flowers will develop normally after the weather warms up. Patience is the only remedy for proliferation.

Balling (from page 83). Cool, humid days cause certain roses (*Rosa*) to ball (fail to open properly). Roses with many petals are subject to balling in regions with long, cool springs. The outer petals become limp, and begin to turn brown while still enclosing the rest of the flower. Plant roses with fewer petals, if you live in a climate with long, cool spring weather.

Cool weather (from page 205). Plant seeds or seedlings of warm season plants, such as tomatoes (*Lycopersicon esculentum*), eggplant (*Solanum melongena*), peppers (*Capsicum*), and green beans (*Phaseolus vulgaris*), after spring weather has settled, all danger of frost is past, and the soil is warm.

Too hot

Diagnoses from Part 1.

CHAPTER	PAGE	DIAGNOSIS
2 Leaves	30	sulfur phytotoxicity
3 Flowers	88	bolting
3 Flowers	88	wrong temperature regime
3 Flowers	89	poor planting timing
3 Flowers	90	lack of winter chill
6 Roots	164	heat or cold injury
6 Roots	164, 173	excessive heat and uneven moisture

Sulfur phytotoxicity (from page 30). Excessive heat can cause the foliage of plants you have treated with sulfur to turn black. This is a phytotoxic reaction. It does no permanent harm to your plant but does temporarily interfere with photosynthesis and limits productivity. Your plant will grow out of it in time. Do not use sulfur in the middle of summer when high temperatures are expected.

Bolting (from page 88). Plants bolt (flower too soon) when the weather gets too hot. This is especially problematic on biennials like any of the cabbage crops (Brassicaceae), lettuce (*Lactuca*), spinach (*Spinacia*), and several ornamental flowering plants. In most plants, bolting is caused by heat; in photoperiod-sensitive plants, it is induced by the long days and short nights of summer. Select cultivars that are bolt-resistant and follow the recommendations regarding proper planting time. Read the labels on the plants, seed packets, catalog descriptions, or search the Internet for specific information about particular plants or cultivars.

Wrong temperature regime, poor planting timing, lack of winter chill (from page 88, 89, 90). Fruit trees like apples (*Malus*), pears (*Pyrus*), and peaches (*Prunus*), and spring flowering bulbs like tulips (*Tulipa*) and daffodils (*Narcissus*) will not flower in climates where winters are too warm. These plants require a certain amount of winter chilling or they are unable to flower. There are cultivars adapted to mild winter climates, so be certain you select plants suited to your particular climate.

Plant your spring flowering bulbs in the autumn so that they get six weeks to two months of cold, moist weather in order to develop a good root system. If you stick them in the ground in late winter they will not be able to flower well because they have not been able to make good roots.

Heat or cold injury, excessive heat and uneven moisture (from page 164, 173). Onions (*Allium*) and beets (*Beta*) can be damaged when the weather is too hot and watering is irregular. Beets develop concentric rings (like a bull's eye) of alternating dark- and light-colored bands. Onions develop gray outer layers. Avoid these conditions by planting at a time when your crop matures before or after the onset of midsummer heat.

Solutions for managing soil and nutrients

We begin with soil management guidelines because healthy, biologically active soil is a vital component to gardening success. The healthier your soil, the more likely your plants are going to be stress-free. Stress renders plants susceptible to disease infection and to pest infestations. By maintaining healthy soil you reduce moisture and nutrient stress for your plants. This helps the plant avoid insects, disease, and nutritional disorders. Also, maintaining a species-rich, ecologically diverse community of organisms in your soil provides competitive interactions that help to exclude pests and diseases.

Feed your soil with dead, but not diseased, plant material such as compost and mulch. The decomposer community in your soil is what makes your soil a living ecosystem. The foundation of the soil food web consists of bacterial and fungal decomposers that break down organic plant matter. The decomposers themselves are food for larger multicellular microscopic organisms like beneficial nematodes, which are, in turn, food for larger creatures like insects and worms. And so it goes, with larger creatures feeding on smaller ones. All these organisms ultimately utilize the energy captured by plants from the sun, which is stored in the dead plant material. The tremendous number of organisms present in healthy soil outcompetes and fends off pathogens and pests. You gain the added benefit that the more you feed your soil, the less you need to feed your plants with supplementary fertilizers.

▶ **Use compost.** Work compost directly into planting holes and beds. Well-made compost is a biologically rich wonderland of beneficial fungi and bacteria that aggressively outcompete agents of disease, preventing them from gaining a toehold in your garden. Make your own compost at home and turn your kitchen and garden waste into black gold. You can also purchase commercially prepared organic compost that incorporates mycorrhizal fungi into the mix. Mycorrhizae are fungi that form sym-

BASIC STEPS TO MAKE COMPOST

1. Pile up kitchen and garden waste and let it decompose. Be sure that all material you add to compost is pathogen and pest-free. It should also be free of weed seeds, and chemicals of any kind.

2. The pile should be made up of two-thirds "brown" material and one-third "green" material. Brown materials include brown, autumn leaves; straw; shredded paper and cardboard; branches that have been run through a chipper; sawdust from untreated wood; dry pine needles; and similar stuff. Green materials include kitchen waste with no animal products; green leaves; grass clippings; and other stuff. These proportions can be measured by the handful, bucket, or shovelful. It is the proportion that counts. As you build the pile, add 1 part good soil to 3 parts brown/green material mix.

3. Toss the brown, green, and soil material together randomly. Old-style compost recipes made much of placing these ingredients in distinct layers. Modern research has shown that random scattering works better.

4. After you have a pile equal to about one wheelbarrow full of material, add one 40-pound bag of chicken manure.

5. Turn the pile over with a shovel or pitchfork about once a week to speed decomposition.

The bacteria, fungi, and chicken manure breaks down and digests the vegetable matter, turning it into a marvelous, dark, friable material that will bless your garden with its generosity. The process takes time, of course. Also be aware that the pile generates heat.

If your climate is cold and wet, cover the pile with a tarp, and recognize that you may not have rich soil for up to a year. In a warm and moist climate, you could have finished soil in a matter of weeks. In a very dry climate, water the pile to keep it moist.

biotic relationships with plant roots. They are important partners to help you maintain good plant health.

▶ **Make compost.** Compost is easy to make. An excellent recycling program, compost returns to the earth many of the nutrients that are taken out by plants as they grow.

Composting bins, an alternative to making a pile, are readily available at many garden centers. One technique, in use for many years, is the "three-bin" method. Using the same proportions, pile the material into bin A. When the volume of material reduces by half, shovel it into bin B, and refill bin A with fresh material. When the volume in bin B reduces by half, shovel the material into bin C. Shortly after landing in bin C the compost should be ready to go into the garden. With this system you will have constant production of compost.

▶ **Use potting soil for container plants.** Soil from your yard is too dense and heavy to use in pots. Potting soil is an artificial mix that contains perlite, vermiculite, and other materials that create space and air pockets, and retain water. Some plants need special mixes. For example, some orchids thrive in bark, while cacti do better in a gravelly, sandy mix.

▶ **Use mulch.** A mulch is a cover of some kind that you place over the earth around your plants. Mulch your landscape, garden beds, and containers with an organic mulch, which, as it slowly decomposes, feeds the soil. Shredded bark is a good organic mulch, for example, and black plastic is a synthetic mulch.

We recommend organic mulches—shredded bark, coconut fiber, nut hulls, pine needles, straw, newspaper or cardboard—because they decompose slowly and add nutrients to feed your soil. A good mulch prevents many insects and diseases from migrating back and forth between the soil and your plants. It will also control weeds and conserve soil moisture.

▶ **Sterilize your soil.** This harsh treatment should be applied to your garden only in certain limited cases. Sterilization kills off all your beneficial fungi and bacteria as well as the pathogens. Follow these steps, depending on your circumstances:

For seeds: Damping off, the common name for a fungal disease caused by *Pythium*, *Rhizoctonia*, or *Phytophthora*, can be devastating to seedlings, killing whole flats overnight. Start seeds in sterilized soil to virtually eliminate the problem. Be sure to provide adequate drainage.

To obtain sterilized soil, purchase a ready-made, sterilized mix for seed starting. Artificial soil, designed for use in containers, has elements like perlite and vermiculite to create pore spaces and retain water. This mix performs much better in containers of any kind than garden soils.

Sterilize the soil mix yourself if you suspect that the purchased mix is no longer sterile (perhaps the bag has been open for some time, for instance). This is easy to do if you have a pressure cooker. Loosely fill jars, such as one-quart canning jars, with the soil. Place lids on loosely, and cook at 15 pounds of pressure for 15 minutes. It smells like baking Boston brown bread while it is cooking. When it is finished, let it cool, put it in clean containers (pots or flats), and plant your seeds. Note: Do not use garden soil for this. It is too dense for plants in containers.

For soil in the garden: For plants in the garden or landscape, it helps to solarize the soil when a plant has succumbed to a soil-borne fungus disease. Solarizing works best in the heat of summer when the intense rays of the sun heat the soil beneath plastic, killing off the fungal pathogens. Follow these steps to sterilize the soil by solarizing:

1. Remove and destroy the dead plant and as much of its roots and infected soil as you can manage.
2. Turn the soil over, smooth out the hole, and cover the exposed soil with clear plastic.
3. Weigh down the sides of the plastic to hold it in place.
4. After four to six weeks of this solar heat treatment, you can garden in this spot again. Be certain drainage is adequate, and add compost to the soil, when you replant.

▶ **Change the pH of your soil.** pH measures the acidity or alkalinity of anything including soil. Neutral pH is 7.0. Change the pH to treat certain fungus diseases such as **clubroot** (from page 183) and **scab** (page 106, 114, 116, 138, 171) and to provide for specific requirements of certain plants. You don't have to treat your entire property, just the area where you plan to grow blueberries (*Vaccinium*), raspberries (*Rubus idaeus*), rhododendrons, cabbage family (Brassicaceae) plants, onions (*Allium cepa*), or potatoes (*Solanum tuberosum*). If you use a crop rotation scheme, modify the pH when you plant, at the beginning of the growing season, for instance. Modifications to the pH last through one growing season.

Test your soil before you try to change the pH. Use either a simple pH test kit or an electronic pH meter, which you can get at any garden center. They are both easy to use; just follow the instructions on the package.

Make the soil more acid. Blueberries (*Vaccinium*), rhododendrons, camellias, and gardenias require an acid (lower pH) soil. Use coffee grounds for a quick, easy way to acidify the soil and add organic matter while you do so. To combat the fungi that cause potato scab, and to provide proper conditions for blueberries, lower the pH in the soil around the plants to 5.0 to 5.5, by thoroughly working sulfur or aluminum sulfate into the soil (if you do not have enough coffee grounds to do the job). Continue to retest the soil until it reaches the correct pH. Both these products are available at garden centers.

Make the soil more alkaline. Raspberries (*Rubus idaeus*) prefer a more alkaline (higher pH) soil, about 6.0 to 6.5. For the fungus disease clubroot of cabbage and all its relatives (Brassicaceae), the soil should be even more alkaline, about pH 7.2. Add dolomite lime to your soil wherever you plan to grow any of these plants. In addition to raising the pH, dolomite lime provides calcium and magnesium, which are essential nutrients.

▶ **Use organic fertilizer, if necessary.** Well-managed soil, amended with rich compost and supplemented with a good organic fertilizer (blood meal, bone meal, seaweed), should be adequate to meet your plant's needs. If you find you have a nutritional emergency, use a liquid organic fertilizer in the form of a foliar spray, such as fish emulsion. The plant can absorb nutrients through its leaves very quickly.

All fertilizers, both organic and synthetic, have three numbers with letters on the front of the package—for example, 24-8-16 or 20-20-20. The first number listed tells you the percentage of nitrogen (N), the second number the percentage of phosphorus (P), and the third the percentage of potassium (K) in the mix. High-nitrogen fertilizers stimulate vegetative growth and can sometimes suppress flowering and fruiting—good for lawns, bad for tomatoes. Fertilizers with higher phosphorus and potassium promote flowering and fruiting.

Organic fertilizers feed the decomposer community in your soil and release their nutrients slowly over time. This is especially important for nitrogen because nitrogen is highly mobile in the water column and leaches away rather quickly into the ground water. Synthetic fertilizers tend to release nitrogen much too quickly.

Diagnoses from Part 1.

CHAPTER	PAGE	DIAGNOSIS
1 Whole Plant	17	salt damage
1 Whole Plant	24	iron or manganese deficiency
1 Whole Plant	24	nitrogen or magnesium deficiency
2 Leaves	31	salt burn
2 Leaves	32, 43	iron or manganese deficiency
2 Leaves	32, 43	nitrogen or magnesium deficiency

CHAPTER	PAGE	DIAGNOSIS
3 Flowers	86, 90	excess nitrogen
3 Flowers	87, 90	poor nutrition
4 Fruit	104	blossom end rot
4 Fruit	109	bitter pit
4 Fruit	119	insufficient nutrients
6 Roots	164	potassium deficiency
6 Roots	173	boron deficiency of beet
6 Roots	178	cavity spot
6 Roots	184	rocky, lumpy, or compacted soil
7 Seeds	196	manganese deficiency
7 Seeds	204	phosphorus deficiency
7 Seeds	205	pH imbalance

For all diagnoses, see soil management guidelines, page 234.

Salt damage, salt burn (from page 17, 31). Excess salt from too much fertilizer, runoff from road or sidewalk deicing efforts, or salt buildup in the soil from irrigation systems can suck the water out of your plant and make it appear to be suffering from lack of water even though you are watering it. Flood the soil with plenty of water to leach away the salts.

Iron or manganese deficiency (from page 24, 32, 43). Iron and manganese are both important mineral nutrients for plants. Unlike nitrogen deficiency, symptoms of iron and manganese deficiency appear in the youngest leaves, the new, actively growing leaves at the tips of branches. Leaf veins commonly stay green while the rest of the leaf turns yellow, giving the leaf a striped appearance. Both these elements become unavailable to the plant if the pH of the soil goes higher than 7.5. The more alkaline the soil, the less iron and manganese are available. Acidify the soil (lower the pH) by adding sulfur or coffee grounds to the soil around your plant (see page 237). Aluminum sulfate also does a good job of acidifying the soil. The plant will then be able to take up the iron and manganese already present in your soil. Alternatively, add organic fertilizer containing chelated iron to your soil.

Nitrogen or magnesium deficiency (from page 24, 32, 43). Nitrogen is one of the most important mineral nutrients for plants and one of the most difficult to maintain at adequate levels in the soil. It is highly mobile in the water column and rapidly leaches away to ground water. It is also mobile within the plant, and when nitrogen is in short supply, the plant moves nitrogen out of the older leaves at the base of the branches and relocates it to the younger (new, actively growing) leaves at the tips of the branches. The leaves at the base of the branches turn yellow as the nitrogen is removed, but they do not drop off. Apply a good organic fertilizer high in nitrogen to correct this problem. Organic fertilizers take time to break down and release their nutrients slowly. That way, the nitrogen does not leach away before the plant can get what it needs. Within a few weeks the yellow leaves on your plant will turn green again.

Magnesium, another important mineral nutrient, is similar to nitrogen in that it leaches away to ground water and is moved within the plant from older leaves to younger leaves, causing the older leaves to turn yellow. Dolomite is an excellent source of magnesium as well as calcium and is frequently an ingredient in organic fertilizers.

Excess nitrogen (from page 86, 90). Nitrogen generally stimulates vegetative growth of leaves and stems. It can inhibit flowers and fruits. Some plants, tomatoes for example, react to excess nitrogen with wildly excessive vegetative growth at the expense of flowers and fruit. Pay attention to the three numbers on the front of fertilizer packages. The first number is the amount of nitrogen. Do not use high-nitrogen fertilizer on plants you expect to make flowers and fruit for you.

Poor nutrition (from page 87, 90). Poor nutrition results in a wide variety of symptoms, including flowers that are smaller than normal, fewer than normal, poorly colored, or even absent. Managing your soil for healthy, biologically rich soil (see guidelines beginning on page 234) will correct these problems.

Blossom end rot and bitter pit (from page 104, 109). These symptoms look for all the world like fungus diseases, but they aren't. Blossom end rot and bitter pit both develop when the proper amount of calcium is not present inside the developing fruit. Calcium is probably present in adequate amounts in the soil, but irregular watering, poorly drained soil, high-nitrogen fertilizers, or salts in the soil can all make the calcium unavailable to your plant. For discussions on watering wisely and improving drainage, see page 230. Read more at salt damage, page 238. And do not use high-nitrogen fertilizers.

Potassium deficiency (from page 164). Your plant is not able to grow properly if potassium is deficient. Leaf edges turn yellow and develop brown spots, then the leaf turns brown and dies. The third number on the organic fertilizer package tells you what percent of potassium the fertilizer contains. Sprinkle a good-quality fertilizer or green sand around your plant.

Boron deficiency (from page 173). Deficiency of this micro-nutrient causes symptoms in a wide variety of plants varying from cankers and splits to deformed, distorted leaves and fruits; it causes beet roots to develop dark, hard, woody patches inside the flesh of the root. Borax is a good source of this nutrient.

Cavity spot (from page 178). These hollow places develop inside potatoes if they grow rapidly from overwatering and too much fertilizer, and are then subjected to drought. Cavity spot can also develop when potatoes grow in drought conditions and then receive abundant water. Give your potatoes steady, regular moisture to avoid this problem.

Rocky, lumpy, or compacted soil (from page 184). These hard obstructions in the soil cause carrots to fork. Remove rocks, loosen the soil, and add compost.

Phosphorus deficiency (from page 204). Plants must have phosphorus for root, flower, and fruit production. Phosphorus deficient plants grow slowly, leaf veins are purple, and the leaf is often purplish in color. Bone meal is an excellent organic source of this mineral nutrient. Check the label on packaging of fertilizers for the second of the three numbers listed on the package. The second number (reading left to right) tells you the percent of phosphorus (P) in the fertilizer.

pH imbalance (from page 205). Some plants require specific pH ranges in their soils. Acid-loving plants like blueberries, rhododendrons, camellias, and gardenias need to have a low pH, around 5.0 to 5.5. Other plants, like raspberries, prefer a more alkaline pH, around 6.0 to 6.5. See page 237.

9 Fungi

What are fungi?

Fungi are valuable symbiotic partners for nearly all garden plants, but they are also the most frequent cause of plant disease. Fungi are ever-present, worldwide, from mushrooms and toadstools to yeast, molds, and mildew. Formerly thought to be part of the plant kingdom, fungi now occupy their own kingdom, separate from plants or animals.

Useful fungi include the yeasts, our valuable partners for making bread, beer and wine; the edible mushrooms we cultivate or harvest from the wild; and the saprophytes, decomposers of dead plants and animals. Destructive fungi that cause diseases in humans, other animals, and plants are called pathogens. Even these fungi recycle nutrients for new life.

Other important fungi are the ones that make antibiotics. The first one discovered was penicillin, from the fungus *Penicillium*. Since then, many more antibiotics have been developed from fungi. Countless lives have been saved through the use of these valuable medicines.

What do fungi do?

Fungi are fascinating organisms with a lifestyle completely different from any other life form on earth. The distinctive feature of fungi is that they absorb their food, while most plants manufacture theirs from sunlight. With some rare exceptions, animals eat their food.

Most fungi are decomposers that make their living by dissolving and absorbing the tissues of plants or animals that have died. They are called saprophytes because they digest food outside their own bodies. They do this by secreting digestive enzymes that dissolve dead tissues, then absorb the nutrients that are released.

The body of a fungus is composed of slender microscopic threads called hyphae. Imagine a spider web growing through the soil. This living web of threads is called a mycelium. We don't usually see this web. What we do see, and may think of as the fungus, is only the surface eruption. The mushroom that we pick to eat or see growing on the lawn is only the reproductive structure created for the purpose of producing spores.

Reproductive spores are microscopic in size, often colorful, and are distributed by wind or water. Some fungi produce spores that actively swim through water; other spores are passive, floating everywhere in the air we breathe. Leave a slice of bread out on the table anywhere in the world and bread mold spores, *Penicillium*, will settle on it. The blue fuzz developed by bread mold are masses of spores.

The bright side of fungi

Because fungi obtain nutrients by decomposition and absorption, they are valuable partners with plants. These partners live on or in the roots of plants and form mycorrhizal associations with plants. "Myco" means fungus and "rhizal" means roots, and this relationship contributes to the active living community that makes healthy soil. The fungi absorb sugars and other nutrients from the plant. They also absorb water and mineral nutrients from the soil and give them, in turn, to the plant. These mycorrhizal associations are symbiotic relationships in which each partner derives some benefit. They are extremely important to the health of your garden. For this reason, the indiscriminate use of fungicides is a bad idea.

The dark side of fungi

The ability to secrete digestive enzymes has allowed many fungi to actively invade living tissue. In doing so, they become parasites and pathogens instead of saprophytes that passively devour only things that are dead. Many of these parasitic fungi are plant pathogens. Their spores germinate hyphae that invade living tissue. They grow into a mycelium inside the host plant, dissolve the cells of their host, and absorb the nutrients. The mycelium inside the plant tissue is usually not visible until the fungus begins to reproduce or the plant reacts to the invasion.

Types of solutions

For air-borne fungi, solutions begin on page 244.

Air-borne fungi are ubiquitous, on your body, on plants in your home, on plants in outdoor containers, in vegetable gardens, and on plants

Mold actively devours this peach. A saprophyte, it does not cause disease on living plants.

The dark spots on this leaf are lesions produced by a fungal pathogen, which is actively devouring the living tissue.

The leaves of salal (*Gaultheria shallon*) can be infected by fifteen different species of leaf-spot fungi. These infections are not lethal but can weaken the plant.

in the landscape. Some are pathogens. Air-borne pathogens generate a long list of diagnoses from Part 1. In fact, they are the most common pathogens you will encounter in the garden. They cause problems on leaves, flowers, fruits, and stems. Seldom life threatening when they appear on leaves, flowers, and fruits, these fungi can, however, seriously impact a plant's health and weaken it. The plant's life is in jeopardy when air-borne fungi attack stems.

For soil-borne fungi, solutions begin on page 252.

Soil-borne fungi assault the roots of your plants, and are the second most common fungus problem you will encounter. Most of the time you will not know soil-borne pathogens are on the attack until you see symptoms on plant parts that are above-ground. These infections can also kill plants.

For sooty mold, solutions begin on page 254.

The methods for treating sooty mold differ from other air-borne fungal infection solutions, even though the infestation arises from air-borne spores. Sooty mold is neither a parasite nor a pathogen. It is feeding on the sweet honeydew excreted by insects such as aphids, scale, or mealybugs. Controlling the insects is the secret to managing this fungus. Because the solutions have more to do with insect control than fungus control, sooty mold is in its own solution category here.

For wood-destroying fungi, solutions begin on page 257.

Wood-destroying fungi thrive inside living trees, devouring the wood and killing the tree from the inside out. You often won't know your tree is in trouble until the fungus begins to produce conchs or mushrooms out of the side of the trunk or at its base.

For mold on stored bulbs, tubers, corms, or rhizomes, solutions begin on page 257.

Fleshy underground plant parts can become moldy with blue, pink, yellow, or white mold, either in storage or in the ground. Bulbs that become moldy in storage are discussed in this section; for bulbs that become moldy in the

Root rot fungi kill roots. Roots turn gray, then black as they die and become mushy. These fungal infections are life threatening to your plants.

The leaves of this camellia turn black due to sooty mold growing on the honeydew excreted by the aphids infesting the tree above it. The mold easily washes off temporarily, but a permanent solution requires treating the insects.

Tulip (*Tulipa*) bulbs can become moldy in storage due to infection by air-borne spores of fungi. If sick bulbs are planted, you will introduce this disease to your garden.

ground, see solutions for soil-borne fungi beginning on page 252.

Solutions for air-borne fungi

The most common fungi that harm your plants float through the air. You can see by the long list of diagnoses in the accompanying table that by dispersing their spores in this way, fungi have found a very successful reproductive strategy.

The chronology of a fungus infection of roses (*Rosa*) provides a classic example of how airborne fungi work (see photos, opposite). When a rose leaf is infected by the fungus *Diplocarpon rosae*, a characteristic fringed purple-black spot develops as the mycelium grows inside the leaf. The spots enlarge and sometimes develop a yellow halo. As the mycelium grows it begins to produce spores in the center of the spot. The spores are released and infect healthy leaves. The fungus continues to produce spores on the dead leaves on the ground. These spores are splashed up onto the foliage of neighboring roses by rain drops and sprinklers and continue the cycle of infection.

Diagnoses from Part 1.

CHAPTER	PAGE	DIAGNOSIS
2 Leaves	30	leaf gall
2 Leaves	36	black spot
2 Leaves	36, 38, 57	rust
2 Leaves	36, 41, 54, 59	leaf-spot
2 Leaves	36, 59	powdery mildew
2 Leaves	46	verticillium wilt
2 Leaves	39, 43, 54	fungus
2 Leaves	45	brown rot

CHAPTER	PAGE	DIAGNOSIS
2 Leaves	46	cankers
2 Leaves	46	botrytis (aka gray mold)
2 Leaves	59	peach leaf curl
3 Flowers	67, 69, 83, 123	botrytis (aka gray mold)
3 Flowers	67, 77	powdery mildew
3 Flowers	68, 120	anthracnose
3 Flowers	69, 82	camellia flower blight
3 Flowers	69, 83, 122, 123	brown rot
4 Fruits	98, 102	powdery mildew
4 Fruits	100, 106	shot hole fungus
4 Fruits	101, 117	cedar-apple rust
4 Fruits	103	botrytis (aka gray mold)
4 Fruits	103	white mold
4 Fruits	105	fly speck
4 Fruits	105	anthracnose
4 Fruits	105, 121	black rot
4 Fruits	106, 114, 116	scab
4 Fruits	108	late blight
4 Fruits	108	brown rot
4 Fruits	109	bitter rot
4 Fruits	120	black rot of grape, blueberry mummy berry, brown rot
5 Stems	131	fusarium wilt
5 Stems	132	coral spot, European canker
5 Stems	132, 137	brown rot, cankers, eutypa dieback
5 Stems	132, 138	rose canker and dieback
5 Stems	132, 142	botrytis (aka gray mold)
5 Stems	133	papery bark
5 Stems	135, 154	smut
5 Stems	135, 154	black knot
5 Stems	137	raspberry cane spot
5 Stems	138	endothia canker
5 Stems	138	scab

CHAPTER	PAGE	DIAGNOSIS
5 Stems	138	sycamore maple sooty bark disease
5 Stems	139	apple canker, pear canker
5 Stems	139, 146	rust
5 Stems	146	cankers
5 Stems	153	cedar-apple rust
5 Stems	155	gall rust of pines
6 Roots	169	onion smudge
6 Roots	170	late blight of potato
6 Roots	171	tulip fire
7 Seeds	196	smut

Change the growing conditions

Prevention is the most reliable technique for treating fungus infections. By using these solutions you prevent the spread of fungus disease throughout your entire plant collection, and you protect your plants from future infections. From the recommendations that follow, choose those that fit your circumstances. These steps should be taken before you use any chemical remedies.

▶ **Sanitize.** This is one of the most important steps you can take to keep your plants healthy. In the world of plant pathology, to sanitize means to remove infected or infested plant material. You should always sanitize before you take any other step to deal with fungal infections. Infected tissue is a source of spores. Spores infect healthy tissue and spread through the garden or through your container plants. Indeed, if you sanitize first, the infection may not spread to healthy parts of your plant.

Remove infected plant material. Once you have plucked leaves or pruned branches, discard all the material. Do not put it into your compost pile unless the pile is very hot, at least 160°F (71°C). Do not contribute it to a municipal green waste collection program. If you live where it is legal to burn waste, and can safely do so, burn infected material. Otherwise, put the material in garbage destined for a landfill.

▶ **Mulch.** See page 236. Mulch is material used to cover the surface of the soil around plants. Mulch for container plants, called topdressing, is usually more decorative than outdoor mulch.

Mulches and topdressings prevent watersplash. Plant parts close to the ground or growing media are most susceptible to infection from fungal spores splashing up from the ground in water, so this is an extremely important step to

fringed purple-black margin

raised black fungal structures producing spores

Black spot of rose (*Rosa*) is a fungus infection on leaves and stems.

take. Mulches and topdressings also help prevent weeds, conserve moisture, and control pests and other diseases.

▶ **Provide air movement.** See page 219. Whether they're on your windowsill, on your deck, or out in the garden, plants crowded together and plants with dense foliage are more susceptible to fungal diseases. So, prune woody plants to open the center, space plants well apart, and prune surrounding plants.

▶ **Put the right plant in the right place.** See page 215. A good plant in the wrong location is a plant under stress. Stress increases susceptibility to pests and diseases. Consult plant labels and packaging, and reliable books, magazines, and Internet sites to determine a plant's requirements for water, sunlight, temperature, and soils.

▶ **Choose resistant cultivars.** See page 215. Many new varieties of popular vegetables and

Ivy geraniums (*Pelargonium*) are favorite subjects for hanging baskets and containers of all types. This leaf is infected with botrytis, or gray mold, a fungus disease. It has been removed from the plant and will be discarded.

ornamental plants are genetically resistant to fungus diseases. Certain cultivars of roses, for example, are resistant to leaf fungus diseases like black spot, powdery mildew, or rust. Incorporating disease-resistant plants helps ensure various fungal diseases won't get a toehold in your home and garden.

▶ **Manage water.** See page 229. Managing water effectively often means the difference between gardening success or failure. Too much water, and the roots are subject to invasion by root rot fungi. Too little water, and your plant will die of drought. Even the method you choose to apply supplemental water can affect the incidence of fungus disease in your garden or on your container plants.

Keep the foliage dry when watering. Apply water to the root zone of the plant, not the foliage. Fungi usually need a film of moisture on the surface of the plant in order to infect the host. Soaker hoses and watering cans with long narrow spouts deliver water to the roots instead of the foliage.

▶ **Plant polycultures, not monocultures.** See page 216. A polyculture helps to inhibit the spread of disease. Distributing flowers, herbs, and vegetables throughout garden beds, so each plant's closest neighbor is different, greatly reduces the incidence of fungus diseases.

If necessary, use organic fungicides

You may decide to utilize chemicals to help control fungus on your plants, indoors or out. Various chemicals are certified for use in organic gardening. Many of these organic treatments are relatively safe for you and the environment. Some have been in use for hundreds of years, others are quite new. Look for OMRI (Organic Materials Review Institute) certification on the label.

Remedy recommendations

Always change the growing conditions (see page 245) before using any of these remedies.

Evaluate your circumstances and the plant you are treating to choose the right product for you. Use products with signal words (CAUTION, WARNING, DANGER) only when you need them. Do not apply them according to a predetermined schedule; instead, observe your plants and use chemicals only as necessary. These are

SAFETY FIRST

1. Always keep all these products **out of the reach of children and pets.**

2. **Read the label.** Use only chemicals that list the plants or type of plant you wish to protect on their labels. For example, a label may say "For use on ornamentals." Do not use this on a food plant.

3. **Follow the directions on the label.** Remember that more is not better. Many chemicals can actually damage some plants. This kind of damage is called a phytotoxic reaction. It is important to read the label and follow the manufacturer's instructions. If you put too much of the active ingredient on your plant, or if you put it on the wrong plant, you may do more harm than good.

   Every package or bottle of a garden remedy product has a label on the back that peels open. Unfold it and read the

tiny print inside to learn what the product is used for, which plants to use it on, when to use it, and how much to use. Some of these labels unfold into long pages of instructions. Be patient, get out your magnifying glass, and read them carefully. Follow those directions.

4. **Always use the least toxic product first.** Look for a signal word on the label. These signal words are required by federal law under the Federal Insecticide, Fungicide and Rodenticide Act (FIFRA). All commercially sold pesticides must be registered with the Environmental Protection Agency (EPA), the registration authority for pesticides, and tested for modes of transmission into the body: inhalation, ingestion, dermal contact, primary eye, and primary skin. Toxicity Category IV requires no signal

word because tests have shown the product to be non-toxic; these products, such as baking soda spray and insecticidal soap, are the safest, least toxic products you can use. Any pesticide determined to be in Toxicity Category III must be labeled **CAUTION**. Any in Toxicity Category II must carry the label **WARNING**. Those in Category I must be labeled either **DANGER** (the most toxic product available to the home gardener) or **DANGER— POISON**, with an image of a skull and crossbones. The last is most toxic of all. It is available only to licensed pesticide applicators.

5. **Wear protective gear and clothing.** Wear goggles, a respiratory face mask, a long-sleeved shirt, long pants, and shoes. Wash your clothes when you are finished using any product with a signal word.

listed from least toxic to most toxic, but all are approved for organic gardening. The first six remedies prevent but do not cure fungal infections; the seventh, lime-sulfur, has some curative properties. If you sanitize (see page 245) and then use any of these products, you will eliminate fungus infections.

▶ **Baking soda spray**
  Signal word? None.
  What is it? In 1846 two bakers created baking soda by combining sodium carbonate and carbon dioxide. Today, baking soda comes in two forms: potassium bicarbonate ($KHCO_3$) and sodium bicarbonate ($NaHCO_3$). Both are natural minerals. The sodium form is more common in nature and comes from mineral springs. Potassium bicarbonate is rarely found in nature and is manufactured by combining potassium carbonate, carbon dioxide, and water.

  What does it do? These bicarbonates protect against fungal diseases on many plants. They will not cure fungus infections, so use them as preventive measures. Research shows that both sodium and potassium bicarbonate cause the cell walls of fungus to collapse. The exact action is unknown.

  What are the side effects? Baking soda has no known side effects for people, other mammals, insects, or fish. Some plants may be sensitive to this mixture. It can burn leaves. To test the reaction of your specific plant, always spray a few leaves and wait a day or two before wide application. Baking soda spray also leaves a white residue on the plant.

  Choose potassium bicarbonate if you can, because potassium is a major plant nutrient, in other words, a fertilizer. Sodium bicarbonate can lead to higher concentrations of sodium in the soil and may eventually cause plant problems.

  How do I use it? Garden centers carry ready-to-use products. To make your own, follow this recipe:

  Recipe for Baking Soda Spray
  1 gal water
  1 Tbsp baking soda (potassium or
      sodium bicarbonate)
  2.5 Tbsp vegetable oil
  1 tsp liquid soap (not detergent)

  Mix the baking soda, oil, and soap into the water. Put it in a spray bottle or pump-up sprayer.

  Use indoors or out. Spray thoroughly, covering all sides of leaves, fruits, and stems. Spray your plants as soon as symptoms appear and repeat every two weeks to protect new growth. Reapply if rain washes it off the leaves.

▶ **Compost tea**
  Signal word? None.
  What is it? Compost tea is mature, finished compost that is steeped in water, aerated, and filtered to make a rich liquid source of beneficial bacteria and fungi. Brew the best product by adding nutrients such as molasses. In addition, while steeping you must aerate the tea. Use an aquarium pump to bubble air through the water and keep it agitated. If you steep the compost in water without aerating it, an anaerobic product—known as an extract—results. This is much less effective than the actively brewed, aerobic one. In addition, the extract might con-

tain anaerobic pathogens that could make you or your plant sick.

What does it do? Compost tea diminishes fungal infections because many of the microorganisms in compost are active, aggressive competitors against pathogenic fungi. Compost tea also feeds organic nutrients to your plants. It prevents but does not cure fungal infections.

What are the side effects? Aerobic compost tea has no side effects. Anaerobic compost tea can have microorganisms living in it that can make you sick and may damage your plants.

How do I use it? Spray fresh, filtered, aerobic compost tea on foliage, stems, fruits, and mulch or soil around the plant. Use it the day you make it. It is safe to use indoors. The odor may be objectionable. Test it and decide for yourself. Ready-to-use compost tea is sometimes available at garden centers. To use this product safely, you should make sure that it has been aerated and that it is fresh. You need to buy it and use it the day that it is made. Reapply a fresh batch when rain washes it away.

▶ **Bacterial fungicide**

Signal word? Caution.

What is it? This relatively new product uses a naturally occurring strain of a bacterium, *Bacillus subtilis* QST713, to prevent fungal disease on plants. It is not a chemical. It is a living bacterial culture.

What does it do? Bacterial fungicide kills the fungal pathogens that cause disease. The bacteria compete for nutrients and growth space on plants. They also attach themselves to cell walls of fungus, and form large colonies that eventually kill the fungus. The bacteria cannot cure

existing infections but are very good at preventing infections.

What are the side effects? Bacterial fungicide is non-toxic to humans, birds, fish, and other aquatic organisms. Some people react to this product, so you should wear protective clothing and a respiratory mask to protect against possible inhalation or skin irritation. It is a safe, non-toxic remedy for ailing houseplants, as well as for general use in the garden.

How do I use it? Follow the directions on the label. You can get bacterial fungicide in a ready-to-use spray bottle or as a concentrate that you must mix with water according to the directions on the label. Spray the liquid directly on the foliage, flowers, fruits, and stems of your plant. Reapply approximately every two weeks, as needed, to protect new growth. Also reapply whenever rain has washed it off. Remember, this is alive. Do not mix this product with

Miltoniopsis, or pansy orchids, are popular flowering houseplants that need bright light, cool temperatures, and humidity. *Bacillus subtilis* is a safe fungicide to use on these plants in your home.

other chemicals because they will kill the living bacteria.

▶ **Neem**

Signal word? Caution.

What is it? Neem is extracted from the seeds of the neem tree (*Azadirachta indica*), an evergreen tree endemic to India. It is a close relative of the chinaberry tree (*Melia azedarach*). The oil is extracted by crushing seeds, usually in a cold-press process.

What does it do? Neem inhibits fungal spores from germinating, and prevents fungal infections. It is, therefore, a preventive measure, not a cure.

What are the side effects? The seeds of both the neem tree and the chinaberry tree are poisonous. Neem rapidly biodegrades. Safety and environmental impact testing is incomplete. Some tests have shown that neem is non-toxic to mammals, bugs, ladybird beetles, and honey bees. Yet labels warn that it should not be used on or near water. In addition, you should not use it when bees are actively foraging. The EPA considers it safe to use indoors. The smell can be quite objectionable.

How do I use it? Follow the directions on the label. Neem by itself will not mix with water, but commercial preparations contain a surfactant that enables the oil to disperse in water. Mix the neem preparation with water, and spray the plant thoroughly about every 7 to 14 days, as needed, during the growing season.

▶ **Sulfur**

Signal word? Caution.

What is it? Sulfur is a yellow mineral mined from the earth, a naturally occurring element, like oxygen, nitrogen, or iron. Ancient Greeks and Romans used sulfur to control fungal diseases on grains and other crops. It is one of the oldest fungicides known.

What does it do? Sulfur prevents fungal spores from germinating. Tests have shown that sulfur controls fungus disease on a wide range of plants. Though it is not a cure, it works as well as synthetic fungicides to limit the spread of fungal pathogens.

What are the side effects? Sulfur is somewhat toxic to mammals like us, so wear protective gear to keep it out of your eyes and lungs and off your skin. If you have asthma or allergies, you may be sensitive to sulfur. The EPA considers sulfur safe to use indoors. Sulfur can kill beneficial insects and fish, so use it when beneficial bugs are less active (that is, when it is cool outside) and keep it away from ponds, streams, and lakes.

Sulfur can harm your plants in two circumstances: when it is too hot, or when you have recently sprayed your plants with an oil. Do not use sulfur if the temperature is above 80°F (26.6°C), or if you have sprayed your plant with horticultural oil in the last month. Avoid using sulfur for one month before and one month after using horticultural oil on your plant. Furthermore, if you use sulfur regularly, it can build up in the soil and make the soil more acid.

How do I use it? Follow the directions on the label. Sulfur is available as a ready-to-use spray, or as a concentrate that you mix with water, or as a dust. Apply thoroughly to all aboveground plant parts. In order to prevent new infections you must apply sulfur before fungal spores spread. You may need to apply it fairly frequently, about every 7 to 14 days, because it washes off the plant.

▶ Copper

Signal word? Caution.

What is it? Copper is a natural mineral element mined from the earth. It has been used as a fungicide for more than 200 years. Copper hydroxide and copper sulfate are the two forms used to protect plants.

What does it do? Copper is a natural and very effective fungicide. Like sulfur, it prevents fungal spores from germinating; therefore, it is a preventive measure, not a cure. The copper compounds made to protect plants from fungus are as effective as synthetic fungicides. It is one of the few products that also fights off bacterial infections.

What are the side effects? Copper is somewhat toxic to humans. It irritates eyes and skin. It is poisonous if ingested in sufficient quantity. Use adequate protection (goggles, respirator, gloves, long sleeves, long pants). Copper is highly toxic to aquatic invertebrates, fish, and amphibians. Do not use it near water. We could not find any studies about its effect on birds. Copper can damage plants if they remain wet too long after spray application. According to standards set for certified organic gardening, you can use copper on fruit and vegetables up to one day before harvest. If you decide to use these products, it is a good idea to alternate copper and sulfur. This prevents either mineral from building up in the soil.

How do I use it? Follow the directions on the label. Copper compounds are available as ready-to-use liquids, as wettable powders, and as dust. Mix wettable powder with water and a spreader-sticker. Some ready-to-use sprays have the spreader-sticker in it and some do not, so check the label. Apply the liquids with spray bottles or pump-up sprayers. Use specially made "dusters" to apply the dust. If you apply it at the first signs of infection it prevents additional infections. Apply early in the morning to allow leaves to dry quickly.

▶ Lime-sulfur

Signal word? Danger.

What is it? Lime-sulfur is made by boiling calcium hydroxide with sulfur. In use as a fungicide since 1845, it was particularly popular in the late 1800s and early 1900s.

What does it do? Lime-sulfur kills fungal spores that have already germinated. The properties of sulfur change when it is mixed with lime. The mixture allows sulfur to penetrate plant tissue, so that the sulfur is able to eradicate fungus as well as to protect against it. In other words, lime-sulfur is a cure as well as a preventive.

What are the side effects? Lime-sulfur is toxic to mammals: you, your children, and your pets. It causes severe eye damage and skin irritation. Use appropriate personal protection (goggles, respirator, gloves, etc.). Keep pets and children away when applying it. Lime-sulfur can cause more severe damage to your plants than sulfur alone. Use it only when temperatures are below 85°F (29.4°C). Do not use it on houseplants. Do not get it on your house or garage because it discolors wood and paint.

How do I use it? Follow the directions on the

label. It is a liquid that you mix with water and spray on your plants. Use it on deciduous trees and shrubs or evergreens before new growth starts, that is, when plants are dormant. This dormant season is late winter or early spring. You can also use it, at a lower concentration, after plants start new growth in early spring when buds are just beginning to turn green. If buds have broken dormancy, that is, are turning green, do **not** use this at full strength.

Solutions for soil-borne fungi

Pathogenic fungi that attack underground plant parts are the second most common disease problem that you will encounter in the garden. A varied lot, some of these fungi are water molds, some are mushrooms, and one is a slime mold. What they have in common is the soil environment. Because the fungi are underground the most effective solutions are those that manage the growing conditions. Chemical remedies do not work.

Diagnoses from Part 1.

CHAPTER	PAGE	DIAGNOSIS
1 Whole Plant	18	fusarium, verticillium
1 Whole Plant	18	botrytis (aka gray mold)
1 Whole Plant	19	armillaria root rot
1 Whole Plant	19	white mold
1 Whole Plant	21	damping off
2 Leaves	46	verticillium wilt
3 Flowers	80	fusarium yellows
4 Fruit	103, 152	white mold
5 Stems	140, 157	armillaria root rot
5 Stems	142, 151	phytophthora root rot, crown rot
5 Stems	142	white mold
5 Stems	151	stem rot
6 Roots	164, 168	root rot
6 Roots	166,172,174,190	onion fusarium basal rot
6 Roots	166, 187	onion pink root
6 Roots	168	potato silver scurf
6 Roots	168	scurf
6 Roots	170, 172, 189	bulb rot, soft rot, root rot
6 Roots	171	scab
6 Roots	175, 184	potato spraing
6 Roots	183	clubroot
6 Roots	189	crown rot
7 Seeds	197	damping off

Change the growing conditions

There is no cure for soil-borne fungus disease. By changing the growing conditions, however, you can interrupt the progress of an infection and keep it from spreading through your plant collection. You can also prevent a recurrence of the disease. Always begin with the first step, sanitize. The rest appear in the order in which you are most likely to need them to address soil-borne fungi. Choose the ones that work best in your circumstances.

▶ **Sanitize.** In the world of plant pathology, to sanitize means to remove infected or infested plant material. This step is crucial to stop the spread of root fungal infections and to keep plants healthy. Infected plants are a source of fungal spores. Soil-borne fungus kills plants, so you must stop it from spreading to your other plants.

Remove and destroy infected plants. Plants dying of root rot or any other fungus disease of the underground plant parts should be removed from your garden and destroyed. Some of these fungi are capable of living in the soil or inside the dead and dying roots for many years, so remove as much of the root system as possible. Also remove a large amount of the soil immediately surrounding the dead or dying plant. Do not put the infected material into your compost pile. Do not contribute it to a municipal green waste collection program. If you live where it is legal to burn waste, and can safely do so, burn infected material. Otherwise, put the material in garbage destined for a landfill.

Replace the dead plant with a resistant variety. Many plants are genetically resistant to soil-inhabiting fungus diseases such as phytophthora, verticillium, fusarium, armillaria, clubroot of cabbage, potato scab, or onion pink root. Do not put the same kind of plant back in the infected planting hole. Select a completely different kind of plant, one that is resistant to the fungus.

Replace with disease-free seeds and plants. Inspect bulbs, tubers, corms, and rhizomes. Look for brown spots, moldy patches, or shriveled tissue. Buy only those that are firm and free of spots or mold. Examine the leaves, stems, and flowers of plants you want to purchase and check for discolored spots, distorted tissues, wilting or other problems. Buy only plants that are healthy and free of obvious defects.

▶ **Manage water.** See page 229.

Allow the soil to dry out. Do not allow the soil to stay too wet for too long. This solution applies to plants in the ground as well as those in containers. Some root rot fungi, called water molds, thrive in soggy soil. *Phytophthora* and *Pythium* are the most frequently encountered

genera of water molds. You do not need to identify the fungus to treat the problem, but overly wet soil stresses plants, making them susceptible to invasion by deadly pathogens.

Water wisely. To determine the right amount of water for a particular plant, read the tag that came with your plant, or consult the Resources at the back of this book. Most good garden books list the water requirements of each plant they discuss.

Check drainage. Dig a hole near the area where the soil seems too wet for too long. This should be near any affected plant, but not so close that you will cut roots. Fill the hole with water and time how long it takes for the water to drain away. If it takes longer than an hour, then you need to improve drainage.

Improve drainage. See page 230. You must determine which technique best fits your situation.

▶ **Manage the soil.** See page 234. Healthy, biologically active soil is a vital component to address fungus diseases. The healthier your soil, the more likely your plants are going to be stress-free. In addition, maintaining a species-rich, ecologically diverse community of organisms in soil provides competitive interactions that help to exclude destructive fungi. Feed your soil with dead, but not diseased, plant material such as compost and mulch.

Use compost. Well-made compost is a biologically rich wonderland of beneficial fungi and bacteria that aggressively outcompete agents of disease, preventing them from gaining a toehold in your garden.

Change the pH of your soil.

▶ **Rotate plants.** See page 217. Do not put the same plants or the same kinds of plants in the same location year after year. For annuals, vegetables, and bulbs this is an effective way to avoid soil-borne diseases caused by fungi.

▶ **Plant polycultures, not monocultures.** See page 216. In the root zone, different kinds of plants exploit slight differences in the environment. Some are deep-rooted, some shallow-rooted. Therefore, roots of different plants mix together more happily in a polyculture (different kinds of plants together) than in a monoculture (one kind of plant all together). For example, the root zones of tomatoes planted close together, in a monoculture, overlap. They all attempt to exploit exactly the same niche in the soil environment. They all compete for resources and will be stunted and stressed, making them more susceptible to disease. So, interplant tomatoes with other crops, like green beans and marigolds, to create a simple polyculture. Also, give the plant enough room for its root system to fully develop and exploit the available resources.

Native Americans of the Pueblos in the American Southwest used polyculture practices widely. They planted corn, beans, and squash in classic polycultures, creating a productive agricultural system.

Solutions for sooty mold

Sooty mold is a black coating on leaves and fruit that easily rubs off. The black coating is a fungus, but it isn't a pathogen. It does not cause disease and is not life threatening to your plant. However, if it covers up too much of the leaf sur-

face, it cuts out the sunlight and can seriously affect the plant's ability to make food through photosynthesis. Besides, it's unsightly.

Diagnoses from Part 1.

CHAPTER	PAGE	DIAGNOSIS
2 Leaves	30	sooty mold
4 Fruits	98, 104	sooty mold

Sooty mold develops when an infestation of insects (usually aphids, but also scale, mealybugs, or psyllids) occurs on your plant or on a plant nearby. These insects have piercing/sucking mouthparts that the insects insert into the plant veins to suck out the sugar-containing sap. As they feed, the insects excrete large amounts of sugary poop, called honeydew, which falls like rain on everything underneath. You may have noticed that a car parked beneath a maple or birch tree can become quite sticky due to the rain of aphid poop falling down. Similarly, a camellia "parked" in the shade of a maple tree can also become sticky. Black sooty mold feeds on this sticky, sugary substance.

Change the growing conditions

Since the following solutions are safe and relatively simple, you may choose to try each one without identifying the insect and see if it works, so that—as always—you do not use chemicals unless you really need them. Chapter 10 contains more detailed information on identifying and treating insect pests.

▶ **Wash your plants.** Rub or wash sooty mold off leaves and fruits. Hose off the plant and wash away the sugary honeydew, so that the mold has no food and cannot continue to grow. Do this in the morning so that the plants have time to dry out, since wet foliage can spread other fungus diseases. Washing the plant is a temporary solution until you deal with the insect infestation.

▶ **Encourage beneficial organisms.** See page 269. This solution treats aphids and mealybugs. Attract beneficial predators to your garden by planting dill, fennel, or buckwheat—all plants that provide nectar for parasitic wasps, ladybird beetles, syrphid, and hover flies. These insects feast on aphids and mealybugs. Alternatively, you can purchase eggs of beneficial insects, like lacewings. Place them in the garden. The larvae hatch out and are voracious predators of the pests.

▶ **Look for ants among the insects.** Inspect aphid or scale colonies for ants. Several kinds of ants are "dairy farmers" who herd, protect, and milk their "cows"—the insect pests. Ants eat the honeydew excreted by the aphids or scale. These ants carry the pests from plant to plant. If you see ants, put sticky barriers (see page 271) around the stems of your plants to trap the ants and prevent them from climbing the stems.

▶ **Treat the insects.** Try these solutions in the order presented.

Blast insects with water spray. Blast aphids and mealybugs off the plant with a strong spray of water. As with washing your plants, this is usually only a temporary solution.

Stop using high-nitrogen fertilizer. A lot of nitrogen in the soil or on foliage promotes aphid reproduction.

If necessary, use organic remedies

If you decide to use chemicals to help control insects associated with sooty mold, please read the safety considerations on page 247.

Remedy recommendations

Always change the growing conditions (see page 252) before using any of these remedies. Evaluate your circumstances and the plant you are treating to choose the right product for you. Use products with signal words (CAUTION, WARNING, DANGER) only when you need them. Do not apply them according to a predetermined schedule; instead, observe your plants and use chemicals only as necessary. These are listed from least toxic to most toxic, but all are approved for organic gardening.

The dark mold growing on the leaves of this camellia can be washed off the plant fairly easily. Also try treating the insects. It is their sweet poop on which the mold feeds.

▶ **Insecticidal soap.** Try this on aphids, scale, mealybugs, and psyllids. See page 262 for information on identifying insects.

Signal word? None.

What is it? Chemically, soap is a salt made by combining an acid (vegetable oil or animal fat, both of which consist of fatty acids) with a base (potassium, sodium hydroxide, or lye). When an acid and a base mix, they react to form a salt. In this case, the salt is what we call soap. Commercial insecticidal soaps list the active ingredient as "potassium salts of fatty acids," in other words, soap.

What does it do? A mixture of soap and water sprayed directly onto insects kills quickly. The soap penetrates the cuticle that protects the pests and causes their cells to collapse. However, soap has no residual activity. Once it dries it is no longer effective.

What are the side effects? Soap is a broad-spectrum insecticide and miticide that kills beneficial insects like ladybird beetles (ladybugs), honey bees, green lacewings, and others, if you spray them. Protect your beneficial critters by spraying only the insects you wish to kill. Soap is not toxic to mammals or birds, and it degrades rapidly in the soil. It is not harmful to aquatic organisms or ecosystems.

How do I use it? Insecticidal soaps are commercially available as ready-to-use products in handy spray bottles at most garden centers. Concentrates that you mix with water and apply with a pump-up sprayer are also available.

If you wish to make your own liquid spray, first get some soap. It pays to be careful here because many of the things we call soap, like dishwashing liquid, are actually detergents (synthetic soaps), which can be harmful to plants. Look for products like pure castile liquid soap, which is available in most stores. If you have the time and inclination, you can make your own soap out of ingredients you personally select for the qualities you desire. There are numerous recipes and instructions on the Internet.

Mix 1 tablespoon of liquid soap with 1 quart (1 liter) of water in a spray bottle or a pump-up sprayer and drench the pests with this mix.

▶ **Neem.** See page 250.

▶ **Pyrethrin**

Signal word? Caution.

What is it? Pyrethrin is a natural botanical insecticide/miticide made from the dried flowers of *Chrysanthemum cinerariifolium*, a perennial relative of the garden mum. This species was formerly placed in the genus *Pyrethrum*, and the natural product obtained from it still carries the older name, pyrethrum.

The flower heads are harvested and dried, then ground to powder. The active ingredients extracted from the powder are given a new name, pyrethrin. Pyrethrin is a mixture of several different chemicals that act as broad-spectrum nerve poisons, killing both insects and mites on contact. Some insects have enzymes that detoxify the natural chemical and allow the insects to recover after their initial paralysis. Synthetic versions of these natural chemicals are called pyrethroids. Pyrethroids are less toxic to mammals than the natural product but are more toxic to insects.

What does it do? Pyrethrin paralyzes the

insects on contact. The dried product on the leaves and stems of your plants retains its potency for several days, affecting beneficial as well as harmful insects.

What are the side effects? Pyrethrin is mildly toxic to mammals, pyrethroids less so. They are considered one of the safest pesticides to use in the home, around food. People with asthma or hay fever may need to be cautious as it may cause allergic reactions. It kills ladybird beetles, but not honey bees. Pyrethrin is harmful to fish and other aquatic organisms.

Be aware that some commercial products contain additives to boost the potency of the natural product, such as piperonyl butoxide, a synergist. A synergist is a somewhat toxic compound by itself, which acts in concert with another compound to make the combination more toxic than either component used alone. Protect yourself with appropriate clothing and safety-wear when spraying.

How do I use it? Read the label and follow directions. Pyrethrin is generally applied as a liquid spray. It is available as ready-to-use hand-held spray bottles at garden centers everywhere, and as concentrates that you mix with water and apply with a spray bottle or pump-up sprayer. Spray thoroughly, the undersides as well as the top sides of the leaves.

Solutions for wood-destroying fungi

Wood-destroying bracket fungi or heart rots, like armillaria, oak wilt, chestnut blight, Dutch elm disease, and ganoderma, kill trees and shrubs. By the time you see mushrooms or bracket (shelf-like) fungi sprouting from the side of any tree trunk, it is too late to save the tree. It may be several years before the tree finally dies, but eventually it will die, decaying from the inside out, and it will fall over. Remove it before it falls on your house, car, or the family dog.

Several different fungi cause these problems. All are lethal. All are best managed through preventive care. Keep your trees and shrubs healthy by meeting their requirements for light, water, temperature, and nutrients. See Chapter 8 and consult the Resources at the back of this book.

Diagnoses from Part 1.

CHAPTER	PAGE	DIAGNOSIS
5 Stems	152	heart rot
5 Stems	157	bracket fungus

▶ **When you see fungi starting to sprout from your tree or shrub, remove the plant and destroy it.** Replace the plant with one that is resistant to fungus infections. Do not put the same kind of plant back in the infected planting hole. Select a completely different kind of plant, one that is resistant to the fungi that afflicted it.

Solutions for mold on stored bulbs, tubers, corms, or rhizomes

Blue mold of bulbs; tuber, bulb and corm rots; and potato gangrene can grow while the bulbs are in storage. These same diseases can sometimes infect fleshy storage organs while they are still in the ground; if that is the case, see page 252.

Diagnoses from Part 1.

CHAPTER	PAGE	DIAGNOSIS
6 Roots	165	gladiolus corm rot
6 Roots	165, 190	dahlia tuber rot
6 Roots	170	fungus
6 Roots	171	bulb fungus
6 Roots	172, 190	bulb blue mold
6 Roots	175	potato gangrene

This daffodil (*Narcissus*) bulb has become so badly infected by a fungus during storage that it is soft and rotten. Discard all bulbs infected by mold.

▸ **Discard moldy bulbs.** If your bulbs have become moldy in storage, discard them. Obtain new, healthy material in order to replant.

▸ **Prevent mold on bulbs in storage.** At the proper time of year, dig up bulbs. To determine the proper time of year, read the plant tag or consult the Resources at the back of this book. Do not crush, bruise, or cut the bulbs. Shake or wash the soil off the bulbs and let them air dry to cure for two weeks.

After two weeks put the bulbs into a plastic bag with a tablespoon of sulfur (the same product used to control air-borne fungi, see page 250). Hold the top closed and shake. Wear a dust mask and rubber gloves for this process, and be aware that some people are allergic to sulfur.

Put the dusted bulbs into paper bags. Be sure to include labels naming the kind of plant and the cultivar. Store the paper bags of bulbs in dry, cool conditions. Do not put them in air-tight containers.

10 Insects

What are insects?

Insects come in many shapes, forms, and sizes. From egg to adult they transform their appearance like no other group of creatures on earth. What defines them as insects is that as adults they have six jointed legs, a hard outer skeleton, a body divided into three parts, and one or two pairs of wings.

Insects do not have bones. Their exoskeleton encloses and protects them like a suit of armor. Naturally, this outer skeleton cannot get bigger as the animal grows. As a larva or nymph, an insect is actively growing and must periodically crawl out of its exoskeleton and grow a new one.

Insects are an incredibly varied lot, from busy bees and beautiful butterflies to the sedentary and unlovely scale. Some insects walk, some swim, and some can fly. They are, in fact, the only invertebrate animal that has developed the ability to fly. More species of insects inhabit the earth than any other kind of animal. Entomologists, the scientists who study insects, have described more than a million species, and most believe there may be 10 million species in all.

What do insects do?

Adult insects and their young, known as larvae or nymphs, often look completely different from each other. A worm-like caterpillar becomes a winged butterfly, a C-shaped white grub becomes a colorful beetle, and a squirming legless maggot becomes a fly zooming through the air. This process, whereby one thing becomes another, is called metamorphosis. In insects

The adult dragonfly exhibits the main features of the insect body plan. The body is divided into three parts: head, thorax, and abdomen. Six legs and four wings attach to the thorax.

head

thorax

abdomen

complete metamorphosis has four stages: egg, larva, pupa, and adult. Incomplete metamorphosis has three stages: egg, nymph, and adult. Knowing about this life cycle helps you recognize the insect pest in its different forms, as well as giving you the ability to disrupt the cycle and manage pest problems.

No matter which stage of life they are in, insects, like all living things, must eat and find shelter. As adults, insects must also mate and lay eggs. Each stage of life is designed to help them successfully engage in these activities. In the garden, on houseplants, or on outdoor container plants, insects' success depends on the kind of mouthparts they have, their preferred habitat, and their range of host plants.

The bright side of insects

Insects are extremely helpful partners to us in many ways. They pollinate our food crops. Bees give us honey, and silkworms provide us with clothing. Because many are scavengers, they

A cicada nymph cast off its exoskeleton which was left behind and has dried out. Because it does not have bones, as an insect grows larger it must periodically crawl out of its exoskeleton and grow a new one.

This hover fly, also called a syrphid, tries to look dangerous, like a bee or wasp to fool predators, but is, in fact, a harmless pollinator of flowers.

Beautiful butterflies feed on purple cone flowers (Echinacea purpurea) sipping nectar and pollinating the flowers.

These ugly yellow and brown lumps are also insects known as scale. Scale have piercing, sucking mouthparts with which they suck sap out of plants.

This caterpillar is the larval stage of a moth or butterfly. It feeds on the leaf of a purpleleaf plum (Prunus cerasifera).

The caterpillar becomes a pupa when it enters a quiescent state of transformation. It does not eat or move about; during this stage, its entire body is reorganized into the adult form. At the appropriate time the adult insect will emerge from this pupa.

are also extremely important members of the decomposer community, recycling waste, detritus, and other organisms, and contributing to healthy soil. Insects are also food for birds, fish, and other animals—an indispensable filament in the web of life.

One of the most important services they provide us is pest control. There is a host of beneficial carnivorous insects ready, willing, and able to kill and eat the pests that wreak havoc among your favorite plants. Lacewings, ladybird beetles, big-eyed bugs, minute pirate bugs, syrphid flies, and many others are predators that hunt down and attack those insects that calmly destroy your prize sweet corn or that cherished windowsill orchid. Some of these predators have truly voracious children. Their larvae eat more pests than the adults.

Other beneficial insects that kill destructive insects are the parasites, called parasitoids. Several species of very tiny wasps seek out their prey and lay an egg or eggs inside the pest's body. When the egg hatches, the wasp larva eats the pest from the inside out. When the larva is mature, it exits the dying insect prey and pupates, continuing the life cycle.

The dark side of insects

Insects can, of course, be insidious pests as well. Lice are parasites on many animals. Mosquitoes and flies transmit deadly diseases. Termites damage wooden structures. And many, many species damage our food crops.

Many insect pests chew and eat plant parts of their choice. Other plant-damaging insects suck the life out of your plants by inserting their needle-like mouthparts directly into the plant's veins. In some of these, their saliva is toxic and causes plants to distort. As if all this isn't bad enough, insects transmit several very nasty plant diseases (aster yellows and bacterial wilt, among many others).

The simple truth is this: If you have a problem with pests on plants in your garden, home, or greenhouse, it is most likely an insect that is causing the problem. Plant-eating insects

The winged adult form of a monarch butterfly breaks out of the pupa to fly away, mate, and lay eggs. Its body illustrates the main structures of most adult insects. Like the dragonfly, the body is divided into three parts: head, thorax, and abdomen.

Bumblebees, along with honeybees and blue orchard mason bees, are energetic and efficient pollinators of many plants. Without the services of these beneficial insects many of our food crops would fail completely.

As an adult this ladybird beetle (also known as a lady bug) feeds on aphids, but her babies are voracious little aphid-eating dragons.

account for about 80 percent of the damage done by pests to plants.

Friend or foe: identifying insects

Use this guide to identify pests and beneficial insects on your plants.

▶ **Beetles, weevils, and curculios.** All members of this group belong to the order Coleoptera, meaning sheath (coleo) wing (ptera). In this group, the wing covers (the two forewings) are hard, often shiny and colorful, and completely shield the abdomen. These insects have complete metamorphosis. The ladybird beetle (aka lady bug) is a familiar representative of this group and one of the most beneficial insects in your garden. Many destructive pests are found in this group as well. As a group, they are rather clumsy fliers compared to many other insects. They have mouthparts adapted for chewing.

An adult green lacewing, like the ladybird beetle, eats aphids. Its larvae devour whole colonies of aphids.

This minute parasitic wasp on a fennel (*Foeniculum*) flower lays its eggs inside living caterpillars. When the egg hatches, the baby eats the caterpillar from the inside out.

Aphids gather in huge numbers on this rose (*Rosa*) bud. A large colony, such as this one, can seriously impact a plant's health.

Beetle eggs hatch into larvae that are distinctly different in appearance from the adult insect. Some are C-shaped white grubs with brown heads and three pairs of jointed legs; they live in the soil and feed on plant roots. Others, like ladybird beetle larvae, look like tiny monsters crawling over the leaves of your plants searching for aphids to eat.

An adult Japanese beetle illustrates the main features for identifying beetles in general. Notice that the head is blunt and rounded, not elongated into a snout, and that the wing covers shield the whole abdomen.

Curculios and weevils are closely related to beetles, but their eggs hatch into larvae that lack the three pairs of jointed legs. Many are C-shaped white grubs with brown heads, like beetle larvae, but the absence of jointed legs is their distinguishing feature.

▶ **Flies.** Flies are members of the order Diptera, meaning they only have two wings instead of four. This group includes many beneficial insects such as syrphid or hover flies, and tachinid flies, both of which are predators of destructive insect pests. Destructive flies include a host of different fruit flies from med flies to apple maggots. Nuisance pests in this order include mosquitoes. Members of this order have complete metamorphosis. Flies are extremely adept at aerial navigation. Hover flies, for example, are as adept as hummingbirds in their aerial maneuvers. Fly mouthparts are adapted for sucking up food. They cannot chew.

▶ **True bugs.** The true bugs are all members of the order Hemiptera, meaning half wing. All insects and many other small animals are often called "bugs" colloquially, but genuine bugs are found only in this order. The forewings of true bugs are hard and sometimes colorful, as in the beetles, but they only partially cover the abdomen. Destructive bugs include squash bugs, stink bugs, tarnished plant bugs, and others. Beneficial bugs include assassin bugs, big-eyed bugs, and minute pirate bugs. Nuisance bugs include bed bugs. Members of this order have incomplete metamorphosis. The larvae are nymphs that resemble miniature adults without wings. All members of this order have piercing/sucking mouthparts. Squash bug nymphs somewhat resemble the adults and are often found in mixed populations feeding with adults. Nymphs and adults stick their needle-like beaks into plant cells and suck out the contents.

▶ **Bees, wasps, and ants.** All these insects belong to the order Hymenoptera, meaning membrane wing. They have four membranous, transparent, and durable wings. They are excellent fliers. Ants develop wings only briefly, and just in the young queens and males, preparing for their mating flight. Adult bees and wasps have permanent wings. Destructive insects in this order include sawflies and carpenter ants. The order also includes several species of ants that are "dairy farmers," who

Adult curculios and weevils have a distinctive long snout, a feature that beetles lack, making them fairly easy to identify.

The larval form in the order Diptera is a maggot, a worm-like animal with no obvious head and no legs. Maggots are often whitish or yellowish, small, and slimy.

An adult fly's wings are often held out at an angle, away from the body, as opposed to lying flat along the back of the insect. The position of the wings frequently serves for rapid identification of this group.

cultivate and care for their "cows" (aphids, scale, mealybugs) to milk them for honeydew.

Beneficial hymenopterans include honey bees, of course, and many minute wasps that are parasitoids of destructive insects like caterpillars. Many larger wasps feed on caterpillars or spiders. Nuisance insects in this group include yellowjackets and wasps that are attracted to sweet fruit. All hymenopterans have complete metamorphosis. Hymenopteran larvae resemble maggots except that they have an obvious head. For many bees and wasps, the larvae live in individual cells constructed of wax, paper, mud, or wood. They pupate inside the cell and emerge only as adults. Adults have mouthparts enabling them to both chew and to suck up liquids. Many members of this group protect themselves by stinging when threatened. Many are also social insects that live in large colonies founded by a fertile queen.

▶ **Butterflies and moths.** All these insects belong to the order Lepidoptera, meaning scale-wing, because their wings are covered with min-

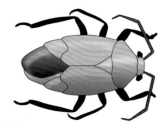

Squash bug adults are wary and are excellent fliers.

Adult grasshoppers have well-developed wings.

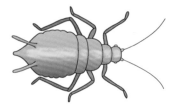

Aphid nymphs look much like the adult aphids except for the lack of wings.

Adult yellowjackets are frequent nuisances at picnics and around fruit trees when the fruit is ripe. They eat fruit that has been pecked open by birds, but generally cannot break open fruit on their own. They are not destructive to your plants, but they are aggressive and their sting is severe.

Baby grasshoppers, or nymphs, resemble adults, but their wings are undeveloped.

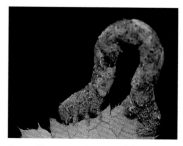

Caterpillars come in many different colors and sizes. Some are very furry, some are quite smooth. Some are brightly colored, and some match their background so perfectly they are very difficult to find.

The adult butterfly exhibits the features of both butterflies and moths. Most moths are active at night, and most butterflies are active in the daytime.

ute, often colorful scales. Adults have four large wings and are often much appreciated for their grace and beauty. Their larvae, on the other hand, are caterpillars, cutworms, hornworms, corn earworms, tomato fruitworms, and many other very destructive pests of our food crops and ornamental plants. All lepidopterans have complete metamorphosis with larvae that are worm-like caterpillars which pupate in a chrysalis, cocoon, or in the soil. The larvae have chewing mouthparts, and the adults have straw-like mouthparts for sucking up nectar.

▶ **Grasshoppers and earwigs.** These insects belong to the order Orthoptera, meaning straight wing. The order also includes the cockroach, praying mantis, and cricket. Adults of some species have four large, often membranous wings, while other species have very small wings, or no wings at all. These insects have incomplete metamorphosis. Their young are nymphs that resemble miniature adults without wings. Nymphs and adults have chewing mouthparts and eat the same food. Of all the insects in this order, grasshoppers and locusts are perhaps the most destructive.

▶ **Thrips.** Thrips are insects in the order Thysanoptera, meaning fringe wing, because their four slender wings are fringed with tiny hair-like projections. Thrips are extremely small insects, long and slender, and often very hard to see with the naked eye. Thrips have incomplete metamorphosis. The nymphs resemble the adults but have no wings. They have rasping and sucking mouthparts, and nymphs and adults are often found feeding together on their host plants. Thrips nymphs, like the adults, rasp away the surface tissue of plants, leaving telltale patches of silvery dead cells behind. Adult thrips can fly but are not strong fliers. If you suspect a thrips infestation, hold paper under the suspect plant and tap the plant. If thrips are present they will fall onto the paper.

▶ **Aphids, leafhoppers, psyllids, whiteflies, scale, and adelgids.** All these insects belong to the order Homoptera, meaning whole wing. They have four membranous wings. All are plant eaters, and many are quite destructive. Most are readily identifiable as insects, but scale and adelgids look more like bumps or cotton wads than insects. They have incomplete metamorphosis.

Winged aphid adults appear late in the season to mate and lay eggs for the next generation the following year.

This Japanese beetle, which only occurs east of the Mississippi river in the U.S., munches a strawberry (*Fragaria*) flower. As a consequence the fruit will not develop.

A borer's hole and frass (poop) are obvious on this asparagus stem. Because the damaging insect is inside the plant, protected by the plant tissue, you can not reach it with a chemical remedy.

The nymphs in some species resemble minia-ture adults without wings. In other species the nymphs are quite different in appearance and are called crawlers. All have piercing/sucking mouthparts. Many are sedentary as adults, sit-ting in one spot with their beaks inserted into a plant's vein while they suck out the life-giv-ing sap. They often occur in large numbers in colonies.

Types of solutions

For insects on above-ground plant parts, solutions begin on page 267.

Insects feeding on the surface of leaves, stems, flowers, or fruit, are not enclosed and protected by the plant, and are relatively easy to reach with various control measures. These are the most commonly encountered insect pests on your plants. Many beneficial insects also occupy this niche on your plants because the beneficials are predators and their prey is the very pest caus-ing you grief. You must be careful to select solu-tions that protect the beneficials as best you can. Insect pests in this section are rarely life threatening to your plant, but they can seriously impact the harvest of your food crops or the aes-thetic appeal of your flowers and landscape.

For insects inside above-ground plant parts, solutions begin on page 282.

Insect pests that get inside the plant to do their damage are very difficult to control and can be life threatening to your plants. Borers and bark beetles, for example, by tunneling under the bark, can completely girdle the stem and kill all the plant parts above the infestation. In many cases, entire trees die. Fruitworms and maggots inside fruit will not kill your plant but can cer-tainly ruin your crop. Because they are inside the tissues of your plant, you cannot reach them with a chemical remedy.

For insects in the soil environment, solu-tions begin on page 284.

Insects in the soil environment can either be in the soil itself or inside your plant's underground plant parts. Root-eating larvae like the straw-berry root weevil or the Japanese beetle are in the soil. Potato tuberworms and wireworms can be inside the underground plant parts, pro-tected by the plant. For home gardeners, chem-ical remedies to the soil are ineffective. Fortu-nately, effective organic biological remedies are available for this problem.

For insects inside galls, solutions begin on page 285.

Most, but not all, galls on above-ground plant parts are caused by insects. The adult insect lays its eggs inside the plant. When the eggs hatch the larvae secrete plant growth-regulating chemicals that stimulate the plant to create a structure (a gall) to house the insects. When the insects mature they fly away, leaving the empty gall behind. Galls are rarely severe enough to prompt remedial action and are not life threat-ening to your plant.

Solutions for insects on above-ground plant parts

Diagnoses from Part 1.

CHAPTER	PAGE	DIAGNOSIS
2 Leaves	35, 37, 50	leafhoppers
2 Leaves	35, 54	skeletonizers
2 Leaves	37	lace bugs
2 Leaves	37	thrips
2 Leaves	38, 55	mealybugs, adelgids, cottony scale
2 Leaves	38, 55	scale
2 Leaves	40	leafminers
2 Leaves	48	sawfly larvae
2 Leaves	48, 52, 53	caterpillars
2 Leaves	49, 51	weevils
2 Leaves	49, 52	beetles
2 Leaves	49, 52	grasshoppers
2 Leaves	49, 53	earwigs
2 Leaves	50	whiteflies
2 Leaves	50, 59	aphids
2 Leaves	51	leafcutter bees
2 Leaves	53	flea beetles
2 Leaves	58	leafrollers
2 Leaves	58	psyllids
2 Leaves	60	midges
3 Flowers	71	thrips
3 Flowers	72, 76	earwigs
3 Flowers	73	climbing cutworms
3 Flowers	73, 74	caterpillars
3 Flowers	74	spittlebugs
3 Flowers	74, 79	aphids
3 Flowers	75	beetles
3 Flowers	75	squash bugs, stink bugs, spittlebugs
3 Flowers	76	ants
3 Flowers	76	grasshoppers
3 Flowers	76	weevils, curculios
3 Flowers	78	flower thrips

CHAPTER	PAGE	DIAGNOSIS
3 Flowers	80	lace bugs
3 Flowers	84	rose midge
3 Flowers	92	plum curculios
3 Flowers	92	rose curculios
3 Flowers	92	strawberry weevil
4 Fruit	97, 102	citrus thrips
4 Fruit	101	San Jose scale
4 Fruit	101	stink bugs
4 Fruit	106	tarnished plant bugs
4 Fruit	110, 118, 124	plum curculios
4 Fruit	111	tomato fruitworms, corn earworms, European corn borers, army worms
4 Fruit	113	wasps, yellowjackets
4 Fruit	116	rosy apple aphids
4 Fruit	118	cherry or cranberry fruitworms
4 Fruit	118	fruit flies
4 Fruit	118	pear midge
4 Fruit	125	blueberry maggots, currant fruit flies, cherry fruitworms
5 Stems	135, 158	lecanium scale, San Jose scale, juniper scale, oyster scale
5 Stems	140, 158	cottony scale, woolly aphids, adelgids, mealybugs
5 Stems	141, 150	Cooley spruce gall adelgid (on Douglas fir)
5 Stems	141, 150	oleander aphid (aka milkweed aphid)
5 Stems	143	asparagus beetles
5 Stems	155	spittlebugs
5 Stems	158	aphids
5 Stems	158	San Jose scale, oyster scale, juniper scale
7 Seeds	196	husk flies
7 Seeds	198	earwigs
7 Seeds	200	cutworms, grasshoppers

As you can see by the list of diagnoses, many kinds of insects attack above-ground plant parts. As with all plant problems, prevention is the cheapest and easiest way to reduce insect infestations. If you have used the flow charts in Part 1, and you already know you have a problem, you probably want to move immediately to a cure. If so, please be sure to return to Chapter 8 and use the preventive measures presented there. You will have far fewer insect pest problems in the future.

Change the growing conditions

These solutions begin with a list of preventive measures treated more fully in Chapter 8. Prevention is always the best way to combat insect attacks. Preventive measures also keep insects from spreading to plants that are not yet under siege, so undertake these steps as soon as possible. Immediately following the preventive techniques, you will find measures to control pests on your plant; use these techniques in the order presented, if possible. Each method builds on the results of the previous one.

Preventive measures

▶ **Put the right plant in the right place.** See page 215.

▶ **Choose resistant cultivars.** See page 215.

▶ **Inspect and quarantine plants.** See page 216.

▶ **Plant polycultures, not monocultures.** See page 216.

▶ **Rotate plants.** See page 217.

▶ **Plant at the right time.** See page 218.

▶ **Manage the soil.** See page 234.

▶ **Remove weeds.** See page 221.

▶ **Mulch.** See page 220.

Control measures

▶ **Sanitize.** This is one of the most important steps you can take to keep plants healthy. In the world of plant pathology, to sanitize means to remove infected or infested plant material. Infested plant parts are a source of insect pests.

Once you remove infested plant material, using any of the steps below, discard all the material. Do not put infested material into your compost pile. Do not contribute it to a municipal green waste collection program. If you live where it is legal to burn waste, and can safely do so, burn infested material. Otherwise, put the material in garbage destined for a landfill.

Remove and destroy insect-infested leaves, stems, or fruit. Remove insect-infested plant material by plucking leaves or pruning branches. Destroy these plant parts before the nymphs or larvae inside them have a chance to mature, mate, lay eggs, and reinfest your plants. The objective is to disrupt the life cycle so that the pest cannot reproduce. Examples:

- Pull or pluck those leaves with the heaviest infestations of aphids, whiteflies, or other insects. Leave lightly infested foliage in place in order to provide food for beneficial predators and parasitoids.
- Remove tent caterpillars by pruning away infested branches and destroying them before the insects mature.

Clean up debris. Clean your garden at the end of the season after harvest. A number of insect pests overwinter on or in the plant debris left behind at the end of the growing season. By removing and destroying this material in the autumn, you can eliminate many pests before they mature in the spring.

▶ **Encourage beneficial organisms.** To attract beneficial organisms to your garden, grow species of plants these animals prefer as sources of food or shelter. Also provide water in very shallow containers, such as a bird bath or plant saucer. Some examples of plants to grow:

- The carrot family (Apiaceae): coriander, dill, fennel, parsley
- The mint family (Lamiaceae): catnip, thyme, rosemary, hyssop, lemon balm
- The daisy family (Asteraceae): cosmos, yarrow, coneflower

Spiders and birds are also efficient predators of insects and other pests. A spider's web may be a nuisance if its location is inconvenient for you, but it's better not to kill the spider. She's just doing her job—to catch and eat as many insects as she can. Many birds eat insects exclusively, while some are part-time insect eaters. Other birds relish snails and slugs. Attract birds of all kinds to your garden with water and shelter. They are valuable allies.

To increase your chances of controlling pests with beneficial organisms, purchase them at your local garden center or through mail-order suppliers. Check with the supplier to determine which species is the best choice for your particular problem, host plants, and environmental conditions. Some examples:

- Green lacewings, ladybird beetles, praying mantises, mealybug destroyers, and minute pirate bugs hunt, kill, and eat many pests.
- Parasitoids—such as *Trichogramma* wasps for caterpillars, *Encarsia formosa* for whiteflies, and several aphid parasites—are tiny insects that lay their eggs inside other insects.
- Beneficial nematodes control insects that dwell in the soil for all or a portion of their life cycle.

At garden centers, purchase a packet that contains a card that you mail to a supply company. The company then sends you 200 or more eggs or pupae. Put many of the eggs or pupae where the pests are most abundant, but be sure to distribute the rest throughout your plants. You can also buy praying mantis eggs at many garden centers. Keep the eggs indoors until they hatch (four to six weeks), then release the babies outdoors. Adult ladybird beetles (lady bugs) are also available. Be sure to release these in the early evening only, so that they turn to settling in instead of flying off to your neighbor's yard.

▶ **Remove pests.**

Blast insects with water spray. Even if the adults fly away before you get to them, wash the eggs and larvae or nymphs to the ground, where they will die. This works well for aphids, whiteflies, and leafhoppers, among others. Hose down your plants about once a week to keep these populations at a low level. Although this appears to contradict the advice to keep foliage dry, it does not, if you use this technique on clear days, in the morning, so that leaves have time to dry.

Pick pests off by hand. Picking up insects or their larvae in your hands makes some people squeamish, but it's a good way to deal with some insects. You can use your bare hands, wear rubber gloves, or use a tool to pick them up. In any case, physically removing the insect from the plant helps to manage the population and reduce damage.

- Use kitchen tongs to pick up tomato hornworms, caterpillars, or other large larvae. Drop them into a jar of soapy water. They will die quickly.
- Hold a wide-mouthed jar of soapy water under Japanese beetles (you have to sneak up on them first) then knock the beetles down into the jar. They too will die quickly. This also works on Colorado potato beetles and any other insects that let you get close enough.
- Scale insects can be rubbed or scraped off with your thumbnail. This has no effect on the eggs or crawlers that you can't see. Swabbing the area with cotton soaked in rubbing alcohol or soapy water will deal with the little ones.
- For plants with boring insects inside, slit open stems or vines with a sharp knife. Remove the pests. Drop them into a jar of soapy water.
- Insert a thin, flexible wire into a borer's hole to hook the pest and drag it out. Drop it into a jar of soapy water to kill it.

Shake your plants. Vigorously shaking your plants will sometimes dislodge insects. Plum curculios and rose curculios, for example, drop to the ground and play dead when disturbed.

- Put a light-colored drop cloth or an old sheet underneath your plant in the morning when temperatures are cool. Shake the plant, and many insects will drop onto your cloth. Gather up pests and put them in soapy water. Alternatively, put them in a plastic bag in the freezer. Leave them there for three days, then put the whole bag in the trash.

Use your vacuum cleaner. Some insects, particularly whiteflies on houseplants, are easily sucked up by vacuum cleaners with a hose attachment. Disturb the bugs to make them fly and scoop them right out of the air with the vacuum cleaner hose.

▶ **Control pests with physical barriers.**

Floating and rigid row covers. Grow your plants under a protective covering, one that lets light, water, and air in but keeps insects out. Row covers made especially for this purpose are lightweight spun-bonded polyester materials that work quite well. Fiberglass window screening, mosquito netting, or sheer fabrics also work but can be heavier and less flexible. Pay attention to the size of the weave; a coarse weave will permit small insects to get through, and a very tight weave restricts air flow, which you do not want.

- Floating row covers. Drape a lightweight material over your seed bed or seedlings. Make it baggy. Leave enough slack so that your plants have room to grow. They push the material up as they grow. Weigh the material down around the edges with dirt, boards, or rocks; or fasten it with U-shaped metal pins made from coat hangers. Caution: any insects already present in the soil as eggs, larvae, or overwintering adults will be protected from predators inside this tent, so be sure to get rid of them by rotating your crops. Also, you'll have to remove the cover when plants begin to flower for any crop that needs to be pollinated by bees.

- Rigid row covers. Use the same materials noted above but attach them to a frame made of wood, PVC pipe, or some other framework. Alternatively, roll or fold aluminum window screening into shape and staple the edges together to make a freestanding cone or cover. Make the frames or cones large enough to accommodate the mature height of your plants. The frame holds the material up off the leaves and will last for many seasons.

Sticky stem wraps. Sticky substances smeared onto paper, plastic, or metal strips and wrapped around the stems or trunks of your plants can trap insects, mites, or other pests attempting to climb up the stem to reach the foliage. Products that have been on the market for many years are widely used in organic gardening.

- Apply the sticky material directly to the stems. As it becomes loaded with trapped insects and dirt, remove it and replace with fresh material.

- Wrap a strip of plastic around the stem of your plant and put the sticky stuff on top of the plastic. Refresh the sticky goo as needed. Note: Trees with coarse bark can have gaps under the plastic that allow insects to crawl through.
- Trunk bands have a foam back and can be wrapped around trees with coarse bark to form a tight fit. Smear the band with one of the sticky products and replace with fresh bands as needed.

Sticky cards or boards. Sticky cards or boards are yellow because yellow attracts insects. The board is then coated with sticky stuff to trap the insects. Use them indoors in the home or greenhouse to control whiteflies and other insect pests. Use them outdoors to manage strong fliers like fruitflies, which will control fruitfly maggots in your blueberries, currants, cherries, cranberries, or other fruits. They are less effective outdoors as a control method for weak fliers like whiteflies. Outdoors, whiteflies have to go where the wind blows them. Indoors, without wind, whiteflies can control their direction and will land on your cards.

Purchase cards ready-made for this purpose or make your own. Make cards for indoor use out of heavy paper or plastic. Outdoors, use plywood or masonite. Make them 3 × 5 inches (7.5 × 12.5 cm) or larger. Paint one side with bright yellow paint. After the paint dries, attach it to a garden stake on the unpainted side. Coat the painted side with a commercially prepared sticky material and place the card near your plants. Scrape off the dead insects and dirt as needed and reapply fresh sticky material. Place the cards so that the leaves of your plant don't get stuck to the cards.

Paper bags. For **cutworms** (from page 73), **fruitworms** (page 107, 111, 118, 125), **army worms** (page 111), **European corn borers** (page 111, 124), **corn earworms** (page 202), **grape berry moth** (page 111), **navel orange worm** (page 112), and **codling moth larvae** (page 112, 124). Enclose young fruitlets of pear or apple trees in paper bags and staple the bags shut. The bag prevents codling moth larvae and other caterpillars, cutworms, fruitworms, army worms, earworms, and apple maggots from doing significant damage to your fruit. On large trees this may not be physically possible because it's too hard to reach all the fruit. But it works very well on dwarf, semi-dwarf, and espaliered trees. Do not use plastic bags for this purpose, they get too hot and they do not breathe. Use small, brown paper lunch sacks or purchase inexpensive small cloth bags made especially for this purpose. Either one will help control insect damage to apples and pears.

Cutworm collars. For **cutworms** (from page 200) and **army worms** (page 202). Put a simple cardboard collar around the base of your seedlings to protect against cutworms. Tear the bottom out of tiny paper cups or cut toilet paper tubes into 1 to 2 inch (2.5 to 5 cm) sections. Place these around the base of young seedlings and push the collars down into the ground so that they stand upright. Tuna fish cans with the bottoms removed also work.

Earwig traps. For **earwigs** (from page 49, 53, 72, 76, 198). Earwigs come out at night to feed on soft plant tissue like tender new leaves and flower petals. They hide during the daytime under pots, rocks, mulch—any place that is dark and moist. Earwigs provide some beneficial services for you by eating some insects that are plant pests. But if they are causing significant damage to your plants, you may wish to manage their populations.

One simple technique is to roll a single sheet of newspaper into a cylinder and use rubber bands to keep it from unwinding. Dampen the cylinder slightly and place it on the ground. Leave it overnight. Earwigs will hide inside. Pick the cylinder up in the morning and get rid of it. Make sure the earwigs don't escape.

Small, brown, paper lunch bags enclose the fruit on an apple tree (*Malus*), protecting the fruit from apple maggots and codling moths.

Apple maggot traps. For **apple maggots** (from page 125) and **husk flies** (page 196). Trap apple maggot adult flies by hanging a red sphere coated with sticky material in your apple trees in the middle of June. The flies get stuck and die before they have a chance to lay eggs. The same technique works on husk flies of your walnuts. When the flies are ready to lay eggs, they are searching for round apple-like objects. They will home in on your trap, believing it to be an apple and will become mired in the goo.

Purchase ready-made apple maggot traps made of red plastic or make your own. You need a round object (shaped like an apple) like a plastic, rubber, or wood ball. Paint it red. Attach a screw eye to one end and hang it in your tree. Apply the sticky stuff and you're good to go. Scrape off dead insects and reapply fresh sticky material every two weeks or so.

Screens. Window and door screens keep insects from flying into your home and attacking your houseplants. If you have a greenhouse, remember to screen the vents so that bugs cannot get inside.

If necessary, use organic insecticides

You may decide to utilize chemicals to help control insects on your plants, indoors or out. Various chemicals are certified for use in organic gardening. Many of these organic treatments are relatively safe for you and the environment. Some have been in use for hundreds of years, others are quite new. Look for OMRI (Organic Materials Review Institute) certification on the label.

Remedy recommendations

Always change the growing conditions (see page 268) before using any of these remedies. Evaluate your circumstances and the plant you are treating to choose the right product for you. Use products with signal words (CAUTION, WARNING, DANGER) only when you need them. Do not apply them according to a predetermined schedule; instead, observe your plants and use chemicals only as necessary. These are listed from least toxic to most toxic, but all are approved for organic gardening.

▶ **Pheromone traps**

Signal word? None for most products. Check the label to be sure.

What is it? A pheromone is a chemical signal emitted by animals to provide clues to sexual receptivity or other behavior. Even humans emit pheromones. Laboratories have created a number of synthetic pheromones, which are useful for insect monitoring and control.

What does it do? Synthetic pheromones disrupt the reproductive cycle of many destructive insect pests, and prevent them from reproducing. Synthetic pheromones duplicate highly specific chemical signals emitted by female insects when they are ready to mate. The males detect this scent from very far away and home in on it, looking to mate with females. The synthetic pheromone tricks the males, luring them into a trap. No mating occurs, and the females never lay fertile eggs. This eliminates destructive larvae. Preventing reproduction or reducing pests' ability to reproduce controls pest populations. Pheromones are also used to monitor insect populations, so that you can apply an insecticide at the most effective time.

What are the side effects? No adverse effects have been reported. Pheromones pose no risk to human health or to non-target animals (mammals, birds, and aquatic organisms).

These affect only the target group for which they were made. For example, pheromones created for lepidopteran larvae (codling moth, army worm, grapeberry moth, for example) have no effect on bark beetles. Pheromones used to control bark beetles have no effect on lepidopteran

SAFETY FIRST

1. Always keep all these products **out of the reach of children and pets.**

2. **Read the label.** Use only chemicals that list the plants or type of plant you wish to protect on their labels. For example, a label may say "For use on ornamentals." Do not use this on a food plant.

3. **Follow the directions on the label.** Remember that more is not better. Many chemicals can actually damage some plants. This kind of damage is called a phytotoxic reaction. It is important to read the label and follow the manufacturer's instructions. If you put too much of the active ingredient on your plant, or if you put it on the wrong plant, you may do more harm than good.

   Every package or bottle of a garden remedy product has a label on the back that peels open. Unfold it and read the tiny print inside to learn what the product is used for, which plants to use it on, when to use it, and how much to use. Some of these labels unfold into long pages of instructions. Be patient, get out your magnifying glass, and read them carefully. Follow those directions.

4. **Always use the least toxic product first.** Look for a signal word on the label. These signal words are required by federal law under the Federal Insecticide, Fungicide and Rodenticide Act (FIFRA). All commercially sold pesticides must be registered with the Environmental Protection Agency (EPA), the registration authority for pesticides, and tested for modes of transmission into the body: inhalation, ingestion, dermal contact, primary eye, and primary skin. Toxicity Category IV requires no signal word because tests have shown the product to be non-toxic; these products, such as baking soda spray and insecticidal soap, are the safest, least toxic products you can use. Any pesticide determined to be in Toxicity Category III must be labeled **CAUTION.** Any in Toxicity Category II must carry the label **WARNING.** Those in Category I must be labeled either **DANGER** (the most toxic product available to the home gardener) or **DANGER— POISON,** with an image of a skull and crossbones. The last is most toxic of all. It is available only to licensed pesticide applicators.

5. **Wear protective gear and clothing.** Wear goggles, a respiratory face mask, a long-sleeved shirt, long pants, and shoes. Wash your clothes when you are finished using any product with a signal word.

larvae. Neither one of those pheromones has any effect on honey bees, lacewings, or ladybird beetles.

How do I use it? Read the label and follow directions. Pheromones are available to homeowners at garden centers and over the Internet. The package you purchase will come with complete instructions for use. Pheromones come as traps, sprays, and pouches.

- Pheromone traps. Look for specific traps for specific insects. For example, if you have moths, find a trap that lists moths on the label. Trap kits are inexpensive and easy to use. The kit provides a plastic, reusable trap along with the appropriate pheromone. Put the pheromone on the sticky substance inside the trap. Males enter the trap looking for females. They get stuck in the sticky goo and die. Because pests never mate, the females lay infertile eggs, thus controlling insect populations without the use of poisons. Also use traps to monitor insect populations by trapping and counting males.
- Pheromone sprays. Choose pheromone sprays for flying insect pests. Follow instructions on the label to spray when males are flying to find females. Males become disoriented and cannot locate the females; their opportunity to mate is lost.
- Pheromone pouches attach to plants and give off chemical signals that tell insects, "Do not gather in groups here." Insects disperse and leave your plants alone.

▶ **Insecticidal soap**
Signal word? None.

What is it? Chemically, soap is a salt made by combining an acid (vegetable oil or animal fat, both of which consist of fatty acids) with a base (potassium, sodium hydroxide, or lye). When an acid and a base mix, they react to form a salt. In this case, the salt is what we call soap. Commercial insecticidal soaps list the active ingredient as "potassium salts of fatty acids," in other words, soap.

What does it do? A mixture of soap and water sprayed directly onto insects kills quickly. The soap penetrates the cuticle that protects the pests and causes their cells to collapse. However, soap has no residual activity. Once it dries it is no longer effective.

What are the side effects? Soap is a broad-spectrum insecticide and miticide that kills beneficial insects like ladybird beetles (ladybugs), honey bees, green lacewings, and others, if you spray them. Protect your beneficial critters by spraying only the insects you wish to kill. Soap is not toxic to mammals or birds, and it degrades rapidly in the soil. It is not harmful to aquatic organisms or ecosystems.

How do I use it? Insecticidal soaps are commercially available as ready-to-use products in handy spray bottles at most garden centers. Concentrates that you mix with water and apply with a pump-up sprayer are also available.

If you wish to make your own liquid spray, first get some soap. It pays to be careful here because many of the things we call soap, like dishwashing liquid, are actually detergents (synthetic soaps), which can be harmful to plants.

Look for products like pure castile liquid soap, which is available in most stores. If you have the time and inclination, you can make your own soap out of ingredients you personally select for the qualities you desire. There are numerous recipes and instructions on the Internet.

Mix 1 tablespoon of liquid soap with 1 quart (1 liter) of water in a spray bottle or a pump-up sprayer and drench the pests with this mix.

▶ *Nosema locustae*

For **grasshoppers** (from page 49, 52, 76, 200)

Signal word? None.

What is it? This product is a living protozoan, a microscopic single-celled animal.

What does it do? *Nosema locustae* is a parasite that infects grasshoppers and crickets, causing them to sicken and die. The protozoan is incorporated into a bran bait, which grasshoppers and crickets eat; it also infects grasshopper eggs so that the young are already infected when they hatch. The grasshopper population is, therefore, affected for years.

What are the side effects? There are no side effects to any organism other than grasshoppers and crickets.

How do I use it? Read the label and follow directions. Use nosema when grasshoppers have become particularly abundant and troublesome. When you see juvenile grasshoppers less than 3/4 inch (18 mm) long, broadcast the bait by hand.

Nosema may effectively kill all the grasshopper pests on your property, but grasshoppers are highly mobile and will migrate into your yard from your neighbors' and from the surrounding countryside. This pesticide can be quite effective when used in a community-wide effort to combat an invasion of grasshoppers.

▶ Diatomaceous earth

For **beetles** (from page 49, 52, 75, 143, 202), **weevils** (page 49, 51, 76), **curculios** (page 76, 92, 110, 118), and **earwigs** (page 49, 53, 72, 76, 198).

Signal word? Caution.

What is it? Diatomaceous earth is a white powder with a gritty feel. It comes from microscopic plants called diatoms that have a skeleton made of silicon dioxide, the same material as glass and quartz. These algae are found everywhere on earth in fresh and salt waters, and in moist soil. Where ancient seas or lakes have dried up, the skeletons of these plants have built up to thick deposits that are mined.

To protect against crawling insects, select diatomaceous earth that is labeled for use as an insecticide; some diatomaceous earth products are used for filters for swimming pools and are ineffective against insects.

What does it do? To an insect, diatomaceous earth is sharp, like ground glass. Any insect that tries to walk across it will be wounded by the sharp particles and will die. It also repels and kills slugs and snails.

What are the side effects? Applied to the soil surface, this product affects only insects that normally crawl across the ground (as well as slugs and snails). Honey bees and butterflies are unaffected. It is unlikely to affect mammals, birds, or aquatic organisms that do not crawl on the ground.

You must wear proper gear to protect yourself while applying diatomaceous earth. Because it is a fine dust-like powder, particles float in the air and get into your eyes and lungs. Wear a face mask to avoid breathing it and wear goggles. Wear gloves and long-sleeved shirts and pants to keep diatomaceous earth off your skin because it can be an irritant.

How do I use it? Pour the powder onto the soil around your plants to protect against any crawling insects. It is particularly effective against insects like black vine weevils and earwigs that crawl up the stem every night and return to the soil at dawn to hide. The powder is most effective when dry. Place it under boards, upside-down pots, or other objects to keep it dry.

▶ BTSD or *Bt san diego*

For **beetles** (from page 49, 52, 75, 143, 202), **weevils** (page 49, 51, 76), and **curculios** (page 76, 92, 110, 118).

Signal word? Caution.

What is it? BTSD is a living biological insecticide that kills beetles and their grubs. *Bt* stands for *Bacillus thuringiensis*, a bacterial parasite that infects and kills specific insects. Several different strains of this bacterium have been identified. BTSD is the specific strain that kills beetles and their grubs. It has no effect on caterpillars, mosquitoes, and black flies. The bacteria are suspended in inert ingredients that are not listed on the label.

What does it do? Applied to the surface of plant leaves, stems, and fruits, the bacteria are ingested when beetles or their larvae eat the treated plant parts. The bacteria infect the insect's gut and kill it over a period of days. Usually the insect stops eating long before it dies.

It is important to read the label to determine which variety of *Bt* the package contains. BTK (*Bt kurstaki*) kills caterpillars; BTI (*Bt israelensis*) kills mosquito larvae, which live in stagnant water.

What are the side effects? No side effects are known at the present time. This bacterium is highly targeted to specific hosts and has no effect on non-target organisms. Caution is necessary, however, because the inert ingredients in the preparation can sometimes cause allergic reactions. Tests have shown the bacterium itself to be harmless to mammals, birds, and all other non-target animals, including many beneficial insects.

How do I use it? Read the label and follow directions. *Bt* var. *san diego*, for beetles, is hard to find but worth the search. Look for ready-to-use sprays, liquid concentrate, or dust. Remember that the bacteria in this product are alive. Do not mix the product with anything that will kill them, such as copper, bleach, or soap. To store the product, follow the recommended temperature guidelines on the package and do not overheat.

▶ BTK or *Bt kurstaki*

For **caterpillars** (from page 48, 52, 53, 73, 74), **cutworms** (page 73, 200), **fruitworms** (page 107, 111, 112, 118, 125), **army worms** (page 111), **European corn borers** (page 111, 124), and **earworms** (page 111, 202).

Signal word? Caution.

What is it? BTK is a living biological insecticide that kills caterpillars. *Bt* stands for *Bacillus thuringiensis*, a bacterial parasite that infects and kills specific insects. The bacteria are suspended in inert ingredients that are not listed on the label.

Several different strains of this bacterium have been identified. BTK is the specific strain that kills caterpillars of all kinds (butterfly and moth larvae); it has no effect on beetles, mosquitoes, and black flies. BTSD (*Bt san diego*) kills beetles, and BTI (*Bt israelensis*) kills mosquito larvae, which live in stagnant water.

What does it do? Applied to the surface of plant leaves, stems, and fruits, the bacteria are ingested when a caterpillar eats the treated plant parts. The bacteria infect the insect's gut and kill it over a period of days. Usually the caterpillar stops eating long before it dies.

What are the side effects? No side effects are known at the present time. This bacterium is highly targeted to specific hosts and has no effect on non-target organisms. Caution is necessary, however, because the inert ingredients in the preparation can sometimes cause allergic reactions.

Caterpillars are the larvae of butterflies and moths, with chewing mouthparts that feed on leaves, fruit, and stems of plants. Adult butterflies and moths have sucking mouthparts and feed on nectar, if they eat anything at all. BTK harms adult butterflies and moths insofar as it is very effective at killing their offspring.

How do I use it? Read the label and follow directions. *Bt* var. *kurstaki* is available as a ready-to-use handy spray bottle at garden centers everywhere. It is also available as a liquid concentrate and as a dust.

Once the caterpillar is safely hidden inside your plant, BTK will not work unless you are able to inject it into borer holes. However, many susceptible pests lay their eggs on the surface of your plant. If you have sprayed BTK before the eggs hatch, the newly hatched caterpillars will ingest it when they try to chew their way into your plant, and they will die.

Remember that the bacteria in this product are alive. Do not mix the product with anything that will kill them, such as copper, bleach, or soap. To store the product, follow the recommended temperature guidelines on the package and do not overheat.

▶ **Milky spore**

For **Japanese beetles** (from page 20, 180, 181)

Signal word? Caution.

What is it? Milky spore is a bacterial disease of Japanese beetles and their relatives. The disease is caused by *Bacillus popilliae* and *B. lentimorbus*. These bacteria are cultivated in commercial laboratories, and packaged and sold in garden supply stores and over the Internet.

What does it do? Japanese beetle larvae are white grubs with brown heads that live in the soil and feed on the roots of your plants. The grubs are particularly troublesome in lawns. When the bacteria are present, the beetle grubs ingest the bacteria as they feed. The bacteria infect the grubs and kill them.

What are the side effects? There are no side effects to mammals, birds, or any animal other than Japanese and related beetles. Milky spore has no effect on other pest beetles, or any other insect such as honey bees and butterflies.

How do I use it? Read the label and follow directions. Milky spore bacteria are prepared as a dust or as granules. Apply the dust in spots, using about a teaspoon of powder every 4 feet or so, with a total of about 10 ounces for 2,500 square feet. You can use a spreader for the granular material at a rate of about 4 pounds for 2,500 square feet.

Unfortunately, Japanese beetle adults are excellent fliers and, even though you may kill all their grubs in the soil in your yard, all the beetles in your neighborhood can still fly to your yard and eat your flowers. Milky spore can provide really excellent control, however, if you can get your whole community to apply it. The adults will still migrate in from the surrounding countryside, but you can get ahead of the beetle destruction if everyone in the neighborhood cooperates.

▶ Neem

Signal word? Caution.

What is it? Neem is extracted from the seeds of the neem tree (*Azadirachta indica*), an evergreen tree endemic to India. It is a close relative of the chinaberry tree (*Melia azedarach*). The oil is extracted by crushing seeds, usually in a cold-press process.

What does it do? Insects with chewing or piercing/sucking mouthparts damage plants. When these kinds of insects ingest neem, they are affected in a variety of ways. Neem prevents some insects from molting, so that they cannot mature. Neem prevents other insects from laying eggs and causes many insects to stop feeding, so that they starve. Neem also repels insects. All these effects can take time before you observe effective population control, so be patient.

What are the side effects? The seeds of both the neem tree and the chinaberry tree are poisonous. Neem rapidly biodegrades. Safety and environmental impact testing is incomplete. Some tests have shown that neem is non-toxic to mammals, honey bees, and predatory insects like ladybird beetles. Yet labels warn that it should not be used on or near water. In addition, you should not use it when bees are actively foraging. The EPA considers it safe to use indoors. The smell can be quite objectionable.

How do I use it? Follow the directions on the label. Neem by itself will not mix with water, but commercial preparations contain a surfactant that enables the oil to disperse in water. Mix the neem preparation with water, and spray the plant thoroughly about every 7 to 14 days, as needed, during the growing season.

▶ Horticultural oil, dormant oil, superior oil

Signal word? Caution.

What is it? All three oils can be made from either vegetable oil or petroleum oil. You will encounter all three names on packaging. The words "dormant" or "superior" on labels refer to the season of use, not to the type of oil from which it is made. Dormant oil is sprayed on plants in winter, when plants are leafless. Superior oil can be sprayed on green leaves during the growing season or in winter. If the labels reads "horticultural oil" only, then look at the directions to find out when to use it.

We recommend products made with vegetable oil, but they can be hard to find. Search for them on the Internet and ask for them at your local garden center. Most garden centers carry several different horticultural oils made from petroleum, some of which are OMRI certified for organic gardening.

What does it do? These oils coat, smother, and kill insects and mites as well as their eggs. The oil is effective when used as a dormant spray in winter, when plants are not in active growth, and at a lower concentration during the growing season.

What are the side effects? Oils can be harmful if swallowed or absorbed through the skin. Prolonged skin contact can cause allergic reactions in some individuals. They can cause moderate eye irritation. Avoid breathing the mist. Wear protective clothing, goggles, and a respiratory mask when using these products. Protect your pets and your children while spraying.

Oils are toxic to fish. Do not apply directly to water.

Oils are considered safe to use indoors on houseplants or in the greenhouse.

Some plants can be sensitive to oils, especially when the temperature is high. Test spray a small portion of your plant and wait a few days to be sure it is able to tolerate the treatment. Maple (*Acer*), hickory (*Carya*), black walnut (*Juglans nigra*), smoke tree (*Cotinus*), and plume tree (*Cryptomeria*) are known to be sensitive. Light yellowing of the foliage is a symptom of sensitivity.

Any oil will turn a blue spruce (*Picea pungens*) green. It does not harm the plant but certainly alters its aesthetic appeal. The blue color of blue spruce is due to a waxy coating on the surface of the leaves. When oil penetrates the blue coating, the blue coat becomes transparent and you can see the green leaf under it. The plant will regain its blue color in two or three years.

The combination of oil and sulfur is harmful to green leaves and will damage them, causing a phytotoxic reaction. Do not use horticultural oil on your plants during the growing season for one month before and one month after you treat your plant with sulfur.

How do I use it? Read the label and follow directions. Ready-made horticultural oil products available at garden centers contain an emulsifier that allows the oil to mix with water. Mix the emulsified horticultural oil with water, following the directions on the label, and apply by spraying. Be sure to coat the plant thoroughly because these products work on contact. Insects, mites, and their eggs have to be covered in oil for it to kill them. The label will tell you how to make a heavier concentration to use as a dormant spray in winter, and how to make a lighter concentration to use when plants are in active growth.

You can make your own horticultural oil with a vegetable oil, like soybean or cottonseed oil, to which you add soap or other emulsifier. Be sure to use a true soap, not a detergent. Always test spray a small area of your plant to be sure it can tolerate the application. Wait a few days before applying a wider application. Add 1 tablespoon of liquid soap to 1 cup of vegetable oil to make a concentrate. Put 1 tablespoon of this concentrate in 1 gallon of water to make a lighter mix to apply to plants during the growing season. Use half a cup of concentrate in 1 gallon of water to make a heavier mix to apply to plants when they are dormant in winter.

Use horticultural oils only when temperatures are below 85°F (29.4°C) in the daytime and above freezing at night. Do not apply any oils to drought-stressed plants. Make sure your plants, including houseplants, are well hydrated before you treat them with oil.

▶ **Sulfur**

Signal word? Caution.

What is it? Sulfur is a yellow mineral mined from the earth, and is a naturally occurring element, like oxygen, nitrogen, or iron. Ancient Greeks and Romans used sulfur to control fungal diseases on grains and other crops. It is one of the oldest pesticides known.

What does it do? Sulfur kills a variety of insects, including some beneficials, by disrupting their metabolism. It is particularly effective against thrips, psyllids, and aphids.

What are the side effects? Sulfur is somewhat toxic to mammals like us, so wear protective gear to keep it out of your eyes and lungs and off your skin. If you have asthma or allergies, you may be sensitive to sulfur. The EPA considers sulfur safe to use indoors. Sulfur can kill beneficial insects and fish, so use it when beneficial bugs are less active (that is, when it is cool outside) and keep it away from ponds, streams, and lakes.

Sulfur can harm your plants in two circumstances: when it is too hot, or when you have recently sprayed your plants with an oil. Do not use sulfur if the temperature is above 80°F (26.6°C), or if you have sprayed your plant with horticultural oil in the last month. Avoid using sulfur for one month before and one month after using horticultural oil on your plant. Furthermore, if you use sulfur regularly, it can build up in the soil and make the soil more acid.

How do I use it? Follow the directions on the label. Sulfur is available as a ready-to-use spray, or as a concentrate that you mix with water, or as a dust. Apply thoroughly to all above-ground plant parts. In order to prevent new infestations you must apply sulfur before insect eggs hatch. You may need to apply it fairly frequently, about every 7 to 14 days, because it washes off the plant.

▶ **Pyrethrin**

Signal word? Caution.

What is it? Pyrethrin is a natural botanical insecticide/miticide made from the dried flowers of *Chrysanthemum cinerariifolium*, a perennial relative of the garden mum. This species was formerly placed in the genus *Pyrethrum*, and the natural product obtained from it still carries the older name, pyrethrum.

The flower heads are harvested and dried, then ground to powder. The active ingredients extracted from the powder are given a new name, pyrethrin. Pyrethrin is a mixture of several different chemicals that act as broad-spectrum nerve poisons, killing both insects and mites on contact. Some insects have enzymes that detoxify the natural chemical and allow the insects to recover after their initial paralysis. Synthetic versions of these natural chemicals are called pyrethroids. Pyrethroids are less toxic to mammals than the natural product but are more toxic to insects.

What does it do? Pyrethrin paralyzes the insects on contact. The dried product on the leaves and stems of your plants retains its potency for several days, affecting beneficial as well as harmful insects.

What are the side effects? Pyrethrin is mildly toxic to mammals, pyrethroids less so. They are considered one of the safest pesticides to use in the home, around food. People with asthma or hay fever may need to be cautious as it may cause allergic reactions. It kills ladybird beetles, but not honey bees. Pyrethrin is harmful to fish and other aquatic organisms.

Be aware that some commercial products contain additives to boost the potency of the natural product, such as piperonyl butoxide, a synergist. A synergist is a somewhat toxic compound by itself, which acts in concert with another compound to make the combination more toxic than either component used alone. Protect yourself with appropriate clothing and safety-wear when spraying.

How do I use it? Read the label and follow directions. Pyrethrin is generally applied as a liquid spray. It is available as ready-to-use hand-held spray bottles at garden centers everywhere, and as concentrates that you mix with water and apply with a spray bottle or pump-up sprayer. Spray thoroughly, the undersides as well as the top sides of the leaves.

Solutions for insects inside above-ground plant parts

Diagnoses from Part 1.

CHAPTER	PAGE	DIAGNOSIS
1 Whole Plant	20, 22	borers, bark beetles
2 Leaves	33, 45	borers
2 Leaves	40, 54	skeletonizers
2 Leaves	40	leafminers
2 Leaves	58	leafrollers
4 Fruit	100, 125	European apple sawfly
4 Fruit	107	raspberry fruitworm

CHAPTER	PAGE	DIAGNOSIS
4 Fruit	111	grape berry moths
4 Fruit	111	tomato fruitworms, corn earworms, army worms
4 Fruit	112	navel orange worms
4 Fruit	112	oriental fruitworms
4 Fruit	112, 124	codling moth larvae
4 Fruit	118	cherry or cranberry fruitworms
4 Fruit	118	fruit flies
4 Fruit	118	pear midge
4 Fruit	124	European corn borer
4 Fruit	125	apple maggots, blue berry maggots, currant fruit flies
5 Stems	131	peachtwig borers, oriental fruit moths
5 Stems	131	raspberry cane borers
5 Stems	131	twig girdlers, twig pruners
5 Stems	134, 144	two-lined chestnut borers
5 Stems	134, 145	Nantucket pine tip moth, oriental fruit moth, peachtwig borers
5 Stems	139	borers
5 Stems	144	flatheaded borers, dogwood borers, carpenter ants, pecan borers, European corn borers, rhododendron borers, squash vine borers, shot hole borers
5 Stems	145	bark beetles
5 Stems	145, 150	common stalk borers
5 Stems	150	white pine weevils
7 Seeds	196	husk flies
7 Seeds	198	white maggots
7 Seeds	199	codling moth larvae, pecan shuckworms, hickory shuckworms

CHAPTER	PAGE	DIAGNOSIS
7 Seeds	199	seed weevils, nut weevils
7 Seeds	201	pea moth larvae
7 Seeds	201	pecan nut casebearers
7 Seeds	202	corn earworms
7 Seeds	202	sap beetles
7 Seeds	202	army worms

As you can see by the list of diagnoses, many kinds of insects bore their way into above-ground plant parts. But, with one exception (beneficial nematodes), all the solutions for such boring insects must be used when the insects are on their way into or out of the plant. They are therefore the same as those in the previous section, solutions for insects on above-ground plant parts, beginning on page 267. Always change the growing conditions before using any of the remedies suggested there. If you decide to use chemicals to help control insects inside your plants, please read the safety considerations on page 274.

▶ **Beneficial nematodes**

Signal word? None.

What is it? Nematodes are microscopic round worms, invisible to the naked eye, that are present everywhere on earth. Some are destructive plant parasites of roots or foliage, others feed on bacteria and fungi in the soil, and some are parasites. Two species that attack soil-dwelling insects are produced commercially and are readily available to homeowners: *Steinernema carpocapsae*, which inhabits a relatively shallow layer of the soil, close to the surface, and *Heterorhabditis bacteriophora*, which ranges deeper into the soil. These beneficial nematodes can control the populations of some 200 insect pests that live on or in the soil.

What does it do? Both these nematodes seek out insect adults or larvae that dwell in or on the soil for part of their life cycle. They also provide temporary control of boring insects. Japanese beetle grubs, plum curculios, onion maggots, and strawberry root weevils are only a few of the insects controlled by these nematodes. The nematodes swim through the film of moisture in the soil, seeking out insect prey. They enter the bodies of their prey through natural openings, such as the insect's mouth. Once inside the insect, the nematodes release a bacterium that they carry in their gut. The bacterium kills the insect within two to four days. The nematodes feed on the insect the whole time, eating it from the inside out and reproducing inside the carcass. When the dead insect is depleted of nourishment, swarms of new nematodes migrate out of the dead insect, searching for more prey.

What are the side effects? There are no side effects known for any vertebrates (mammals, birds, reptiles, amphibians, or fish) or for any plants. Insects that do not spend some portion of their life cycle on or in the soil, such as honey bees, are unaffected.

How do I use it? Follow the instructions on the label. The package you purchase at your garden center contains living nematodes and must be handled carefully to keep them alive. The package contains infective larvae suspended in a storage medium (moist peat, vermiculite, gel). The package needs to be refrigerated until you are ready to use the nematodes. In general, you should apply them to areas where you know the pest insects are present. Like any predator, nematodes need an adequate food supply in order to do their job effectively. Normally, mix the larvae suspension with water and spray or sprinkle the liquid on the selected area. Beneficial nematodes can persist in the soil for as long as five years, if the soil is warm and moist and there is plenty of food. This solution is very cost effective.

Beneficial nematodes can also be injected directly into the entry hole made by tunneling pests. The nematodes kill destructive boring insects but cannot persist inside the plants. If the plant becomes reinfested, repeat the treatment.

Solutions for insects in the soil environment

Diagnoses from Part 1.

CHAPTER	PAGE	DIAGNOSIS
1 Whole Plant	20	root weevil larvae, Japanese beetle larvae
6 Roots	179	wireworms
6 Roots	179	iris borers, potato tuberworms
6 Roots	180	carrot weevils, flea beetle larvae, sweet potato weevils, Japanese beetle larvae
6 Roots	180	white-fringed beetle larvae, cucumber beetles
6 Roots	180	narcissus bulb fly
6 Roots	180	root maggots, cabbage maggots, onion maggots, rust flies
6 Roots	181	wireworms, corn rootworms, strawberry root weevils, black vine weevils, Japanese beetle larvae

CHAPTER	PAGE	DIAGNOSIS
6 Roots	182, 191	root aphids
6 Roots	182, 191	root mealybugs
7 Seeds	197	corn rootworms, seed-corn beetles, white grubs
7 Seeds	197	wireworms

Insect larvae or adults in the soil environment can damage the roots or underground storage organs of your plants by eating them, burrowing inside them, or sucking nutrients out of their veins. Since most of these pests, usually in the adult phase, live above ground for part of their life cycle, use the techniques starting on page 268 as part of your management strategy. Solutions that manage these pests underground are limited, but extremely effective.

As with all plant problems, prevention is the cheapest and easiest way to reduce insect infestations. If you have used the flow charts in Part 1, and you already know you have a problem, you probably want to move immediately to a cure. If so, please be sure to return to Chapter 8 and use the preventive measures presented there. You will have far fewer insect pest problems in the future.

Change the growing conditions
These solutions begin with a list of preventive measures that you will find in Chapter 8. Prevention is always the best way to combat insect attacks. Preventive measures also keep insects from spreading to plants that are not yet under siege, so undertake these steps as soon as possible to control pests on your plant.

Preventive measures

▶ **Use physical barriers.** See page 270.

▶ **Choose resistant cultivars.** See page 215.

▶ **Rotate plants.** See page 217.

Control measure

▶ **Sanitize.** Use the techniques starting on page 268 and destroy infested plant parts while the insects or larvae are still inside them.

If necessary, use organic insecticides

If you decide to use chemicals to help control insects in the soil environment of your plants, please read the safety considerations on page 274.

Remedy recommendations

Always change the growing conditions (see page 284) before using either of these remedies. Evaluate your circumstances and the plant you are treating to choose the right product for you. Use products with signal words only when you need them. Do not apply them according to a predetermined schedule; instead, observe your plants and use chemicals only as necessary. Both these products are approved for organic gardening.

▶ **Beneficial nematodes.** See page 283.

▶ **Pyrethrin.** See page 281.

Solutions for insects inside galls

Diagnoses from Part 1.

CHAPTER	PAGE	DIAGNOSIS
2 Leaves	56	kinnikinnik leaf gall aphid
2 Leaves	56	mossyrose gall
2 Leaves	56	spiny rose gall
2 Leaves	57	galls
5 Stems	141, 148	Cooley spruce gall adelgid (on spruce)
5 Stems	157	mossyrose gall

Most plant galls are caused by insects or mites which produce chemicals that cause the plant to create a structure, known as a gall, in which the insects live. Some galls enclose insect larvae only; other galls enclose whole populations of adults and offspring. As long as the insects are inside the gall, they are protected.

Fortunately, plant damage due to galls caused by insects is rarely serious and is easily controlled by simply pruning away the affected plant parts. Prune off and destroy the galls before the pests inside mature, while the gall is still fresh. If the gall is dried up, or if you see exit holes on the surface of the gall, the pests have already matured and abandoned the structure. Pruning is an effective strategy for mossyrose gall, spiny rose gall, and various other galls on roses (*Rosa*), oaks (*Quercus*), and other plants.

If pruning fails, try an organic remedy. Applications of insecticidal soap (see page 275) can help to control galls by killing the insects before they are completely enclosed by the gall. Remove any existing galls and spray the plants with insecticidal soap when new growth starts in the spring.

11 Mites

What are mites?

Mites are part of the class of animals known as arachnids, which means they have eight legs and are closely related to spiders and ticks. Mites are not insects, which have six legs. Mites (Acari) are everywhere, and most of them are so tiny you will never see them.

Scientists have described and named more than 48,000 species of mites and suspect there are actually more than 500,000 species around the world. Of invertebrate animals they are second only to insects in diversity, that is, in their number of species. In fact, if you took a square yard (about one square meter) of soil from beneath a mixed deciduous-coniferous forest, you would strike it rich in mites. If you examined that soil under a microscope, you would find about a million mites belonging to 200 species from some 50 families.

Mites are one of the most ancient of terrestrial animals, and paleontologists have found fossil mites that are nearly 400 million years old. An Egyptian papyrus from 1550 BC discusses treatment of a disease caused by mites, and ancient Greek scholars studied mites. Linnaeus, the man who invented the binomial system of nomenclature, described the first mite of

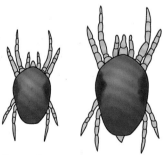

The small mite on the left is the male, the large one on the right is the female two-spotted spider mite.

Under the microscope you can see that this tiny red spider mite has eight legs like a spider.

Nearly invisible, these two-spotted spider mites scurry about on the underside of a croton (*Codiaeum*) leaf.

western scientific literature in 1758. It was *Acarius siro*.

Most mites are invisible to the naked eye, and live an almost secret life among us. But one mite we encounter every day is the ubiquitous dust mite (*Dermatophagoides pteronyssinus*), which does very well in the warm, humid habitat of our bed linens.

What do mites do?

Mites inhabit every major ecosystem and live successfully in the arctic, the tropics, temperate climates, deserts, rain forests and, even under water—both fresh and salt. They have been found 32 feet (10 meters) underground in hard mineral soil, and in deep marine trenches 16,000 feet (5,000 meters) below the surface of the sea. They thrive in an amazing diversity of habitats from geothermal hot springs, to under the skin of reptiles, to inside our own hair follicles. Most mites live freely in the soil, but many are parasites on plants, fungi, bacteria, and other animals.

The characteristics that have led to such amazing success include their diversity and adaptability to so many different ecological niches; their high egg production; their short life cycles; and their incredible array of transportation modes.

A female mite lives between 14 and 30 days, and lays 100 or more eggs during her lifetime. Some female mites need to find males to fertilize the eggs, but others do not. They rely instead on parthenogenesis, which just means that a female can produce offspring without sex.

Mites have piercing/sucking mouthparts, which allow them to penetrate the cell wall of plants and suck out the cell's contents. Several different kinds of mites attack plants in the landscape, home, or greenhouse. Some, like spider mites, two-spotted spider mites, and cyclamen mites, feed on the surface of leaves, stems, and fruits. Other kinds of mites, such as blister mites, gall mites, and rust mites, crawl inside the plant's tissues and feed on leaves and fruits.

The bright side of mites

Some species of mites feed on leaf litter, rotting wood, microbes, bacteria, fungi, and other detritus in the soil. Other mites are predators that eat larger micro-fauna. Thus, mites contribute to the rich stew that makes a good organic soil. In addition, some predatory mites hunt down and eat mites that damage plants. These are useful bio-controls and are available from companies that supply beneficial organisms for the garden.

The dark side of mites

Mites can be damaging parasites, can carry disease from one organism to another, and can cause allergies. Dust mites live in our homes, feeding on the detritus of dead skin cells that rains from our bodies. Though they do not bite, they cause hay fever, asthma, and contact dermatitis in many people. And there are others. Scabies and chiggers pierce your skin to feed on your blood, causing intense itching. Ear mites, mange, and a variety of other mites plague dogs and cats, while still other species infest chickens and other birds. *Varoa* mites infect the European honey bee (*Apis mellifera*) and have wreaked havoc among bees and their keepers.

Types of solutions

For mites on above-ground plant parts, solutions begin on this page.

Mites that feed on the exterior of plants pierce plant cells and suck out the cell's contents, leaving an empty shell behind. With spider mites, the walls of the empty cell reflect light and appear to be minute white or yellow specks that sparkle slightly in sunlight. Spider mites frequent gardens, regularly infesting outdoor plants. They occasionally attack houseplants as well. Often they spin webs over the surface of plants and are especially troublesome where conditions are dry and dusty.

Cyclamen mites have toxic saliva that causes plants to become distorted, stunted, and discolored as they feed. Cyclamen mites mostly infest greenhouses, although they can attack strawberry plants in the garden. Despite their name, cyclamen mites feed on a wide variety of plants.

For mites inside above-ground plant parts, solutions begin on page 295.

Blister mites, gall mites, and rust mites burrow into the tissues of leaves and fruits of outdoor plants. Because they are hidden and protected by the tissues of their host plant, they are difficult to reach with control measures.

For mites in bulbs, solutions begin on page 296.

Bulb mites feed on fleshy underground structures like bulbs, corms, and tubers, either in the ground or in storage. Control measures differ from the other two types of solutions.

Solutions for mites on above-ground plant parts

Diagnoses from Part 1.

CHAPTER	PAGE	DIAGNOSIS
2 Leaves	37	spider mites
2 Leaves	60	mites
3 Flowers	78	cyclamen mites

Change the growing conditions

Try these steps before resorting to a chemical solution. Mites can be eliminated if you watch for their signs and take the time to make these changes. Choose the solutions that work best for your circumstances. This list of techniques begins with a preventive measure that keeps mites from getting access to your plant collection in the first place; control measures follow.

Preventive measure

▶ **Quarantine new plants.** Two-spotted spider mites and cyclamen mites often gain entry to your garden, home, or greenhouse on infested bedding plants, strawberries, and houseplants. Inspect your plant material prior to purchasing it. Turn the leaves over and look for webs and yellow or white speckles. Check the growing tips for distorted, discolored, and stunted new growth. Purchase only material that appears to be healthy.

You cannot see most mites, and a plant may be symptomless in the early stages of infestation. Whenever you buy a new plant or receive a gift plant, if you have any doubts about its health, keep your new plant in quarantine. Isolate it from existing plants until you are sure it is free of pests or disease.

Be sure to move the quarantined plant far away from all your other plants even if those plants are not related to the sick plant. Mite-borne plant diseases can frequently cross genetic barriers and infect many different kinds of plants. Be sure to clean your tools and wash your hands after working with any plant in quarantine.

Control measures

▶ **Sanitize.** This is one of the most important steps you can take to keep plants healthy. In the world of plant pathology, to sanitize means to remove infected or infested plant material. Such plant parts are a source of fungal spores, nematode larvae, bacteria, insects, and mites.

Remove and destroy mite-infested leaves, stems, or fruit. Remove mite-infested plant material by plucking leaves or pruning branches. Destroy these plant parts before the nymphs inside them have a chance to mature, mate, lay eggs, and reinfest your plants. The objective is to disrupt the life cycle so that the pest cannot reproduce. Do not put infested material into your compost pile. Do not contribute it to a municipal green waste collection program. If you live where it is legal to burn waste, and can safely do so, burn infested material. Otherwise, put the material in garbage destined for a landfill.

Hot water for cyclamen mites. A hot water treatment can kill **cyclamen mites** (from page 78). We recommend attempting this technique only on high-value perennials or houseplants that you can't bear to discard. Trim off and discard all badly infested tissue and wash away any dirt. Immerse the plant in hot water held at a constant temperature of 115°F (46°C) for seven minutes. Treatments reported in scientific papers vary from 110°F (43.3°C) for 15 to 30 minutes, to 120.3°F (49.0°C) for one to 10 minutes. The hotter the water, the less time it takes to kill the mites. Be very careful, however: too hot and your plant will die, too cool and the mites will survive.

Commercial growers use a constant temperature recirculating water bath for this purpose. At home you could use a large pan of water on a gas stove. Do not use an electric burner because it cycles on and off and the temperature fluctuates too much. You will need an accurate thermometer (digital readout preferred) and you will need to gently stir the entire time.

Bladder gall mites live inside the tissue of this cherry (*Prunus*) leaf. Their toxic saliva causes the plant to react by growing these long, strange structures filled with mites.

This rose (*Rosa*) leaf is covered with the webs of spider mites. The tiny red dots on the webbing and leaf are the mites themselves.

Blister mites inside this pear (*Pyrus*) leaf cause the leaf to distort and die.

▶ **Remove pests.**

Blast mites with water spray. Knock **mites** (from page 37, 60) off your plants with a strong stream of water from your hose. Hose down your plants about once a week to keep these populations at a low level. Although this appears to contradict the advice to keep foliage dry, it does not, if you use this technique on clear days, in the mornin g, so that leaves have time to dry.

Wash plants. For **cyclamen mites** (from page 78), trim off and destroy all badly damaged plant parts, then gently wash the plants with water.

▶ **Encourage beneficial organisms.** To attract beneficial mites and insects to your garden, grow species of plants these animals prefer as sources of food or shelter. Also provide water in very shallow containers, such as a bird bath or plant saucer. Some examples of plants to grow:

- The carrot family (Apiaceae): coriander, dill, fennel, parsley
- The mint family (Lamiaceae): catnip, thyme, rosemary, hyssop, lemon balm
- The daisy family (Asteraceae): cosmos, yarrow, coneflower

To increase your chances of controlling pests with beneficial organisms, purchase them at your local garden center or through mail-order suppliers. Check with the supplier to determine which species is the best choice for your particular problem, host plants, and environmental conditions. Some examples:

- Predatory mites attack and kill spider mites and cyclamen mites. Species of

Phytoseiulus, Amblyseius, or *Metaseiulus* are available.
- Green lacewings, ladybird beetles, praying mantises, mealybug destroyers, and minute pirate bugs hunt, kill, and eat many pests.

If necessary, use organic miticides

You may decide to utilize chemicals to help control mites on your plants, indoors or out. Various chemicals are certified for use in organic gardening. Many of these organic treatments are relatively safe for you and the environment. Some have been in use for hundreds of years, others are quite new. Look for OMRI (Organic Materials Review Institute) certification on the label. Keep in mind that mites are not insects. Many pesticides that kill insects do not kill mites. Whatever product you choose, read the label and look for the word "miticide." Miticides kill mites. Insecticides kill insects.

Remedy recommendations

Always change the growing conditions (see page 288) before using any of these remedies. Evaluate your circumstances and the plant you are treating to choose the right product for you. Use products with signal words (CAUTION, WARNING, DANGER) only when you need them. Do not apply them according to a predetermined schedule; instead, observe your plants and use chemicals only as necessary. These are listed from least toxic to most toxic, but all are approved for organic gardening.

▶ **Insecticidal soap**
   Signal word? None.
   What is it? Chemically, soap is a salt made by

combining an acid (vegetable oil or animal fat, both of which consist of fatty acids) with a base (potassium, sodium hydroxide, or lye). When an acid and a base mix, they react to form a salt. In this case, the salt is what we call soap. Commercial insecticidal soaps list the active ingredient as "potassium salts of fatty acids," in other words, soap.

What does it do? Insecticidal soap works on mites. A mixture of soap and water sprayed directly onto mites kills quickly. The soap penetrates the cuticle that protects the pests and causes their cells to collapse. However, soap has no residual activity. Once it dries it is no longer effective.

What are the side effects? Soap is a broad-

SAFETY FIRST

1. Always keep all these products **out of the reach of children and pets.**

2. **Read the label.** Use only chemicals that list the plants or type of plant you wish to protect on their labels. For example, a label may say "For use on ornamentals." Do not use this on a food plant.

3. **Follow the directions on the label.** Remember that more is not better. Many chemicals can actually damage some plants. This kind of damage is called a phytotoxic reaction. It is important to read the label and follow the manufacturer's instructions. If you put too much of the active ingredient on your plant, or if you put it on the wrong plant, you may do more harm than good.

   Every package or bottle of a garden remedy product has a label on the back that peels open. Unfold it and read the tiny print inside to learn what the product is used for, which plants to use it on, when to use it, and how much to use. Some of these labels unfold into long pages of instructions. Be patient, get out your magnifying glass, and read them carefully. Follow those directions.

4. **Always use the least toxic product first.** Look for a signal word on the label. These signal words are required by federal law under the Federal Insecticide, Fungicide and Rodenticide Act (FIFRA). All commercially sold pesticides must be registered with the Environmental Protection Agency (EPA), the registration authority for pesticides, and tested for modes of transmission into the body: inhalation, ingestion, dermal contact, primary eye, and primary skin. Toxicity Category IV requires no signal word because tests have shown the product to be non-toxic; these products, such as baking soda spray and insecticidal soap, are the safest, least toxic products you can use. Any pesticide determined to be in Toxicity Category III must be labeled **CAUTION**. Any in Toxicity Category II must carry the label **WARNING**. Those in Category I must be labeled either **DANGER** (the most toxic product available to the home gardener) or **DANGER— POISON**, with an image of a skull and crossbones. The last is most toxic of all. It is available only to licensed pesticide applicators.

5. **Wear protective gear and clothing.** Wear goggles, a respiratory face mask, a long-sleeved shirt, long pants, and shoes. Wash your clothes when you are finished using any product with a signal word.

spectrum insecticide and miticide that kills beneficial insects like ladybird beetles (ladybugs), honey bees, green lacewings, and others, if you spray them. Protect your beneficial critters by spraying only the pests you wish to kill. Soap is not toxic to mammals or birds, and it degrades rapidly in the soil. It is not harmful to aquatic organisms or ecosystems.

How do I use it? Insecticidal soaps are commercially available as ready-to-use products in handy spray bottles at most garden centers. Concentrates that you mix with water and apply with a pump-up sprayer are also available.

If you wish to make your own liquid spray, first get some soap. It pays to be careful here because many of the things we call soap, like dishwashing liquid, are actually detergents (synthetic soaps) which can be harmful to plants. Look for products like pure castile liquid soap, which is available in most stores. If you have the time and inclination, you can make your own soap out of ingredients you personally select for the qualities you desire. There are numerous recipes and instructions on the Internet.

Mix 1 tablespoon of liquid soap with 1 quart (1 liter) of water in a spray bottle or a pump-up sprayer and drench the pests with this mix.

▶ **Neem**

Signal word? Caution.

What is it? Neem is extracted from the seeds of the neem tree (*Azadirachta indica*), an evergreen tree endemic to India. It is a close relative of the chinaberry tree (*Melia azedarach*). The oil is extracted by crushing seeds, usually in a cold-press process.

What does it do? Neem controls mites by preventing the mites from molting and laying eggs. In addition, it causes mites to stop feeding. Mite eggs also fail to hatch. It takes time before you observe positive results, so be patient.

What are the side effects? The seeds of both the neem tree and the chinaberry tree are poisonous. Neem rapidly biodegrades. Safety and environmental impact testing is incomplete. Some tests have shown that neem is non-toxic to mammals, honey bees, and predatory insects like ladybird beetles. Yet labels warn that it should not be used on or near water. In addition, you should not use it when bees are actively foraging. The EPA considers it safe to use indoors. The smell can be quite objectionable.

How do I use it? Follow the directions on the label. Neem by itself will not mix with water, but commercial preparations contain a surfactant that enables the oil to disperse in water. Mix the neem preparation with water, and spray the plant thoroughly about every 7 to 14 days, as needed, during the growing season.

▶ **Horticultural oil, dormant oil, superior oil**

Signal word? Caution.

What is it? All three oils can be made from either vegetable oil or petroleum oil. You will encounter all three names on packaging. The words "dormant" or "superior" on labels refer to the season of use, not to the type of oil from which it is made. Dormant oil is sprayed on plants in winter, when plants are leafless. Superior oil can be sprayed on green leaves during the growing season or in winter. If the label reads "horticultural oil" only, then look at the directions to find out when to use it.

We recommend products made with vegetable oil, but they can be hard to find. Search for them on the Internet and ask for them at your local garden center. Most garden centers carry several different horticultural oils made from petroleum, some of which are OMRI certified for organic gardening.

What does it do? These oils coat, smother, and kill insects and mites as well as their eggs. It is effective when used as a dormant spray in winter when plants are not in active growth, and at a lower concentration during the growing season.

What are the side effects? Oils can be harmful if swallowed or absorbed through the skin. Prolonged skin contact can cause allergic reactions in some individuals. They can cause moderate eye irritation. Avoid breathing the mist. Wear protective clothing, goggles, and a respiratory mask when using these products. Protect your pets and your children while spraying.

Oils are toxic to fish. Do not apply directly to water.

Oils are considered safe to use indoors on houseplants or in the greenhouse.

Some plants can be sensitive to oils, especially when the temperature is high. Test spray a small portion of your plant and wait a few days to be sure it is able to tolerate the treatment. Maple (*Acer*), hickory (*Carya*), black walnut (*Juglans nigra*), smoke tree (*Cotinus*), and plume tree (*Cryptomeria*) are known to be sensitive. Light yellowing of the foliage is a symptom of sensitivity.

Any oil will turn a blue spruce (*Picea pungens*) green. It does not harm the plant but certainly alters its aesthetic appeal. The blue color of blue spruce is due to a waxy coating on the surface of the leaves. When oil penetrates the blue coating, the blue coat becomes transparent and you can see the green leaf under it. The plant will regain its blue color in two or three years.

The combination of oil and sulfur is harmful to green leaves and will damage them, causing a phytotoxic reaction. Do not use horticultural oil on your plants during the growing season for one month before and one month after you treat your plant with sulfur.

How do I use it? Read the label and follow directions. Ready-made horticultural oil products available at garden centers contain an emulsifier that allows the oil to mix with water. Mix the emulsified horticultural oil with water, following the directions on the label, and apply by spraying. Be sure to coat the plant thoroughly because these products work on contact. Insects, mites, and their eggs have to be covered in oil for it to kill them. The label will tell you how to make a heavier concentration to use as a dormant spray in winter, and how to make a lighter concentration to use when plants are in active growth.

You can make your own horticultural oil with a vegetable oil, like soybean or cottonseed oil, to which you add soap or other emulsifier. Be sure to use a true soap, not a detergent. Always test spray a small area of your plant to be sure it can tolerate the application. Wait a few days before applying a wider application. Add 1 tablespoon of liquid soap to 1 cup of vegetable oil to make a concentrate. Put 1 tablespoon of this concentrate in 1 gallon of water to make a lighter mix to apply to plants during the growing season. Use half a cup of concentrate in 1 gallon of water to make a heavier mix to apply to plants when they are dormant in winter.

Use horticultural oils only when temperatures are below 85°F (29.4°C) in the daytime and above freezing at night. Do not apply any oils to drought-stressed plants. Make sure your plants, including houseplants, are well hydrated before you treat them with oil.

▶ **Sulfur**

Signal word? Caution.

What is it? Sulfur is a yellow mineral mined from the earth, a naturally occurring element, like oxygen, nitrogen, or iron. Ancient Greeks and Romans used sulfur to control fungal diseases on grains and other crops. It is one of the oldest pesticides known.

What does it do? Sulfur kills the eggs, larvae, and adults of mites by disrupting their metabolism. Its efficacy increases as temperature and relative humidity increase, so it is most effective on days that are warm and humid.

What are the side effects? Sulfur is somewhat toxic to mammals like us, so wear protective gear to keep it out of your eyes and lungs and off your skin. If you have asthma or allergies, you may be sensitive to sulfur. The EPA considers sulfur safe to use indoors. Sulfur can kill beneficial insects and fish, so use it when beneficial bugs are less active (that is, when it is cool outside) and keep it away from ponds, streams, and lakes.

Sulfur can harm your plants in two circumstances: when it is too hot, or when you have recently sprayed your plants with an oil. Do not use sulfur if the temperature is above 80°F (26.6°C), or if you have sprayed your plant with horticultural oil in the last month. Avoid using sulfur for one month before and one month after using horticultural oil on your plant. Furthermore, if you use sulfur regularly, it can build up in the soil and make the soil more acid.

How do I use it? Follow the directions on the label. Sulfur is available as a ready-to-use spray, or as a concentrate that you mix with water, or as a dust. Apply thoroughly to all above-ground plant parts. In order to prevent new infestations you must apply sulfur fairly frequently, about every 7 to 14 days, because it washes off the plant. In addition, sulfur is more effective on days that are warm and humid.

▶ **Pyrethrin**

Signal word? Caution.

What is it? Pyrethrin is a natural botanical insecticide/miticide made from the dried flowers of *Chrysanthemum cinerariifolium*, a perennial relative of the garden mum. This species was formerly placed in the genus *Pyrethrum*, and the natural product obtained from it still carries the older name, pyrethrum.

The flower heads are harvested and dried, then ground to powder. The active ingredients extracted from the powder are given a new name, pyrethrin. Pyrethrin is a mixture of several different chemicals that act as broad-spectrum nerve poisons, killing both insects and mites on contact. Synthetic versions of these natural chemicals are called pyrethroids. Pyrethroids are less toxic to mammals than the natural product but are more toxic to insects and mites.

What does it do? Pyrethrin paralyzes the mites on contact. The dried product on the leaves and stems of your plants retains its potency for several days, affecting beneficial as well as harmful mites and insects.

What are the side effects? Pyrethrin is mildly toxic to mammals, pyrethroids less so. They are considered one of the safest pesticides to use in the home, around food. People with asthma or hay fever may need to be cautious as it may cause allergic reactions. It kills ladybird beetles, but not honey bees. Pyrethrin is harmful to fish and other aquatic organisms.

Be aware that some commercial products contain additives to boost the potency of the natural product, such as piperonyl butoxide, a synergist. A synergist is a somewhat toxic compound by itself, which acts in concert with another compound to make the combination more toxic than either component used alone. Protect yourself with appropriate clothing and safety-wear when spraying.

How do I use it? Read the label and follow directions. Pyrethrin is generally applied as a liquid spray. It is available as ready-to-use hand-held spray bottles at garden centers everywhere, and as concentrates that you mix with water and apply with a spray bottle or pump-up sprayer. Spray thoroughly, the undersides as well as the top sides of the leaves.

Solutions for mites inside above-ground plant parts

Diagnoses from Part 1.

CHAPTER	PAGE	DIAGNOSIS
2 Leaves	56	bladder gall mites
2 Leaves	39, 57	blister mites
4 Fruit	101	redberry mites

Change the growing conditions

As in all disease management, prevention is your best defense. Once mites have burrowed into plant tissue, there is very little you can do about it; they are protected by the plant tissue that surrounds them. Only one control technique is effective.

▶ **Sanitize.** This is one of the most important steps you can take to keep plants healthy. In the world of plant pathology, to sanitize means to remove infected or infested plant material. Such plant parts are a source of fungal spores, nematode larvae, bacteria, insects, and mites.

Remove and destroy mite-infested leaves, stems, or fruit. Remove mite-infested plant material by plucking leaves or pruning branches. Destroy these plant parts before the nymphs inside them have a chance to mature, mate, lay eggs, and reinfest your plants. The objective is to disrupt the life cycle so that the pest cannot reproduce. Do not put infested material into your compost pile. Do not contribute it to a municipal green waste collection program. If you live where it is legal to burn waste, and can safely do so, burn

Left: Bladder gall mites live inside the strange growths on this maple (*Acer*) leaf. Right: Redberry mites inside the tissue of this blackberry (*Rubus*) fruit cause some of the drupelets to stay red and fail to ripen.

infested material. Otherwise, put the material in garbage destined for a landfill.

If necessary, use organic miticides

If you decide to utilize chemicals to help control mites on your plants, please read the safety considerations on page 291. Keep in mind that mites are not insects. Many pesticides that kill insects do not kill mites. Whatever product you choose, read the label and look for the word "miticide." Miticides kill mites. Insecticides kill insects.

Remedy recommendations

Choose either product to treat mites inside above-ground plant parts. Both are approved for organic gardening.

▶ **Horticultural oil, dormant oil, superior oil.** See page 292. Horticultural oil, used properly, is one of your best bets in dealing with these kinds of mites. Female mites and eggs are hidden in cracks and crevices of the bark of your trees and shrubs over the winter. Spraying oil into the cracks coats, smothers, and kills the mites along with their eggs. By decimating the over-wintering population in this way, you seriously reduce the incidence of mite attack the following spring.

▶ **Sulfur.** See page 294. Sulfur will not kill the mites that are already safely sipping away inside the plant tissue. It will, however, kill any young mites on the surface of your plants who are looking for a place to settle down.

Solutions for mites in bulbs

Diagnoses from Part 1.

CHAPTER	PAGE	DIAGNOSIS
6 Roots	188	bulb mites

▶ **Start with mite-free bulbs.** Always purchase your bulbs and tubers from reliable sources that certify them to be free of pests at the time of purchase. Inspect bulbs, tubers, corms, and rhizomes when you buy them, and select only those that are plump, firm, and free of spots or rough discolored areas. Bulb mites are too small to see with the naked eye (they look like tiny grains of very fine white sand), but infested bulbs will be soft and blackened or spotted.

A healthy, mite-free daffodil (*Narcissus*) bulb is firm and white beneath the brown scales, and has numerous roots at the base.

A mite-infested daffodil (*Narcissus*) bulb is squishy and black beneath the brown scales, and has no roots at the base.

This photomicrograph shows a bulb mite feeding on the black, decayed tissue of a daffodil (*Narcissus*) bulb.

▶ **Protect bulbs in storage.** Dust stored bulbs with sulfur to protect them from mites as well as from fungus diseases.

1. At the proper time of year, lift (dig up) bulbs carefully from the ground, taking care not to crush, bruise, or cut them.
2. Lift spring bulbs (tulips, daffodils, crocus) when all the foliage has turned yellow and died away in early summer. You do not have to lift spring bulbs every year, only when they have become too crowded and are no longer flowering well.
3. Lift summer bulbs (cannas, begonias, dahlias) in the autumn if you live in a climate where a hard freeze will kill them.
4. Shake or wash all the soil off the bulbs and let them air dry for a couple of weeks.
5. When they are sufficiently cured, put them into a plastic bag with a little sulfur, hold the top closed, and shake. Wear a dust mask and rubber gloves for this process and be aware that some people are allergic to sulfur. See page 294.
6. Put the dusted bulbs into paper bags and be sure to include labels naming the kind of plant and the cultivar. Add vermiculite if desired and close the bags.
7. Store your bulbs under dry, cool conditions. Do not put them in air-tight containers.

12 Bacteria

What are bacteria?

Bacteria are extremely small microorganisms that usually consist of a single cell. A typical bacterium measures 1/25,000th of an inch or 0.01 mm. For most bacteria you would need an electron microscope to see that the cell has an outer wall lined with a membrane. Within that membrane you would find the cytoplasm with a single chromosome. This chromosome is a tangled thread of DNA that is not contained within a nucleus. This unique feature places bacteria in their own kingdom, Prokaryotae, separate from other biological kingdoms such as Plantae, Animalia, or Fungi.

Bacterial cells come in many different shapes, from spherical to rod-shaped to spiral or tightly coiled. The bacterium's shape affects how it moves through liquid, which in turn influences how it infects other organisms or escapes predators.

Bacteria are ubiquitous and are found in every environment on the planet, including some of the most inhospitable sites on earth. They live in volcanic vents at the bottom of the ocean, in rocks deep within the earth, and even in radioac-

tive waste. They also thrive in other living organisms; our bodies, in fact, contain more bacterial cells than human cells. The number of bacterial species is unknown; only 1,600 have been named and described. The number of bacteria on earth is almost inconceivable; a teaspoon of soil typically contains about 40 million bacteria. Indeed, bacteria make up a vast portion of the earth's biomass.

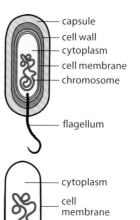

capsule
cell wall
cytoplasm
cell membrane
chromosome

flagellum

Bacteria are microscopic, single-celled organisms encased within a cell wall. They have only one chromosome, which is not contained within a nucleus.

cytoplasm
cell membrane
chromosome

Mollicutes share many of the features of bacteria, however, they lack a cell wall. Unlike bacteria, all mollicutes are parasites.

Mollicutes are close relatives of bacteria. They have the same features as bacteria except that they lack a cell wall. Their cells are simply contained in a cell membrane. All mollicutes are pathogens, meaning they cause disease in animals and plants. Mollicutes that cause plant disease were discovered in 1967 and were originally thought to be mycoplasma-like-organisms (MLO), a term you might encounter in older references. Most plant diseases caused by mollicutes are transmitted by leafhoppers, or occasionally by psyllids.

What do bacteria do?

Bacteria are extremely important members of the decomposer community. Most species are saprophytes, meaning they decompose dead animals and plants, recycling and reusing the nutrients of which plant and animal bodies are made. Saprophytic bacteria obtain their energy by digesting organic matter. They secrete digestive enzymes into their environment and absorb the resultant "soup." Other species get their energy through photosynthesis, just like plants do, and some bacteria, such as those in deep-sea trenches, get energy from inorganic chemical reactions. Bacteria become pathogenic when they invade a living host, either plant or animal, and begin to digest the host's cells. Few species are plant pathogens, but some of these cause serious, sometimes fatal, plant diseases. Some bacterial pathogens are soil-borne, some are carried by wind-driven rain, and some are transmitted by insects.

An important feature of bacteria is their astoundingly rapid reproduction rate. Most reproduce by fission, a process in which a cell simply divides into two daughter cells. Under ideal conditions of warmth and moisture, bacteria can double their population in as little as 20 minutes. Fortunately, environmental conditions are rarely ideal, and their growth slows down as their population builds and their waste products accumulate. This efficient means of proliferation is one reason pathogenic bacteria can be deadly. Bacterial infections can quickly overwhelm a host's defenses.

The bright side of bacteria

Two species in one genus, *Bacillus thuringiensis* (a very important insecticide) and *B. subtilis* (a new fungicide), are extremely helpful partners in managing destructive insects and fungal diseases in your garden.

Saprophytic bacteria are beneficial microorganisms. As decomposers of garden waste, they are valuable partners when you want to make compost. Compost builds biologically active, healthy soil, and helps fend off pathogenic fungi and bacteria.

Species of one special genus of bacteria, *Rhizobium*, are able to "fix" nitrogen by taking it out of the air and changing it into a form available to plants. Nitrogen is an important macronutrient for plants, because it is an essential component of all amino acids, and all proteins are composed of amino acids. Plants in the bean and pea family (Fabaceae) have a special symbiotic relationship with *Rhizobium* bacteria, which live inside small, round, pinkish nodules on the roots of these plants.

We also use bacteria to make sourdough bread, yogurt, certain cheeses, sauerkraut, and pickles. The species *Streptomyces griseus* is the original source of the antibiotic, streptomycin. And, of course, special strains of *E. coli* bacteria, which live symbiotically inside our gut, are bacteria we cannot live without. Some bacteria have even been used to help clean up oil spills.

Genetic engineers use bacteria to transfer genes from one organism into another. A favorite tool is *Agrobacterium tumefaciens*, which causes crown gall. For example, it can be used to create genetically modified strains of *E. coli*, a bacterium which can be grown in nutrient broth. Transferring the gene that makes insulin from humans into *E. coli* allows us to generate huge quantities of insulin, which has proven very useful to us. However useful it may be with regard to pharmaceuticals, other aspects of this technology, such as creating genetically modified organisms from our food plants, like corn (*Zea mays*), are dubious.

The dark side of bacteria

The dark side of these organisms is their ability to cause diseases in plants and animals. Because bacteria multiply quickly, bacterial infections can be aggressive and spread rapidly. Even worse, they are very difficult to control and are often fatal. Antibiotics have helped control infections in human populations and have even been used on plants in commercial operations. We absolutely do not recommend using antibiotics on plants. This use helps build resistance to antibiotics in bacteria, and that can be very dangerous indeed.

Types of solutions

About 200 bacteria infect plants, and many factors foster the spread of disease. Humidity, rain, overhead watering, insects, and oozing wounds on the plants themselves all contribute to infections. Most bacteria require moisture, and plant pathologists repeat this phrase like a mantra: If they dry, they die. Keeping foliage dry and never working with wet plants are the two most important steps you can take to combat any type of bacterial infection.

For air-borne bacteria, solutions begin on page 301.

Leafhoppers are wedge-shaped insects with piercing/sucking mouthparts that feed on plant sap. They are primary vectors of many plant diseases caused by mollicutes, such as aster yellows.

These cherry (*Prunus*) leaves wilt because they have an infection caused by *Pseudomonas syringae* bacteria.

Bacterial infection in the leaves of this lilac (*Syringa*) creates angular spots because the bacteria cannot digest the large veins of the leaf.

This group includes bacterial pathogens that are transmitted above-ground by wind-driven rain, splash-up from the ground, overhead watering, contaminated tools, and insects. Fire blight of pear trees provides a good example. In the spring, fire blight cankers on pear trees develop a sweet, sticky ooze that attracts honey bees. The ooze contains millions of bacteria. The ooze and the bacteria stick to the feet and mouthparts of the bees. When the bees visit the pear blossoms to gather nectar and pollen, they transport the bacteria to the flowers. The bacteria rapidly infect the flowers and spread into the tree. In this category, the insect is a transportation device, not an active participant in the infection cycle.

For soil-borne bacteria, solutions begin on page 305.

Soil-borne bacterial pathogens can live in soil for years. They infect opportunistically through wounds or insects. Sometimes they can even invade roots directly in the absence of wounds and insects.

For insect-borne bacteria, solutions begin on page 306.

Most of the bacteria and all the mollicutes in this group live inside the bodies of insects, which carry the pathogens from plant to plant. The insects feed on a contaminated plant, perhaps a weed, and the pathogens enter the body of the insect as they suck sap out of the sick plant. The pathogens grow and multiply inside the insect for a time, eventually residing in the salivary glands. When the insect feeds on the next plant, it injects the pathogen in its saliva into the healthy plant.

Solutions for air-borne bacteria

Diagnoses from Part 1.

CHAPTER	PAGE	DIAGNOSIS
1 Whole Plant	16	bacteria
2 Leaves	35	bacterial leaf-spot
2 Leaves	45	fire blight
2 Leaves	45, 54	bacteria
3 Flowers	84	fire blight
4 Fruit	105	bacterial spots
4 Fruit	108	bacterial blight
4 Fruit	109, 122	bacterial leaf-spot
5 Stems	132	lilac blight, fire blight
5 Stems	137	bacterial blight
7 Seeds	196	walnut blight

There are no cures for bacterial infections on plants. Preventive measures are extremely important, however, because they will keep bacteria from spreading through all your plants. If you have used the flow charts in Part 1, and you already know you have a problem, you probably want to move immediately to some kind of control. If so, please be sure to return to Chapter 8

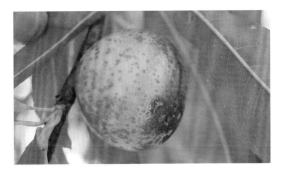

This plum (*Prunus*) exhibits a multitude of small spots, characteristic of bacterial spot disease. Preventive measures can reduce the incidence of this disease, but there are no effective remedies to cure the plant once it has become sick.

and use the preventive measures presented there, so that bacteria does not become a persistent problem on your plants.

Change the growing conditions

These solutions begin with a list of preventive measures that you will find in Chapter 8. Prevention is always the best way to combat bacteria. Preventive measures also keep bacteria from spreading to plants that are not yet under siege, so undertake these steps as soon as possible. Immediately following the preventive techniques, you will find bacterial control measures.

Preventive measures

▶ **Choose resistant cultivars.** See page 215.

▶ **Start with disease-free seeds, plants, and bulbs.** See page 216.

▶ **Manage the soil.** See page 234.

▶ **Mulch.** See page 236.

▶ **Give plants time to toughen up for winter.** In late summer, stop fertilizing, pruning, or even watering your plants so that they can harden up for winter. Soft, succulent new growth is susceptible to bacterial diseases because it is too young to have fully developed its protective barriers. It is also more susceptible to cracking during freezing weather, providing entry points for bacteria to infect the plant.

Control measures

▶ **Sanitize.** In the world of plant pathology, to sanitize means to remove infected or infested plant material. This is one of the most important steps you can take to keep plants healthy. Infected or infested plant parts are a source of bacterial cells.

Once you remove infected plant material using any of the steps below, discard all the material. Do not contribute it to a municipal green waste collection program. If you live where it is legal to burn waste, and can safely do so, burn infected material. Otherwise, put the material in garbage destined for a landfill.

Remove and destroy the whole plant. This is necessary for any non-woody plant. Some of these bacteria can live in the soil or inside dead and dying roots for many years, so remove as much of the root system as possible. Remove and discard the soil immediately surrounding the dead or dying plant. For a container plant, destroy or discard the plant and the potting media; clean the pot with bleach before using it again.

Remove and destroy infected branches of woody plants. Sick plants provide a source of infection that spreads the disease to all susceptible plants in the vicinity. If a stem or limb is infected with bacteria, then amputate it 1 foot (30 cm) below any visible lesion. Woody plants, like fruit trees, may survive bacterial infections by surgically removing infected limbs in this way. Like any surgeon, sterilize your tools.

Clean up debris. Clean your garden at the end of the season after harvest. A number of bacteria overwinter on or in the plant debris left behind at the end of the growing season. By removing and destroying this material in the autumn you can eliminate many bacteria before they attack in the spring.

▶ **Sterilize tools.** Any time you wound a plant with any tool you can inadvertently spread bacterial diseases. If you cut any plant for any reason, sterilize your tools before you use them on another plant. Be especially vigilant if you suspect a plant is sick but have not yet removed and destroyed it.

Pests and diseases can also travel from one location to another on a dirty shovel. After you dig up an infected plant, clean your shovel.

- Soap and water. At a minimum, wash your tools with soap and water, then rinse them off with rubbing alcohol. This may not be 100 percent effective.
- Bleach. Soak pruners, saws, knives, and other tools in a 10 percent solution of household bleach (1 cup of bleach to 9 cups of water) for five minutes. Rinse the bleach off and wipe the tool with a good quality oil. This method will eventually corrode metal tools.
- Heat. Using a blowtorch, heat your tools until they are very, very hot. Let them cool before using them again. This method will not corrode metal tools.

▶ **Manage water.** Remember the plant pathologists' mantra for controlling bacteria: If they dry, they die.

Proper watering techniques. Apply water to the root zone of the plant, not the foliage. Bacteria always need a film of moisture on the surface of the plant in order to infect the host. Some ways to water without getting the plant wet:

- Lay down soaker hoses. These hoses are permeable (leaky). They allow water to slowly drip out of their sides for the entire length of the hose. They are easily hidden from view under mulch.
- For hand watering, use any system that delivers water to the roots and not the leaves, such as hose-attached water wands, or watering cans with a long thin spout to deliver water under the foliage.
- In your vegetable garden, dig shallow trenches (furrows) between the rows and lay a hose at one end of the furrow. Turn the water on to a slow flow and fill the furrow with water.
- Install drip-trickle watering systems that do not use overhead spray nozzles. This solution works best if you are just installing your garden, doing a major renovation, or can install underground portions without destroying existing plants.
- For container plants, use a watering can or hose with a narrow tip and water directly on the growing media at the base of the plant.

Allow the soil to dry out. Do not allow the soil to stay too wet for too long. This solution applies to plants in the ground as well as those in containers.

If necessary, use organic remedies

You may decide to utilize chemicals to help control bacteria on your plants, indoors or out. Various chemicals are certified for use in organic gardening. Many of these organic treatments are relatively safe for you and the environment. Some have been in use for hundreds of years, others are quite new. Look for OMRI (Organic

Materials Review Institute) certification on the label.

Remedy recommendations

Unfortunately, very few chemicals are effective against bacteria or mollicutes. The only one we can recommend is any copper-containing compound. As always, change the growing conditions (see page 302) before using a remedy, and do not apply chemicals according to a predetermined schedule. This product is approved for organic gardening.

SAFETY FIRST

1. Always keep all these products **out of the reach of children and pets.**

2. **Read the label.** Use only chemicals that list the plants or type of plant you wish to protect on their labels. For example, a label may say "For use on ornamentals." Do not use this on a food plant.

3. **Follow the directions on the label.** Remember that more is not better. Many chemicals can actually damage some plants. This kind of damage is called a phytotoxic reaction. It is important to read the label and follow the manufacturer's instructions. If you put too much of the active ingredient on your plant, or if you put it on the wrong plant, you may do more harm than good.

   Every package or bottle of a garden remedy product has a label on the back that peels open. Unfold it and read the tiny print inside to learn what the product is used for, which plants to use it on, when to use it, and how much to use. Some of these labels unfold into long pages of instructions. Be patient, get out your magnifying glass, and read them carefully. Follow those directions.

4. **Always use the least toxic product first.** Look for a signal word on the label. These signal words are required by federal law under the Federal Insecticide, Fungicide and Rodenticide Act (FIFRA). All commercially sold pesticides must be registered with the Environmental Protection Agency (EPA), the registration authority for pesticides, and tested for modes of transmission into the body: inhalation, ingestion, dermal contact, primary eye, and primary skin. Toxicity Category IV requires no signal word because tests have shown the product to be non-toxic; these products, such as baking soda spray and insecticidal soap, are the safest, least toxic products you can use. Any pesticide determined to be in Toxicity Category III must be labeled **CAUTION**. Any in Toxicity Category II must carry the label **WARNING**. Those in Category I must be labeled either **DANGER** (the most toxic product available to the home gardener) or **DANGER— POISON**, with an image of a skull and crossbones. The last is most toxic of all. It is available only to licensed pesticide applicators.

5. **Wear protective gear and clothing.** Wear goggles, a respiratory face mask, a long-sleeved shirt, long pants, and shoes. Wash your clothes when you are finished using any product with a signal word.

▶ **Copper**

Signal word? Caution.

What is it? Copper is a natural mineral element mined from the earth. It has been used as a bactericide for more than 200 years. Copper hydroxide and copper sulfate are the two forms used to protect plants.

What does it do? Copper is a natural and very effective fungicide and one of the few products that also fights off bacterial infections.

What are the side effects? Copper is somewhat toxic to humans. It irritates eyes and skin. It is poisonous if ingested in sufficient quantity. Use adequate protection (goggles, respirator, gloves, long sleeves, long pants). Copper is highly toxic to aquatic invertebrates, fish, and amphibians. Do not use it near water. We could not find any studies about its effect on birds. Copper can damage plants if they remain wet too long after spray application. According to standards set for certified organic gardening, you can use copper on fruit and vegetables up to one day before harvest.

How do I use it? Follow the directions on the label. Copper compounds are available as ready-to-use liquids, as wettable powders, and as dust. Mix wettable powder with water and a spreader-sticker. Some ready-to-use sprays have the spreader-sticker in it and some do not, so check the label. Apply the liquids with spray bottles or pump-up sprayers. Use specially made "dusters" to apply the dust. If you apply it at the first signs of infection it prevents additional infections. Apply early in the morning to allow leaves to dry quickly.

Solutions for soil-borne bacteria

Diagnoses from Part 1.

CHAPTER	PAGE	DIAGNOSIS
1 Whole Plant	22	crown gall
5 Stems	135	crown gall
5 Stems	152	slime flux
5 Stems	154	aerial crown gall
6 Roots	165, 175, 188	potato bacterial ring rot
6 Roots	170	soft rot
6 Roots	176	bacterial ring rot
6 Roots	189	bacterial rot
6 Roots	191	crown gall, root gall

There are no cures for bacterial infections on plants. Preventive measures are extremely important, however, because they will keep bacteria from spreading through all your plants. Please be sure to turn to Chapter 8 and use the preventive measures presented there, so that bacteria does not become a persistent problem on your plants.

Change the growing conditions

Prevention is the only way to combat soil-borne bacteria. Preventive measures also keep bacteria from spreading to plants that are not yet under siege, so undertake these steps as soon as possible.

▶ **Choose resistant cultivars.** See page 215.

▶ **Start with disease-free seeds and plants.** See page 216.

▶ **Sanitize.** See page 302.

▶ **Rotate plants.** See page 217.

▶ **Minimize wounding.** Take care not to wound your plant when hoeing weeds, mowing the lawn, or working with a weed-eater. Small wounds, especially near the soil, provide entry points for bacteria to get into your plants.

▶ **Sterilize tools.** See page 303.

Solutions for insect-borne bacteria

Diagnoses from Part 1.

CHAPTER	PAGE	DIAGNOSIS
2 Leaves	45	fire blight
3 Flowers	77, 78	aster yellows
3 Flowers	84	fire blight
4 Fruit	120	cucurbit bacterial wilt
5 Stems	148	fasciation
5 Stems	152	slime flux
6 Roots	186	aster yellows

There are no cures for insect-borne bacterial infections on plants. Preventive measures are extremely important, however, because they will keep bacteria from spreading through all your plants. If you have reached this section from the diagnostic flow charts in Part 1, your plant has a bacterial disease that is transmitted by insects. The key to managing these problems is to control the insects. See Chapter 10 for complete information on controlling insects, and look to Chapter 8 for preventive measures, so that bacteria does not become a persistent problem on your plants.

Change the growing conditions

Prevention is always the best way to combat bacteria. Preventive measures keep bacteria from spreading to plants that are not yet under siege, so undertake these steps as soon as possible.

▶ **Choose resistant cultivars.** See page 215.

▶ **Start with disease-free seeds, plants, and bulbs.** See page 216.

▶ **Manage insect populations.** See page 268.

A bacterial rot has infected this potato (*Solanum tuberosum*). Preventing this disease is the only way to treat your plants.

A calendula exhibits wilting and proliferation, typical symptoms of aster yellows. This lethal disease is caused by mollicutes and transmitted by insects such as leafhoppers.

13 Viruses

What are viruses?

To see a virus you must use an electron microscope. And what you'd see is a molecule of genetic information protected by a coat of protein.

Viruses are so unlike any other biological entity on earth that for many years scientists have disagreed on whether viruses are even alive. Viruses do not have cells of their own. They carry out none of the metabolic processes that characterize living beings. And unlike other living organisms, the only way they can reproduce is to infect somebody else's living cells. In other words, they hijack the metabolic machinery of others and force their hosts to produce more virus particles.

Viruses can survive in the most extraordinary circumstances. Some, like tobacco mosaic virus, can be crystalized, stored on a shelf like a gemstone for years, and still retain the power to infect living cells. Others, like the AIDS virus, can only survive inside the living cells of a host.

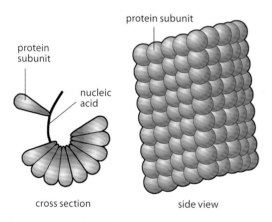

A virus is extremely small and very simple. It consists of a molecule of nucleic acid, the genetic information, surrounded and protected by a coat of protein.

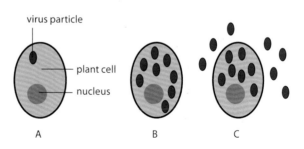

The life cycle of a virus: A. The initial infection of a plant cell by a virus particle. B. The virus forces the host cell to make more virus particles. C. The virus particles escape the cell to infect other cells of the host plant.

All the more than 2,000 known viruses are parasites, and all cause disease of some living being that is their unwilling host. Viruses that infect people cause a wide range of diseases, including the common cold, influenza, polio, smallpox, rabies, and AIDS. Other species of virus attack mammals, birds, insects, plants, bacteria, and fungi. Some viruses can jump across species' barriers and attack dozens of different kinds of animals, allowing such diseases as bird flu to infect both people and birds. On the other hand, viruses that infect plants cannot infect human beings.

A virus infection usually spreads throughout an entire plant: A. The blue leaf indicates the site of the initial infection. B. The infection rapidly spreads to the root system. C. The infection moves upward into the main stems. D. The entire plant now has a systemic virus infection.

Some scientists have decided that viruses are not alive until they infect a host cell. Other scientists treat viruses as living organisms with their own kingdom in the classification system used for biological organisms.

What do viruses do?

The molecule of genetic information called a nucleoprotein that dwells inside a virus is a snippet of DNA (deoxyribonucleic acid) or RNA (ribonucleic acid). The DNA or RNA contains the instructions to manufacture more virus particles. Most plant viruses have only RNA. Viruses can infect their host plant in a number of ways.

- Sharing the root system of an infected neighbor.
- Receiving pollen from an infected plant.
- Having a parasitic plant, such as mistletoe or dodder, growing on a healthy host.
- These are rare occurrences. The most common forms of transmission are wounds from tools, insects, or nematodes.

Once inside a plant cell, viruses grab control of the host cell's genetic information and subvert its normal processes, causing it to manufacture more virus particles. Viruses do not divide like cells, and they produce no reproductive structures. New virus particles, created by the host plant cells, migrate to new cells within the plant and spread the infection. Within two to five days, a virus infection moves from the original inoculation site into the phloem. Once it reaches the phloem, the virus rapidly infects the entire plant. Virus infections are systemic.

Solutions for viruses

Diagnoses from Part 1.

CHAPTER	PAGE	DIAGNOSIS
1 Whole Plant	23	virus
2 Leaves	42, 60	virus
3 Flowers	68, 71	virus
3 Flowers	79	double blossom
4 Fruit	97, 102, 117	mosaic virus
4 Fruit	116	pear stony pit virus
4 Fruit	119	crumbly berry virus
5 Stems	149	witches' broom
6 Roots	186	curly top virus

For all virus infections, symptoms vary widely and can mimic other conditions. There is no cure; there are no chemical anti-viral sprays. As always, prevention is the best long-term solution. If you have reached this diagnosis using the flow charts in Part 1, and if your plant is valuable or treasured, you may want to confirm the diagnosis by sending a sample to a diagnostic laboratory. If the lab confirms the diagnosis, you can then decide whether you want to take on the expense of having your plant cloned by a tissue culture lab, the last of the four types of solutions for virus infections recommended here.

▶ **Destroy the infected plant.** This protects your other plants from the virus. Remove the infected plant from the ground. Burn or discard it in the garbage. Do not compost it or contribute it to a municipal green waste collection program. Replace the plant with an unrelated plant, as if you were rotating your crops (see page 217). This avoids the possibility of the virus infecting the new plant. For a container plant, destroy or discard the plant, the potting media, and the pot.

▶ **Manage the infected plant.** If you have a virus-infected plant that you cannot bear to part with, follow these steps.

1. Isolate your plant. Be sure to move the plant far away from all your other plants even if those plants are not related to the sick plant. Plant viruses frequently cross genetic barriers and infect many

This rose (*Rosa*) may have picked up a virus infection if the pruners were not sterilized properly. Pruning shears can transmit virus infections from a sick plant to a healthy one.

Mosaic virus infection causes small patches of white tissue to develop over the leaf of this bean plant (*Phaseolus*).

The bean plant (*Phaseolus*) with the infected leaf also has infected fruit. Mosaic virus causes white patches to develop on the fruit as well as the leaves.

different kinds of plants. Once again, this technique protects your other plants. Be sure to clean your tools and wash your hands after working with any plant in quarantine.

2. Sterilize your tools. Any time you wound a plant with any tool you can inadvertently spread viruses, bacterial diseases, or nematodes. If you cut any plant for any reason, sterilize your tools before you use them on another plant. Be especially vigilant if you suspect a plant is sick but have not yet removed and destroyed it.

Pests and diseases can also travel from one location to another on a dirty shovel. After you dig up an infected plant, clean your shovel.

- Soap and water. At a minimum, wash your tools with soap and water, then rinse them off with rubbing alcohol. This may not be 100 percent effective.
- Bleach. Soak pruners, saws, knives, and other tools in a 10 percent solution of household bleach (1 cup of bleach to 9 cups of water) for five minutes. Rinse the bleach off and wipe the tool with a good quality oil. This method will eventually corrode metal tools.
- Heat. Using a blowtorch, heat your tools until they are very, very hot. Let them cool before using them again. This method will not corrode metal tools.

▶ **Prevent future virus infections.** Whether you destroy the plant or not, you should take steps to prevent future virus infections. Tools, insects, nematodes, and handling sick plants transmit virus diseases. Each thing that carries a virus particle is called a vector. Managing the vector or disrupting its ability to reach and infect plants is the only way to keep your plants virus-free.

Start with disease-free seeds, plants, and bulbs. Inspect bulbs, tubers, corms, and rhizomes. Look for brown spots, moldy patches, or shriveled tissue. Buy only those that are firm and free of spots or mold. Examine the leaves, stems, and flowers of plants you want to purchase, and check for discolored spots, distorted tissues, wilting, or other problems. Buy only plants that are healthy and free of obvious defects.

Vectors that spread virus infections include tools, insects, nematodes, and careless handling. This apple tree (*Malus*) is infected with a complex of viruses.

Handling roses when they are wet can lead to the spread of virus infections as on this hybrid tea rose (*Rosa*).

You may find the cheap 59-cent specials at the supermarket very attractive because of the extremely low price. But beware, supermarkets rarely have the personnel or the knowledge to maintain healthy plants. These bargain basement plants can easily have serious problems that make them far more trouble than they are worth.

Choose resistant cultivars. If you remove a dead or dying plant due to a lethal virus infection, replace your dead plant with one that is resistant to the problem. Do not put the same kind of plant back in the infected planting hole. Select a completely different kind of plant, one of the many new varieties of popular vegetables and ornamental plants that are genetically resistant to viruses. To find disease-resistant varieties, check with your Cooperative Extension Service and your local Master Gardener organization. Local knowledge is invaluable. Look in catalogs from suppliers, or do an Internet search. Read labels on plants, bulbs, tubers, or seed packets:

- A package of green bean (*Phaseolus vulgaris*) seeds may read, "An extra bonus is the proven disease resistance of 'Slenderette' to bean mosaic and curly top virus." 'Slenderette' is the cultivar name.
- Other packaging might read, "Green bean 'Slenderette', BCMV." BCMV signifies resistance to bean common mosaic virus.
- Packaging of vegetables might have the letters N for nematode resistance, TMV for tobacco mosaic virus resistance, F for fusarium fungus resistance, and V for verticillium fungus resistance.

Some cultivars of corn (*Zea mays*) are more resistant to corn earworms than others because their husks are tighter and keep insects out. Some cultivars of tomato (*Lycopersicon esculentum*) are more resistant to aphids than others. Pest and disease organisms often have host plant preferences, and you can use this knowledge to your advantage. Whiteflies, for example, love hibiscus but do not like pepper plants (*Capsicum*) nearly so much. If a catalog description does not say a plant or seed is disease- or pest-resistant, then it probably isn't.

Plant at the right time. Insects are major vectors for transmitting viral diseases, but insect populations fluctuate according to the seasons. For many insects, their numbers generally increase as spring turns into summer and decrease as summer yields to fall. Therefore, it is sometimes possible to time your planting to lessen the insects' effect on the health of your plant. For example, plant peas (*Pisum*) in early spring so that the peas mature before the weather gets warm enough for the pea aphid population to build up. This avoids virus diseases that aphids transmit to your pea crop.

Exact timing depends on the climate in your specific geographic location, the kinds of pest insects present in your area, and which kinds of plants you want to grow. Again, search the Internet, or check with your Cooperative Extension Service and your local Master Gardener organization. These are all sources of information specific to your particular location and pest species.

Sterilize tools. Any time you wound a plant with any tool you can inadvertently spread viral diseases. If you cut any plant for any reason, sterilize your tools before you use them on another plant. Be especially vigilant if you suspect a plant is sick but have not yet removed and destroyed it.

Pests and diseases can also travel from one location to another on a dirty shovel. After you dig up an infected plant, clean your shovel.

- Soap and water. At a minimum, wash your tools with soap and water, then rinse them off with rubbing alcohol. This may not be 100 percent effective.
- Bleach. Soak pruners, saws, knives, and other tools in a 10 percent solution of household bleach (1 cup of bleach to 9 cups of water) for five minutes. Rinse the bleach off and wipe the tool with a good quality oil. This method will eventually corrode metal tools.
- Heat. Using a blowtorch, heat your tools until they are very, very hot. Let them cool before using them again. This method will not corrode metal tools.

Wash your hands frequently. Some viruses can be transmitted by contact. Tobacco mosaic virus, one of the most common, is easily transmitted on fingers and has a wide range of host plants.

Handling cigarettes, cigars, or other tobacco products made with infected tobacco leaves puts TMV particles on your fingers. Simply touching the foliage of your plant transmits TMV particles to the plant and can infect them with the virus. If you use tobacco products, you must wash your hands before handling any plants.

Avoid touching plants when they are wet. Virus particles are very easily transmitted by contact when plants are wet. Thus, go out into the garden when plants are dry. Handle plants, indoors and out, only when they are dry.

Control pests. See page 268.

▶ **Clone your plant.** Viruses rarely kill their host plants outright, but plants cannot be cured. Some virus-infected plants can persist for years, limping along, never performing as well as they might. Plants in this condition are sometimes overlooked. Orchid collections worldwide, for example, house plants with odontoglossum ring-spot virus or cymbidium mosaic virus. Although a cure is not possible, plants that are valuable can be cloned to eliminate the virus's genetic information. The original plant does not improve, but its duplicates, created in a tissue culture laboratory, can be free of the virus.

14 Nematodes

What are nematodes?

Nematodes are worm-like microscopic animals. Most are colorless and invisible to the naked eye. Their bodies are generally eel-like and smooth. They move with an undulating side-to-side movement, much like a snake or an eel. Although they are minute, they have a complete digestive system and a simple nervous system. Nematodes are the most abundant multicellular animal on earth. They are found in every habitat from frigid polar extremes to tropical heat and from the highest mountains to the deepest oceans.

About 20,000 species live in soil or water, either fresh or salt. They feed on the microscopic bacteria, fungi, plants, and animals of those environments.

What do nematodes do?

Nematodes are very important members of the soil ecosystem. As they eat bacteria and fungi, nematodes break down their food and release nutrients into the soil.

Like other animals, most nematodes are either male or female. Adults of both sexes must find each other and mate, then the female will lay fertile eggs. Some species of plant pathogenic nematodes, however, have no males. In this case, all adults are females which have developed the ability to lay eggs that develop into new individuals in the absence of fertiliza-

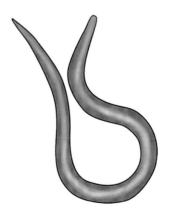

Microscopic, worm-like animals, nematodes are ubiquitous. Of the thousands of species only a few are plant parasites.

tion (parthenogenesis). The entire life cycle of nematodes is about two to four weeks.

The bright side of nematodes

You can enlist nematodes that are parasites of destructive insects to control pests. Nematodes help control over 200 species of soil-inhabiting grubs and maggots. Other beneficial nematodes are predators of plant pathogenic nematodes.

The dark side of nematodes

A number of nematodes are parasites of animals. Trichinosis, a disease of humans, rats, and pigs, is caused by a nematode. Other nematode diseases are hookworms, pinworms, and whipworms.

A few hundred species of nematodes cause plant disease. Plant parasitic nematodes generally have a needle-like mouthpart called a stylet. They pierce plant cells with the stylet, inject saliva, and suck dissolved nutrients out of the plant. The saliva they inject is toxic and causes the plant's tissues to swell, distort, and eventually die.

Plant parasitic nematodes can be very destructive to your garden, and once established can be very difficult to control. The root-knot nematode, for example, has a very wide host range, infecting more than 2,000 species of plants. Symptoms vary but include stunting, yellowish leaves, few flowers, and fruits of poor quality. Foliar nematodes can also result in severe losses, primarily on chrysanthemums, strawberries (*Fragaria*), and dahlias.

Some plant pathogenic nematodes feed on the surface of the plant (ectoparasites); others feed from inside the plant tissue (endoparasites). Both kinds can be migratory, moving freely on or inside the plant, or sedentary (they attach to the plant, settle down, and stop moving).

Almost all plant pathogenic nematodes spend part of their life cycle in the soil. The eggs and adult males are found in the soil. Young juveniles, before they become parasites, are found in the soil for all or a portion of their lives. Consequently, soil conditions such as moisture, aeration, and temperature greatly affect nematode abundance, viability, and spread. Most nematodes are limited to the top 6 to 12 inches (15 to 30 cm) of the soil. Soil nematodes migrate slowly from place to place except when they are helped along by shovels, hoes, boots, or anything else that can carry particles of soil from one place to another. On their own power, they have to swim through a film of water to get from one place to another. They can also be splashed from the soil up onto the foliage by raindrops or overhead irrigation.

Bud and leaf nematodes (*Aphelenchoides*) rarely, if ever, enter the soil. They survive inside the plant tissues they infect. When plants are wet these nematodes can climb up plant stems by swimming through a film of water. If wet plants touch each other, the nematodes can then spread to nearby plants.

The female root-knot nematode (*Meloidogyne*) is a sedentary internal parasite but the male is only sedentary until it matures. Feeding by both sexes causes the plant cells to enlarge, forming knot-like swellings on the roots.

Solutions for nematodes

Diagnoses from Part 1.

CHAPTER	PAGE	DIAGNOSIS
1 Whole Plant	16	root-knot nematodes
2 Leaves	41	foliar nematodes
5 Stems	149	phlox nematodes
6 Roots	174, 184, 186	nematodes
6 Roots	191	root-knot nematodes

The solutions for plant pathogenic nematodes are presented in the sequence of actions you need to take in order to prevent nematodes from spreading throughout your plant collection, and to keep nematodes out in the first place. There is one organic remedy available to treat nematodes (see page 320), but as with all plant pests and diseases, prevention, by changing cultural conditions, is by the far the best solution.

Change the growing conditions

▶ **Verify that nematodes are present.** Whether they infect the root system or the leaves, nematodes cause symptoms on above-ground plant parts that masquerade as many other plant problems, including virus infections. Before you destroy plants suspected of harboring nematodes, verify the diagnosis with a microscope examination. Nematodes are easy to see with a microscope. Use a microscope with a minimum of a 10× objective. Some home science kit microscopes come with this power. Schools, community colleges, and universities often have microscopes you can use in their laboratories.

Nematodes that infect plants have a needle-like mouthpart called a stylet, a structure visible under the microscope. Nematodes without a stylet are not plant pathogens. You could also take your samples to a Master Gardener

The root-knot nematode can infect numerous plants, and, as the name implies, it causes knot-like swellings on the root system.

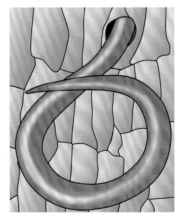

Some nematodes burrow into root tissue, where they feed, which causes the swellings on the roots.

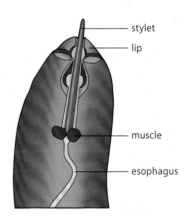

stylet
lip
muscle
esophagus

Microscopic examination of the head of a plant parasitic nematode reveals its needle-like stylet, which the animal uses to pierce plant cells to feed.

clinic, or to your Cooperative Extension Agent for verification. You can skip this step, but you may destroy plants that do not actually have nematodes.

▶ **Sanitize.** This is one of the most important steps you can take to keep plants healthy. In the world of plant pathology, to sanitize means to remove infected or infested plant material. Such plant parts are a source of nematode larvae, fungal spores, bacteria, insects, and mites.

Remove and destroy infected plants. Plants dying of nematode disease, whether from root or foliar infections, should be removed from your garden and destroyed. Do not put the infested material into your compost pile. Some of these nematodes are capable of living in the soil or inside the dead and dying roots or leaves for many years. Remove as much of the root system as possible along with a large amount of the soil immediately surrounding the dead or dying plant. For a container plant, destroy or discard the plant and the potting media; clean the pot with bleach before using it again.

Replace the dead plant with a resistant variety. Do not put the same kind of plant back in the infected planting hole. Select a completely different kind of plant, one that is resistant to nematodes. An "N" following the plant name on a label or in a catalog description means that the plant is resistant to nematodes.

▶ **Sterilize tools.** Nematodes can easily travel from one location to another on a dirty shovel or pruning shears. Any time you wound a plant with any tool, you can inadvertently spread viruses, bacterial diseases, or nematodes. If you cut any plant for any reason, sterilize your tools before you use them on another plant. Be especially vigilant if you suspect a plant is sick but have not yet removed and destroyed it.

Pests and diseases can also travel from one location to another on a dirty shovel. After you dig up an infected plant, clean your shovel.

- Soap and water. At a minimum, wash your tools with soap and water, then rinse them off with rubbing alcohol. This may not be 100 percent effective.
- Bleach. Soak pruners, saws, knives, and other tools in a 10 percent solution of household bleach (1 cup of bleach to 9 cups of water) for five minutes. Rinse the bleach off and wipe the tool with a good quality oil. This method will eventually corrode metal tools.
- Heat. Using a blowtorch, heat your tools until they are very, very hot. Let them cool before using them again. This method will not corrode metal tools.

▶ **Sterilize the soil.** This harsh treatment cannot generally be applied to your garden except in certain limited cases, such as this solarization technique. Sterilization kills off all your beneficial fungi and bacteria as well as the pathogens. Soil sterilization can help to control root-knot nematodes but will not affect foliar nematodes. To sterilize the soil by solarizing:

1. Remove and destroy the dead plant and as much of its roots and infected soil as you can manage.
2. Turn the soil over, smooth out the hole, and cover the exposed soil with clear plastic.
3. Weigh down the sides of the plastic to hold it in place.

4. After four to six weeks of this solar heat treatment, you can garden in this spot again. Be certain drainage is adequate, and add compost to the soil when you replant.

▶ **Manage the soil.** See page 234.

▶ **Use marigolds as a cover crop.** A cover crop is a crop that you plant with the intention of plowing it under while it is still green and fresh. Marigolds (*Tagetes*) are powerfully aromatic in all plant parts and have long had an excellent reputation for nematode control. If you sow marigold seeds over an area, let the plants grow to maturity, and then plow them under and let them decompose. They release into the soil chemicals that nematodes cannot tolerate.

▶ **Choose resistant cultivars.** Many new varieties of popular vegetables and ornamental plants are genetically resistant to pests or diseases. In addition, pest and disease organisms often have host plant preferences, and you can use this knowledge to your advantage. Whiteflies, for example, love hibiscus but do not like pepper plants (*Capsicum*) nearly so much. Incorporating pest- or disease-resistant plants helps ensure pests and diseases won't get a toehold in your home and garden.

To find pest- or disease-resistant varieties, check with your Cooperative Extension Service and your local Master Gardener organization. Local knowledge is invaluable. Look in catalogs from suppliers, or do an Internet search. Read labels on plants, bulbs, tubers, or seed packets:

- Packaging of vegetables might have the letters N for nematode resistance, TMV for tobacco mosaic virus resistance, F for fusarium fungus resistance, and V for verticillium fungus resistance.

If a catalog description does not say a plant or seed is disease- or pest-resistant, then it probably isn't. Internet searches will yield vast amounts of information, and you will quickly find appropriate varieties and locations where you can purchase them.

▶ **Rotate plants.** Do not put the same plants or the same kinds of plants in the same location year after year. For annuals, vegetables, and bulbs this is an effective way to avoid soil-borne diseases caused by fungi and bacteria, and pests such as insects and nematodes. Do not put susceptible plants in nematode-infested soil for three years.

Vegetables. Many experienced vegetable gardeners have well-thought-out plans for rotating their crops. For example, they may grow tomatoes (*Lycopersicon esculentum*) every year, but each year, for three years, they put them in a different location. In the fourth year, they go back to the first tomato plot. Plan for polycultures in your crop-rotation scheme; when you plant each bed or container, be sure to interplant with different kinds of plants. For example, include marigolds (*Tagetes*) between your tomatoes, and when you move your tomato planting bed each year, move your marigolds along with it.

Annuals. Flowers such as petunias, marigolds, or impatiens that live for a single season are called annuals. Like vegetables, you should not plant the same kind of plant in the same location every year. Make a plan that allows you to follow a rotation schedule similar to the one you use for vegetables.

Spring and summer bulbs. Some bulbs must be dug up each season and stored until replanted. Rotate their planting sites just as you would for vegetables or annuals. Spring bulbs, like tulips (*Tulipa*), daffodils (*Narcissus*), or crocus, are lifted in summer, after the foliage dies down, when they have become crowded and no longer flower well. Summer bulbs or tubers, like gladiolus, dahlias, or begonias, are lifted (dug up) in fall to protect them from freezing. In either case replant in new locations.

Perennials, trees, and shrubs. Plants such as perennials, trees, and shrubs, which are permanently planted in the landscape, clearly cannot be rotated in the same way as annual vegetables can. But should you lose a tree or shrub to a root-destroying fungus, nematodes, or insect pests, do not replace it with the same species in the same planting hole. Some fungi and nematodes can live in the soil for years. If you really must have the same plant in that hole, wait five years before attempting to do so. It is better to find an acceptable substitute which is resistant to the pest or disease that killed your original tree.

▶ **Plant polycultures, not monocultures.** See page 216. A polyculture helps to inhibit the spread of pests and diseases. Distributing flowers, herbs, and vegetables throughout garden beds, so each plant's closest neighbor is different, greatly reduces the incidence of diseases (fungal, bacterial, and viral) and pests (insects, mites, and nematodes).

Incorporating flowers and herbs into the vegetable garden provides multiple benefits in the form of effective pest and disease management. Herbs such as fennel (*Foeniculum*) and dill (*Anethum*) attract beneficial insects to help control insect pests. Flowers like yarrow (*Achillea*), cosmos, and rudbeckia also attract beneficial insects, and marigolds (*Tagetes*) repel root-knot nematodes.

▶ **Mulch.** Mulch is material used to cover the surface of the soil around plants. Mulch for container plants, called topdressing, is usually more decorative than outdoor mulch.

Mulch and topdressing help prevent weeds, conserve moisture, and control pests and diseases. These materials also prevent water-splash. Plant parts close to the ground or growing media are most susceptible to infection from fungus spores, bacteria, and nematodes splashing up from the ground in water. Mulch or topdressing also helps control insect pests that hide in the soil during the day and come out at night to devour your plants. Many materials can be used for mulch:

- Biodegradable materials, such as sustainably harvested bark mulch, crushed coconut and other nut husks, pine needles, straw, newspaper, and cardboard. As these materials decompose, they nourish a host of soil microorganisms that help to control nematodes. Cardboard should be top-dressed with a more attractive material. Do not use "Beauty Bark," since it may be treated with herbicides.
- Fine gravel, decorative stone, or sand. Use as a topdressing on container plants to control fungus gnats. Use as a mulch

around lavender (*Lavandula*) or other plants to control root rot.

- Grass clippings. But be careful: You must be certain no weed killer was used on the grass, and you must also be sure that the clippings contain no weed seeds.

▶ **Manage water.** See page 229.

If necessary, use organic remedies

You may decide to utilize chemicals to help control nematodes on your plants, indoors or out. A number of chemicals are certified for use in organic gardening, but very few are certified for nematode control. Look for OMRI (Organic Materials Review Institute) certification on the

SAFETY FIRST

1. Always keep all these products **out of the reach of children and pets.**

2. **Read the label.** Use only chemicals that list the plants or type of plant you wish to protect on their labels. For example, a label may say "For use on ornamentals." Do not use this on a food plant.

3. **Follow the directions on the label.** Remember that more is not better. Many chemicals can actually damage some plants. This kind of damage is called a phytotoxic reaction. It is important to read the label and follow the manufacturer's instructions. If you put too much of the active ingredient on your plant, or if you put it on the wrong plant, you may do more harm than good.

   Every package or bottle of a garden remedy product has a label on the back that peels open. Unfold it and read the tiny print inside to learn what the product is used for, which plants to use it on, when to use it, and how much to use. Some of these labels unfold into long pages of instructions. Be patient, get out your magnifying glass, and read them carefully. Follow those directions.

4. **Always use the least toxic product first.** Look for a signal word on the label. These signal words are required by federal law under the Federal Insecticide, Fungicide and Rodenticide Act (FIFRA). All commercially sold pesticides must be registered with the Environmental Protection Agency (EPA), the registration authority for pesticides, and tested for modes of transmission into the body: inhalation, ingestion, dermal contact, primary eye, and primary skin. Toxicity Category IV requires no signal word because tests have shown the product to be non-toxic; these products, such as baking soda spray and insecticidal soap, are the safest, least toxic products you can use. Any pesticide determined to be in Toxicity Category III must be labeled **CAUTION.** Any in Toxicity Category II must carry the label **WARNING.** Those in Category I must be labeled either **DANGER** (the most toxic product available to the home gardener) or **DANGER—POISON**, with an image of a skull and crossbones. The last is most toxic of all. It is available only to licensed pesticide applicators.

5. **Wear protective gear and clothing.** Wear goggles, a respiratory face mask, a long-sleeved shirt, long pants, and shoes. Wash your clothes when you are finished using any product with a signal word.

label. One such OMRI certified organic remedy for nematode control is included here.

Remedy recommendations

Always change the growing conditions (see page 315) before using this remedy. Evaluate your circumstances and the plant you are treating. Observe your plants. Do not apply chemicals according to a predetermined schedule.

▶ **Biological nematicide**

Signal word? Caution.

What is it? *Myrothecium verrucaria* is a fungus that is grown in cultures in a laboratory and then killed. The active ingredient in this nematicide is the dead fungus and the medium in which it was cultured. It is available as a dry flowable (DF) formulation that is easy to mix with water.

As a living fungus, *Myrothecium verrucaria* causes plant disease. Therefore, the EPA requires that products used for nematode control may not contain the living fungus.

What does it do? The dried, dead fungus and the culture medium work together to kill nematodes. Neither component works by itself; the entire mixture is required. The exact mode of action is still under investigation. It kills only plant pathogenic nematodes.

What are the side effects? The EPA has found no evidence of harmful effects to humans, or to any other terrestrial non-target organism. It does not kill beneficial nematodes. However, tests are ongoing, and you should not use it near bodies of water because of possible toxicity to aquatic organisms. Tests also show that mild, reversible skin and eye irritation occurs on test animals, so wear protective gear when using this product.

How do I use it? Read the label and follow directions. Apply the dry product directly to the soil, incorporating it into the upper 3 to 6 inches (7.5 to 15 cm). The powder can also be mixed with water and applied to the soil as a spray. You can apply it any time during your plant's life cycle: before planting, during planting, or after planting.

15 Other Pests

What are other pests?

Many of us take great delight in inviting wildlife into our gardens. We are perfectly willing to share the wealth with songbirds, hummingbirds, butterflies, and honey bees. For many of us, the garden is our only contact with the natural world, and interaction with wild things is wonderful. Some of these creatures, however, are like guests who do not know when to go home. They overstay their welcome and become pests.

Pests in the garden include a wide variety of wildlife such as slugs, snails, birds, and mammals of many kinds. Parasitic plants and mechanical damage are also "pests" we discuss in this chapter.

Slugs and snails are related to clams, oysters, octopus, and squid. All these animals are mollusks that share numerous anatomical and biological features. A subgroup of mollusks, the gastropods, includes all the snail-like animals with spiral shells, such as abalone and conchs. Slugs are also gastropods. They look like snails without shells, even though they actually have a very small internal shell.

Wildlife, including butterflies, frequent our gardens if we grow flowers with abundant nectar or other food sources, and provide opportunities for shelter.

Slugs and snails are part of the gastropod (stomach foot) subgroup of mollusks. They glide across the garden on a slimy trail of mucus and eat as they go.

Many of the wildlife creatures we enjoy can overstay their welcome. Deer are common garden pests.

From the beautiful hummingbird to the bizarre ostrich, birds bring pleasure and grief to many. They are colorful, they sing beautifully, and they provide hours of entertainment for birdwatchers. Many birds eat destructive insects and are welcome beneficial wildlife. Others eat fruit and seeds and, therefore, can become pests.

Mammals are a large group of animals that are warm blooded, have hair instead of feathers, and feed their young milk produced in special glands called mammary glands. Mammals we enjoy but that can nevertheless become pests in the garden include deer, squirrels, rabbits, and raccoons.

Mistletoes and other parasitic plants derive all or most of their nourishment from their host plant.

Machines we've developed to mow down vegetation, like lawnmowers and weed-eaters, can be troubling. Improperly used, they damage prize plants at the soil line, creating wounds that invite disease.

What do other pests do?

Slugs and snails generally come out of hiding at night or on moist overcast days. On sunny, hot days they hide in cool, moist, dark places. You can find them under rocks, logs, or pots. Slugs and snails glide on a ribbon of slime across the grass and rocks to get to your prize hostas, lettuce (*Lactuca*), or strawberries (*Fragaria*). They feed by rasping ragged holes in leaves, flowers, and fruit. They also eat cardboard, paper, and algae. Since they show up at night to make holes in your plants and then hide, you don't often see them in action, only the damage and slime trails they leave behind.

Most birds are welcome in the garden. We enjoy them, not only because we like their songs and their antics, but because many of them eat insect pests. Many of us find it worthwhile to attract birds into the garden, by providing food, water, and shelter. We encourage them to nest and raise their young. Putting up bird feeders and bird houses adds a whole new dimension to our gardens as nexus between the human world and the world of nature.

Birds that eat fruit, however, can do extensive damage in a short time when they descend onto your garden. Woodpeckers and sapsuckers don't eat fruit, but do their own special kind of damage. Sapsuckers peck shallow holes in a grid pattern on the trunks of trees and then eat the sap which flows out of the wounds. These holes can provide entry points for fungal diseases and insect pests, both of which have the potential to kill your tree.

The most common mammals that invade our gardens are deer, rodents (squirrels, mice, rats, voles, gophers, porcupines), rabbits, and raccoons. But there are many other mammals, such as bears, coyotes, opossums, moles, and even mountain lions and elk, that occasionally enter gardens, even in suburbia. Apart from squirrels, few mammals are truly welcome in the garden as they can be quite destructive.

Parasitic plants also pose problems, just like tapeworms are for mammals. They penetrate the tissues of your plant and suck nutrients out. Lichens and algae are not parasites and do not cause plant problems. We discuss them here because many people do not know what they are, and they worry about their presence.

Lawnmowers and weed-eaters are pests when they damage your plant stems at the soil line. Careless use of equipment can remove chunks of bark from tree trunks and exposed roots. These open wounds invite diseases and insect pests that can kill your tree. Take care when using equipment like this, and protect your plants from damage.

Types of solutions

For slugs and snails, solutions begin on page 325.

When you see large, irregular, ragged holes in the middle of leaves and the responsible party is nowhere in sight, suspect slugs or snails. If you also find shiny dried slime trails then your suspicions are confirmed. These pests hide during the daytime unless the weather is cool and moist.

Slugs and snails can squeeze into small spaces and hide inside potted plants. They can enter through the drainage hole in the bottom of a pot. They can hide anywhere on the plant or under the topdressing in the pot. Because of this ability to hide, you can inadvertently bring some home any time you buy a potted plant or receive one as a gift.

For birds, solutions begin on page 328.

Birds can eat all the cherries from your cherry (*Prunus avium*) tree before you have a chance to harvest any fruit for yourself. They also devour grapes (*Vitis*), figs (*Ficus*), blueberries (*Vaccinium*), papayas (*Carica*), apples (*Malus*), and any

While slugs love moist, overcast days and soft, mossy ground, they usually come out at night. You can tell they've been there by the ragged holes in leaves, flowers, and fruit, and the slime trails they leave behind.

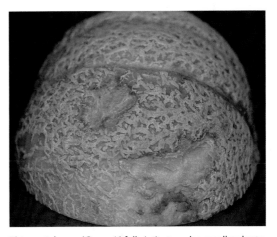

This cantaloupe (*Cucumis*) fell victim to voles, small rodents who strike at night. Parallel grooves of tooth marks indicate the perpetrator.

other sweet fruit they can sink their beaks into. Jays can harvest all the nuts from your nut trees too. Some birds will dig up and eat the seeds you have just planted in your garden or in your freshly seeded new lawn, or eat the seedlings as they sprout. Many birds like to eat greens too. Usually, wild greens are enough to satisfy them, but on occasion they will eat lettuce or other greens right out of your garden.

For mammals, solutions begin on page 329.

Mammals commonly enter the garden at dawn or dusk, or at night. Deer, rodents, and rabbits eat leaves, flowers, fruits, and nuts, and chew bark off trees in winter. Burrowing rodents eat roots and underground fleshy storage organs like tulip (*Tulipa*) bulbs. Raccoons are mostly after fruit and will eat your corn (*Zea mays*), blueberries (*Vaccinium*), and strawberries (*Fra-*

garia) precisely on the night before the day you planned to harvest your crop.

For parasitic plants, solutions begin on page 331.

Leafy mistletoe (*Phoradendron*), dwarf mistletoe (*Arceuthobium*), and dodder (*Cuscuta*) are all true parasites. They invade plant tissue to obtain nutrition. Because leafy mistletoe has green leaves, it is able to manufacture some of its own food. Dwarf mistletoe and dodder make no food of their own and obtain all their nutrition from their host. Lichens and algae are epiphytes, not parasites. Epiphytes use other plants as a perch, but they do not obtain nutrition from their host plant. They do not cause plant problems.

For lawnmowers and weed-eaters, solutions begin on page 331.

Lichens are not plant parasites and do not cause plant problems. In fact, they are accurate indicators of good air quality.

Gather up the strange orange or yellow strings of dodder (*Cuscuta*) as soon as you see them—ideally, before the plant flowers and sets seed—and dispose of them in the trash. Do not compost this material.

Damage to your plants from equipment can remove patches of bark near the soil line leaving open wounds that invite infection by diseases or invasion by insect pests.

Solutions for slugs and snails

Diagnoses from Part 1.

CHAPTER	PAGE	DIAGNOSIS
2 Leaves	48, 53	slugs or snails
3 Flowers	72, 75	slugs or snails
4 Fruit	110	slugs or snails
6 Roots	178	slugs or snails
7 Seeds	198	slugs or snails

Change the growing conditions

▶ **Eliminate hiding places and make traps.** Slugs and snails hide under pots, boards, rocks, logs, weeds, and cardboard boxes. Remove as many of these as you can. Place a few in strategic locations, so that you can gather up the slugs and snails during the day and destroy them.

Turn a flowerpot upside down or place a flat board on the ground. Use pebbles to prop the pot or board off the ground by 1 inch (2.5 cm). This creates a moist, shaded location. Slugs and snails will congregate in these places during the day. Check your traps every day to gather up and dispose of these animals (see the next suggestion). Alternatively, put diatomaceous earth under the traps to kill these pests (see page 276).

▶ **Remove pests by hand.** Pick up slugs and snails every time you see them. Pick up snails by their shell. Use kitchen tongs to pick up slugs. Drop both into a jar of soapy water, or put them in a sturdy paper bag and stomp on it. Dispose of the remains in the compost heap or the trash. Also go slug hunting at night with a flashlight.

▶ **Copper tape.** After you have removed the slugs and snails, wrap a strip of copper tape around a pot, planter box, or a tree trunk. Slugs and snails will not crawl across copper.

▶ **Encourage beneficial predators.** Predators of slugs and snails that you might want in your yard include garter snakes, toads, moles, and some beetles. Skunks also eat these pests, but we don't recommend that you encourage their presence. You can also raise beneficial predators such as chickens, ducks, and geese. Be sure you live in a location that permits keeping these animals. Finally, you can purchase predatory snails. Be aware, however, that in many locations, buying and releasing these is illegal. Check for local government regulations.

If necessary, use organic remedies

You may decide to utilize chemicals to help control slugs and snails on your plants. Various chemicals are certified for use in organic gardening. Many of these organic treatments are relatively safe for you and the environment. Some have been in use for hundreds of years, others are quite new. Look for OMRI (Organic Materials Review Institute) certification on the label.

Remedy recommendations

Always change the growing conditions before using either of these remedies. Evaluate your circumstances and the plant you are treating. Observe your plants. Do not apply chemicals according to a predetermined schedule. Both products are approved for organic gardening.

▶ **Iron phosphate**

Signal word? Caution.

What is it? Iron phosphate is a natural ingredient found in soil. It is composed of the mineral elements iron and phosphorus combined with oxygen and is used in fertilizers. An attractant (bait) is added to induce snails and slugs to

---

SAFETY FIRST

1. Always keep all these products **out of the reach of children and pets.**

2. **Read the label.** Use only chemicals that list the plants or type of plant you wish to protect on their labels. For example, a label may say "For use on ornamentals." Do not use this on a food plant.

3. **Follow the directions on the label.** Remember that more is not better. Many chemicals can actually damage some plants. This kind of damage is called a phytotoxic reaction. It is important to read the label and follow the manufacturer's instructions. If you put too much of the active ingredient on your plant, or if you put it on the wrong plant, you may do more harm than good.

   Every package or bottle of a garden remedy product has a label on the back that peels open. Unfold it and read the tiny print inside to learn what the product is used for, which plants to use it on, when to use it, and how much to use. Some of these labels unfold into long pages of instructions. Be patient, get out your magnifying glass, and read them carefully. Follow those directions.

4. **Always use the least toxic product first.** Look for a signal word on the label. These signal words are required by federal law under the Federal Insecticide, Fungicide and Rodenticide Act (FIFRA). All commercially sold pesticides must be registered with the Environmental Protection Agency (EPA), the registration authority for pesticides, and tested for modes of transmission into the body: inhalation, ingestion, dermal contact, primary eye, and primary skin. Toxicity Category IV requires no signal word because tests have shown the product to be non-toxic; these products, such as baking soda spray and insecticidal soap, are the safest, least toxic products you can use. Any pesticide determined to be in Toxicity Category III must be labeled **CAUTION**. Any in Toxicity Category II must carry the label **WARNING**. Those in Category I must be labeled either **DANGER** (the most toxic product available to the home gardener) or **DANGER—POISON**, with an image of a skull and crossbones. The last is most toxic of all. It is available only to licensed pesticide applicators.

5. **Wear protective gear and clothing.** Wear goggles, a respiratory face mask, a long-sleeved shirt, long pants, and shoes. Wash your clothes when you are finished using any product with a signal word.

eat it. Uneaten, it will degrade into fertilizer and become part of the soil.

What does it do? Iron phosphate is a molluscicide that kills snails and slugs. Slugs and snails eat it, get sick, and stop feeding. It takes several days for them to die. However, the damage to your plants will have stopped because they stop eating. Generally, they crawl away to hide and die so you will not see large numbers of dead or dying snails or slugs after you apply this product. You will, however, notice that your plants are doing much better and are sustaining much less damage than before.

What are the side effects? It can cause moderate eye irritation, so wash your hands thoroughly after applying this product. It does not harm pets, wildlife, or other terrestrial non-target organisms, but it may affect aquatic systems. Do not apply it directly to water or dispose of it in water.

How do I use it? Read the label and follow directions. It is safe to use on all fruit, vegetable, and ornamental plants. Scatter it on the ground near the plants to be protected. It will lure slugs and snails out of hiding, and they will eat it. Apply it to moist soil. If the soil is dry, wet it down before scattering the product, but do not apply it to standing water. Use it up to the day of harvest.

Note: Many gardeners have relied for years on an older generation of products containing metaldehyde, which is poisonous to pets, wildlife, and children as well as to slugs and snails. We cannot and do not recommend the use of these older products. Iron phosphate is by far the better choice.

▶ **Diatomaceous earth**
Signal word? Caution.

What is it? Diatomaceous earth is a white powder with a gritty feel. It comes from microscopic plants called diatoms that have a skeleton made of silicon dioxide, the same material as glass and quartz. These algae are found everywhere on earth in fresh and salt waters, and in moist soil. Where ancient seas or lakes have dried up, the skeletons of these plants have built up to thick deposits that are mined.

To protect against slugs and snails, select diatomaceous earth that is labeled for use as an insecticide; some diatomaceous earth products are used for filters for swimming pools and are ineffective against slugs and snails.

What does it do? Diatomaceous earth repels and kills slugs and snails. It is sharp, like ground glass. Any slug or snail that tries to crawl across it will be wounded by the sharp particles and will die.

What are the side effects? Applied to the soil surface, this product affects only slugs, snails, or insects that normally crawl across the ground. Honey bees and butterflies are unaffected. It is unlikely to affect mammals, birds, or aquatic organisms that do not crawl on the ground.

You must wear proper gear to protect yourself while applying diatomaceous earth. Because it is a fine dust-like powder, particles float in the air and get into your eyes and lungs. Wear a face mask to avoid breathing it and wear goggles. Wear gloves and long-sleeved shirts and pants to keep diatomaceous earth off your skin because it can be an irritant.

How do I use it? Pour the powder onto the soil around your plants. The powder is most effective when dry. Place it under boards, upside-down pots, or other objects to keep it dry.

Solutions for birds

Diagnoses from Part 1.

CHAPTER	PAGE	DIAGNOSIS
2 Leaves	52	birds
4 Fruit	113	birds
5 Stems	144	woodpeckers
5 Stems	145	sapsuckers
7 Seeds	200, 203	birds

Change the growing conditions

▶ **Nets.** Drape nets over your fruit or nut trees, berry bushes, or grape vines to prevent birds from harvesting your entire crop. Lightweight nets made of inexpensive black plastic work well for this purpose, but you must prevent access from below. For berry bushes and grape vines, carry the nets all the way to the ground and fasten them down so that birds cannot squeeze underneath the net to get inside. For fruit or nut trees, gather the net on the bottom edge to close it around the trunk. Fasten it closed with tape or staples.

▶ **Floating and rigid row covers.** Grow your plants under a protective covering, one that lets light, water, and air in but keeps birds out. Row covers made especially for this purpose are lightweight spun-bonded polyester materials that work quite well. Fiberglass window screening, mosquito netting, or sheer fabrics also work but can be heavier and less flexible. Pay attention to the size of the weave; a very tight weave restricts air flow, which you do not want.

- Floating row covers. Drape a lightweight material over your seed bed or seedlings. Make it baggy. Leave enough slack so that your plants have room to grow. They push the material up as they grow. Weigh the material down around the edges with dirt, boards, or rocks; or fasten it with U-shaped metal pins made from coat hangers.
- Rigid row covers. Use the same materials noted above but attach them to a frame made of wood, PVC pipe, or some other framework. Alternatively, roll or fold aluminum window screening into shape and staple the edges together to make a free-standing cone or cover. Make the frames or cones large enough to accommodate the mature height of your plants. The frame holds the material up off the leaves and will last for many seasons.

▶ **Burlap wrap.** When you spot **sapsuckers** (from page 145) in your trees or you find the tell-tale grid of shallow holes on your tree trunks or branches, wrap the area with burlap. The birds should become discouraged and find some other tree to feed on. Sapsuckers are difficult to control, however, because they are persistent. When they decide a particular tree is their favorite food in the whole world, they will keep coming back.

▶ **Fright tactics: visual.** Hang shiny, reflective objects that dance in the wind from your fruit trees and around your garden. Aluminum pie pans, reflective tape, old CDs or DVDs—anything that moves in the breeze and flashes light—can reduce the damage birds do. Plastic owls mounted in the trees can also serve as a deterrent. Birds become accustomed to such things however, especially if they are stationary. We have seen birds nesting on a porch right beside flashy CDs hanging from the porch eaves. We have also seen birds perched on top of a plastic owl calmly preening themselves. To be really effective you will have to move these objects to new locations every other day or so.

▶ **Fright tactics: sounds.** Broadcast the cries of bird-eating hawks at random intervals. This is a very effective way to scare birds away from your fruit. We have seen this technique employed very efficiently on commercial berry farms. It might dismay your neighbors in suburban close quarters, however.

Electronic devices that broadcast a sound that birds can hear (but humans cannot) also work. Many different brands of both kinds of electronic equipment are readily available to homeowners.

Solutions for mammals

Diagnoses from Part 1.

CHAPTER	PAGE	DIAGNOSIS
1 Whole Plant	20	gophers, rabbits, other mammals
2 Leaves	51	deer, other mammals
3 Flowers	73	deer
4 Fruit	113	bears, coyotes, deer, raccoons, children
4 Fruit	113	rodents

CHAPTER	PAGE	DIAGNOSIS
5 Stems	133, 143	rodents
5 Stems	133	deer
6 Roots	181	rodents
7 Seeds	200	burrowing mice
7 Seeds	200	rabbits
7 Seeds	203	raccoons, bears, humans
7 Seeds	203	squirrels

Change the growing conditions

▶ **Fences.** Build a fence 8 feet (2.5 m) tall to keep deer out of your garden. Enclose your whole property or just the plants you want to protect. The fence does not need to be solid, just sturdy enough to keep deer out and tall enough that they cannot jump over it.

Electric fences also work well to keep deer and other large animals out of your garden. Solar-powered systems are available so you do not need to plug these into your house for power. An electric fence needs to be only about 4 feet (1.2 m) tall.

A 2-foot-high (0.6 m) strip of chicken wire attached to your fence at the bottom will keep out rodents. Bury the chicken wire 1 foot (30 cm) deep in the soil to keep out rodents that burrow.

Fences will not keep raccoons out of your garden. They climb right over them.

▶ **Row covers.** See page 328.

▶ **Deer-resistant plants.** Put plants in your garden that deer do not like. Aromatic plants in particular seem to be avoided by deer. They will not eat rosemary (*Rosmarinus*), thyme (*Thymus*), sage (*Salvia*), or lavender (*Lavandula*). Lavender may even have a repellent effect on deer. There are many published lists of deer-resistant plants. Check the Internet or a good garden reference book.

▶ **Dogs.** A barking dog in the yard deters deer, rodents, raccoons, and all other mammals. (A barking dog in the house deters no one.) If you own an outdoor dog who barks, it will do a good job of protecting your garden from Bambi's bunch or Thumper's thugs.

▶ **Motion-activated sprinklers.** Set a motion-activated impulse sprinkler in the yard where deer are likely to enter. The motion detector turns the sprinkler on when a deer shows up. The sudden loud noise and splash of cold water scares the deer away. Avoid placing it where it will be activated by arriving guests or spouses.

Smaller units of this type are made to keep your neighbor's cat out of your yard. They also work for raccoons and other small mammals.

▶ **Electronic sounds.** Place an electronic device in the garden that produces supersonic sounds that humans cannot hear. These units can be adjusted to emit sounds at a frequency targeted to particular animals. You can set it for deer, raccoons, or rodents.

▶ **Live trap and remove.** Put baited traps in the garden that spring shut when the offending animal enters the trap. The trap does not kill the animal. You can pick up the trap with the animal inside and take it to a remote location to set it free. Traps can be purchased in any of various sizes.

Remedy recommendations

These two remedy recommendations do not have signal words and fall outside the purview of registration requirements. The first is a spray and the second is lethal. Always handle these products and devices with care and use them safely. Please read the safety considerations on page 326.

▶ **Repellents.** Keep these out of the reach of children and pets. There are many commercially prepared products available at garden centers. Most of them contain putrescent egg solids (rotten eggs), capsaicin (hot pepper oil), and garlic. Spray these nasty-tasting liquids on your plants to keep animals from eating them. Rain washes these products off. In addition, sometimes very hungry pest mammals get used to the flavor. It helps to switch back and forth between different products.

▶ **Lethal traps.** Electronic traps that electrocute their victims work well for small rodents. It is illegal to kill deer in some locations and without a hunting license. This applies to many other mammals as well. It is usually legal to kill voles, mice, gophers, and rats. It is often illegal to kill raccoons or squirrels. Check your state, county, and municipal regulations.

Mechanical traps that spring shut to kill burrowing animals, such as gophers, also work well. You need to find their burrow, dig down to it, and place the trap in such a way that the offending animal will walk through the trap and be killed.

Note: Moles do not eat plants. They eat only insects, worms, and other underground animals. Moles are actually beneficial. A mole may accidentally harm your plant when burrowing through the soil after its prey. Gophers on the other hand eat nothing but plants and are quite destructive to your garden. If you have a problem with moles, treat your garden with beneficial nematodes to kill all the soil-inhabiting insects the moles are eating. If there is no more food for them, they'll move away, and you do not have to kill them.

Solutions for parasitic plants

Diagnoses from Part 1.

CHAPTER	PAGE	DIAGNOSIS
5 Stems	140, 156	dwarf mistletoe
5 Stems	156	leafy mistletoe

Change the growing conditions

▶ **Prune.** Both leafy mistletoe (*Phoradendron*) and dwarf mistletoe (*Arceuthobium*) are controlled by pruning away the branch they grow on. Dispose of this material by chipping and composting it, or discard it in the trash.

Solutions for lawnmowers and weed-eaters

Diagnoses from Part 1.

CHAPTER	PAGE	DIAGNOSIS
5 Stems	133, 143	lawnmowers, weed-eaters

Change the growing conditions

▶ **Protective barriers.** Put rocks, wooden stakes, or some other barrier around your trees and shrubs. Keep the machines away from your plants.

▶ **No-mow zones.** Remove all the grass in a circle around trees and shrubs, and replace the grass with a mulch or a layer of gravel, pebbles, decorative bricks, or pavers. This provides a space for the wheels of the equipment to roll over without damaging your plant.

PART 3

What Does It Look Like?

A Photo Gallery of Common Problems

Problems on whole plants

Have you checked the flow charts before consulting these photographs? Symptoms can look alike but have vastly different causes. The flow charts help you eliminate other possible, but incorrect, diagnoses.

The whole plant is wilted

For diagnosis, turn to the flow charts beginning on page 16.

GROWING CONDITIONS

Transplant shock (from page 17). This pine (*Pinus*) could not recover when it was moved to a new location. Many circumstances contribute to this failure, so for a good solution, see page 231.

Mechanical damage (from page 18). A new fence and garage built close to this arborvitae (*Thuja occidentalis*) disturbed the roots, so that the tree could not hang on. For solution, see page 225.

Rootbound (from page 20). Someone forgot to up-pot this large-flowered tickseed (*Coreopsis grandiflora*) when it needed it, and the roots were not able to find enough moisture in the small volume of soil. For solution, see page 227.

Drought (from page 17). This viburnum didn't stand a chance on a hot, windy day when the soil was already dry. For solution, see page 231.

Salt damage (from page 17). Frequent doses of fertilizer allowed excessive salt to build up in the soil around this bean (*Phaseolus*) seedling. For solution, see page 238.

Botrytis aka **gray mold** (from page 18). Fuzzy gray-brown mold grows on the dead stem tissue of this zinnia. For solution, see page 252.

Fusarium, verticillium (from page 18). When you cut into a stem of this arborvitae (*Thuja occidentalis*), you find dark streaks in the wood. The tree suffers from a fungus infection of the vascular system. For solution, see page 252.

Bacteria (from page 16). Branches on this pear (*Pyrus*) are dying one at a time in a random pattern throughout the tree's canopy, a clear-cut symptom of a bacterial infection. For solution, see page 301.

Borers (from page 20). Looking closely, you see the telltale hole in the stem of this acorn squash (*Cucurbita pepo*) and can safely conclude that a borer is at work. For solution, see page 282.

Problems on whole plants

The whole plant is not wilted, but some or all of the leaves are discolored

For diagnosis, turn to the flow charts beginning on page 21.

For diagnosis, turn to the flow charts beginning on page 21.

GROWING CONDITIONS

Freeze damage (from page 21). These avocados (*Persea*) experienced an unexpected freeze during a severe winter on the coast of California. For solution, see page 232.

Blow down (from page 22). This immature Douglas fir (*Pseudotsuga menziesii*) fell over during a wind storm because the root system was compromised. For solution, see page 225.

Overwatering (from page 21). The roots of this crown of thorns (*Euphorbia*) remained soaking wet because its pot stood in a water-filled saucer. For solution, see page 232.

Herbicide damage (from page 23). The leaves on this blackberry (*Rubus*) are both stunted and oddly shaped, a clear sign of a careless application of herbicide. For solution, see page 226.

Iron or manganese deficiency (from page 24). This young leaf from the tip of a branch on a flowering quince (*Chaenomeles*) has turned yellow because the soil lacked a sufficient amount of iron or manganese. For solution, see page 238.

Nitrogen or magnesium deficiency (from page 24). The older leaves at the base of branches turn yellow when a plant does not have enough nitrogen or magnesium in the soil. For solution, see page 238.

INSECTS

Borers (from page 22). The holes in the bark of this flowering dogwood (*Cornus florida*) are a sure sign that the dogwood borer infests the tree. For solution, see page 282.

BACTERIA

Crown gall (from page 22). This rose (*Rosa*) is not wilted, but a large gall grows at the base of its stems near the soil line. For solution, see page 305.

VIRUSES

Virus (from page 23). Odd yellow markings on this viburnum leaf are classic symptoms of a virus infection. For solution, see page 309.

Problems on leaves and leafy vegetables

Have you checked the flow charts before consulting these photographs? Symptoms can look alike but have vastly different causes. The flow charts help you eliminate other possible, but incorrect, diagnoses.

The whole leaf is discolored

For diagnosis, turn to the flow charts beginning on page 30.

Scorch (from page 33). The branch tips on a Japanese maple (*Acer*) wilt, despite the fact that there has been no disturbance in the root zone of the plant. Extreme heat and high wind cause this condition; sufficient water will prevent it. For solution, see page 231.

GROWING CONDITIONS

Sulfur phytotoxicity (from page 30). Black discoloration that does not rub off coats this pear (*Pyrus*) leaf, which received a dose of sulfur on a hot summer day. The sulfur, combined with heat and sunlight, turned the leaf black. For solution, see page 233.

Salt burn (from page 31). This dieffenbachia received adequate water (so that the soil was not always dry), but someone mistakenly gave it too much fertilizer. The high concentration of fertilizer resulted in too much salt, which drew water through reverse osmosis from the leaves and dried them out. For solution, see page 238.

Drought (from page 31). The soil under this salal (*Gaultheria shallon*) dried out, yet excess salt had not reached the plant. Because of the extreme drought conditions, the entire leaf died and turned brown. For solution, see page 231.

Leaf scorch (from page 31). The leaves at the tips of the branches turned brown because this viburnum could not supply water quickly enough to its leaves. The thinner tissue at the tips and edges of the leaf succumbed first. For solution, see page 231.

Mechanical damage (from page 33). The branches with brown leaves, needles, are all on one side of the plant. Disturbance in the root zone of this Douglas fir (*Pseudotsuga menziesii*) damaged the roots, and interrupted the flow of water and nutrients to its leaves. For solution, see page 225.

Iron or manganese deficiency (from page 32). When young leaves turn yellow while the main veins remain green, you can deduce an iron or manganese deficiency, as seen on this serviceberry (*Amelanchier*). For solution, see page 238.

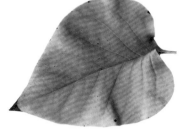

Nitrogen or magnesium deficiency (from page 32). Leaves at the base of branches are the old, mature leaves. When they begin to turn yellow, while the main veins remain green, as they have on this lilac (*Syringa*), suspect nitrogen or magnesium deficiency. For solution, see page 238.

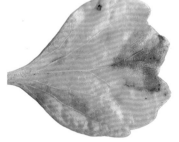

Too much light (from page 32). The leaves at the tip of the branch (in other words, the young leaves) on this pachysandra turned completely yellow. Plants that require partial shade can suffer from this condition in a variety of circumstances. For solution, see page 229.

Overwatering (from page 32). This pothos (*Epipremnum*) grew in soggy soil because its pot stood in a water-filled saucer. The leaves at the base of stems, namely the older leaves, turned yellow and dropped off. For solution, see page 232.

Winter desiccation (from page 33). All the leaves on the windward side of this Oregon grape (*Mahonia*) turned brown during windy, freezing weather. For solution, see page 232.

Problems on Leaves and Leafy Vegetables • **339**

The whole leaf is discolored, GROWING CONDITIONS [*continued*]

Old age (from page 32). The soil was not soggy, yet this leaf at the base of a rhododendron branch turned completely yellow and dropped off. All leaves have a limited life span. Even conifers and broadleaved evergreens like rhodies shed their oldest leaves. For solution, see page 222.

INSECTS

Borers (from page 33). All the leaves on some randomly scattered branches are brown on this peach (*Prunus persica*), indicating that boring insects are attacking the tree. For solution, see page 282.

FUNGI

Sooty mold (from page 30). A black coating that rubs off leaves is actually a fungus that grows on honeydew, the sticky excrement of aphids or scale insects. The nutritious honeydew on this milkweed (*Asclepias*) feeds the fungus, which eventually grows thick enough to block sunlight. For solution, see page 254.

Leaf gall (from page 30). The pale green, swollen leaf on this azalea (*Rhododendron*) indicates leaf gall, a fungus infection. For solution, see page 244.

Problems on leaves and leafy vegetables

The leaf has discrete, rounded spots or speckles of any size

For diagnosis, turn to the flow charts beginning on page 34.

For diagnosis, turn to the flow charts beginning on page 34.

FUNGI

Rust (from page 36). This rose (*Rosa*) leaf has spots that are orange bumps. When you touch these bumps, they release orange dust—the colorful powdery spores of a rust fungus. For solution, see page 244.

Rust (from page 38). The bumps on this hollyhock (*Alcea*) leaf are only on the underside. When touched, they release tiny brown dust particles, the spores from the fungus that causes the growths. For solution, see page 244.

Fungus (from page 39). This poplar (*Populus*) leaf is not deformed, but has an odd concave bubble on the upper surface of the leaf and a yellow convex bubble on the underside. The growth, a fungus infection, is hollow. For solution, see page 244.

GROWING CONDITIONS

Black spot (from page 36). This rose (*Rosa*) leaflet displays one of the most common symptoms any rose grower encounters: black spots with ragged, fringed edges. For solution, see page 244.

Leaf-spot (from page 36). Discrete spots give the first hint of a particular leaf-spot fungus, apple scab, on this apple (*Malus*) leaf. For solution, see page 244.

Physiological leaf-spot (from page 35). Discrete, rounded spots that never cross over veins signal that this is not a disease, but a mysterious condition with an unknown cause. Weather and climate may be factors, but physiological leaf-spot does not affect the health of this photinia. For solution, see page 222.

Powdery mildew (from page 36). White powdery spots and patches on the surface of this lilac (*Syringa*) are classic symptoms of a common fungus infection. For solution, see page 244.

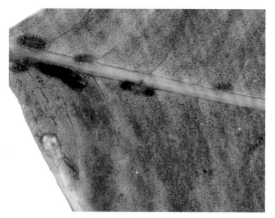

Scale (from page 38). This weeping fig (*Ficus*) has attracted scale insects. The small, shiny, brown bumps, most of which hide on the underside of the leaf, indicate the beginning of a scale infestation. For solution, see page 267.

Lace bugs (from page 37). Turn over the leaves of this sickly rhododendron and discover black specks on the underside, a symptom of lace bugs. For solution, see page 267.

Adelgids (from page 38). This hemlock hosts an adelgid gathering, much against its will. The white, cottony bumps on the underside of leaves, or needles as they are known on conifers, is a call to action. For solution, see page 267.

Skeletonizers (from page 35). While touring the garden you find sunken spots with a lacy network of fibers on this rose (*Rosa*) leaf. Such a symptom indicates that skeletonizer insects are at work here. For solution, see page 267, 282.

Leafhoppers (from page 37). Noticing stippling on the upper surface of this blackberry (*Rubus*) leaf, you turn the leaf over; wedge-shaped bugs instantly fly away, but you do not find black specks. After leafhoppers suck the contents out, the dead cells appear pale. For solution, see page 267.

Leafhoppers (from page 35). Look closely at this honeysuckle (*Lonicera*) leaf. These spots are actually a collection of very tiny speckles. Leafhoppers pierce leaf cells with their straw-like mouthparts and suck out the contents. For solution, see page 267.

MITES

Spider mites (from page 37). Tiny bugs crawl rapidly over fine webbing that looks like a spider's nest on this rose (*Rosa*). Spider mites, like all mites, are not insects but closely related to spiders. For solution, see page 288.

Blister mites (from page 39). Many bumps on both sides of this young pear (*Pyrus*) leaf reveal that blister mites have taken up habitation. As the leaf matures, the symptom changes dramatically. For solution, see page 295.

BACTERIA

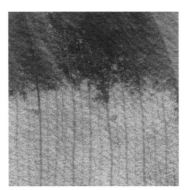

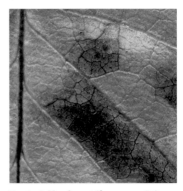

Bacterial leaf-spot (from page 35). The upper portion of the leaf, where it is dark green, is translucent, like grease spots on paper—a classic symptom of bacterial infection. For solution, see page 301.

Bacterial leaf-spot (from page 35) Take a closer look at the lilac (*Syringa*) leaf, and you can easily see the infection confined by the leaf veins. Most fungi can devour leaf veins; most bacteria cannot. For solution, see page 301.

Bacterial leaf-spot (from page 35). The spots on this lilac (*Syringa*) turned translucent at first, as in the previous photograph, but over time they browned, then took on this angular shape because the leaf veins confined them. For solution, see page 301.

343

Problems on leaves and leafy vegetables

The leaf has very large, irregular spots or blotches

For diagnosis, turn to the flow charts beginning on page 40.

GROWING CONDITIONS	FUNGI

Sunburn (from page 40). A classic symptom of sunburn, a large blotch in the middle of the leaf, appeared on this rhododendron when it was exposed to several days of direct sun. Intense sunlight and heat killed the cells, which then turned brown. For solution, see page 229.

Leaf-spot (from page 41). The black, irregular spots on this salal (*Gaultheria shallon*) leaf are surrounded by halos of brown tissue, a significant symptom of fungus infection. For solution, see page 244.

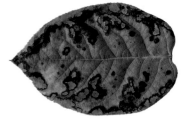

Leaf-spot (from page 41). Brown blotches containing multiple black areas indicate an advanced fungus infection on this salal (*Gaultheria shallon*) leaf. For solution, see page 244.

Insufficient water (from page 41). Completely brown blotches on the tip of this hydrangea leaf means the plant did not get enough water. This plant, grown in a container, became rootbound, and needed a larger volume of soil to plumb for water. For solution, see page 231.

Leaf-spot (from page 41). Close examination of the brown tissue on this photinia leaf reveals hundreds of minute black specks, the fruiting body of fungus that grows in the dead leaf tissue. For solution, see page 244.

Leaf-spot (from page 41). The tip of this viburnum leaf has a large black blotch contained within an even larger brown blotch. Necrotic tissue is a classic symptom of a fungal infection. For solution, see page 244.

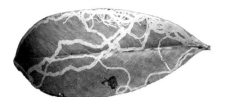

Leafminers (from page 40). Silvery trails, like an abstract painting, decorate this madrone (*Arbutus menziesii*) leaf. In reality an insidious insect is mining the leaf tissue between the upper surface and the underside, robbing the plant of nutrients. For solution, see page 267, 282.

Skeletonizers (from page 40). Exposed veins lie in the bottom of the sunken, brown blotches on this apple (*Malus*) leaf. You can also see the responsible insect, whose jaws are not powerful enough to chew the tough vein tissue. For solution, see page 282.

Leafminers (from page 40). If you pinch the brown blotch on this lilac (*Syringa*) leaf and rub your fingers together, the leaf tissue slides back and forth. Leafminers are at it again, stealing food from this plant's manufacturing facility. For solution, see page 267, 282.

NEMATODES

Foliar nematodes (from page 41). The dramatic blotches on this dock (*Rumex*) reveal that swarms of foliar nematodes are devouring the leaf. For solution, see page 315.

Problems on leaves and leafy vegetables

The leaf has stripes or diffuse mottling

For diagnosis, turn to the flow charts beginning on page 42.

For diagnosis, turn to the flow charts beginning on page 42.

GROWING CONDITIONS

Iron or manganese deficiency (from page 43). On this rose (*Rosa*) leaflet, growing at the tip of a branch, the leaf tissue between the main veins became a mottled yellow, but no brown spots were discovered on the leaf's underside. For solution, see page 238.

Insufficient water (from page 42). The dramatic green stripes along the main veins are the last living tissue in this salal (*Gaultheria shallon*) leaf. The rest of the tissue turned brown and died. For solution, see page 231.

Nitrogen or magnesium deficiency (from page 43). On this rhododendron leaf, which was growing at the base of a branch, the tissue between the main veins became a mottled yellow, and the underside was free of brown spots. For solution, see page 238.

FUNGI

Fungus (from page 43). The upper surface of this rhododendron leaf displayed yellow mottling between the main veins. Closer examination reveals discolored spots and mottling on the underside of the leaf, indicating a fungus infection. For solution, see page 244.

VIRUSES

Virus (from page 42). Subtle circles and zigzag lines course across this lilac (*Syringa*) leaf. Though virus infections rarely kill plants, they disfigure both foliage and flower and are easily spread by insects and pruning shears. For solution, see page 309.

Herbicide damage (from page 42). The striping and dramatic distortion of these rose (*Rosa*) leaves are classic symptoms of herbicide damage. Someone was carelessly applying an herbicide to control nearby weeds. For solution, see page 226.

Problems on leaves and leafy vegetables

The leaf is wilted, limp, and droopy

For diagnosis, turn to the flow charts beginning on page 44.

Insufficient water and death of tissue (from page 44). The brown leaf tissue on the tips of this viburnum leaf has died. These leaves cannot recover, even when watered. For solution, see page 231.

Mechanical damage (from page 46). These rhododendron leaves are on a broken stem. Breakage like this is not always obvious, so look carefully at the stems below wilted leaves. For solution, see page 225.

Insufficient water (from page 44). The wilted leaves on this rose (*Rosa*) retain their normal color. The plant grows in a container and did not receive enough water on a hot summer day. It recovered fully when watered. For solution, see page 231.

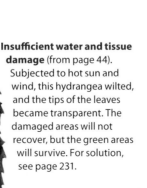

Insufficient water and tissue damage (from page 44). Subjected to hot sun and wind, this hydrangea wilted, and the tips of the leaves became transparent. The damaged areas will not recover, but the green areas will survive. For solution, see page 231.

Freeze damage (from page 46). The leaves and stems turned brown overnight when this rose (*Rosa*) suffered a night of unexpectedly low temperatures. For solution, see page 232.

The leaf is wilted, limp, and droopy,
GROWING CONDITIONS [*continued*]

Cankers (from page 46). The sunken discolored lesion on the stem of this rose (*Rosa*) caused the leaves to wilt and die. The canker girdles the stem, cutting off water and nutrients to the leaves. For solution, see page 244.

Flagging (from page 46). The leaves (scale-like needles) at the base of branches in the interior of this western red cedar (*Thuja plicata*) turned brown. This is a normal process, as many conifers shed their innermost leaves every summer. They drop their older leaves to save nutrients and water for new growth. For solution, see page 222.

Verticillium wilt (from page 46). After discovering wilted leaves on this lilac (*Syringa*), you might cut the stem and discover these dark streaks in the wood. Verticillium is a common soil-dwelling fungus that can infect and kill a wide variety of plants. For solution, see page 244, 252.

INSECTS

Borers (from page 45). The delicate leaves of this asparagus wilt, and you find a hole with a sawdust-like material falling out of it. You can be sure that a boring insect feeds inside. For solution, see page 282.

Botrytis aka **gray mold** (from page 46). Brown blotches surround the botrytis, or gray mold, that grows on the leaves and stems of this wilted zinnia. The fungus invades healthy tissue and slowly kills the plant. For solution, see page 244.

BACTERIA

Brown rot (from page 45). Wilted cherry (*Prunus avium*) leaves that are soft, fuzzy, and moldy illustrate a dramatic symptom of brown rot. These leaves and twigs have died from the disease. For solution, see page 244.

Fire blight (from page 45). The wilted leaves on this cherry (*Prunus avium*) are crunchy and crisp, but there is no mold on them. Fire blight, a bacterial disease (*Erwinia amylovora*), can kill the entire tree. For solution, see page 301, 306.

Bacteria (from page 45). While inspecting the wilted leaves on this cherry (*Prunus avium*) tree, you find a gummy substance oozing from the branch. If you suspect a bacterial infection, you would be right. For solution, see page 301.

Problems on leaves and leafy vegetables

The leaf has holes or chewed edges, or you see pests

For diagnosis, turn to the flow charts beginning on page 47.

For diagnosis, turn to the flow charts beginning on page 47.

FUNGI

Fungus (from page 54). The few, ragged holes in this rhododendron leaf indicate a fungus infection, in which both the fungus and the missing leaf tissue have fallen to the ground. There, the fungus continues to absorb nutrients from the stolen leaf tissue. For solution, see page 244.

Leaf-spot (from page 54). Only a few organisms can eat the tough tissue of leaf veins. Ragged holes and round spots that cross over the veins are therefore important symptoms, this time of a fungal infection, on this dogwood (*Cornus*). For solution, see page 244.

INSECTS

Leafcutter bees (from page 51). This rose (*Rosa*) leaf looks like someone has been after it with the hole punch. Circular holes in the leaf edges tell you that leafcutter bees are working the area. For solution, see page 267.

Leafhoppers (from page 50). Turning a viburnum leaf over, you find this surprisingly pretty wedge-shaped insect. This tiny pest is a leafhopper. For solution, see page 267.

Skeletonizers (from page 54). The cherry (*Prunus avium*) leaf has holes as well as discolored areas that prove to be sunken, lacy patches of uneaten veins. This type of insect is not powerful enough to eat the tough vein tissue. For solution, see page 267, 282.

Sawfly larvae (from page 48). A sawfly larva is eating the soft tissue on this cherry (*Prunus avium*) leaf. This slimy little critter looks like a slug, but it isn't. It has no wrinkles, tentacles, or eyes that you can see. For solution, see page 267.

Whiteflies (from page 50). Whiteflies (20×) are so tiny that you can only get a good look at them under the microscope, but they fly away so fast you will rarely get the chance. For solution, see page 267.

Weevils (from page 49). You find holes in a leaf, and you discover a pest that looks like an insect. You take a closer look and find this critter with a long snout. It is a weevil. For solution, see page 267.

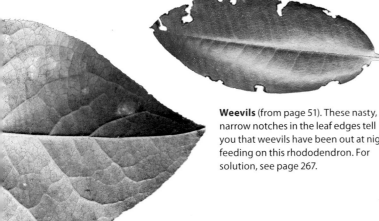

Whiteflies (from page 50). You discover white residue on salal (*Gaultheria shallon*) after tiny white bugs fly away. Using piercing/sucking mouthparts, they suck the sap out of leaf veins. For solution, see page 267.

Weevils (from page 51). These nasty, narrow notches in the leaf edges tell you that weevils have been out at night feeding on this rhododendron. For solution, see page 267.

Earwigs (from page 49). Something is chewing on the tender leaf tissue in your garden, and you have found the pest who is responsible. The pincers on its rear end give away its identity. It is an earwig. For solution, see page 267.

Earwigs (from page 53). Holes in the tender new leaves of this laurel (*Prunus*) tell you that earwigs are lurking. Earwigs hide during the day in moist, dark places and come out at night to ravage the garden. For solution, see page 267.

The leaf has holes or chewed edges, or you see pests, INSECTS [*continued*]

Aphids (from page 50). Green aphids are on this hellebore (*Helleborus*). The color may be different, but their pear-shaped bodies give away their identity. For solution, see page 267.

Grasshoppers (from page 49). There are holes in the leaves of your plants—and an insect close by. It has very long hind legs, so you know it is a grasshopper. This one is young and, therefore, small. For solution, see page 267.

Caterpillars (from page 48). Some worm-like critter—that is not slimy—has found this coral bells (*Heuchera*). A smooth caterpillar is devouring this leaf and any others it can get its jaws into. For solution, see page 267.

Aphids (from page 50). These pear-shaped insects, on an artichoke (*Cynara*) leaf, are black aphids. For solution, see page 267.

Grasshoppers (from page 52). Something is eating this salal (*Gaultheria shallon*) leaf—as you can see, a pest with jaws so powerful, it can eat both small and large vein tissue. For solution, see page 267.

Caterpillars (from page 53). Irregularly shaped, smooth-edged holes in the broccoli (*Brassica*) show you that caterpillars are creeping about while you are not looking. Most eat from the edges of the leaf inward, but cabbage loopers will dine any-where. For solution, see page 267.

Beetles (from page 52). Obviously beetles are eating this potato (*Solanum tuberosum*) leaf, but even if the pest were not present you could tell because the main veins are still here while the small veins are eaten. For solution, see page 267.

Beetles (from page 52). Both small and large veins remain on this grape (*Vitis*), creating a lacy effect; beetles have eaten the softer material between veins. For solution, see page 267.

Bacteria (from page 54). A bacterial infection on this English ivy (*Hedera helix*) leaf makes dry brown spots that are confined by the main veins. The dead tissue falls out, leaving holes in the leaf. For solution, see page 301.

Beetles (from page 49). Inspecting this purpleleaf plum (*Prunus cerasifera*), you discover a critter with shiny hard wing covers on both surfaces of a leaf. If it looks like a beetle and chews like a beetle, there is no doubt that it is a beetle. For solution, see page 267.

Flea beetles (from page 53). The small, round holes on this foamy bells (×*Heucherella*) proclaim that flea beetles feed here. These tiny, shiny, black beetles hop around the garden like fleas, looking for a good dining opportunity. For solution, see page 267.

Slugs or snails (from page 48). You discover that the pests eating your plants are large and wrinkled, and have eyes on tentacles. This slug fits the description of the culprit. For solution, see page 325.

Deer or other mammals (from page 51). These half-eaten photinia leaves are a sure sign that deer, or the neighbor's cow or horse, have been browsing in the garden. For solution, see page 329.

Slugs or snails (from page 53). Faint slime trails around the ragged, large holes in this iris confirm the presence of slugs or snails in the garden. For solution, see page 325.

Deer or other mammals (from page 51). Roses (*Rosa*), as every rose grower knows, are deer candy. This poor specimen needs protection of some kind. For solution, see page 329.

Problems on leaves and leafy vegetables

The leaf has raised bumps, warts, or weird growths

For diagnosis, turn to the flow charts beginning on page 55.

GROWING CONDITIONS

Edema (from page 57). Brown, corky tissue that is rough to the touch grows on this ivy geranium (*Pelargonium*) because the plant received too much water. For solution, see page 232.

FUNGI

Rust (from page 57). Colorful powdery spores from the growths on this St. John's wort (*Hypericum*) smudge the grower's fingers. For solution, see page 244.

INSECTS

Mealybugs, cottony scale (from page 55). White, cottony bumps on a hoya (which is not a conifer) suggest the plant is hosting either mealybugs or cottony scale. For solution, see page 267.

Scale (from page 55). This weeping fig (*Ficus*) has attracted scale insects. The small, shiny, brown bumps, most of which hide on the underside of the leaf, indicate the beginning of a scale infestation. For solution, see page 267.

Adelgids (from page 55). This hemlock hosts an adelgid gathering, much against its will. The white, cottony bumps on the underside of leaves, or needles as they are known on conifers, is a call to action. For solution, see page 267.

Galls (from page 57). Firm, round galls house insect larvae on this willow (*Salix*) leaf. When the larvae mature, they drill holes in the gall and fly away. For solution, see page 285.

The leaf has raised bumps, warts, or weird growths, INSECTS [*continued*]

Mossyrose gall (from page 56). Bumps that appear lacy or mossy—something like tangled yarn—indicate mossyrose gall on a rose (*Rosa*) leaf. For solution, see page 285.

Bladder gall mites (from page 56). The tiny, nipple-shaped bumps on this maple (*Acer*) leaf are bladder gall mites. For solution, see page 295.

Spiny rose gall (from page 56). Bristly balls attached to this rose (*Rosa*) leaf let you know that an insect has tricked the plant into building a house for its larvae. For solution, see page 285.

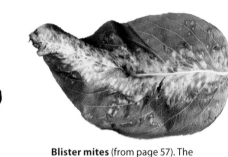

Blister mites (from page 57). The growths on this mature pear (*Pyrus*) leaf are smooth to the touch. Though these are yellow and irregularly shaped, they can be any shape or color. For solution, see page 295.

Kinnikinnik leaf gall aphid (from page 56). Aphids are the culprit on this kinnikinnik (*Arctostaphylos*). Part of the leaf itself has rolled up and turned bright red. The aphids live inside. For solution, see page 285.

Problems on leaves and leafy vegetables

The leaf is distorted

For diagnosis, turn to the flow charts beginning on page 58.

For diagnosis, turn to the flow charts beginning on page 58.

GROWING CONDITIONS

Lack of humidity (from page 58). The strap-shaped leaves of many monocots, like this iris, develop accordion pleating when conditions are too dry. The new growth will be smooth if the plant gets enough humidity. For solution, see page 231.

Irregular watering (from page 59). No insects inhabit this puckered viburnum leaf, but the grower watered it inconsistently, alternately giving it too much, and then too little water. For solution, see page 231.

FUNGI

Powdery mildew (from page 59). This fungus infection hits new growth especially hard, as on this severely distorted rose (*Rosa*) leaf. For solution, see page 244.

Herbicide damage (from page 60). A combination of windy conditions and an inattentive applicator resulted in these badly distorted and stunted grape (*Vitis*) leaves. For solution, see page 226.

The leaf is distorted, FUNGI [*continued*]

Peach leaf curl (from page 59). This distorted peach (*Prunus persica*) leaf is red and purple, so you know which fungus infection has attacked your plant. For solution, see page 244.

Aphids (from page 59). This puckered and twisted viburnum leaf is full of insects, aphids in this case. For solution, see page 267.

Leaf-spot (from page 59). Dark orange spots cover the distorted foliage of this heavenly bamboo (*Nandina*). For solution, see page 244.

Psyllids (from page 58). The leaf edges on this boxwood (*Buxus*) are cupped up-ward, the classic symptom of psyllids. For solution, see page 267.

Leafrollers (from page 58). A caterpillar rolled this rose (*Rosa*) leaf into a cylinder and sewed it together with silk. For solution, see page 267, 282.

MITES

Mites (from page 60). An infestation of mites has caused the new growing tips of this yew (*Taxus*) to become stunted, discolored, and distorted. For solution, see page 288.

VIRUSES

Virus (from page 60). This distorted and extremely stunted apple (*Malus*) leaf is not cupped upward. As a result you can deduce that a virus infection has invaded the tree. Though the tree will probably not die, it will never be vigorous, and the fruit, as well as the leaves, may be damaged. For solution, see page 309.

Problems on flowers, flower buds, and edible flowers

Have you checked the flow charts before consulting these photographs? Symptoms can look alike but have vastly different causes. The flow charts help you eliminate other possible, but incorrect, diagnoses.

The flower is discolored

For diagnosis, turn to the flow charts beginning on page 66.

GROWING CONDITIONS

Sunscald (from page 67). The pale discoloration on the petal tips of this cyclamen are a form of sunburn. For solution, see page 229.

Insufficient water (from page 70). The large brown blotches on this rhododendron may prompt you to take a closer look and discover it has not received adequate water. For solution, see page 231.

Pesticide or herbicide damage (from page 71). Brown streaks and mottles on this Queen Anne's lace (*Daucus carota*) indicate chemical damage. For solution, see page 226.

Pesticide or herbicide damage (from page 68). The brown spots on this rhododendron remain the same size, so you can safely conclude that a harmful chemical damaged the flower. For solution, see page 226.

Frost damage (from page 70). Following a sudden cold snap, this rose (*Rosa*) began to turn brown. For solution, see page 232.

Botrytis aka **gray mold** (from page 67). The grayish-white spots on this pansy (*Viola*) are translucent and not powdery, a sure sign of this common fungus. For solution, see page 244.

Botrytis aka **gray mold** (from page 69). Brown moldy blotches grew on this geranium (*Pelargonium*) flower. Then it fell off the plant. Both symptoms point to botrytis. For solution, see page 244.

Old age (from page 70). The first flowers to open on this camellia have turned brown, while the most recent blossoms are fresh. Conclusion? The flowers have succumbed to old age, but the plant itself has not. For solution, see page 222.

Powdery mildew (from page 67). The grayish-white spots on this clematis are opaque and powdery. You guessed it, your plant has a common fungus infection. For solution, see page 244.

Anthracnose (from page 68). Small purple spots on this dogwood (*Cornus*) indicate this fungal disease. For solution, see page 244.

The flower is discolored, FUNGI [*continued*]

Camellia flower blight (from page 69). Grayish-brown mold never grows on the brown spots on this camellia flower; however, the spots do get larger as the fungus grows. For solution, see page 244.

Thrips (from page 71). The silvery-white streaks and mottles on this gladiolus are dead giveaways that thrips thrive here. For solution, see page 267.

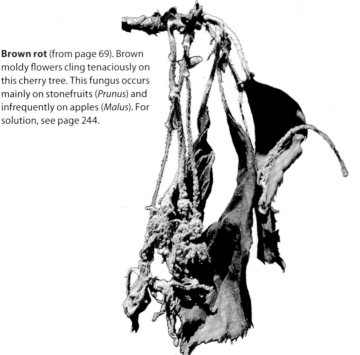

Brown rot (from page 69). Brown moldy flowers cling tenaciously on this cherry tree. This fungus occurs mainly on stonefruits (*Prunus*) and infrequently on apples (*Malus*). For solution, see page 244.

Problems on flowers, flower buds, and edible flowers

The flower has holes or chewed edges, or you see pests

For diagnosis, turn to the flow charts beginning on page 72.

INSECTS

Raspberry fruitworms (from page 75). These adults, here munching their way through the pollen of a thimbleberry (*Rubus*), cause less damage than their larvae, so it is a good idea to treat the problem before the beetles lay too many eggs. For solution, see page 267.

Weevils, curculios (from page 76). These pests have long snouts and feed on all flower parts. This rose curculio, currently feeding on the pollen of a rose (*Rosa*), has left evidence of its earlier meal of petals. For solution, see page 267.

Aphids (from page 74). Small, pear-shaped pests cluster on one side of this rose (*Rosa*) bud. With careful examination, you discover two tubes on the pests' rear ends. For solution, see page 267.

Squash bugs (from page 75). Squash bugs feeding on this zucchini (*Cucurbita pepo*) left yellow marks on the leaves. For solution, see page 267.

Ants (from page 76). Though ants rarely damage flowers, they may bring aphids, which do. Here they feed on sugar from an apple (*Malus*). For solution, see page 267.

Grasshoppers (from page 76). With their huge hind legs and skill at leaping, grasshoppers are pretty easy to spot. Here they're enjoying a black-eyed Susan (*Rudbeckia*). For solution, see page 267.

The flower has holes or chewed edges, or you see pests, INSECTS [*continued*]

Spittlebugs (from page 74). A yarrow (*Achillea*) sports a glob of foamy spittle; there, a small soft-bodied bug hides, sucking sap from the plant's veins. For solution, see page 267.

Spittlebugs (from page 75). The adult spittlebug sucks plant juice from the leaves and stems of many plants. For solution, see page 267.

Earwigs (from page 76). An earwig's distinctive features are the pincers on its rear end. They feed at night and love the tenderest part of flower petals. This one hides during the day on a milkweed (*Asclepias*). For solution, see page 267.

Earwigs (from page 72). Holes in the middle of the tender petals of this petunia mean earwigs feed in your garden under cover of night. For solution, see page 267.

Caterpillars (from page 74). The green wormy creature on the front of this rose (*Rosa*) bud disguises itself as a sepal. Examine your plants carefully to look for such camouflaged invaders. For solution, see page 267.

Caterpillars (from page 73). You've seen the holes in the flowers, but find no caterpillars. Instead you see these little black pellets on the leaves of your rose (*Rosa*). For solution, see page 267.

Blister beetles (from page 75). These pests secrete a poisonous chemical that can cause blisters on skin and poison animals that consume them in feed. This one sits on an apple (*Malus*) blossom. For solution, see page 267.

Blister beetles (from page 75). Some of the more than 2,500 species of blister beetles are beneficial because they eat grasshopper eggs. This one treads lightly on thimble-berry (*Rubus*). For solution, see page 267.

Japanese beetles (from page 75). In the United States, these pests occur only east of the Mississippi River, consuming the flowers and leaves of over 200 different kinds of plants, including those of strawberries (*Fragaria*), as here. For solution, see page 267.

Spotted cucumber beetles (from page 75). These beetles eat the leaves and flowers of plants in the squash family (Cucurbitaceae), as well as some other vegetables. For solution, see page 267.

Slugs or snails (from page 72). The telltale slime trail on this barberry (*Berberis*) tells you that slugs or snails are lurking nearby. For solution, see page 325.

Slugs or snails (from page 75). After seeing the slime trail on this barberry (*Berberis*), you look around until you spot this snail. Although beautiful, it will harm the flowers. For solution, see page 325.

Deer (from page 73). There is no caterpillar poop, and the one remaining petal on this rockrose (*Cistus*) has been bitten in half, a calling card from a deer. For solution, see page 329.

Problems on flowers, flower buds, and edible flowers

The flower is distorted or stunted

For diagnosis, turn to the flow charts beginning on page 77.

For diagnosis, turn to the flow charts beginning on page 77.

GROWING CONDITIONS

Proliferation (from page 79). A tiny flower bud grows in the center of a calendula blossom, indicating something has disturbed normal development of the flower. For solution, see page 232.

Lack of disbudding (from page 81). Plants use a lot of energy to create flowers. As a result, if you leave all the buds on a plant, the flowers will frequently be too small, as on this floribunda rose (*Rosa*). For solution, see page 227.

Herbicide damage (from page 80). The distorted petals and small size of this rose (*Rosa*) clearly illustrate the signs of an unfortunate encounter with an herbicide. For solution, see page 226.

Herbicide damage (from page 79). Dry brown spots on this deformed rhododendron point to an accidental spraying with an herbicide. For solution, see page 226.

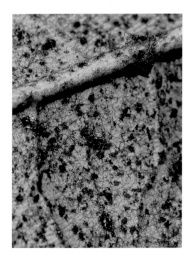

Flower thrips (from page 78). This deformed rose (*Rosa*) flower has turned brown, and tiny insects fall out when you shake it over a white piece of paper. Thrips, which are extremely small but long and narrow, like a tiny rod, live inside the flower. For solution, see page 267.

Lace bugs (from page 80). The stunted flower on this rhododendron alerts you to a problem. Turning the leaf over you find these shiny black and brown dots, a distinctive sign of these all too common pests. For solution, see page 267.

Aphids (from page 79). You pick apart this stunted and deformed viburnum flower and discover pear-shaped insects inside. You recognize aphids because of the two tubes on their rear ends. For solution, see page 267.

Problems on flowers, flower buds, and edible flowers

The flower is rotten, wilted, or decayed

For diagnosis, turn to the flow charts beginning on page 82.

For diagnosis, turn to the flow charts beginning on page 82.

GROWING CONDITIONS

Balling (from page 83). Roses (*Rosa*) with many petals may fail to open properly in humid weather. The outer petals become limp and turn brown, and the bud persists on the plant. For solution, see page 232.

Ethylene (from page 85). If your moth orchids (*Phalaenopsis*) are indoors, they may be exposed to ethylene gas generated by ripening fruit or natural gas. This growth regulator causes orchid flowers, but not plants, to wilt. For solution, see page 222.

Insufficient water (from page 85). Wilting of the tender new growth and flower buds frequently signals water stress, as on this rose (*Rosa*). For solution, see page 231.

Pollination (from page 85). Only one flower on this moth orchid (*Phalaenopsis*), on the left, has wilted; the rest are fine. Once pollination has occurred orchid flowers always wilt. For solution, see page 222.

Rose midge (from page 84). This rose (*Rosa*) bud turned black at the base, so you take a closer look and find small white maggots (midge larvae) feeding inside. For solution, see page 267.

Camellia flower blight (from page 82). Your camellia flower turns brown, rots, and falls from the plant. This fungal disease attacks only camellias. For solution, see page 244.

Brown rot (from page 83). Creamy brown mold covers these cherry blossoms. This serious fungal disease occurs mainly on stonefruits (*Prunus*) and infrequently on apples (*Malus*). For solution, see page 244.

Botrytis aka **gray mold** (from page 83). Brownish-gray mold covering the petals of this rose (*Rosa*) signals the presence of this common fungal infection. For solution, see page 244.

Fire blight (from page 84). Dry crispy flowers and buds hang onto this cherry (*Prunus avium*) after turning black. Entire branches may be affected and eventually kill the tree. This bacteria attacks only members of the rose family, such as pears (*Pyrus*), apples (*Malus*), quince (*Cydonia*), mountain ash (*Sorbus*), hawthorn (*Crataegus*), pyracantha, cotoneaster, and the stonefruits. For solution, see page 301, 306.

Problems on flowers, flower buds, and edible flowers

The plant has flowered poorly, has failed to flower, or has dropped buds

For diagnosis, turn to the flow charts beginning on page 86.

GROWING CONDITIONS

Transplant shock (from page 86). This recently transplanted magnolia did not flower this year but will once it is established in its new location. For solution, see page 231.

Poor pruning timing (from page 89). Knowing when to prune which plant, such as this clematis, may make all the difference to the success or failure of floral display. Prune at the wrong time of year, and you might accidentally remove all the developing flower buds. For solution, see page 227.

Bolting (from page 88). This ornamental cabbage (*Brassica oleracea*) has flowered, or bolted, sooner than expected because environmental conditions (temperature and daylength) triggered the flowering response. For solution, see page 233.

Poor planting timing (from page 89). Many of our favorite bulbs, like this daffodil (*Narcissus*), require six weeks of cold in order to grow roots and develop properly. Without a cold treatment, they will not flower. For solution, see page 233.

Lack of deadheading (from page 88). When a plant such as this rhododendron flowers in alternate years, it does so because it puts so much energy into making seeds that it takes a year to recover. For solution, see page 227.

The plant has flowered poorly, has failed to flower, or has dropped buds,
GROWING CONDITIONS [*continued*]

Poor nutrition (from page 87). Yellowing between the veins in the leaves and poor flowering of this rhododendron indicate a serious lack of mineral nutrients in the soil. For solution, see page 238.

Poor nutrition (from page 90). Leaves yellowing between the veins on this mock orange (*Philadelphus*) tell you the plant is malnourished and does not have the strength to flower. For solution, see page 238.

Excess nitrogen (from page 86). An overgenerous application of a high-nitrogen fertilizer caused these strawberries (*Fragaria*) to grow lush foliage but very few flowers or fruit. For solution, see page 238.

Excess nitrogen (from page 90). Too much fertilizer or high-nitrogen fertilizer stimulates abundant vegetative growth, as of these tomatoes (*Lycopersicon esculentum*), at the expense of flowering. For solution, see page 238.

Lack of winter chill (from page 90). Many fruit trees, such as this plum (*Prunus*), require a specific amount of winter cold in order to flower. This lack of flowering may also happen if you live in a warm climate and do not have a suitable cultivar. For solution, see page 233.

Wrong temperature regime (from page 88). If a plant's temperature needs have not been met, as for this cymbidium orchid, it can appear healthy but never flower abundantly. For solution, see page 233.

Frost damage (from page 92). A sudden freeze caused this rhododendron flower bud to abort. For solution, see page 232.

Too much shade (from page 90). If your rosemary (*Rosmarinus*) is thin, weak, and spindly, like this one, it needs more sunlight. For solution, see page 229.

Too much shade (from page 87). This lithodora remains tall and spindly with pale green leaves and very few flowers because it was planted in the shade of dense conifers. For solution, see page 229.

The plant has flowered poorly, has failed to flower, or has dropped buds,
GROWING CONDITIONS [*continued*]

Too much shade (from page 91). If your plant needs full sun, like these tomatoes (*Lycopersicon esculentum*), but the location is too shady, your plant may grow weak and spindly and drop its flower buds. For solution, see page 229.

Excess water (from page 91). Leaves of this mock orange (*Philadelphus*) turn yellow because the soil is saturated with water. Flowers and buds fall off the plant. For solution, see page 232.

Insufficient water (from page 91). These dry, shriveled apple (*Malus*) blossoms died from severe drought. For solution, see page 231.

Insufficient water (from page 91). Dried, shriveled flower buds are a clue that your plant is unable to get enough water quickly enough to meet its needs. For solution, see page 231.

Insufficient water (from page 87). The leaves of this bird of paradise (*Strelitzia nicolai*) turned brown at the tips, and the plant flowered poorly. This is the result when plants cannot obtain enough water. For solution, see page 231.

Lack of water (from page 90). Leaves turning brown at the tips or edges, as on this rose (*Rosa*), indicate an inability to obtain adequate water, a condition that can seriously impact flowering performance and even the life of the plant. For solution, see page 231.

INSECTS

Plum curculios (from page 92). Flower buds of fruit trees that are nicked, gouged, or eaten before falling to the ground indicate plum curculios are attacking your trees. For solution, see page 267.

Rose curculios (from page 92). Flower buds of roses (*Rosa*) riddled with holes by rose curculios will eventually turn brown and drop to the ground. For solution, see page 267.

Strawberry bud weevil (from page 92). Strawberry (*Fragaria*) or bramble (*Rubus*) flowers that turn brown and fall may have a small hole in the side, indicating a strawberry bud weevil has laid an egg inside the bud. For solution, see page 267.

Problems on fruits and vegetables

Have you checked the flow charts before consulting these photographs? Symptoms can look alike but have vastly different causes. The flow charts help you eliminate other possible, but incorrect, diagnoses.

The whole fruit is discolored

For diagnosis, turn to the flow charts beginning on page 97.

GROWING CONDITIONS

Greenback (from page 97). These tomatoes failed to ripen and remained green at stem end. Cool temperatures caused this condition, known as greenback. For solution, see page 232.

Citrus freeze damage (from page 98). Brown spots on this orange indicate that a cold snap caught the grower by surprise. The flesh of the orange is dry and pulpy. For solution, see page 232.

Problems on fruits and vegetables

The fruit has spots of any size

For diagnosis, turn to the flow charts beginning on page 99.

GROWING CONDITIONS

Sunscald (from page 103). Tomatoes (*Lycopersicon esculentum*), exposed to harsh sunlight, have smooth white patches that become dry and papery. For solution, see page 229.

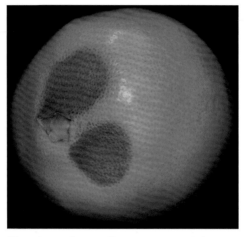

Citrus freeze damage (from page 107). Light brown spots, the color of a brown paper bag, dot these mature citrus. It just got too cold for these oranges. For solution, see page 232.

Russeting (from page 106). Corky spots spread over the surface of this apple (*Malus*). The fruit stayed wet for too long. For solution, see page 224.

Russeting (from page 106). This tomato (*Lycopersicon esculentum*) also suffers from corky spots spreading across its surface; it too was wet for too long. For solution, see page 224.

The fruit has spots of any size,
GROWING CONDITIONS [*continued*]

Blossom end rot (from page 104). A large brown spot encircles the blossom end of a tomato (*Lycopersicon esculentum*). Irregular watering is part of the problem here. For solution, see page 238.

Botrytis aka **gray mold** (from page 103). This blackberry (*Rubus*) had soft watery spots that later developed the gray mold you see here. For solution, see page 244.

Brown rot (from page 108). The large, brown, moldy area under the skin of this peach (*Prunus persica*) is firm and dry, indicating this common fungus. For solution, see page 244.

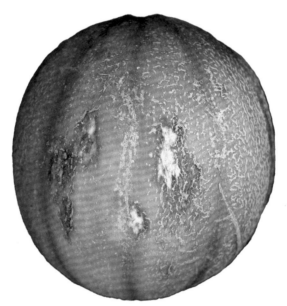

White mold (from page 103). The soft watery spots on this melon (*Cucumis*) later erupted with white mold. For solution, see page 244, 252.

Black rot (from page 105). Spots on these grapes (*Vitis*) start out dark brown, later becoming large black blotches that rot the fruit. For solution, see page 244.

Scab (from page 106). This apple (*Malus*) has large spots of corky tissue on the surface. Scab is a common fungus infection. For solution, see page 244.

Fly speck (from page 105). Small, shiny spots cluster into a patch on the surface of this apple (*Malus*). The clustering is a distinct feature of this fungal disease. For solution, see page 244.

Late blight (from page 108). The large brown areas under the skin of this tomato (*Lycopersicon esculentum*) are soft and wet, telltale signs of this fungal disease. For solution, see page 244.

INSECTS

Tarnished plant bugs (from page 106). As this peach (*Prunus persica*) matures, a "cat face" distortion takes place around the corky tissue these insect pests caused. For solution, see page 267.

MITES

Redberry mites (from page 101). A patch of red unripened tissue on an otherwise ripe blackberry (*Rubus*) is a sure sign of these tiny spider relatives. For solution, see page 295.

Cedar-apple rust (from page 101). Spots on this apple (*Malus*) leaf start out yellow but later become orange. The fruit nearby suffers from the same fungus. For solution, see page 244.

BACTERIA

Bacterial spots (from page 105). The spots on this peach (*Prunus persica*) are very small, raised, black bumps—typical symptoms of a bacterial infection. For solution, see page 301.

Bacterial blight (from page 108). Walnuts (*Juglans*) illustrate a sure sign of bacteria—translucent spots that become dry, brown patches. For solution, see page 301.

VIRUSES

Bacterial leaf-spot (from page 109). Spots surrounded by yellow haloes on this tomato point to a bacterial leaf-spot infection. For solution, see page 301.

Bacterial blight (from page 108). Translucent spots that become dry, brown patches on this cucumber (*Cucumis sativus*) are classic symptoms of a bacterial infection. For solution, see page 301.

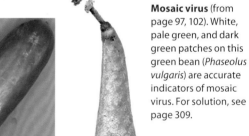

Mosaic virus (from page 97, 102). White, pale green, and dark green patches on this green bean (*Phaseolus vulgaris*) are accurate indicators of mosaic virus. For solution, see page 309.

Problems on fruits and vegetables

The fruit has holes or is missing, partly eaten, or cracked

For diagnosis, turn to the flow charts beginning on page 110.

GROWING CONDITIONS

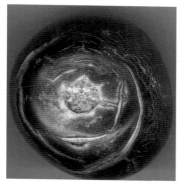

Growth cracks (from page 114). The scabbed-over, dry cracks that encircle the stem end of this tomato are simply growth cracks. For solution, see page 231.

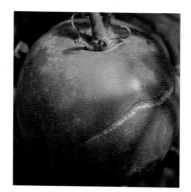

Excess water (from page 114). The crack on this tomato is moist, indicating that the plant got too much water while the fruit was growing. For solution, see page 232.

FUNGI

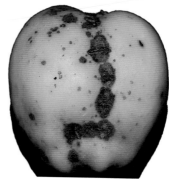

Scab (from page 144). The crack on this apple is filled with brown corky tissue, and it runs lengthwise along the fruit. Both are sure signs of this fungus infection. For solution, see page 244.

INSECTS

Plum curculios (from page 110). The shallow, crescent-shaped hole in this apple (*Malus*) is a sign of this tiny insect. For solution, see page 267.

Tomato fruitworm (from page 111). If you find a wormy-looking creature inside the fruit of a non-woody plant, such as this tomato (*Lycopersicon esculentum*), suspect a fruitworm. For solution, see page 267, 282.

Wasps, yellowjackets (from page 113). Wasps and yellowjackets are often drawn to the sweet flesh of apples (*Malus*). For solution, see page 267.

The fruit has holes or is missing, partly eaten, or cracked, INSECTS [*continued*]

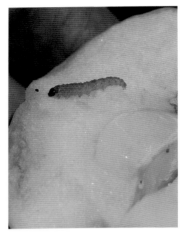

Corn earworm (from page 111). A common pest dwells inside the fruit of a non-woody plant, in this case corn (*Zea mays*). For solution, see page 267, 282.

Codling moth larvae (from page 112). Dry, sawdust-like material fills the ugly hole on this apple (*Malus*). The hole is surrounded by dry, papery, black or brown tissue. For solution, see page 282.

Codling moth larvae (from page 112). A codling moth larva lurks inside this apple (*Malus*). For solution, see page 282.

OTHER PESTS

Birds (from page 113). Birds pecked pointy holes in the flesh of this apple (*Malus*), no doubt relishing the sweet flavor as much as we do. For solution, see page 328.

Rodents (from page 113). This apple (*Malus*) has been eaten by rodents; parallel grooves mark the spot. For solution, see page 329.

Slugs or snails (from page 110). Slime trails and holes larger than 1/4 inch (6 mm) in diameter tell you that slugs or snails are foraging at night. For solution, see page 325.

Slugs or snails (from page 110). This melon (*Cucumis*) is being hammered by slugs or snails in the dark of night. For solution, see page 325.

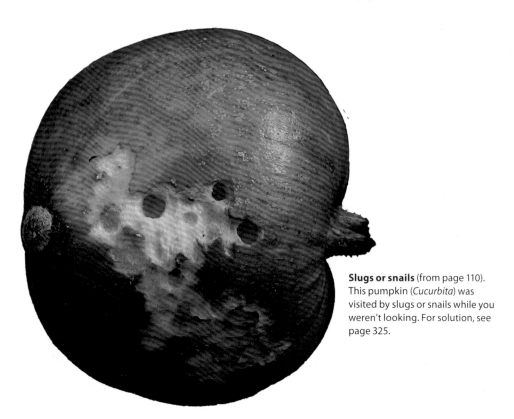

Slugs or snails (from page 110). This pumpkin (*Cucurbita*) was visited by slugs or snails while you weren't looking. For solution, see page 325.

Problems on fruits and vegetables

The fruit is distorted, stunted, or shriveled

For diagnosis, turn to the flow charts beginning on page 115.

For diagnosis, turn to the flow charts beginning on page 115.

GROWING CONDITIONS

Too much fruit (from page 119). There is so much fruit on this very healthy apple (*Malus*) tree that the fruit is stunted. For solution, see page 227.

Environmental stress (from page 119). These tomatoes (*Lycopersicon esculentum*), which are under stress for a variety of reasons, have very few fruits. For solution, see page 224.

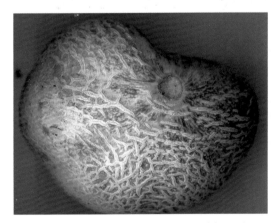

Poor pollination (from page 117). One side of this melon (*Cucumis*) is stunted and misshapen, while the other end appears normal. Not enough seeds developed because of inadequate pollination. For solution, see page 227.

Insufficient nutrients (from page 119). There are very few fruits on this apple (*Malus*) tree because it did not receive enough nutrition. The apples also don't taste very good. For solution, see page 238.

Scab (from page 116). This hideous apple (*Malus*) has no insect larva inside but does have corky scabs on its surface. A common fungus has infected it. For solution, see page 244.

Cedar-apple rust (from page 117). The fruit of an apple (*Malus*) has pale yellow spots that enlarge and turn orange. The leaves nearby show the same symptoms. For solution, see page 244.

Anthracnose (from page 120). Anthracnose, another fungus infection, affects this pepper (*Capsicum*) the way brown rot does some other fruit. The fruit shrivels, dries out, and turns black but falls from the plant. For solution, see page 244.

Anthracnose (from page 120). An immature melon (*Cucumis*) also suffers from anthracnose. For solution, see page 244.

Brown rot (from page 120). These two peaches (*Prunus persica*) have dried out and turned black but remain on the tree—the typical course for this fungus. For solution, see page 244.

Rosy apple aphids (from page 116). This mature apple (*Malus*) is distorted and pinched in at the blossom end; a certain type of aphid is no doubt present. For solution, see page 267.

Fruit flies (from page 118). This distorted walnut (*Juglans*) is full of maggots (but no grubs). The walnut ripens normally, however, masking this unpleasant surprise. For solution, see page 267, 282.

BACTERIA

Cucurbit bacterial wilt (from page 120). This poor, shriveled cucumber (*Cucumis sativus*) fell from the plant. If you cut the stem, the sap is milky and sticky. For solution, see page 306.

Problems on fruits and vegetables

The fruit is mushy, wormy, moldy, or rotten

For diagnosis, turn to the flow charts beginning on page 121.

FUNGI

Black rot (from page 121). This apple (*Malus*) displays all the symptoms of black rot: brown rotten areas that slowly turn black. For solution, see page 244.

Black rot (from page 121). These grapes (*Vitis*) suffer the same fate as the apple (*Malus*). Insects are not responsible for this rotten fruit. For solution, see page 244.

Botrytis aka **gray mold** (from page 123). Mold on this raspberry (*Rubus idaeus*) is grayish brown. Yes, the berry has botrytis. For solution, see page 244.

Brown rot (from page 122). This pair of mummified plums (*Prunus*) hangs on to the tree through the winter. For solution, see page 244.

Brown rot (from page 123). The cream color of the mold growing on this peach (*Prunus persica*) indicates brown rot. For solution, see page 244.

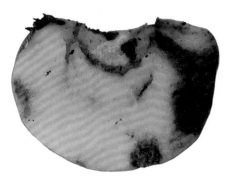

Apple maggot (from page 125). This mature apple (*Malus*) is mushy, and a maggot lives inside. For solution, see page 267, 282.

Codling moth larvae (from page 124). A black decayed area in the center of this apple (*Malus*) indicates the presence of these caterpillars. Note the tunnel leading to the surface. For solution, see page 282.

Bacterial leaf-spot (from page 122). This plum (*Prunus*) is moist and soft, symptoms of bacterial leaf-spot infection. For solution, see page 301.

European apple sawfly (from page 125). The shriveled, immature apple (*Malus*) fruitlet, on the left, has maggots inside and will fall from the tree. For solution, see page 282.

Bacterial leaf-spot (from page 122). Another rotten tomato, with moist, soft areas that are sunken pits with yellow haloes. For solution, see page 301.

Problems on stems, trunks, and branches

Have you checked the flow charts before consulting these photographs? Symptoms can look alike but have vastly different causes. The flow charts help you eliminate other possible, but incorrect, diagnoses.

The whole stem is discolored, dying, or dead

For diagnosis, turn to the flow charts beginning on page 130.

Rose canker and dieback (from page 132). A canker has completely encircled the stem of this rose (*Rosa*). For solution, see page 244.

FUNGI

Fusarium wilt (from page 131). The stems on only one side of this juniper (*Juniperus*) are turning yellow. These stems will drop off as this fungus infection progresses. For solution, see page 244.

Botrytis aka **gray mold** (from page 132). Fluffy gray mold grows on this slender rose (*Rosa*) twig, which is afflicted with botrytis. For solution, see page 244.

389

The whole stem is discolored, dying, or dead, FUNGI [*continued*]

Coral spot (from page 132). Raised, hard, red-orange balls the size of pinheads erupt from a canker on this apple (*Malus*) tree. For solution, see page 244.

Brown rot (from page 132). Sticky gum oozes from the twig at the base of these dead, skeletonized leaves on a purple-leaf plum (*Prunus cerasifera*). For solution, see page 244.

Black knot (from page 135). A rough, long, tumor-like growth encases the stem of a cherry (*Prunus avium*) tree. This fungus is often easy to spot. For solution, see page 244.

Papery bark (from page 133). The bark on this apple (*Malus*) peels off in papery strips and flakes. At least for apple (*Malus*) and pear (*Pyrus*) trees, an air-borne fungus (*Trametes versicolor*) is to blame. For solution, see page 244.

Raspberry cane borer (from page 131). Looking closely at the cane of this raspberry (*Rubus idaeus*), you find two rows of punctures, classic signs of cane borers. For solution, see page 282.

Peachtwig borer (from page 131). Investigating the cause of these weird leaves on your peach (*Prunus persica*), you find a caterpillar inside the stem. For solution, see page 282.

Lecanium scale (from page 135). The stems on this zelkova are encrusted with small, hard bumps—lecanium scale. For solution, see page 267.

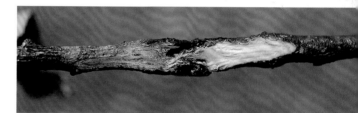

Peachtwig borer (from page 134). If you slit open this peach (*Prunus persica*) stem when you see a hole, you will find a wormy larva inside. For solution, see page 282.

Crown gall (from page 135). Rough, globular, tumor-like growths rupture the stem at the base of this rose (*Rosa*). For solution, see page 305.

Fire blight (from page 132). The new shoots on this pear (*Pyrus*) tree wilt, blacken, and die. Fire blight is an all too common bacterial infection. For solution, see page 301.

OTHER PESTS

Lawnmowers (from page 133). Patches of missing bark on the trunk of this elm (*Ulmus*) tell the story of an unfortunate encounter with a lawnmower. For solution, see page 225, 331.

Problems on stems, trunks, and branches

The stem has spots of any size

For diagnosis, turn to the flow charts beginning on page 136.

For diagnosis, turn to the flow charts beginning on page 136.

FUNGI

Brown rot (from page 137). A canker encircles the twig of this cherry (*Prunus avium*) just below the dying leaves, a symptom of brown rot. For solution, see page 244.

Phytophthora root rot, crown rot (from page 142). Cinnamon-brown, rotten areas at the base of this lavender (*Lavandula*) indicates these fungal infections. For solution, see page 252.

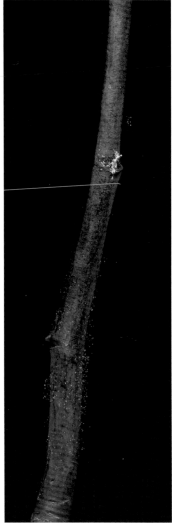

Botrytis aka **gray mold** (from page 142). Fluffy, gray mold grows on the spots on this rose (*Rosa*) twig. For solution, see page 244.

The stem has spots of any size, FUNGI [*continued*]

Rose canker and dieback (from page 138). This piece of rose (*Rosa*) stem has dark brown patches. The leaves above the canker have dried up, turned yellow-brown, and died. For solution, see page 244.

Apple canker, pear canker (from page 139). The stem of this cherry (*Prunus avium*) shows concentric rings of black tissue inside the crack. For solution, see page 245.

Canker (from page 137). Gum oozes from the canker on this peach (*Prunus persica*) stem. For solution, see page 244.

Bacterial blight (from page 137). New shoots on this cherry (*Prunus avium*) wilt, turn brown-black, and die. For solution, see page 301.

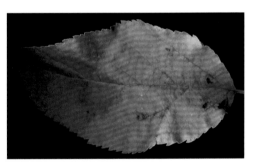

Scab (from page 138). Both the stem and leaves of this apple (*Malus*) tree have olive-brown spots. For solution, see page 244.

Cooley spruce gall adelgid (from page 141). Adelgids produce these pineapple-shaped, brown galls attached to stem of this spruce (*Picea*). For solution, see page 285.

Borers (from page 139). Holes in the bark on this dogwood (*Cornus*) tell you that borers are tunneling under the bark. The tunnels are filled with sawdust. For solution, see page 282.

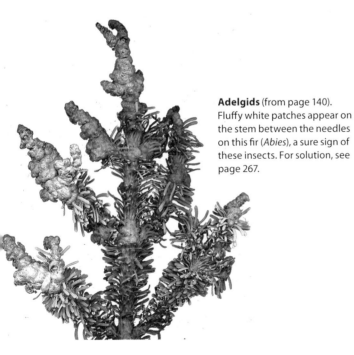

Adelgids (from page 140). Fluffy white patches appear on the stem between the needles on this fir (*Abies*), a sure sign of these insects. For solution, see page 267.

Problems on stems, trunks, and branches

The stem has holes or is chewed, split, cracked, or broken

For diagnosis, turn to the flow charts beginning on page 143.

For diagnosis, turn to the flow charts beginning on page 143.

GROWING CONDITIONS

Heavy fruit crop (from page 146). Branches that break where they join the main trunk indicate that there is too much fruit on this peach (*Prunus persica*) tree. For solution, see page 227.

Irregular watering (from page 147). If longitudinal cracks and splits develop during the growing season, as on this plum (*Prunus*), it is a sure sign of irregular watering. For solution, see page 231.

Frost cracks (from page 147). If longitudinal cracks and splits develop during the winter, as on this apple (*Malus*), frost is to blame. Such cracks usually close in summer. For solution, see page 232.

FUNGI

Cankers (from page 146). This canker on a peach (*Prunus persica*) has split and cracked, forming concentric rings of flaky bark. For solution, see page 245.

Bark beetles (from page 145). If you peel away the bark on this dead Douglas fir (*Pseudotsuga menziesii*), you would find tunnels radiating out from a central line running through the trunk. For solution, see page 282.

Borers (from page 144). Sawdust or what looks like sawdust spills from the holes on the stems of this viburnum. You can bet borers are inside. For solution, see page 282.

Asparagus beetle (from page 143). When patches of surface tissue go missing from an asparagus, you can be sure that beetles are foraging. For solution, see page 267.

Woodpeckers (from page 144). Holes larger than 1 inch (2.5 cm) in diameter on this Douglas fir (*Pseudotsuga menziesii*) tell you that woodpeckers seek insect larvae here. For solution, see page 328.

Sapsuckers (from page 145). A grid pattern of parallel rows of shallow holes indicate sapsuckers are looking for the sap of this hemlock (*Tsuga*). For solution, see page 328.

Lawnmowers (from page 143). An old injury to the trunk of this tree tells you a lawnmower came too close to this elm (*Ulmus*). For solution, see page 225, 331.

Rodents (from page 143). Investigating the cause of missing tissue from this beet (*Beta*) stem, you find tooth marks. For solution, see page 329.

Problems on stems, trunks, and branches

The stem is distorted or stunted

For diagnosis, turn to the flow charts beginning on page 148.

GROWING CONDITIONS

Herbicide damage (from page 149). These dense clusters of stunted twigs persist for only a season or two on a rose (*Rosa*). For solution, see page 226.

Herbicide damage (from page 149). Careless use of an herbicide has caused the stem of this lupine (*Lupinus*) to spiral, twist, and loop crazily. For solution, see page 226.

INSECTS

Cooley spruce gall adelgid (from page 148). The toxic saliva of adelgids is behind the dry, brown pineapple-shaped galls on the branches of this spruce (*Picea*). For solution, see page 285.

VIRUSES

Witches' broom (from page 149). Closely packed clusters of stunted twigs persist year after year on a cherry (*Prunus avium*) tree. For solution, see page 309.

Fasciation (from page 148). Wide, flat, ribbon-like stems on this cotoneaster are caused by a virus. For solution, see page 306.

Problems on stems, trunks, and branches

The stem is moldy, mushy, rotten, or slimy

For diagnosis, turn to the flow charts beginning on page 151.

For diagnosis, turn to the flow charts beginning on page 151.

FUNGI

Heart rot (from page 152). Shelf-like growths emerge from the trunk of this beech (*Fagus*), telling you that its heart is rotting. For solution, see page 257.

Crown rot (from page 151). Branches of this maple (*Acer*) are dying one by one, which indicates that the base of the trunk, as well as the roots, are brown and rotten. For solution, see page 252.

BACTERIA

Stem rot (from page 151). Noticing that the stem of this watermelon (*Citrullus*) is slimy and decayed, you find tiny, black pellets at the base of the plant. For solution, see page 252.

Slime flux (from page 152). The fluid oozing from the side of this oak (*Quercus*) tree trunk smells really bad, a telltale symptom of a bacterial infection. For solution, see page 305, 306.

Problems on stems, trunks, and branches

The stem has lumps or foreign growths, or you see pests

For diagnosis, turn to the flow charts beginning on page 153.

For diagnosis, turn to the flow charts beginning on page 153.

FUNGI

Black knot (from page 154). Black, cylindrical, corky growths, to 12 inches (30 cm) long and 1 inch (2.5 cm) in diameter, tell you this fungus has infected your cherry (*Prunus avium*). For solution, see page 244.

Bracket fungus (from page 157). Shelf-like organisms grow from the trunk of this maple (*Acer*). For solution, see page 257.

INSECTS

San Jose scale, oyster scale, juniper scale (from page 158). Hard, circular or oval bumps encrust the stem on a ficus. For solution, see page 267.

Aphids (from page 158). Small, pear-shaped insects with two tubes on their rear ends cluster on the stem of this rose (*Rosa*). You know you have aphids. For solution, see page 267.

Lecanium scale (from page 158). You see brown lumps about ¼ inch (6 mm) in diameter clustered on the stem and conclude that scale infects this zelkova. For solution, see page 267.

Mossyrose gall (from page 157). Insects inhabit the soft, mossy, green ball on this rose (*Rosa*). For solution, see page 285.

Adelgids (from page 158). White, fluffy wax that looks like cotton or mold covers adelgids on this hemlock (*Tsuga*). For solution, see page 267.

Spittlebugs (from page 155). Globs of frothy white spittle stuck to the stems mean that spittlebugs live on this achillea. For solution, see page 267.

OTHER PESTS

Leafy mistletoe (from page 156). Green, leafy, branched plants grow directly out of the stems of an oak (*Quercus*). For solution, see page 331.

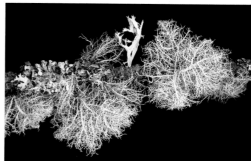

Lichens (from page 156). Lichens (as these growing on an apple, *Malus*) are harmless organisms that usually indicate good air quality. They are green, gray, brown, orange, or chartreuse organisms that are dry and firm or leafy.

BACTERIA

Aerial crown gall (from page 154). Rough, rounded growths burst from the stem of this plum (*Prunus*), rupturing it. For solution, see page 305.

Problems on roots, bulbs, and root vegetables

Have you checked the flow charts before consulting these photographs? Symptoms can look alike but have vastly different causes. The flow charts help you eliminate other possible, but incorrect, diagnoses.

The whole root is discolored

For diagnosis, turn to the flow charts beginning on page 164.

GROWING CONDITIONS

FUNGI

BACTERIA

Heat injury (from page 164). Onion (*Allium cepa*) bulbs turn gray when subjected to too much heat while still in the ground. For solution, see page 233.

Root rot (from page 164). The brown discoloration and the type of root that it is (a fibrous feeder root, not a fleshy storage organ) indicate that a fungus infects this gardenia root. For solution, see page 252.

Potato bacterial ring rot (from page 165). The potato (*Solanum tuberosum*) is a large fleshy storage organ, and it begins to turn brown. These two clues tell you that a bacteria infects the potato. For solution, see page 305.

Problems on roots, bulbs, and root vegetables

The root has discolored areas of any size

For diagnosis, turn to the flow charts beginning on page 167.

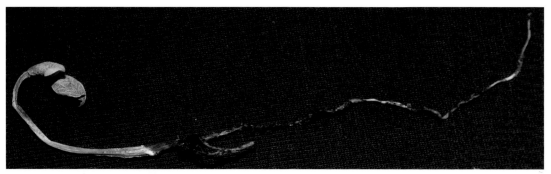

Root rot (from page 168). Because the root of this green bean (*Phaseolus vulgaris*) seedling is a fibrous feeder root with a large, flat, brown discoloration, you know that fungus has infected the seedling. For solution, see page 252.

Scab (from page 171). Raised, round, tough, and corky areas on this potato (*Solanum tuberosum*) give a clear indication of fungus. For solution, see page 252.

Fungus (from page 170). The discolored area on this tulip (*Tulipa*) bulb is sunken, firm, and dry; it is also brown-black (not purplish). All symptoms point to fungus. For solution, see page 258.

Bulb rot (from page 172). Blue-green mold grows on sunken, brown areas on a daffodil (*Narcissus*) bulb. For solution, see page 252.

The root has discolored areas of any size, FUNGI [*continued*]

Late blight of potato (from page 170). Purplish-brown, sunken, firm, and dry discoloration on the left end of this potato (*Solanum tuberosum*) indicates this fungus, which affects only potato. For solution, see page 245.

Late blight of potato (from page 170). A variation of the appearance of this fungus infection still shows the purplish hue of the discoloration. For solution, see page 245.

Bulb blue mold (from page 172). The red-brown lesions on this tulip (*Tulipa*) bulb are moldy. For solution, see page 258.

NEMATODES

BACTERIA

GROWING CONDITIONS

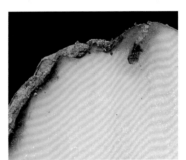

Nematodes (from page 174). If you cut this onion (*Allium cepa*) from side to side (not top to bottom, as here), you would see concentric rings of brown, decaying tissue. For solution, see page 315.

Bacterial ring rot (from page 176). The start of a bacterial infection: yellowish rings begin to develop around brown spots inside this potato (*Solanum tuberosum*). For solution, see page 305.

Exposure to sunlight (from page 169). This carrot (*Daucus*) has a light green discolored area at the top, revealing that the carrot got too much sun. For solution, see page 229.

Problems on roots, bulbs, and root vegetables

The root has holes; is chewed, cracked, or split; is partially or entirely missing; or you see pests

For diagnosis, turn to the flow charts beginning on page 177.

GROWING CONDITIONS	INSECTS

Wireworms (from page 179). This potato (*Solanum tuberosum*) has scab, as evidenced by the corky tissue. But if you look closely you also see holes. Cut it open and you will discover wireworms, long, yellowish-orange or gray larvae. These are grubs that live in tunnels. For solution, see page 284.

Wireworms (from page 179). Long, yellowish-orange or gray grubs live in tunnels inside this carrot (*Daucus*). For solution, see page 284.

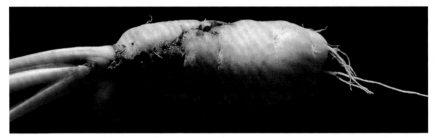

Root maggots (from page 180). The slimy tunnels and channels in this carrot (*Daucus*) reveal the presence of white maggots. The tunnels are scarred with brown lesions. For solution, see page 284.

Irregular watering (from page 177). This carrot (*Daucus*) has split open because sometimes it got too much water and sometimes too little. For solution, see page 231.

The root has holes; is chewed, cracked, or split; is partially or entirely missing; or you see pests, INSECTS [*continued*]

Potato tuberworms (from page 179). The larvae inside the tunnels in this potato (*Solanum tuberosum*) are pinkish. For solution, see page 284.

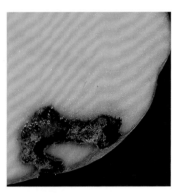

Potato tuberworms (from page 179). Cut open the potato (*Solanum tuberosum*) in the last photograph, and you will discover the pinkish larvae of potato tuberworms. For solution, see page 284.

Slugs or snails (from page 178). The hole on the surface leads to a large chamber within this carrot (*Daucus*). For solution, see page 325.

Rodents (from page 181). The tooth marks of rodents mar the surface of the radish (*Raphanus*). For solution, see page 329.

Rodents (from page 181). This carrot (*Daucus*) is partially eaten and you see tooth marks that are parallel grooves, indications of snacking by a rodent. For solution, see page 329.

Problems on roots, bulbs, and root vegetables

The root is distorted, stunted, or shriveled

For diagnosis, turn to the flow charts beginning on page 183.

For diagnosis, turn to the flow charts beginning on page 183.

GROWING CONDITIONS

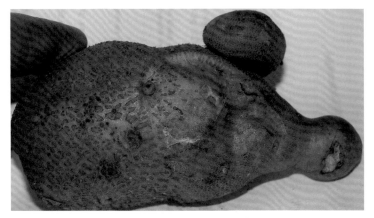

Uneven moisture (from page 185). Grow your own deformed, knobby "Mr. Potato Head" by giving your potatoes too much, then too little water. For solution, see page 231.

Rocky soil (from page 184). This forked carrot (*Daucus*) indicates that the soil it was grown in was too rocky. For solution, see page 238.

Problems on roots, bulbs, and root vegetables

The root is moldy or rotten

For diagnosis, turn to the flow charts beginning on page 188.

FUNGI

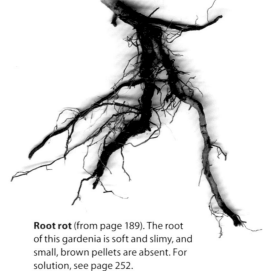

Bulb rot (from page 189). This daffodil (*Narcissus*) bulb is soft and slimy. Investigation turns up no small, brown pellets in the soil. For solution, see page 252.

Root rot (from page 189). The root of this gardenia is soft and slimy, and small, brown pellets are absent. For solution, see page 252.

Bulb blue mold (from page 190). A tulip (*Tulipa*) bulb has sunken, reddish-brown lesions with blue-green mold growing on them. For solution, see page 258.

Crown rot (from page 189). This beet (*Beta*) is soft and crumbly, and small, brown pellets the size of mustard seeds are on the root or in the soil. For solution, see page 252.

BACTERIA

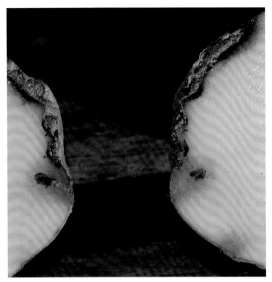

Bacterial ring rot (from page 188). The stem end of this potato (*Solanum tuberosum*) has a rotten black ring inside. For solution, see page 305.

Bacterial rot (from page 189). The stem end of the carrot (*Daucus*) on the upper right is filled with a thick foul-smelling ooze. For solution, see page 305.

MITES

Bulb mites (from page 188). Break open this daffodil (*Narcissus*) bulb to find white mites inside. For solution, see page 296.

Problems on seeds and seedlings

Have you checked the flow charts before consulting these photographs? Symptoms can look alike but have vastly different causes. The flow charts help you eliminate other possible, but incorrect, diagnoses.

Seeds or seedlings are discolored, distorted, or shriveled

For diagnosis, turn to the flow charts beginning on page 196.

For diagnosis, turn to the flow charts beginning on page 196.

BACTERIA

Walnut blight (from page 196). Walnut (*Juglans*) fruits with hard, black, sunken blotches on the exterior have a bacterial infection (*Xanthomonas*). For solution, see page 301.

Walnut blight (from page 196). A close look at a walnut (*Juglans*) fruit with a bacterial infection (*Xanthomonas*). For solution, see page 301.

GROWING CONDITIONS

Manganese deficiency (from page 196). A manganese deficiency causes green bean (*Phaseolus vulgaris*) seeds to have brown spots and hollow spaces in the interior. For solution, see page 238.

INSECTS

Husk flies (from page 196). Walnut (*Juglans*) fruit with soft, rotten, black blotches inside the husk have maggots, the larvae of husk flies. For solution, see page 267, 282.

Seeds or seedlings are discolored, distorted, or shriveled

Seeds or seedlings have holes of any size, or fail to emerge after planting

For diagnosis, turn to the flow charts beginning on page 197.

INSECTS

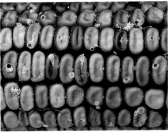

Seed weevils, nut weevils (from page 199). This almond (*Prunus dulcis*) seed has a circular hole bored into it by a seed or nut weevil. For solution, see page 283.

Nut weevils (from page 199). This acorn has a circular exit hole where a nut weevil larva escaped when it reached maturity, having eaten the acorn's contents. For solution, see page 283.

Seed weevils (from page 199). Some kernels on these ears of Indian corn (*Zea mays*) have small circular exit holes left by escaping seed weevils. For solution, see page 283.

FUNGI

Damping off (from page 197). The seeds of this bean (*Phaseolus*) rotted in the soil before they germinated. For solution, see page 252.

Seeds or seedlings are discolored, distorted, or shriveled

Seeds or seedlings are chewed or missing

For diagnosis, turn to the flow charts beginning on page 200.

INSECTS

Corn earworms (from page 202). Yellow-, brown-, or green-striped caterpillars are feeding at the tips of corn (*Zea mays*) ears, inside the husk. For solution, see page 283.

OTHER PESTS

Birds (from page 203). The husk of this ear of corn (*Zea mays*) has been ravaged by birds eating the kernels inside. Corn kernels are missing but none lie on the ground. For solution, see page 328.

Squirrels (from page 203). Shells from a nearby walnut (*Juglans*) tree litter the ground. For solution, see page 329.

Seeds or seedlings are discolored, distorted, or shriveled

Seedlings grow poorly

For diagnosis, turn to the flow charts beginning on page 204.

GROWING CONDITIONS

Excess water (from page 204). The deep roots of this green bean (*Phaseolus vulgaris*) seedling have drowned and are dead. Only the surface, shallow roots remain, and the plant has been infected by a root rot fungus. For solution, see page 232.

Insufficient light (from page 204). The green bean (*Phaseolus vulgaris*) seedling on the right was grown in shade, the one on the left under normal sunlight. Plants are the same age and same cultivar. The shade-grown plant is tall, spindly, and pale green. For solution, see page 229.

Appendix: What's Wrong With My Lawn?

A lawn is a colony of plants, all living in very close proximity. This colony is a monoculture just like an apple orchard or a cornfield. All members of the colony are subject to the same disorders, diseases, and pests, and because the population is so dense, the problem can spread like wildfire. Any problem that arises affects every member, not just an individual.

Oddly enough the first step in lawn care may well be to get rid of it entirely. In the United States the lawn is nearly sacrosanct, and most plant lovers rarely ask themselves, "Do we really need a lawn?" We recommend that you go ahead and ask, and consider this—lawns consume a disproportionate and unacceptable amount of resources. While doing so, they can add an alarming amount of pollution to ground water. In the United States, $8.4 billion a year is spent on lawn care. Drinking water, which is now a diminishing and valuable commodity, is wasted in vast quantities watering the lawn. And untold hours are spent mowing, weeding, fertilizing, and taming the lawn.

If we all tore out our lawns and used the same

The grand sweep of this perfect lawn requires constant maintenance in the form of mowing, thatching, fertilizing, watering, weeding, edging, and pest and disease control.

A well-cared for lawn is lovely, but is safe for children only if we use non-toxic, organic chemicals. Nevertheless, caring for a lawn consumes many resources and lots of time.

money, time, and natural resources on other plants, the result would be fresh, locally grown fruit, vegetables, herbs, and flowers. We would also contribute to cleaner water and air, and more abundant and healthier habitat for birds, butterflies, and bees.

That being said, a well-cared-for lawn is lovely to look at, to walk on, to sit and picnic on. It is a wonderful place for children and pets to play, but only if we do not use unsafe chemicals. While we recommend that you visit a public park to enjoy these benefits, we do offer guidelines for lawn care.

Lawn care guidelines

The key to a healthy lawn is that grass must be in active, vigorous growth throughout the growing season. This means it must be in the right temperature environment and get the right amount of light, water, and nutrients.

▶ **Make the lawn as small as possible.** If you already have a lawn, remove as much as possible by converting it to planting beds. Raised beds combined with sheet mulching is the easiest method to use. First, mow or cut the weeds and grass to ground level. Cover the area with flattened cardboard boxes or several thicknesses of newspaper. Do not allow any sunlight to penetrate through to the ground. Cover the cardboard with a layer of organic compost. Build up the sides of the bed to the height you desire, and fill the space with a good organic soil mix. Plant in the beds and use a good organic mulch 1 to 3 inches (2.5 to 7.5 cm) thick.

▶ **Size and shape the lawn to fit your sprinkler.** Make the lawn the same size and shape as the pattern of water delivered by your sprinkler. This shape is often an oval or circle. Set up your sprinkler and turn it on. Watch to see exactly where the water goes. Cut the lawn back to fit this pattern. You will avoid wasting water (not to mention money) on the sidewalk or street.

▶ **Choose the right grass for your location.** The family of grasses (Poaceae) is often divided into two distinct types: cool season and warm season. Cool season grasses are green in autumn, winter, and spring when temperatures are cool. They turn brown in summer when it gets hot and dry; therefore, to keep them green in summer, you have to water them. Warm season grasses are green in spring, summer, and early autumn when temperatures are warm; they turn brown when it gets cold.

Cool season grasses: Kentucky bluegrass (*Poa pratensis*), red fescue (*Festuca rubra*), tall fescue (*Schedonorus phoenix*), bentgrasses (*Agrostis*), crested wheatgrass (*Agropyron cristatum*), and perennial ryegrass (*Lolium perenne*).

Warm season grasses: Bermuda grass (*Cynodon dactylon*), blue grama (*Bouteloua gracilis*), buffalo grass (*Bouteloua dactyloides*), St. Augustine grass (*Stenotaphrum secundatum*), and zoysia grass (*Zoysia*).

Areas with mild winters are prime locations for warm season grasses. Cool season grasses perform well in cold winter areas. Some experts recommend a mix of cool and warm season grasses, because some grass will always be green regardless of the season. We do not recommend this, however, because the amount of brown that is always present is unsatisfactory.

▶ **Choose resistant cultivars.** If you are starting a brand new lawn, or reseeding an area, look for cultivars that are disease- and/or pest-resistant. Read the label and catalog descriptions. One or both of these should say to what problem the grass is resistant. If the label or catalog description is silent on the subject, assume the grass is not resistant and choose another variety.

▶ **Use a polyculture approach.** Mix white clover (*Trifolium repens*) seeds with grass seeds when you plant. The mix of different kinds of plants in close proximity helps to retard the spread of pests and disease. Clover has the added benefit of being a nitrogen fixer; it actually takes nitrogen out of the air and makes it available for plant uptake as nitrogen fertilizer.

▶ **Make sure the lawn gets the right amount of sun.** Most lawn grasses need full sun to look their best and will grow poorly in partial shade to shade. If there is too much bare ground, the grass is not getting enough sun. Without enough light the grass does not cover well, and the large amount of bare ground encourages weeds.

Some grasses (red fescue, bentgrass, St. Augustine grass) tolerate more shade than others and will grow adequately in light shade. No grass will survive in heavy shade. Look at the label to find out the light requirements of grasses you buy. Reseed bare areas with an appropriate variety.

▶ **Manage water**. See page 229. Lawn grasses vary widely in their water needs. Grasses native to the prairies of the American West (blue grama, buffalo grass) are the most drought tolerant grasses, requiring as little as 12 inches (30 cm) of water a year to do well. Kentucky bluegrass, by contrast, needs about 48 inches (120 cm) of water during the growing season in order to stay green.

Look at packaging, labels, or a good garden resource to find out how much water your grass needs. If you don't know what kind of grass you have, and your lawn keeps turning brown during the growing season, it is not getting enough water.

Do not hand water your grass. Most people do not have enough patience to water as thoroughly as grass needs.

Use a sprinkler. Determine how much time it takes to deliver 1 inch (2.5 cm) of water. Set out a row of empty, uniformly sized, straight-sided containers (empty tuna fish cans work well). Measure the depth of water in each container at the end of 15 minutes. Divide 1 inch (2.5 cm) by the depth of water in the cup. Multiply this number by 15 (minutes). The result is the time it takes to deliver 1 inch (2.5 cm) of water to your lawn. Use this information to give your lawn the right amount of water.

Apply the water long enough for it to penetrate deeply. Do not water again until the soil is dry. This will encourage deep rooting and facilitate drought tolerance. Frequent, shallow watering results in shallow rooting, no ability to withstand drought, and increased frequency of fungal diseases.

▶ **Manage the soil.** See page 234.

Use a high-nitrogen organic fertilizer. The nitrogen promotes vegetative growth, which is exactly what you want a lawn grass to do. Fertilize the lawn once a year, in spring in cold winter areas, in spring or summer in mild winter areas. Organic fertilizers feed the decomposer community in your soil and release their nutrients slowly over time. This is especially important for nitrogen because nitrogen is highly mobile in the water column and leaches away rather quickly into the ground water. Synthetic fertilizers tend to release nitrogen much too quickly.

Test the pH of your soil. Most grasses appreciate a pH range from 6.0 to 7.0. Use either a simple pH test kit or an electronic pH meter, which you can get at any garden center. They are both easy to use; just follow the instructions on the package.

Adjust the pH of your soil, **if necessary.** Modifications to the pH last through one growing season. To make the soil more alkaline (that is, with a higher pH number), spread dolomite lime across the lawn. Follow instructions on the label. In addition to raising the pH, dolomite lime provides calcium and magnesium, which are essential nutrients. To make the soil more acid (that is, with a lower pH number), spread sulfur on the lawn. Follow the directions on the label to find out how much to use.

▶ **Use proper mowing techniques.** Consider planting or reseeding with a grass that needs mowing infrequently. Blue grama, buffalo grass, and red fescue are about 6 to 8 inches (15 to 20 cm) tall and look good even when mowed only once a year in the fall.

Do not mow your grass too short. This can cause serious damage. Every grass species has a recommended mowing height. Look at labels, packaging, and good references to find out the correct height for your grass. If you don't know what kind of grass you have, take a sample to your local Master Gardener organization for identification.

Leave grass clippings on the lawn, if they are light. Heavy globs of grass will cut off light and air and should be raked away. Light clippings, however, are very good for the grass because they decompose and enrich the soil, becoming free organic fertilizer.

▶ **Encourage beneficial organisms.** A number of insect pests and mites attack lawn grasses, and you can enlist the aid of beneficial organisms to help you control them. To attract beneficial organisms to your garden, grow species of plants these animals prefer as sources of food or shelter in the surrounding garden beds. Also provide water in very shallow containers, such as a bird bath or plant saucer. Some examples of plants to grow:

- The carrot family (Apiaceae): coriander, dill, fennel, parsley
- The mint family (Lamiaceae): catnip, thyme, rosemary, hyssop, lemon balm
- The daisy family (Asteraceae): cosmos, yarrow, coneflower

Spiders and birds are also efficient predators of insects and other pests. A spider's web may be a nuisance if its location is inconvenient for you, but it's better not to kill the spider. She's just doing her job—to catch and eat as many insects as she can. Many birds eat insects exclusively, while some are part-time insect eaters. Other birds relish snails and slugs. Attract birds of all kinds to your garden with water and shelter. They are valuable allies.

To increase your chances of controlling pests with beneficial organisms, purchase them at your local garden center or through mail-order suppliers. Check with the supplier to determine which species is the best choice for your particular problem, host plants, and environmental conditions. Some examples:

- Green lacewings, ladybird beetles, praying mantises, mealybug destroyers, and minute pirate bugs hunt, kill, and eat many pests.
- Parasitoids—such as *Trichogramma* wasps for caterpillars, *Encarsia formosa* for whiteflies, and several aphid parasites—are tiny insects that lay their eggs inside other insects.
- Beneficial nematodes control insects that dwell in the soil for all or a portion of their life cycle.
- Predatory mites attack and kill spider mites and cyclamen mites. Species of *Phytoseiulus*, *Amblyseius*, or *Metaseiulus* are available.

At garden centers, purchase a packet that contains a card that you mail to a supply company. The company then sends you 200 or more eggs or pupae. Put many of the eggs or pupae where the pests are most abundant, but be sure to distribute the rest throughout your plants. You can also buy praying mantis eggs at many garden centers. Keep the eggs indoors until they hatch (four to six weeks), then release the babies outdoors. Adult ladybird beetles (lady bugs) are also available. Be sure to release these in the early evening only, so that they turn to settling in instead of flying off to your neighbor's yard.

▶ **Remove weeds.** Weeds compete with your lawn grasses for water, nutrients, and sunlight. Getting rid of weeds is a big help in managing diseases, insect populations, and other pests like slugs and snails in your lawn. Many weeds harbor plant diseases, harmful insects, and other pests. Some viral, bacterial, and mollicute diseases, for example, that infect weeds are brought into your garden by insects that first feed on the infected weeds and then feed on your plants. Weeds also provide hiding places for slugs and snails. Some techniques to control weeds:

- Sheet mulch. An excellent way to eliminate pernicious perennial weeds (but will also eliminate all the grass in the treated area). First, mow or cut the weeds and grass to ground level. Cover the area with flattened cardboard boxes or several thicknesses of newspaper. Do not allow any sunlight to penetrate through to the ground. Cover the cardboard with a layer of organic mulch. Within a few months to a year, so long as the weeds cannot get any sunlight, they will die. The cardboard will decompose to fertilizer. Then you can reseed the area with the grass of your choice.
- Hoe or pull weeds. This works well in established lawns and leaves the grasses

you want to keep. Some weeds such as Canada thistle (*Cirsium*), field bindweed (*Convolvulus*), or horsetail (*Equisetum*) regenerate from tiny pieces of root that you leave behind. This can be absolutely maddening, but diligence is rewarded with eventual success. For dandelion (*Taraxacum*) or cat's ear (*Hypochaeris*) be sure to remove the crown at the top of the tap root so that the weed cannot grow back. When weed removal leaves a patch of bare ground, reseed the area with a good grass seed.

- Use a pre-emergent herbicide (germination inhibitor). Corn gluten prevents weed seeds (and any other seeds) from germinating. It has no effect on established plants. It is an organic product that feeds the soil as it degrades and provides nitrogen to enrich the soil. Non-GMO corn gluten is available for those concerned about using genetically modified corn products in gardens. Search for it on the Internet.

▶ **Aerate.** Aerating the lawn means to poke holes in the ground to allow air to get to the grass roots. This is important in areas where the soil is compacted due to foot traffic, machinery, or equipment. Lawn aerating machines can be rented and are motorized for ease of use. You can also use a spading fork to punch holes in the lawn.

Resources

The following businesses are useful sources for ● organic remedies and biological controls; ▲ seeds and plants of resistant cultivars; and gardening equipment and supplies, including organic fertilizer.

Adams County Nursery, Inc.
P.O. Box 108
Aspers, PA 17304
www.acnursery.com
▲

Ames' Orchard and Nursery
18292 Wildlife Rd.
Fayetteville, AR 72701
▲

A. M. Leonard, Inc.
P.O. Box 816
Piqua, OH 45356
http://www.amleo.com

Applied Bionomics
11074 W. Saanich Rd.
Sidney, BC V8L 5P5
Canada
www.appliedbio-nomics.com

Bear Creek Nursery
P.O. Box 411
Northport, WA 99157
www.bearcreeknursery.com
▲

Beneficial Insectary
14751 Oak Run Rd.
Oak Run, CA 96069
http://www.littleengine.com/
   biz/beneficial-insectary-
   oak-run/

Biofac Crop Care, Inc.
P.O. Box 87
Mathis, TX 78368
www.biofac.com

Buena Biosystems
P.O. Box 4008
Ventura, CA 93007

W. Atlee Burpee & Co.
300 Park Ave.
Warminster, PA 18974
www.burpee.com
● ▲

C & O Nursery
P.O. Box 116
Wenatchee, WA 98807-0116
▲

Country Heritage Nursery, Inc.
P.O. Box 536
Hartford, MI 49057
▲

Cumberland Valley Nurseries,
   Inc.
P.O. Box 471
McMinnville, TN 37110
▲

Farmer Seed and Nursery Co.
818 N.W. 4th St.
Faribault, MN 55021
www.farmerseed.com

Foothill Agricultural Research
510½ West Chase Dr.
Corona, CA 91720

Freedom Tree Farms
P.O. Box 69
Pelham, TN 37366
www.freedomtreefarms.com

Gardener's Supply Co.
128 Intervale Rd.
Burlington, VT 05401
www.gardeners.com

Gardens Alive!
5100 Schenley Pl.
Lawrenceburg, IN 47025
www.gardensalive.com

Gurney's Seed & Nursery Co.
110 Capital St.
Yankton, SC 57079
www.gurneys.com

Harmony Farm Supply
P.O. Box 460
Graton, CA 95444
www.harmonyfarm.com

Harris Seeds
P.O. Box 22960
60 Saginaw Dr.
Rochester, NY 14692
www.harrisseeds.com

Henry Field's Seed & Nursery
  Co.
415 N. Burnett St.
Shenandoah, IA 51602
www.henryfields.com

Hydro-Gardens, Inc.
P.O. Box 25845
Colorado Springs, CO 80936
www.hydro-gardens.com

Johnny's Selected Seeds
310 Foss Hill Rd.
Albion, ME 04910
www.johnnyseeds.com

J. W. Jung Seed Co.
335 S. High St.
Randolph, WI 53957
www.jungseed.com

Kelly Nurseries
Division of Plantron, Inc.
410 8th Ave. NW
Faribault, MN 55021
www.kellynurseries.com

The Kinsman Co., Inc.
River Rd.
Point Pleasant, PA 18950
www.kinsmangarden.com

Liberty Seed Co.
P.O. Box 806
461 Robinson Rd.
New Philadelphia, OH 44663

Mantis Manufacturing Corp.
1028 Street Rd.
Southampton, PA 18966

Mellinger's, Inc.
2310 W. South Range Rd.
North Lima, OH 44452
www.mellingers.com

J. E. Miller Nurseries, Inc.
5060 W. Lake Rd.
Canandaigua, NY 14424
www.millernurseries.com

The Natural Gardening Co.
217 San Anselmo Ave.
San Anselmo, CA 94960
www.naturalgardening.com

Nature's Control
P.O. Box 35
Medford, OR 97501
www.naturescontrol.com

Nichols Garden Nursery
1190 N. Pacific Hwy.
Albany, OR 97321
www.nicholsgardennursery.com

North Star Gardens
19060 Manning Trail North
Marine on St. Croix, MN 55047

Ohio Earth Food, Inc.
5488 Swamp St. NE
Hartville, OH 44632
www.ohioearthfood.com

One Green World
28696 S. Cramer Rd.
Molalla, OR 97038
www.onegreenworld.com

Orcon Organic Control, Inc.
5132 Venice Blvd.
Los Angeles, CA 90019
www.organiccontrol.com

Orol Ledden & Sons
P.O. Box 7
Center & Atlantic Aves.
Sewell, NJ 08080

Park Seed Co.
P.O. Box 31
Cokesbury Rd.
Greenwood, SC 29647
www.parkseed.com

Peaceful Valley Farm Supply
P.O. Box 2209
Grass Valley, CA 95945
www.groworganic.com

Pinetree Garden Seeds
Box 300
New Gloucester, ME 04260
www.superseeds.com

Plants of the Southwest
3095 Aqua Fria St.
Santa Fe, NM 87507
www.plantsofthesouthwest.com

Raintree Nursery
391 Butts Rd.
Morton, WA 98356
www.raintreenursery.com

Richters
P.O. Box 26, Hwy. 47
Goodwood, ON L0C 1A0
Canada
www.richters.com

Rincon-Vitova Insectaries, Inc.
P.O. Box 1555
Ventura, CA 93002
www.rinconvitova.com

Seeds Blüm
H.C. 33, Box 2057
Boise, ID 83706

Shepherd's Garden Seeds
30 Irene St.
Torrington, CT 06790

Smith & Hawken
P.O. Box 6900
2 Arbor Ln.
Florence, KY 41022
www.smithandhawken.com

Southern Exposure Seed
   Exchange
P.O. Box 170
Earlysville, VA 22936
www.southernexposure.com

Southmeadow Fruit Gardens
10603 Cleveland Ave.
Baroda, MI 49101
www.southmeadowfruitgardens.
   com

Stark Bro's Nurseries &
   Orchards Co.
P.O. Box 10
Louisiana, MO 63353
www.starkbros.com

Stokes Seeds, Inc.
P.O. Box 548
Buffalo, NY 14240
www.stokeseeds.com

Territorial Seed Co.
P.O. Box 157
20 Palmer Ave,
Cottage Grove, OR 97424
www.territorialseed.com
▲

Thompson & Morgan, Inc.
P.O. Box 1308
Jackson, NJ 08527
www.tmseeds.com
▲

The Urban Farmer Store
2833 Vicente St.
San Francisco, CA 94116
www.urbanfarmerstore.com
◼

Westgro Sales, Inc. and Agrico
  Sales, Ltd.
7333 Progress Way
Delta, BC V4G 1E7
Canada
www.growercentral.com
●

Glossary

acid soil. Soil with a pH lower than 7.0. Required by rhodies and azaleas (*Rhododendron*), blueberries (*Vaccinium*), camellias, gardenias, and other acid-loving plants.

acidify. To make a soil more acid by adding an amendment, such as coffee grounds, sulfur, or aluminum sulfate.

aeration. 1. To bubble air through a liquid. 2. To make holes in a lawn to allow air to penetrate the soil.

aerobic. Conditions that provide access to oxygen, or processes that require oxygen.

alkaline soil. Soil with a pH higher than 7.0.

amendment. A substance, such as compost or organic fertilizer, that is incorporated into soil to improve its condition, nutrient status, structure, or pH.

anaerobic. Conditions that deny access to oxygen, or processes that require the absence of oxygen.

anther. The part of the flower stamen that generates, contains, and releases pollen

anthracnose. Diseases of leaves, fruits, or stems caused by several related fungi (*Colletotrichum*, *Glomerella*) and characterized by symptoms of dark, sunken lesions that often develop black concentric rings.

Bacillus. A genus of rod-shaped bacteria. Several species are valuable beneficial organisms for the control of insect pests (*Bacillus thuringiensis* var. *kurstacki*, *Bt israelensis*, *Bt san diego*, *B. popilliae*, *B. lentimorbus*) or fungal diseases (*B. subtilis*).

bacteria. Prokaryotic organisms, usually single-celled, with a cell wall and without a nucleus, bacteria are ubiquitous. A few species cause serious plant diseases, including *Erwinia amylovora* (fire blight), *E. carotovora* (soft rot), *Pseudomonas syringae* (blight), *Xanthomonas campestris* (blight), and *Agrobacterium tumefaciens* (crown gall).

beneficial organisms. Any of a number of insects, mites, nematodes, and bacteria that are valuable partners to help control pests and diseases in the garden. They should be encouraged.

biennial. Plants that only live for two years, such as cabbage (*Brassica oleracea*). In the first year they manufacture and store food to provide the energy for the second year, when they flower profusely, set abundant seed, and die.

biological remedies. Any of a number of beneficial organisms that are commercially produced and available for purchase in retail outlets or via the Internet.

blight. Diseases characterized by the rapid death

of leaves, stems, and flowers caused by various bacteria or fungi.

bolting. Unexpected early flowering of certain plants (lettuce, spinach, cabbage) due to improper conditions of temperature and daylength.

bract. A modified leaf or leaf-like appendage, smaller or larger than normal leaves, sometimes colorful, that grows immediately below flowers or inflorescences. The bright red "flowers" of *Poinsettia* are bracts that subtend the insignificant flowers.

bulb. An underground storage structure (onion, tulip) with highly modified leaves attached to a very small nubbin of stem tissue.

canker. A sunken lesion, often dark and necrotic, on stems, twigs, or branches.

canopy. The aerial crown of leaves of a tree or shrub.

capsule. A type of fruit (seed pod) that is dry and opens to release the seeds.

chelated iron. Iron combined with a compound like EDTA (ethylenediaminetetraacetic acid) to make it more readily available for rapid plant uptake.

clone. An identical duplicate of a plant created through vegetative (asexual) or tissue culture propagation.

compaction. The elimination of pore spaces in soil by heavy equipment or by working the soil when it is too wet.

compost. Plant debris (from kitchen or garden waste) digested by beneficial bacteria and fungi into a nutrient-rich, dark, crumbly substance used as a soil amendment to renew fertility and restore healthy biological activity. This action repels pathogenic fungi and bacteria that cause plant disease.

compost tea. Compost and molasses added to water, then aerated and filtered. The mixture encourages beneficial bacteria and fungi to proliferate. Fresh compost tea used immediately after brewing as a foliar spray helps to repel pathogenic fungi and bacteria.

conifer. A large group of non-flowering plants that bear their seeds in cones. Pine (*Pinus*), fir (*Abies*), spruce (*Picea*), redwood (*Sequoia*), cedar (*Cedrus*), and juniper (*Juniperus*) are examples of conifers, plants which have no flowers and no fruit.

cork, corky. Corky tissue is rough in texture and often orange-brown in color. It usually develops on leaves, fruit, or stems in response to excess water or, sometimes, to disease.

cotyledon. The seed leaf of a plant embryo in which food is stored.

corm. Resembles a bulb but is actually stem tissue. Common corms are gladiolus and crocus.

crop rotation. The practice of installing annual plants in different locations every year to avoid soil-borne pests and diseases.

crown. 1. The point of leaf attachment on those plants that have a basal rosette of leaves and lack above-ground stems. Examples include strawberry (*Fragaria*) and lettuce (*Lactuca*). 2. Synonym for the canopy of trees and shrubs.

cultivar. A specific variety of cultivated plant (derived from the words "cultivated" and "variety").

damping off, damp off. This condition occurs when seeds or seedlings die from any of several different fungal infections that invade the root system.

deadheading. The practice of removing spent flowers in order to prevent seed formation and conserve energy.

deciduous. Woody plants (trees, shrubs, vines) that drop their leaves in autumn and are leafless in winter.

diatomaceous earth. The microscopic skeletons of diatoms that kill insects, slugs, and snails by abrasion.

dicot. Short for dicotyledon. One of the two large groups of flowering plants. The seeds of this group have two cotyledons. The other large group is the monocots.

dieback. Stems that die, turn brown, and then blacken, starting at the tip and working down toward the roots. If stubs remain on a stem because of poor pruning, dieback often results.

disbudding. The practice of removing some of the side buds of an inflorescence so that the remaining flower(s) grow larger.

disorder. A plant disease caused by environmental imbalances rather than by a pathogen or pest. Nitrogen deficiency is an example.

dolomite. A specific kind of limestone (calcium carbonate) that contains a high amount of magnesium.

dormancy. A state of suspended animation where metabolic processes are reduced to the bare minimum needed to keep the plant alive. Seeds are commonly dormant, for example, until the proper environmental conditions signal the process of germination to begin. Many trees and shrubs are dormant in winter.

dormant oil. A horticultural oil sprayed on trees and shrubs while they are leafless and dormant in winter to smother and kill overwintering insects and mites, and their eggs.

ectoparasite. A parasite that attaches itself to the exterior of a host plant and obtains its nutrients from its host.

endoparasite. A parasite that gets inside the interior of a host plant and obtains its nutrients from its host.

epidermis. The external, protective, skin-like tissue that covers all parts of a plant's body.

epiphyte. A plant that attaches itself to the exterior of a host plant but, unlike parasites, obtains none of its nutrients from its host.

espalier. The practice of pruning a tree or shrub so that it grows in two dimensions, flat against a wall or fence for example. A space-saving technique that allows one to have fruit trees in very small spaces.

evergreen. A plant that keeps its leaves all winter long. Broadleaved evergreens are flowering plants and may be herbaceous perennials, or woody trees and shrubs. Coniferous evergreens are conifers (not flowering plants) and are all trees and shrubs.

family. A term often misused to loosely mean a group of related things. In botany, family means a specific level of relationship. All plant family names end in -aceae. The aster family, Asteraceae, for example, includes many ornamental genera (*Cosmos, Dahlia, Gaillardia*) as well as edibles, such as endive (*Cichorium*), artichoke (*Cynara*), and lettuce (*Lactuca*).

fertilizer. Substances rich in certain mineral elements required for plant growth and which are applied to the soil for uptake by plants.

fertilization. 1. The practice of applying fertilizer to enrich soil and enhance plant growth. 2. The union of sperm and egg to create a zygote, which grows and matures into a plant or animal.

fruit. A ripened, mature ovary containing seeds. Fruits can be fleshy, such as grape (*Vitis*), cantaloupe (*Cucumis melo*), and tomato (*Lycopersicon esculentum*), or dry, such as a poppy capsule (*Papaver*) or peanuts (*Arachis*) inside the shell.

fruiting bodies. Reproductive structures containing spores, which are produced by fungi.

fungicide. A substance used to kill fungi.

fungus. One of a very large group of organisms reproducing by means of spores and with a filamentous growth habit. Placed in their own kingdom, Fungi, many of these organisms are serious plant pathogens, while many others are beneficial and highly desirable.

gall. An overgrowth of plant tissue, sometimes tumor-like, induced by insects or bacteria.

genus. A group of closely related species. *Rosa damascena*, *R. gallica*, and *R. centifolia*, for example, are all members of the genus *Rosa*, the rose.

germination. The process of growth initiated when environmental conditions stimulate a seed to metabolize stored food and break dormancy.

grafting. A technique of attaching cut pieces of one plant (the scion) to the root system of another plant (the rootstock).

hardiness. The ability to tolerate a certain amount of freezing winter temperatures without dying.

herbicide. Various substances used to kill plants.

honeydew. A sweet, sticky liquid excrement produced by such insects as aphids, scale, or mealybugs.

horticultural oil. Oil sprayed on plants to kill insects. Prepared from vegetable oil or petroleum oil, it is applied at higher concentration as a dormant spray in winter, or at lower concentration during the growing season.

host. A plant infected or infested by pathogens or other parasites.

hybrid. A cross between two species or strains, either natural or artificial.

hypha, hyphae. The filaments comprising the body of a fungus.

infected, infection. A plant is infected when invaded by a fungal, viral, or bacterial pathogen.

infested, infestation. A plant is infested when attacked by insect, mite, or nematode pests.

inflorescence. All the flowers, collectively, on a single stem.

insecticidal soap. A soap (potassium salt of fatty acids), not a detergent, used to kill insects.

internode. The section of a stem between leaves or nodes.

larva, larvae. The immature or juvenile stages of organisms like insects, mites, or nematodes.

leaf. The primary organ of photosynthesis, a leaf is usually a flat, green organ held out to the sun to capture solar energy.

leaflet. A small leaf-like unit, one of several in a compound leaf. Clover (*Trifolium*), for example, typically has three leaflets on each leaf.

lesion. A damaged or dead area of any part of a plant, usually discolored.

lime. Calcium carbonate (limestone), a soil amendment to raise pH and to add calcium.

margin. The edge of a leaf.

microclimate. Subtle variations in environmental conditions resulting in warmer or colder, wetter or dryer, sunny or shady locations in the garden.

mildew. See **powdery mildew**.

mold, moldy. Fungal pathogens that produce visible fuzzy mold on the exterior of plant parts.

mollicutes. Prokaryotes related to bacteria but lacking cell walls. Mollicutes are obligate pathogens of plants and animals. Aster yellows, for example, is a plant disease caused by a mollicute.

monocot. Short for monocotyledon. One of the two large groups of flowering plants. This group has seeds with a single cotyledon. Dicot is the other group.

monoculture. A planting area containing only one kind of plant. Apple (*Malus*) orchards, cornfields (*Zea mays*), and lawns of a single grass species are good examples of monocultures.

mosaic. A virus disease characterized by discrete patches of discolored tissue.

mottling. Diffuse discolored areas.

mulch. A material applied to the surface of the soil to conserve water, control weeds, prevent disease, and feed the soil.

mummy. Dead, brown or black, decayed fruit that hangs on the plant.

mycelium. The web-like mass of hyphae comprising the body of a fungus.

mycorrhizae. Special fungi that live symbiotically on or in the roots of plants. Mycorrhizal fungi absorb water and mineral nutrients from the soil and give them to the plant, while the plant makes sugar, which it gives to the fungus.

necrosis, necrotic. Necrosis describes dead, brown or black tissue.

nematode. A very large group of microscopic animals, some of which are plant parasites.

nitrogen. A natural element and a major plant nutrient.

node. The point where a leaf attaches to a stem, containing a bud.

NPK. The three letters and numbers on all packages of fertilizer referring to nitrogen (N), phosphorus (P), and potassium (K).

nucleic acid. DNA or RNA containing genetic information.

nutrient. Natural mineral elements weathered from rock particles in soil or decaying organic matter and absorbed by plant roots.

obligate pathogen. A disease-causing agent that cannot live outside of its host, such as a virus, a mollicute, and certain fungi or bacteria.

organ. Structures of the plant body composed of several different tissues. The leaf, the flower, and the fruit, for example, are organs.

organic fertilizer. Mineral nutrients derived from natural biological or mineral sources that have been subjected to minimal processing. Examples include blood meal, bone meal, and seaweed.

organic matter. Materials derived from natural biological sources.

organic mulch. Natural biological materials, such as shredded bark, coconut fiber, nut hulls, wood chips, pine needles, shredded newspaper, or cardboard spread over the surface of the soil.

overwinter. The capacity of some organisms to survive freezing for extended periods.

pathogen. An organism that causes disease.

perennial. A plant that survives more than two years.

pest. Any animal feeding on parts of your plants.

pesticide. Various chemicals designed to kill certain organisms, for example, insecticides kill insects, miticides kill mites, fungicides kill fungi, and herbicides kill plants.

petiole. The leaf stalk that attaches a leaf to a stem.

pH. Stands for the "potential of hydrogen." Aqueous solutions with a pH less than 7 are acidic, while those with a pH greater than 7 are alkaline.

pH scale. The pH scale ranges from 0 to 14, with 7 in the middle at the neutral position.

pheromone. Chemicals produced by organisms to attract a mate or to signal specific behavior such as aggregation. Synthetic pheromones are man-made versions of natural pheromones used to disrupt the life cycle of specific insects.

phloem. The living cells of the vascular tissue that conduct food to all parts of the plant body.

phytotoxic. Injury or death of plant cells from various substances under certain environmental conditions.

pistil. The female sex parts of a flower, composed of an ovary, style, and stigma.

pollen. The sperm-bearing units produced in the male sex parts of flowering plants or in the male cones of a conifer.

pollination. The process of transporting sperm-bearing pollen to the egg-bearing female sex parts of a flower or a cone. Transportation can be by wind, or by an animal vector, such as a bee, hummingbird, or human.

polyculture. The practice of positioning different kinds of plants next to each other in order to slow down the transmission of diseases and pests from one plant to another.

powdery mildew. Any of several different kinds of fungal pathogens that grow as a whitish substance on the surface of plant parts.

pre-emergent herbicide. A substance used to control weeds by preventing seeds from germinating.

predatory mites. Beneficial mites that eat plant-damaging mites.

prokaryotes. Simple microorganisms (bacteria, mollicutes), usually single-celled and without a membrane-bound nucleus.

propagate. To increase the number of plants by sexual or asexual reproduction.

prune. To selectively remove plant parts to improve the health or shape of a plant.

resistant. Plants that are inherently resistant to certain pests or diseases, resulting in a lower incidence of infection or infestation.

rhizome. A highly modified underground stem, such as iris rhizomes.

rot. The softening, discoloration, and disintegration of plant tissue as a result of bacterial or fungal infection.

russet. Brown to orange, roughened areas of plant parts due to the formation of cork cells.

rust. A disease caused by any one of many different rust fungi.

sanitize. The process of removing infected or infested plant material from a plant or from the garden.

saprophyte. An organism that uses dead organic material for food.

scab. Any of several fungal diseases that cause raised, corky lesions on plant parts.

scale. Insects that are immobile at maturity, often covered by a shield-like scale.

scarify. The mechanical abrasion of the seed coat by nicking or filing to facilitate germination.

scorch. Browning and death of the tips and margins of leaves as a result of unfavorable environmental conditions.

sepal. The first whorl of appendages surrounding a flower, often green, that subtend the petals.

shot hole. A symptom; small diseased patches of leaf tissue fall out of the leaf, creating small, ragged holes in the leaf.

smut. A disease, caused by any of several different smut fungi, characterized by masses of dark-colored, powdery spores.

solarize. To cover soil with plastic in order to free it of certain pathogens using the heat of the sun.

sooty mold. A fungus that lives on the surface of plant parts, feeding on the sugary excrement (honeydew) produced by insects such as aphids. It is not a parasite and does not cause infection.

species. A unit of scientific classification consisting of a group of related individuals in a freely interbreeding population.

spore. The reproductive unit of a fungus, analogous to the seed of a plant.

stamen. The male sex parts of a flower, consisting of a filament and a pollen-containing anther.

sterilization. The elimination of pathogens from soil, tools, or plant parts using heat or chemicals.

sticky trap. Viscous, sticky substances used to entrap insects by miring them in goo.

stigma. The structure at the tip of the flower pistil which receives pollen and facilitates the transfer of sperm from pollen to the egg inside the ovary.

stolon. A highly modified above-ground stem, such as strawberry (*Fragaria*) runners, by which a plant spreads.

stress. Limited or excessive environmental resources that restrict metabolic and physiological processes within the plant, weakening it and rendering it more susceptible to attack by pathogens or pests.

style. The stalk-like appendage of the pistil, between the ovary and the stigma.

stylet. The hypodermic-needle-like mouthparts of nematodes and certain insects.

superior oil. A highly refined horticultural oil that can be used on plants during the growing season in order to kill insects and mites.

symptom. The external and internal reactions or alterations of a plant as a result of a disorder, pest, or disease.

systemic. Any pathogen or substance that moves through the vascular tissue to all parts of the plant. Many infections from viruses, bacteria, or mollicutes can be systemic.

tender. Plants that are unable to survive freezing winter cold.

thinning. 1. The process of removing excess fruit while still immature. 2. The process of selectively pruning away excess branches of a tree or shrub. 3. The process of pulling up excess seedlings, leaving a select few to mature.

tissue. Groups of cells that perform particular functions. Epidermal tissue, for example, is the skin-like tissue that covers all plant parts. Vascular tissue conducts water, food, and mineral nutrients to all parts of the plant body.

tolerant. Plants that are not incapacitated by infection or infestation and suffer little damage.

topdressing. An attractive substance, such as horticultural sand or gravel, applied to the surface of the potting soil in a container.

tuber. A highly modified stem as an underground food storage organ. The potato (*Solanum tuberosum*) is a tuber.

tuberous root. A highly modified root as an underground food storage organ. The sweet potato (*Ipomoea batatas*) is a tuberous root.

tumor. The uncontrolled, overgrowth of disorganized tissues into a swollen mass.

variety. A variant or form of a plant that is different from the normal type. Sometimes given Latin names, varieties are often applied to connote specific differences in habit (*pendula* for weeping), flower color (*alba* for white), or foliage color (*variegata* for variegated).

vascular. The fluid-conducting system of a plant body, analogous to the blood or vascular system of our own bodies.

vector. An animal or tool that transports a pathogen from one plant to another.

vegetable. A non-botanical, culinary term indicating an edible plant or plant part, usually not sweet.

virus. An obligate parasite consisting of nucleic acid and protein. Visible only by an electron microscope.

wilt. Drooping of plant parts due to insufficient water caused by a lack of water, by high concentrations of fertilizer or other salts in the soil, or by death of the roots due to excess water, fungal disease, nematodes, or compaction of the soil.

witches' broom. Dense clusters of short stems in a ball-like mass that persist year after year.

xylem. The water and mineral nutrient-conducting cells of the vascular tissue which are dead at maturity.

yellows. Plant disease characterized by stunting and yellowing.

zygote. The fertilized egg cell of a plant or animal.

References

Books listed here are ones we have found to be particularly helpful. An asterisk (*) denotes books that focus solely on organic gardening techniques.

Agrios, George N. 2005. *Plant Pathology*. 5th ed. Burlington, Massachusetts: Elsevier Academic Press.

Brenzel, Kathleen Norris, ed. 2007. *Sunset Western Garden Book*. 8th ed. Menlo Park, California: Sunset Publishing Corporation.

*Coleman, Eliot. 1989. *The New Organic Grower*. Chelsea, Vermont: Chelsea Green Publishing.

*Ellis, Barbara W., and Fern Marshall Bradley, eds. 1996. *The Organic Gardener's Handbook of Natural Insect and Disease Control*. Emmaus, Pennsylvania: Rodale Press.

Gillman, Jeff. 2008. *The Truth About Garden Remedies*. Portland, Oregon: Timber Press.

———. 2008. *The Truth About Organic Gardening*. Portland, Oregon: Timber Press.

Grissell, Eric. 2001. *Insects and Gardens: In Pursuit of a Garden Ecology*. Portland, Oregon: Timber Press.

Lowenfels, Jeff, and Wayne Lewis. 2006. *Teaming with Microbes*. Portland, Oregon: Timber Press.

McKinley, Michael, ed. 2001. *Ortho's Home Gardener's Problem Solver*. Des Moines, Iowa: Ortho Books.

Olkowski, William, Sheila Daar, and Helga Olkowski. 1991. *Common-Sense Pest Control*. Newtown, Connecticut: Taunton Press.

Westcott, Cynthia. 1973. *The Gardener's Bug Book*. Garden City, New York: Doubleday & Co.

———. 1990. *Westcott's Plant Disease Handbook*. 5th ed., rev. by R. Kenneth Horst. New York: Van Nostrand Reinhold Co.

Index

Note: Page numbers in **bold** indicate illustrations or photographs.

Abies, 12, **395**, 428
Abies procera, **26**
Acer
  bladder gall mites, **356**
  bracket fungus, **401**
  crown rot, **400**
  flowering plant, 12
  in forests, **128**
  fruit of, 93, **95**
  papery bark, **133**
  scorch, **338**
  solutions, 280
  sooty bark disease, **138**
Acer circinatum, **26**, **138**
Achillea, 63, 217, 269, **364**, **402**
acidify, 427
acid soil, 222, 237, 239, 240, 250, 427
acorns, 193, **413**
acorn squash, **335**
Adams County Nursery, Inc., 423
adelgids. *See also* Cooley spruce gall adelgids
  identification of, 265–266
  leaves damaged, **38**, **55**, **342**, **355**
  solutions, 267

stems damaged, **140**, **141**, **158**, **395**, **402**
aeration, 248, 314, 427
aerial crown gall, **154**, 305, **403**
aerobic, 249, 427
African violets, **63**
agave, **13**
Agrobacterium tumefaciens, 300, 427
Agropyron cristatum, 418
Agrostis, 418
air movement, 219, 246
Alcea, **341**
algae, **156**
alkaline soils, 237, 239, 240, 427
Allium cepa. See onions
almonds, **413**
Amblyseius, 219
Amelanchier, **339**
amendments, 427
Ames' Orchard and Nursery, 423
A. M. Leonard, Inc., 423
anaerobic, 248–249, 427
Anethum, 217, 218, 269
annuals, 217
anthers, **62**, 427
anthracnose, **68**, **105**, **120**, 244–252, **361**, **385**, 427
ants, 76, **144**, 263–264, 267, 282, **363**

Aphelenchoides, 314
aphids
  flowers damaged, 74, 79, **262**, **363**, 368
  fruits damaged, **116**, 267, **386**
  identification of, **264**, 265–266
  lacewings and, **262**
  leaves damaged, **50**, **56**, **59**, 285, **352**, **356**, **358**
  parasites of, 219
  roots damaged, **179**, **182**, **191**, 284
  solutions, 267
  stems damaged, **140**, **141**, **150**, **158**, **401**
Apiaceae, 218, 269
Apis mellifera, 287
apples
  ants on, **363**
  bacterial diseases, 370, 390
  bitter pit, **109**
  bitter rot, **109**
  blister beetles, **365**
  brown rot, **362**
  canker, **139**, 390, 394
  cedar-apple rust, **101**, **153**, **385**
  European apple sawfly, **125**, **388**
  fire blight, 370
  flowers, 12, 69

apples [*continued*]
  fly speck, **379**
  frost damage, **396**
  fruit of, 93, 94, **384**
  insufficient water, **374**
  leaves damaged, **341**, **345**
  lichens on, **403**
  maggots, **125**, **272**, **273**, **388**
  monocultures, 216
  papery bark, **390**
  plum curculios, **381**
  rosy apple aphids, **116**
  russeting, **224**, **377**
  scab, **379**, **381**, **385**, **394**
  shot hole fungus, **100**, **106**
  solutions, 239, 244–245, 267,
    272, **273**, 282
  virus infections, **310**, **359**
  winter chill, 234
Applied Bionomics, 423
arborvitae, 224, **334**, **335**
Arbutus menziesii, **345**
Arceuthobium, **140**, **156**, 331
Arctostaphylos, **356**
armillaria root rot, 19, **140**, **157**,
  252–254
army worms, **111**, **202**, 267, 272,
  277–278, 282, 283
artichokes, **63**, **352**
Asclepias, **95**, **340**, **364**
asparagus beetles, **143**, 267, 276–
  277, **397**
Asteraceae, 218, 269, 429
aster yellows, 77, 78, **186**, 261, 306
avocado, **213**, **336**
Azadirachta indica, 250, 279, 292
azaleas, 219, **340**, 427

Bacillus, 427
Bacillus lentimorbus, 278
Bacillus popilliae, 278
Bacillus subtilis, 249, 299
Bacillus thuringiensis, 277–278,
  299, 427

bacteria. *See also specific types*
  defined, 427
  leaves damaged, **45**, **54**, 349,
    353
  overview and functions,
    298–300
  solutions, 300–306
  stems damaged, **335**
bacterial blight, **108**, **137**, 301,
  380, **394**
bacterial fungicides, 249–250
bacterial leaf-spot. *See also* leaf-
    spot; physiological leaf-spot
  fruits damaged, **105**, **109**, **122**,
    380, **388**
  leaves damaged, **35**, **343**, **380**
  solutions, 301
bacterial ring rot, **165**, **175–176**,
  188, **189**, 305, **404**, **406**, **411**
bacterial rot, **189**, 305, **411**
baking soda spray, 248
balling, **83**, 233, **369**
banyan trees, 159
barberry, **366**
bark beetles, **22**, **145**, 282, **397**
bark damage, **133**, **138**
beans, 12, **335**, **413**
Bear Creek Nursery, 423
bears, 146, **203**, 228, 329
beeches, 138, **400**
bees, **51**, **228**, **261**, 263–264, 267,
  287, **350**
beetles
  asparagus, **143**, **397**
  bark, **22**, **145**, **397**
  blister, **365**
  cucumber, **180**, **365**
  flea, **53**, **180**, **353**
  flowers damaged, **75**
  identification of, 262
  Japanese, **262**
  ladybird, 219, **261**, 269
  larvae of, **262**
  leaves damaged, **49**, **52**, **353**

sap, **202**
seedcorn, **197**, 284
solutions, 267, 269, 276–279,
  282, 284
white-fringed, **180**
beets, 160, **164**, **173**, **186**, 234,
  398, **410**
begonias, 218
Beneficial Insectary, 423
beneficial nematodes, 219, 269,
  283
beneficial organisms, 218–219,
  269, 283, 290, 427
bentgrasses, 418
Berberis, **366**
Bermuda grass, 418
berries. *See specific varieties*
Beta, 160, **164**, **173**, **186**, 234, **398**,
  410
Betula, 133
biennials, 234, 427
Biofac Crop Care, Inc., 423
biological remedies, 427. *See also*
  beneficial organisms
birches, 133
bird of paradise, **375**
birds
  attracting to garden, 219, 269
  fruits damaged, **113**, **144**, **145**,
    322–323, **382**
  leaves damaged, **52**
  seeds damaged, **200**, **203**, **414**
  stems damaged, **398**
bitter pit, **109**, 239
bitter rot, **109**, 244
blackberries
  botrytis, **378**
  bud weevil, 92
  double blossom, 79
  herbicide damage, **336**
  leafhoppers, **343**
  raspberry fruitworms, **107**
  redberry mites, **101**, **343**, **379**
black-eyed Susans, **363**

black knot, **135**, **154**, 244, **390**, **401**

black rot, **105**, **120**, **121**, 244–252, 378, 387

black spot, 36, 244, **245**, 341

black vine weevils, **181**, 276–277, 284

black walnut trees, 280. *See also* walnut blight; walnuts

bladder gall mites, **56**, **289**, **295**, 356

blight
    bacterial, **108**, **137**, 301, **380**, **394**
    camellia flower, **69**, **82**, 244, **362**, 370
    defined, 427
    fire, **45**, **84**, **132**, 301, 306, **349**, 370, 392
    late, **108**, 170, 244, 379, **406**
    lilac, **132**, 301
    walnut, **196**, 301, **412**

blister beetles, **365**

blister mites, **39**, **57**, 287, 288, **289**, 295, **343**, 356

blossom end rot, **104**, 239, **378**

blow down, **22**, 226, **336**

blueberries, 93, 237, 427

blueberry maggots, **125**, 267, 282

blueberry mummy berry, **120**

blue grama, 418

bluegrass, **26**

blue orchard mason bees, **228**, **261**

blue spruce trees, 280

bolting, 88, 234, **371**, 428

borers
    common stalk, **145**, **150**
    dogwood, **337**
    European corn, **111**, **124**, **144**
    flatheaded, **144**
    identification of, **265**
    iris, **179**
    leaves damaged, **33**, **45**, 340, 348

peachtwig, **131**, **134**, **391**

pecan, **144**

raspberry cane, **391**

rhododendron, **144**

shot hole, **144**, 432

solutions, 267, 272, 282, 284

squash vine, **144**

stems damaged, **20**, **22**, **139**, 335, 337, **395**, **397**

two-lined chestnut, **134**, **144**

boron deficiency, 173, 240

botrytis
    flowers damaged, **67**, **69**, **83**, 361, 370
    fruits damaged, **103**, **123**, 378, 387
    leaves damaged, **18**, **46**, **246**
    solutions for air-borne varieties, 244–252
    solutions for soil-borne varieties, 252–254
    stems damaged, **132**, **142**, 335, 389, 393

Bouteloua dactyloides, 418

Bouteloua gracilis, 418

boxwoods, **358**

bracket fungus, **157**, 257, **401**

bracts, 25, **428**

brambles, **375**

branches broken, **146**, 226, 228. *See also* stems

Brassicaceae, 183, 193, 234, 237, 352

Brassica oleracea, 12, **183**, **371**, 427

broccoli, **183**, 352

brown rot
    flowers damaged, **69**, **83**, **362**, 370
    fruits damaged, **108**, **120**, **122**, **123**, 378, 385, 387
    leaves damaged, **45**, 349
    solutions, 244–252
    stems damaged, **132**, 137, **390**, 393

Brussels sprouts, 217

Bt israelensis (BTI), 278

Bt kurstaki (BTK), 277–278

Bt san diego (BTSD), 277–278

bud nematodes, 314

Buena Biosystems, 423

buffalo grass, 418

bulb blue mold, **172**, **190**, 258, **406**, **410**

bulb fungus, 171, 258

bulb mites, **188**, 288, **296**, 411

bulb rot, **172**, **189**, **405**, **410**

bulbs, 90, 217–218, 234, 257–258, 296–297, 318, 428. *See also* roots and bulbs

burlap wrap, 328

Burpee & Co., 423

burrowing mice, **200**, 329

butterflies, **260**, **261**, **264**, 321

Buxus, 358

cabbage family, 12, 183, **183**, 193, 234, 237, 427

cabbage maggots, **180**, 284

cacti, 127, **128**

calcium, **104**, 239

calendulas, 306, 367

camellia flower blight, **69**, **82**, 244, **362**, 370

camellias, 237, **243**, **255**, 427

canker
    apple, **139**, **390**, **394**
    defined, 428
    endothia, **138**
    leaves damaged, **46**, 348
    pear, **139**, 244
    roses, **132**, **138**, 389, **394**
    solutions, 244–252
    stems damaged, **132**, **137**, **146**, 394, 396

canopy, 33, 428

cantaloupes, **94**

Capsicum, 120, 193, 233, **385**

capsule, 93, 428

carpenter ants, **144**, 282

carrots, 160, **186**, 218, 269, **406–409**, **411**

carrot weevils, **180**, 284

Carya, 280

Carya illinoinensis, **199**, **201**

Carya ovata, **199**

caterpillars
  flowers damaged, **73**, **74**, **364**
  fruits damaged, 121
  identification of, **264**
  leaves damaged, **48**, **52**, **53**, **260**, **352**
  roots damaged, **177**, **179**
  seeds damaged, **201**
  solutions, 267, 277–278
  stems damaged, **134**
  Trichogramma wasps and, 219

catnip, 218, 269

cat's ear, **95**

cauliflower, **183**

cavity spot, **178**, 240

CCD (colony collapse disorder), 228

cedar-apple rust
  fruits damaged, **101**, **117**, **153**, **379**, **385**
  solutions, 244
  stems damaged, **153**

cedar trees, 12, 428

Chaenomeles, **336**

chelated iron, 239, 428

chemicals
  biological nematicides, 320
  fungicides, 246–252, 256–257, 429
  herbicides, 221, 430, 432
  insecticides, 273–282
  miticides, 290, 296
  safety considerations, 209–211, 247, 274, 291

cherries, 94, 232, **349–350**, 370, **390**, **393–394**, **399**, **401**

cherry fruitworms, **118**, **125**, 267, 272, 282

cherry laurel, 224

chestnuts, 138

child-caused damage, 146, 228, 329

chinaberry trees, 250, 279, 292

chlorophyll, 11

Chrysanthemum cinerariifolium, 256, 281, 294

cicadas, **260**

Cistus, **366**

Citrullus, **400**

citrus freeze damage, **98**, **107**, 233, **376**, **377**

Citrus sinensis, 93

citrus thrips, **97**, **102**, 267

clematis, **26**, **361**

Clematis armandii, **26**

climbing cutworms, **73**, 267, 277–278

clones, 312, 428

clubroot, **183**, 237, 252

coconut palm, 126

coconuts, 193

Codiaeum, **286**

codling moth larvae, **112**, **124**, **199**, 272, 282, **382**, **388**

cold injury, **164**. *See also* frost damage

cole crops, 217

Coleoptera, 262

Colletotrichum, 427

colony collapse disorder (CCD), 228

common stalk borers, **145**, **150**, 282

compaction, 18, 184, 240, **409**, 428

compost, 235–236, 253, 428

compost tea, 248–249, 428

coneflowers, 269

cones, **13**

conifers, 12, **55**, **140**, 428. *See also specific varieties*

C & O Nursery, 423

Cooley spruce gall adelgids, **141**, **148**, **150**, 267, 285, **395**, **399**

cool weather, 205, 233

Cooperative Extension Service, 215

copper, 251, 305

copper tape, 325

coral bells, **352**

coral spot, **132**, 244, **390**

Coreopsis grandiflora, **334**

coriander, 218, 269

corky tissue
  defined, 428
  fruits affected, 99, 106, 109, 114, 116, **377**, **379**
  on leaves, 57
  roots affected, 171
  on stems, 154

corms, 127, **165**, 257–258, 428

corn. *See also* corn earworms; corn rootworms
  common stalk borers, **145**
  European corn borers, **111**, **124**, **144**, 267, 272, 282
  fungus diseases, **196**
  growing conditions, 205
  monocultures, 216
  pest resistance, 215
  pollination, 228
  prop roots, 159
  seedcorn beetles, **197**, 284
  seeds, 192, **194**, **413**

corn earworms, **111**, **202**, 267, 272, 282, 283, **382**, **414**

corn rootworms, **181**, **197**, 284

Cornus, **350**, **361**, **395**

Cornus florida, **337**

Cornus nuttallii, **26**

Corylus, 193

cosmos, 217, 269

Cotinus, 280

cotoneaster, **370**, **399**

cottony scale, **38**, **55**, **140**, **158**, 267, **355**

cotyledons, 93, 192–194, 428

Country Heritage Nursery, Inc., 423

coyotes, 329

crab apples, **101**

cranberry fruitworms, **118**, 267, 272, 282

Crataegus, **370**

crested wheatgrass, 418

crop rotation, 217, 254, 428

croton, **286**

crown, 428

crown gall
    aerial, **154**, **305**, **403**
    Agrobacterium tumefaciens, 427
    roots damaged, **191**
    solutions, 305
    stems damaged, **22**, **135**, **337**, **392**

crown of thorns, **336**

crown rot, **142**, **151**, **189**, 252–254, **393**, **400**, **410**

crumbly berry virus, **119**, 309

Cryptomeria, 280

cucumber beetles, **180**, 276–277, 284, **365**

cucumbers, **120**, **380**, **386**

Cucumis, **378**, **383**, **384**, **385**

Cucumis melo, **94**

Cucumis sativus, **120**, **380**, **386**

Cucurbita, 12, **383**

Cucurbitaceae, 193, **365**

Cucurbita pepo, 93, **335**, **363**

cucurbit bacterial wilt, **120**, 306, **386**

cultivars, 428

Cumberland Valley Nurseries, Inc., 423

curculios
    flowers damaged, **76**, **92**, **363**

fruits damaged, **110**, **118**, **124**

identification of, 262, **263**

plum, **92**, **110**, **118**, **124**, **375**, **381**

rose, **92**, **375**

solutions, 267, 276–277

curled leaves, **58–60**

curly top virus, **186**, 309

currant fruit flies, **125**, 267, 282

Cuscuta, **324**

cutworm collars, 272

cutworms, **73**, **200**, 267, 272, 277–278. *See also* army worms

cyclamen mites, **78**, 219, 288–290

cyclamens, **360**

Cydonia, **370**

cymbidium orchids, **373**

Cynara, **63**, **352**

Cynodon dactylon, 418

daffodils, 161, 218, 234, **258**, **296**, **371**, **405**, **410**, **411**

dahlias, 218

dahlia tuber rot, **165**, **190**, 258

daisy family, 218, 269

damping off, **21**, **197**, 236–237, 252, **413**, 428

dandelions, 93, 94, 95, **227**

Daucus, 160, **186**, **406**, **407**, **408**, **409**, **411**

Daucus carota, **360**

daylength, **186**, 229

deadheading, **88**, 227, **371**, 428

death of tissue, **44**

deciduous, 428

deer
    deterence, 215, 217, 329–330
    flowers damaged, **73**, **366**
    leaves damaged, **51**, **354**
    stems damaged, **133**

delphiniums, 12

Dermatophagoides pteronyssinus, 287

diatomaceous earth, 276–277, 327–328, 428

dicotyledons (dicots), 12, 192, 429

dieback, **132**, **137**, **138**, 244, 429

dieffenbachia, **338**

dill, 217, 218, 269

Diplocarpon rosae, 244

Diptera, 263

disbudding, **81**, 227, **367**, 429

disease-resistant plants, 215–216

disorders *vs.* diseases, 213–214, 429

distorted growth
    of flowers, **77–81**, 262, **367–368**
    of fruits, **115–120**, **384–386**
    of leaves, **58–60**, **357–359**
    of roots and bulbs, **183–187**, **409**
    of seeds and seedlings, **148–150**, **399**
    of stems, **148–150**, **399**

DNA, 308, 431

dock, **345**

dodder, **324**

dogs, 330

dogwood borers, 282, **337**

dogwoods, **350**, **361**, **395**

dolomite lime, 237, 429

dormancy, 192–193, 429

dormant oil, 279–280, 292, 296, 429

double blossoms, **79**, 309

Douglas firs, **141**, **150**, **336**, **339**, **397**

dragonflies, **259**

drainage, 230, 253

drip-trickle watering systems, 230

drought
    flowers damaged, **70**, **85**, **87**, **90**, **91**, **360**, **369**, **374**, **375**
    leaves damaged, **31**, **41**, **42**, **44**, **338**, **344**, **346**, **347**, **357**
    plants damaged, **17**, **334**
    roots damaged, **187**

drupes, 193
dust mites, 287
dwarf mistletoe, **140, 156,** 331

earwigs
  flowers damaged, **72, 76,** 364
  identification of, 265
  leaves damaged, **49, 53,** 351
  seeds damaged, **198**
  solutions, 267, 272, 276
earworms. *See* corn earworms
Echinacea purpurea, **260**
E. coli bacteria, 300
ectoparasites, 314, 429
edema, **57,** 355
eggplants, 193, 217, 233
electronic sounds, 330
elms, **392, 398**
Encarsia formosa, 219, 269
endoparasites, 314, 429
endothia canker, **138,** 244
English ivy, **353**
Environmental Protection
  Agency (EPA), 211, 247, 274
environmental stress, **119,** 225,
  384
epidermis, 26, 429
epiphytes, 128, 429
Epipremnum, **339**
Epipremnum pinnatum, **26**
equipment, 210
Erwinia amylovora, **349,** 427
Erwinia carotovora, 427
espalier, 272, 429
ethylene, **85,** 224, **369**
Euphorbia, **336**
European apple sawfly, **100, 125,**
  282, **388**
European canker, **132,** 244
European corn borers
  fruits damaged, **111, 124**
  solutions, 267, 272, 282
  stems damaged, **144**

eutypa dieback, **132, 137,** 244
evergreens, 26, 340, 429
evolution of plants, 11–12
excess fruit, 119, 227, 228, **384,**
  396
excess nitrogen, **86, 90,** 239, **372**

Fagus, **400**
family, 429
Farmer Seed and Nursery Co.,
  424
fasciation, **148,** 306, **399**
Federal Insecticide, Fungicide and Rodenticide Act
  (FIFRA), 211, 247, 274
fennel (*Foeniculum*), 217, 218, **262,**
  269
fertilization, 429
fertilizer, 237–238, 429
Festuca rubra, 418
Ficus, 112, 159, **342, 355, 401**
figs, 112, **342, 355**
fire blight
  flowers damaged, **84,** 370
  leaves damaged, **45,** 349
  solutions, 301, 306
  stems damaged, **132, 392**
fir trees, 12, **395,** 428
flagging, **46,** 222–223, **348**
flame weeding, 221
flatheaded borers, **144,** 282
flea beetles, **53, 180,** 267, 276–277,
  284, **353**
flies. *See also* fly speck
  currant fruit, **125**
  fruit, **118, 386**
  hover, **260**
  husk, **196, 412**
  rust, **180**
  sawflies, **100, 125, 388**
  solutions, 215, 219, 265–267,
    273, 282, 284
  whiteflies, **50, 351**

floating row covers, 270–271, 328
flowering dogwood, **337**
flowering quince, **336**
flowers
  chewed, **72–76, 363–366**
  diagnosis of symptoms, 63–65
  discolored, **66–71, 360–362**
  distorted or stunted, **77–81,**
    262, **367–368**
  function of, 12–13, 62
  morphology, 61–62
  poor or failed, **86–92, 371–375**
  in vegetable gardens, 217
  wilted or rotten, **82–85,**
    369–370
flower thrips, **78,** 267
fly speck, **105,** 244, **379**
foamy bells, **353**
Foeniculum, 217, 218, **262,** 269
foliar nematodes, **41,** 314, 315, **345**
Foothill Agricultural Research,
  424
forsythia, 227
Four-D Rule, 223
Fragaria, 92, 126, **365, 372, 375,**
  428
Freedom Tree Farms, 424
fright tactics, 328–329
frost damage. *See also* cold injury
  to flowers, 70, 89, 92, 361
  flowers damaged, **373**
  in fruits, **98, 107**
  to leaves, **46,** 336, 347
  to plants, 21
  solutions, 232–233
  stems damaged, **147, 396**
fruit flies, **118,** 267, 282, **386**
fruits
  defined, 429
  diagnosis of symptoms, 95–96
  discolored, **97–98**
  distorted or shriveled, **115–**
    120, 384–386

environmental stress, **119**, 225
functions, 94
heavy crops, 119, 227, 228, **384, 396**
holes or cracks in, **110–114**
mushy, wormy, or moldy, **121– 125, 387–388**
spotted, **99–109, 377–380, 381–383**
structure, 93
fruitworms
    cherries and, **118, 125**, 267, 272, 282
    cranberries and, **118**, 267, 272, 282
    oranges and, **112**, 272, 282
    oriental, **112**, 272
    raspberries and, **107**, 272, 282, **363**
    solutions, 277–278
    tomatoes and, **111**, 267, 272, 282, **381**
fungi
    air-borne, 242, 244–252
    bracket, **157, 401**
    bulb, **171**
    on bulbs, tubers, corms, or rhizomes, 243–244, 257–258
    functions, 241–242
    leaves damaged, **39, 43, 54, 341, 346, 350**
    onions damaged, **166, 169, 172, 174, 187, 190**
    roots damaged, **170, 405**
    roses damaged (*See under* roses)
    shot hole, **100, 106**
    soil-borne, 243, 252–254
    solutions for, 246–252, 256–258
    sooty mold, 243, 254–257
    tomatoes damaged, **379**
    water management and, 246, 253
    wood-destroying, 243, 257
fungicides, 246–252, 256–257, 429

fusarium wilt
    solutions for air-borne varieties, 244–252
    solutions for soil-borne varieties, 252–254
    stems damaged, **18, 131, 218, 335, 389**
fusarium yellows, **80**

gall. *See also* Cooley spruce gall adelgids
    bladder gall mites, **56, 289, 295, 356**
    crown (*See* crown gall)
    defined, 430
    insects in, 266, 285, 288
    kinnikinnik leaf gall aphids, **56, 285, 356**
    leaf, **30**, 244, **340**
    leaves damaged, **57, 355**
    mossyrose, **56, 157**, 285, **356**
    solutions, 285
    spiny rose, **56**, 285, **356**
gall mites, 288
gall rust of pines, **155**, 245
Gardener's Supply Co., 424
gardenias, 237, **410**, 427
Gardens Alive!, 424
gastropods, 321
Gaultheria shallon, **242**, 338, 343, **346, 351**
genus, 430
geraniums, **361**
germination, 193, 430
girdling, **23**, 226
gladiolus, 218
gladiolus corm rot, **165**, 258
Glomerella, 427
gophers, **20**, 329
grafting, 127, 430
grape berry moths, **111**, 272, 282
grapes, 111, **120**, 227, 353, 357, **378, 387**

grasses, 12, **26**, 93, 418
grasshoppers
    flowers damaged, **76, 363**
    identification of, **264**, 265
    leaves damaged, **49, 52, 352**
    seeds damaged, **200**
    solutions, 267, 276
gray mold
    flowers damaged, **67, 69, 83, 361, 370**
    fruits damaged, **103, 123, 378, 387**
    leaves damaged, **18, 46, 246**
    solutions for air-borne varieties, 244–252
    solutions for soil-borne varieties, 252–254
    stems damaged, **132, 142, 335, 389, 393**
greenback, **97**, 233, **376**
green beans, 93, **94**, 95, 205, 215, 233, **380, 412, 415**
green lacewings, 219, **262**, 269
growing conditions
    cultural, 222–224
    defined, 212–213
    herbicide or pesticide damage, 226–227
    insect damage and, 268–273
    light conditions, 229
    management, 227–228
    mechanical damage, 225–226
    optimum, 208, 214
    poor, 224–225
    preventing problems, 215–222
    roots damaged, **176, 186**
    soil and nutrient management, 234–240
    temperature, 232–234
    water management, 229–231
    (*See also* water management)
growth cracks, **114**, 231, **381**
grubs, 107, 118, 121, 124, **177, 179**

Gurney's Seed & Nursery Co., 424

hail damage, **108**, 226
hardiness, 213, 430
Harmony Farm Supply, 424
Harris Seeds, 424
hazelnuts, 193
heart rot, **152**, 257, **400**
heat damage
  bolting, **88**, 234
  to roots and bulbs, **164**, **173**,
    234, **404**
  sulfur phytotoxicity, 30, 233–234
heavenly bamboo, 358
heavy fruit crop, 119, 227, 228,
  384, **396**
Hedera helix, **353**
Helleborus (hellebore), **352**
Hemiptera, 75, 263
hemlocks, 342, **402**
Henry Field's Seed & Nursery
  Co., 424
herbicide damage
  to flowers, **68**, **71**, **79**, **80**, **360**,
    367
  to leaves, **23**, **42**, **60**, 336, 357
  to plants, 226–227, **346**
  to stems, **149**, **399**
herbicides, 221, 430. *See also* herbicide damage
Heterorhabditis bacteriophora, 283
Heuchera, **352**
×*Heucherella*, **353**
hickory nuts, **199**
hickory shuckworms, **199**, 282
hickory trees, 280
Homoptera, 265–266
hollyhocks, **341**
honeydew, 243, 430
honeysuckles, **343**
horticultural oils, 279–280, 292, 296
host, 156, 430
hover flies, **260**
hoya, **355**

human-caused damage, 146, 228,
  329
humidity, **58**, 231, **357**
husk flies, **196**, 267, 273, 282, **412**
hybrids, 430
hydrangeas, **347**
Hydro-Gardens, Inc., 424
Hymenoptera, 263–264
Hypericum, **355**
hyphae, 241, 430
Hypochaeris radicata, **95**
hyssop, 218, 269

infection, 430
infestation, 430
inflorescence, 61, 430
insecticidal soaps, 256, 275–276,
  290–292, 430
insecticides, 273–282. *See also*
  insecticidal soaps
insects. *See also specific varieties*
  on above-ground plant parts,
    266–282
  functions, 259–262
  identifying, 262–266
  inside above-ground plant
    parts, 266, 282–284
  inside galls, 266, 285, 288
  seasonal variation, 218
  in the soil, 266, 284–285
internodes, 126, 430
Ipomoea, 160, **161**
iris, 161, **354**
iris borers, **179**, 284
iron deficiency, **24**, **32**, **43**, 238,
  336, **339**, **346**
iron phosphate, 326–327
irrigation. *See* water management
ivy geraniums, 246, **355**

Japanese beetle larvae, **20**, **180**,
  181, 284
Japanese beetles, **262**, **265**, 278–
  279, **365**

Japanese maples, **338**
Johnny's Selected Seeds, 420
Juglans, **199**, **380**, **412**, **414**
Juglans nigra, 280
juniper scale, **135**, **158**, 267, **401**
Juniperus, 12, **218**, **389**, 428
J. W. Jung Seed Co., 424

kale, **183**, 217
Kelly Nurseries, 424
Kentucky bluegrass, 418, 419
kinnikinnik leaf gall aphids, **56**,
  285, **356**
The Kinsman Co., Inc., 424
kohlrabi, 217

lace bugs, 37, **80**, 267, **342**, 368
Lactuca, 88, 234, 428
ladybird beetles, 219, **261**, 269
Lamiaceae, 218, 269
larvae, 259, 430
late blight, **108**, **170**, 244, **379**,
  406
Lathyrus latifolius, **95**
laurels, **351**
lavender, 217, 329, **393**
lawn care, 416–422
lawnmower damage, 133, 143,
  226, 331, **392**, **398**
leafcutter bees, **51**, 267, **350**
leaf gall, **30**, 244, **340**
leafhoppers, **35**, 37, **50**, 265–267,
  299, 300, **343**, **350**
leaflets, 430
leafminers, **40**, 267, 282, **345**
leaf nematodes, 314
leafrollers, **58**, 267, 282, **359**
leaf scorch, **31**, 231, **338**
leaf-spot. *See also* bacterial leaf-
  spot; physiological leaf-spot
  leaves damaged, **36**, **41**, **54**, **59**,
    242, **341**, **344**, **350**, **358**
  solutions, 224, 244
leafy mistletoe, **156**, 331, **403**

leaves
    blotches on, **41**, **344–345**
    bumps on, **55–57**, **355–356**
    chewed, **47–54**, **350–354**
    defined, **430**
    diagnosis of symptoms, 27–29
    discolored, **15**, **21–24**, **30–33**,
        336–340
    distorted, **58–60**, **357–359**
    functions, 26–27
    speckles on, **34–41**, **341–343**
    stripes on, **42–43**, **346**
    structure, 25–26, 27
    stunted, **60**
    wilted, **15–20**, **44–46**, **347–**
        349
lecanium scale, **135**, **158**, 267,
    391, **402**
legumes, 193
lemon balm, 218, 269
Lepidoptera, 264–265
lesions, 430
lettuce, 88, 234, 428
Liberty Seed Co., 424
lichens, **156**, 324, **403**
light
    excessive, 32, 229, **339**
    insufficient, 204, 229, 373, 374,
        415
lilac blight, **132**, 301
lilacs, 227, **300**, **339**, **341**, **343**,
    345, **346**, **348**
Lilium (lilies), 12, **62**
Lilium columbianum, **13**
lime, 430
lime-sulfur, 251–252
Lithodora, **373**
Lolium perenne, 418
Lonicera, **343**
lupines (*Lupinus*), **399**
Lycopersicon esculentum. *See*
    tomatoes

madrones, **345**

maggots
    apple, **125**, **272**, **388**
    blueberry, **125**
    cabbage, **180**
    fruits damaged, 118, 121, 125
    identification of, **263**
    onion, **180**
    root, **180**, **407**
    roots damaged, **177**, **179**, **180**
    solutions, 267, 273, 282, 284
    white, **198**
magnesium deficiency, **24**, **32**,
    239, **336**, **337**, **339**, **346**
magnolias, **371**
Mahonia, **339**
Malus. See apples
mammals, 324, 329–330
manganese deficiency
    leaves damaged, **24**, **32**, **43**,
        336, **339**, **346**
    seeds damaged, **196**, **412**
    solutions, 238
Mantis Manufacturing Corp.,
    424
maples
    bladder gall mites, **356**
    bracket fungus, **401**
    crown rot, **400**
    flowers of, 12
    in forests, **128**
    fruit of, 93, **95**
    papery bark, **133**
    scorch, **338**
    solutions, 280
    sooty bark disease, **138**
margin, 430
marigolds, 217, 317
mason bees, **228**, **261**
mealybug destroyers, 219, 269
mealybugs
    leaves damaged, **38**, **55**, **355**
    roots damaged, **179**, **182**
    solutions, 267
    stems damaged, **140**, **158**

mechanical damage
    to fruits, **108**, 226
    to leaves, **33**, **46**, **347**
    to plants, **18**, **334**
    to roots, **173**, **225–226**, **339**
    to stems, **146**, 226
Melia azedarach, 250, 279, 292
Mellinger's, Inc., 424
Meloidogyne, 314
melons, 120, **378**, **383**, **384**, **385**
Metaseiulus, 219
microclimates, 208, 430
midges, **60**, 267, **370**
milkweed, **95**, **340**, **364**
milkweed aphids, **141**, **150**, 267
milky spore, 278–279
J. E. Miller Nurseries, Inc., 424
Miltoniopsis, 249
mint family, 218, 269
minute pirate bugs, 219, 269
mites
    bladder gall, **56**, **289**, **295**, **356**
    blister, **39**, **57**, **289**, **343**, **356**
    bulb, **188**, **296**, **411**
    cyclamen, **78**
    dust, 287
    leaves damaged, **60**, **359**
    overview and functions,
        286–288
    predatory, 219, **432**
    redberry, **101**, **295**, **379**
    rust, 288
    solutions, 219, 288–297, 295
    spider, **37**, **286**, **343**
    Varoa, 287
miticides, 290, 296
mock orange, 227, **372**, **374**
moisture. *See* water management
mold. *See also* white mold
    bulb blue, **172**, **190**, **406**, **410**
    defined, **430**
    gray (*See* botrytis)
    saphrophytes, **242**
    solutions, 254–258

mold [*continued*]
    sooty, **30**, **98**, **104**, **340**, 432
mollicutes, 299, 430
monocotyledons (monocots), 12,
    357, 430
monoculture *vs.* polyculture, 216,
    246, 254, 430
mosaic virus, **97**, **102**, **117**, **309**,
    380, 430
mossyrose galls, **56**, **157**, 285, **356**
moth orchids, **369**
moths. *See also* codling moth lar-
    vae; pea moth larvae
    grape berry, **111**
    Nantucket pine tip, **134**, **145**
    oriental fruit, **131**, **134**
    overview, 264–265
    solutions, 272, 282–283
motion-activated sprinklers, 330
mottled leaves, **42**–**43**, 430
mountain ash, **370**
mowing, 420
mulching, 220–221, 236, 245–
    246, 430
mummy, 431
mustard, **183**
mycelium, 241, 431
mycorrhizae, 235–236, 242, 431
Myrothecium verrucaria, 320

Nandina, **358**
Nantucket pine tip moths, **134**,
    145, 282
Narcissus, 161, 218, 234, **258**, **296**,
    371, **405**, **410**, **411**
narcissus bulb fly, **180**, 284
The Natural Gardening Co., 424
Nature's Control, 424
navel orange worms, **112**, 272,
    282
necrosis, 431
neem, 250, 279, 292
nematicides, 320

nematodes
    beneficial, 219, 269, 283
    bud, 314
    foliar, **41**, **345**
    leaf, 314
    leaves damaged, **41**
    overview and functions,
        313–314
    phlox, **149**
    plant parasitic, **314**, **315**
    root-knot, **16**, **191**, 217, 314, **315**
    roots damaged, **174**, **184**, **186**
    solutions, 315–320
    stems damaged, **149**
nets, 328
Nichols Garden Nursery, 425
nightshades, 217
nitrogen, defined, 431
nitrogen, excess, **86**, **90**, 239, **372**
nitrogen deficiency, 24, **32**, **43**,
    239, **337**, **339**, **346**
noble firs, **26**
nodes, 431
non-flowering plants, 12
North Star Gardens, 425
Nosema locustae, 276
NPK, 431
nucleic acid, 431
nutrient management
    bitter pit and, **109**, 239
    blossom end rot and, **104**, 239
    boron deficiency, **173**, 240
    cavity spots and, **178**, 240
    flowers damaged, **372**
    fruits damaged, **119**, **384**
    iron deficiency, 24, **32**, **43**, 238,
        336, **339**, **346**
    leaves damaged, **87**, **90**
    magnesium deficiency, 24, **32**,
        239, **336**, **337**, **339**, **346**
    manganese, 24, **32**, **43**, 196, 238
    manganese deficiency (*See*
        manganese deficiency)

nitrogen deficiency, 24, **32**, **43**,
    239, **337**, **339**, **346**
nitrogen excess, **86**, **90**, 239,
    372
phosphorus deficiency, **204**,
    240
potassium deficiency, **164**,
    239–240
roots damaged, **186**, 225
salt burn, **31**, 238
salt damage, **17**, 238
nutrients, defined, 431
nuts
    hazelnuts, 193
    hickory, **199**
    navel orange worms in, 112
    pecan, **199**, **201**
    as seeds, 193 (*See also* seeds and
        seedlings)
    walnuts, **199**, 280, **380**, **412**, **414**
nut weevils, **199**, **413**

oaks, 12, **128**, 138, 285, **400**, **403**
obligate pathogens, 230, 431
Ohio Earth Food, Inc., 425
old age, **32**, 70, 222–224, **340**, **361**
oleander aphids, **141**, **150**, 267
OMRI (Organic Materials
    Review Institute), 209, 273,
    290
One Green World, 425
onions
    daylength effects, **186**
    fungus diseases, **166**, **169**, **172**,
        174, **187**, **190**, 244, 252
    fusarium basal rot, **166**, **172**,
        174, **190**, 252
    heat or cold damage, **164**, 234,
        404
    insect damage, **180**, 284
    maggots on, **180**, 284
    nematode damage, **406**
    pH balance and, 237

pink root, **166**, **187**, 252
roots of, **161**
seedstalk formation, **185**
smudge, **169**, 244
oranges, 93
orchids (Orchidaceae)
aerial roots, 159, **160**
bees and, 62
ethylene and, 85, 224
as flowering plants, 12
flowers damaged, **369**
pseudobulbs, 126, **128**
wilting, 224
Orcon Organic Control, Inc., 425
Oregon grape, **339**
organic fertilizers, 431
Organic Materials Review Institute (OMRI), 209, 273, 290
organic matter, 431
organic mulch, 431
organs, defined, 431
oriental fruit moths, **131**, **134**, 282
oriental fruit worms, **112**, 272
ornamental cabbage, **371**
ornamental grasses, 93
Orol Ledden & Sons, 425
Orthoptera, 265
Oryza sativa, 93
overcrowding, **186**, **225**
overwatering, **21**, **32**, **91**, **114**, **204**, 232, **336**, **339**, **374**, **381**, **415**
overwinter, 269, 431
oyster scale, **135**, 267, **401**

Pacific dogwood, **26**
palms, 12
pansy, 62, **216**, **361**
pansy orchids, 249
Papaver, 93
paper bags, 272
papery bark, **133**, 244, **390**
parasitic plants, 331
parasitic wasps, **262**

parasitoids, 219, 269
Park Seed Co., 425
parsley, 218, 269
pathogens, 242–243, 299, 431
Peaceful Valley Farm Supply, 425
peaches
fruits damaged, 94, **378**, **380**, **385**, **387**
heavy fruit crop damage, **213**
leaf curl, **59**, 244, **358**
leaves damaged, **340**, **358**
seeds of, 193
solutions, 234
stems damaged, **391**, **394**, **396**
peachtwig borers, **131**, **134**, 282, **391**
pea moth larvae, **201**, 283
pears
canker, **139**, 244
flowers damaged, **370**
fruits damaged, **100**, 109
leaves damaged, **338**, **343**, **356**
midges, **118**, 267, 282
plant damaged, **335**
solutions, 234
stems damaged, **392**
stony pit virus, **116**, 309
peas, 218
pecan borers, **144**, 282
pecan nut casebearers, **201**, 283
pecan shuckworms, **199**, 282
pecan trees, **199**, **201**
Pelargonium, 246, **355**, **361**
peppers, 120, 193, 217, 233, **385**
perennial ryegrass, 418
perennials, 218, 318, 431
perennial sweet pea, **95**
Persea, **213**, **336**
pesticide damage, **68**, **71**, 226, **360**
pesticides, 431
pest-resistant plants, 215–216
pests, defined, 431
petiole, 25, 431

petunias, **364**
Phalaenopsis, 224, **369**
Phaseolus, 12, **335**, **413**
Phaseolus vulgaris, 93, **94**, 205, 215, 233, **380**, **412**, **415**
pH balance, 237–239, 253–254, 431
pheromone traps, 273–275, 431
Philadelphus, 227, **372**, **374**
philodendrons, 159
phloem, 126, 431
phlox nematodes, **149**, 315
Phoradendron, **156**, 331
phosphorus deficiency, **204**, 240
photinias, 224, **341**, **354**
photosynthesis, 11, 26, **27**
physiological leaf-spot, 35, 222, **224**, 341. *See also* bacterial leaf-spot; leaf-spot
phytophthora root rot, **142**, **151**, 230, 236, 252, **393**
Phytoseiulus, 219
phytotoxicity, **30**, 233–234, 247, 431
Picea, 12, **141**, **395**, **399**, 428
Picea pungens, 280
Pinetree Garden Seeds, 425
pine trees, 12, **145**, **155**, 224, 428
Pinus sylvestris, **13**
pistils, 431
Pisum, 218
placement of plants, 215, 246
planting times, **89**, 218, **371**
plant parasite nematodes, 314, 315
plant reproduction, 12
Plants of the Southwest, 425
plant spacing, 219
plum curculios, **92**, **110**, **118**, **124**, 267, 276–277, **375**, **381**
plume trees, 280
plums, 193, 301, **353**, **373**, **387**, **388**, **396**, **403**
Poa annua, **26**

Poaceae, 418
Poa pratensis, 418
pollen, 431
pollination
 defined, 431
 ecology, 62
 in orchids, 85, **369**
 poor, **117**, 227–228, **384**
 unwanted, 224
polyculture *vs.* monoculture, 216,
 246, 254, 432
poppy, 93
Populus (poplar), 341
potassium bicarbonate, 248
potassium deficiency, **164**, 239
potatoes
 bacterial ring rot, **165**, 175–176,
 188, 305, **404**, 406, **411**
 bacterial rot, **306**
 beetles, **353**
 cavity spot, 240
 crop rotations, 217
 gangrene, **175**
 growing conditions, 225
 irregular watering, **185**, **409**
 late blight, **170**, **406**
 roots of, **161**
 silver scurf, **168**
 solutions, 245, 252–253, 257–
 258, 266, 270, 284, 305
 spraing, **175**, **184**
 tuberworms, **179**, 284, **408**
potato scab, **405**
pothos, 26, **339**
potting soil, 236
powdery mildew
 defined, 432
 flowers damaged, 67, 77, **361**
 fruits damaged, **98**, **102**
 leaves damaged, 36, **59**, 341,
 357
 solutions, 244–252
praying mantises, 219, 269

predatory mites, 219, 432
pre-emergent herbicides, 221, 432
prevention, 208, 214, 215–222,
 268, 288–289
prokaryotes, 432
proliferation, **79**, 233, **367**
prop roots, 159
pruning, **89**, 219, **220**, 222–223,
 227–228, **371**, 432
Prunus
 aerial crown gall, **403**
 bacterial leaf-spot, **388**
 brown rot, 69, 83, 108, **362**, **387**
 earwigs, **351**
 fire blight, **370**
 irregular watering, **396**
 plum curculios, 92
 shot hole fungus, **100**
 solutions, 301
 winter chill, **373**
Prunus avium
 black knot, **401**
 brown rot, **390**
 canker, **393**, **394**
 fire blight, **349**
 fruits of, 94
 skeletonizers, **350**
 solutions, 232
 witches' broom, **399**
Prunus cerasifera, **260**, **353**, **390**
Prunus laurocerasus, 224
Prunus persica
 bacterial spots, **380**
 borers, **340**
 brown rot, **385**, **387**
 canker, **394**
 fruits of, 94
 heavy fruit crop, **213**
 irregular watering, **396**
 peachleaf curl, **358**
 peachtwig borer, **391**
 seeds of, 193
 solutions, 234

tarnished plant bugs, **379**
Pseudomonas syringae, **300**, 427
Pseudotsuga menziesii, **141**, **150**,
 336, **339**, **397**
psyllids, **58**, 265–266, 267, 299,
 358
pumpkins, **383**
purple cone flowers, **260**
purpleleaf plum, **260**, **390**
pyracantha, **370**
pyrethrin, 256–257, 281–282, 294
Pyrethrum, 256, 281, 294
Pyrus
 bacterial infection, **335**
 bitter rot, 109
 blister mites, **343**, **356**
 European apple sawfly, **100**
 fire blight, **370**, **392**
 papery bark, **390**
 pear stony pit virus, 116
 solutions, 234
 sulfur phytotoxicity, **338**
Pythium, 230, 236

quarantined plants, 216, 288
Queen Anne's lace, **360**
Quercus, 12, **128**, 285, **400**, **403**
quince, **370**

rabbits, **20**, **200**, 329
raccoons, **203**, 329
radishes, **183**, **408**
Raintree Nursery, 425
Raphanus, **408**
raspberries, 92, 119, **131**, 237, **387**
raspberry cane borers, 282, **391**
raspberry cane spot, **137**, 244
raspberry fruitworms, **107**, 272,
 282, **363**
redberry mites, **101**, **295**, **379**
red fescue, 418
redwood trees, 428
repellents, 330

resistant cultivars, 215, 253, 432
Rhizobium, 299
Rhizoctonia, 236
rhizomes, 127, 432
rhododendrons
    borers, **144**, 282
    deadheading, **371**
    defined, 427
    flowers of, 12
    frost damage, **373**
    fungus infection, **350**
    lace bugs, **342**, **368**
    leaf gall, **340**
    mechanical damage, **347**
    nitrogen deficiency, **346**
    pesticide or herbicide damage,
        360, **367**
    poor nutrition, **372**
    solutions, 219, 224, 237
    sunburn, **344**
    weevils, **351**
rice, 93
Richters, 425
Rincon-Vitova Insectaries, Inc.,
    425
RNA, 308, 431
rockroses, **366**
rodents
    fruits damaged, **113**, **382**
    roots damaged, **20**, **181**, **398**, **408**
    seeds damaged, **200**, **203**
    solutions, 329–330
    stems damaged, **133**, **143**
root aphids, **182**, **191**, 284
rootbound plants, **20**, 227, **334**
root gall, **191**, 305
root-knot nematodes, **16**, **191**, 217,
    314, **315**
root maggots, **180**, 284, **407**
root mealybugs, **182**, **191**, 284
root rot
    armillaria, **19**, **140**, **157**,
        252–254

phytophthora, **142**, **151**, 230,
    236, 252, **393**
    roots damaged, **164**, **168**, **189**,
        243, **404**, **405**, **410**
    solutions, 252–254
roots and bulbs
    chewed, with holes or cracks,
        177–182, **407–408**
    diagnosis of symptoms,
        161–166
    discolored, **164–176**, **404–406**
    distorted, stunted, or shriveled,
        183–187, **409**
    function, 160–161
    moldy or rotten, **188–190**,
        410–411
    structures, 159, **160**
root vegetables, 217
root weevil larvae, **20**, 284
rootworms, corn, **181**, **197**, 284
Rosa. See roses
rose family, 84, 370
rosemary (*Rosmarinus*), 217, 218,
    269, 329, **373**
roses
    aphids, **363**, **401**
    balling, **369**
    botrytis, **389**
    canker and dieback, **132**, **138**,
        348, **389**, **393**, **394**
    caterpillars, **364**
    curculios, **92**, **363**, **375**
    deer damage, **354**, **366**
    disease resistance, **209**, 215
    fire blight, **370**
    frost damage, **347**, **361**
    gall, **356**, **392**, **402**
    herbicide damage, **346**, **367**,
        399
    iron deficiency, **346**
    leafcutter bees, **350**
    leafrollers, **359**
    midges, **84**, 267, **370**

powdery mildew, **357**
pruning, 219, **220**
rust, **341**
solutions, 244, **262**, 267, 276–
    277, 285, **289**
thrips, **368**
virus infections, **309**
rosy apple aphids, **116**, 267, **386**
rot. *See also* root rot
    bacterial ring, **165**, **175–176**,
        188, **189**, 305, **404**, **406**, **411**
    black, **105**, **120**, **121**, 244, **378**,
        387
    blossom end, **104**, **239**, **378**
    brown (*See* brown rot)
    bulb, **172**, **189**, **405**, **410**
    crown, **142**, **151**, **189**, 252–254,
        393, **400**, **410**
    dahlia tuber, **165**, **190**, 258
    defined, 432
    gladiolus corm, **165**, 258
    heart, **152**, 257, **400**
    onions and, **166**, **172**, **174**, **190**,
        252
    potatoes and, **165**, **175**, 305,
        404
    soft, **170**, **189**, 305, 427
    stem, **151**, 252, **400**
rotation of plants, 217, 254
row covers, 270–271, 328
Rubus
    blister beetles, **365**
    botrytis, **378**
    bud weevil, 92
    herbicide damage, **336**
    leafhoppers, **343**
    raspberry fruitworms, **107**, **363**
    redberry mites, **101**, **379**
    strawberry bud weevil, **375**
Rubus idaeus, 92, 237, **387**, **391**
Rudbeckia, 217, **363**
Rumex, **345**
russeting, **106**, **224**, **377**, 432

rust
    cedar-apple, **101, 117, 153,** 244, **379, 385**
    defined, 432
    gall, **155,** 245
    leaves damaged, **36, 38, 57, 355**
    plants damaged, **341**
    solutions, 244–252
    stems damaged, **139, 146**
rust flies, **180,** 284
rust mites, 288

Saccharum officinarum, 127
safety considerations, 209–211, 247, 274, 291
sage, 217, 329
Saintpaulia, **63**
salal, **242, 338, 343, 346, 351**
Salix, 355
salt burn, **31,** 238, **338**
salt damage, **17,** 238, **335**
Salvia, 217, 329
sanitizing plants, 245, 252, 268, 289, 432
San Jose scale, **101, 135, 158,** 267, **401**
sap beetles, **202,** 283
saprophytes, 242, 299, 432
sapsuckers, **145, 328, 398**
sawflies, **100, 125,** 282, **388**
sawfly larvae, **48,** 267, **350**
scab
    defined, 432
    fruits damaged, **106, 114, 116, 379, 381, 385**
    pH and, 237
    roots damaged, **171, 405**
    solutions for air-borne varieties, 244–252
    solutions for soil-borne varieties, 252–254
    stems damaged, **138, 394**

scale
    cottony, **38, 55, 140, 158, 355**
    defined, 432
    juniper, **135, 158, 401**
    leaves damaged, **342**
    lecanium, **135, 158, 391, 402**
    oyster, **135, 401**
    San Jose, **101, 135, 158, 401**
    solutions, 265–267
    stems damaged, **260**
scarify, 432
Schedonorus phoenix, 418
scorch, **33,** 161, 231, **338,** 432. *See also* leaf scorch
Scots pine, **13**
scurf, **168,** 252
seedcorn beetles, **197,** 284
seeds and seedlings
    chewed or missing, **200–203, 414**
    diagnosis of symptoms, **194–195**
    discolored, distorted, or shriveled, **196, 412**
    flowers and, 61–62
    fruits and, 93–94, **95**
    functions, 12–13, 193–194
    holes or lack of germination, **197–199, 413**
    poor growth, **204–205, 415**
    structure, 192
Seeds Blüm, 425
seedstalk formation, **185,** 229
seed weevils, **199,** 283, **413**
sepals, **62,** 432
Sequoia, 428
serviceberry, **339**
shade, **87, 90, 91,** 229, 373, **374**
sheet mulches, 221
Shepherd's Garden Seeds, 425
shot hole borers, **144,** 282, 432
shot hole fungus, **100, 106,** 244
shriveled growth
    fruits, **115–120, 384–386**

roots and bulbs, **183–187, 409**
seeds and seedlings, **196, 412**
shrubs. *See* stems
shuckworms, **199,** 282
skeletonizers, **35, 40, 54,** 267, 282, **342, 345, 350**
slime flux, **152,** 305, 306, **400**
slugs and snails
    flowers damaged, **72, 75, 366**
    fruits damaged, **110, 383**
    habits of, 322, **323**
    leaves damaged, **48, 53, 354**
    roots damaged, **178, 408**
    seeds damaged, **198**
    solutions, 321, 325–328
Smith & Hawken, 425
smoke trees, 280
smut, **135, 154, 196,** 244, 432
snow damage, 146, 228
sodium bicarbonate, 248
soft rot, **170, 189,** 305, 427
soil management. *See also* nutrient management
    acid soils, 222, 237, 239, 240, 250, 427
    alkaline soils, 237, 239, 240, 427
    amendments, 427
    botrytis, 243, 252–254
    compacted or rocky, 18, **184,** 240, **409,** 428
    composting, 235–236
    fertilizer, 237–238
    fungi and, 243, 252–254
    fusarium wilt, 252–254
    insects, 266, 284–285
    mulching, 220–221, 236, 245–246
    pH, **205,** 237–239
    potting soil, 236
    sterilizing or solarizing, 236–237, 432
Solanum melongena, 193, 233

Solanum tuberosum
    bacterial ring rot, 175–176, 188, **404, 406, 411**
    bacterial rot, **306**
    beetles, **353**
    irregular watering, **185**
    leaves damaged, **353**
    potato gangrene, **175**
    potato spraing, **175, 184**
    roots of, **161**
    scab, **405**
    solutions, 237, 257–258
    tuberworms, **408**
solarizing soils, 236, **432**
sooty mold, **30, 98, 104,** 254–257, **340, 432**
Southern Exposure Seed Exchange, 425
Southmeadow Fruit Gardens, 425
spacing of plants, 219
species, **432**
spider mites, **37,** 219, **286,** 288, 290, **343**
spiders, 218–219, 269
spinach, 88, 234
Spinacia, 88
spiny rose galls, **56, 285, 356**
spittlebugs, **74, 75, 154,** 267, **364, 402**
spores, 12, **432**
spot
    bacterial (*See* bacterial leaf-spot)
    black, **36,** 244, **245, 341**
    cavity, **178,** 240
    coral, **132,** 244, **390**
    leaf (*See* leaf-spot)
    raspberry cane, **137,** 244
spruce trees, 12, **141, 395, 399,** 428
squash bugs, **75, 264,** 267, **363**
squash vine borers, **144,** 282
squirrels, **203,** 329, **414**
stamens, 61, **432**

Stark Bro's Nurseries & Orchards Co., 425
Steinernema carpocapsae, 283
stem rot, **151,** 252, **400**
stems
    chewed, or with holes, cracks, **143–147, 396–398**
    diagnosis of symptoms, **128–130**
    discolored, dying, or dead, **128–135, 389–392**
    distorted or stunted, 148–150, **399**
    functions, 127–128
    lumpy or with pests, **153, 401–403**
    mechanical damage, **146**
    moldy, rotten, or slimy, **152, 400**
    spotted, **136–142, 393–395**
    structures, 126–127
Stenotaphrum secundatum, 418
sterilizing soils, 236–237, **432**
sterilizing tools, 221–222
sticky traps, 271–272, **432**
stigma, **62, 432**
stink bugs, **75, 101,** 267
St. Augustine grass, 418
St. John's wort, **355**
Stokes Seeds, Inc., 425
stolons, 126, **432**
stonefruits, 69, 83, 92, **100,** 108, **362, 370**
strawberries, 92, 126, **365, 372,** 428
strawberry bud weevils, **92,** 267, 276–277, **375**
strawberry root weevils, **181,** 284
Strelitzia nicolai, **375**
Streptomyces griseus, 299–300
stress, **432**
stunted growth
    of flowers, **77–81,** 262, **367–368**
    of leaves, **60**

    of roots and bulbs, **183–187, 409**
    of stems, **148–150, 399**
style, **62, 433**
stylet, **433**
sugar cane, 127
sulfur, 250–251, 281, 294
sulfur phytotoxicity, **30,** 233–234, **338**
sunburn, **40, 104, 229, 343**
sunlight exposure to roots, **169,** 229, **406**
sunscald
    flowers damaged, **67, 360**
    fruits damaged, **103, 377**
    roots damaged, **169**
    solutions, 229
    stems damaged, **139, 147**
superior oils, 279–280, 292, 296, **433**
sweet potatoes, 160, **161**
sweet potato weevils, **180,** 284
sycamore maple sooty bark disease, **138,** 245
symptoms
    defined, **433**
    flowers chewed, **72–76, 363–366**
    flowers discolored, **66–71, 360–362**
    flowers distorted or stunted, **77–81,** 262, **367–368**
    flowers poor or failed, **86–92, 371–375**
    flowers wilted or rotten, **82–85, 369–370**
    fruits discolored, **97–98**
    fruits distorted or shriveled, **115–120, 384–386**
    fruits mushy, wormy, or moldy, **121–125, 387–388**
    fruits spotted, **99–109, 377–380**

symptoms [*continued*]

fruits with holes or cracks, 110–114, **381–383**

leaves chewed, **47–54**, **350–354**

leaves discolored, **15**, **21–24**, **30–33**, **336–340**

leaves distorted, **58–60**, **357–359**

leaves speckled, **34–41**, **341–343**

leaves striped, **42–43**, 346

leaves wilted, **15–20**, **44–46**, **347–349**

leaves with blotches, 41, **344–345**

leaves with bumps, **55–57**, **355–356**

plant wilted, **15–20**

roots chewed, with holes or cracks, **177–182**, **407–408**

roots discolored, **164–176**, **404–406**

roots distorted, stunted, or shriveled, **183–187**, **409**

roots moldy or rotten, **188–190**, **410–411**

seedlings grow poorly, **204–205**, **415**

seeds chewed or missing, **200–203**, **414**

seeds discolored, distorted, or shriveled, **196**, **412**

seeds have holes or did not germinate, **197–199**, **413**

stems chewed, or with holes, cracks, **143–147**, **396–398**

stems discolored, dying, or dead, **128–135**, **389–392**

stems distorted or stunted, **148–150**, **399**

stems lumpy or with pests, 153, **401–403**

stems moldy, rotten, or slimy, **152**, **400**

stems spotted, **136–142**, **393–395**

stunted growth, **16**, **60**

Syringa, 227, 300, 339, 341, 343, 345, 346, 348

syrphids, **260**

systemic, 433

Tagetes, 217

tall fescue, 418

Taraxacum officinale, 93, 94, 95, **227**

tarnished plant bugs, **106**, 267

Taxus, **359**

temperatures. *See also* frost damage; heat damage

balling, **83**, 369

flowers damaged, **88**, 373

greenback, **97**, 376

proliferation, **79**, 367

solutions, 232–234

winter chill, **90**, 371, 373

winter desiccation, **33**, 339

tender, defined, 433

Territorial Seed Co., 425

thimbleberries, **363**, 365

thinning, defined, 433

Thompson & Morgan, Inc., 425

Three-Protection Regulations, 223

thrips

citrus, **97**, **102**

flowers damaged, **71**, **78**, **362**, **368**

identification of, 265

leaves damaged, 37

solutions, 267

Thuja, 224

Thuja occidentalis, **334**, 335

Thuja plicata, **27**, 348

thyme (*Thymus*), 217, 218, 269, 329

Thysanoptera, 265

tickseed, **334**

timing of planting, **89**, 205, 218, 233

tissue, defined, 433

tissue damage, **44**

tissue death, **44**

tobacco mosaic viruses, 307

tolerant, defined, 433

tomatillo, 217

tomatoes

bacterial diseases, **380**, **388**

blossom end rot, **378**

excess nitrogen, **372**

fruit or vegetable? **94**

fruitworms, **111**, 267, 272, 282, **381**

fungus diseases, **379**

greenback, **376**

growing conditions, 205, **384**

insufficient light, **374**

late blight, **379**

pest resistance, 215

rotation schedules, 217

russeting, **377**

seeds of, 193, **194**

solutions, 232–233

structure, **93**

sunscald, **377**

tools, 221–222, 303

topdressing, 220, 245–246, 433

transplant shock, **17**, **86**, 231, **371**

traps, 330

trees, **22**, **23**, 218, 226, 336. *See also* stems; *specific varieties*

Trichogramma wasps, 219, 269

Trifolium repens, 418

true bugs, 75, 263

trunks. *See* stems

Tsuga, **398**, **402**

tubers, 127, 257–258, 433

tuberworms, potato, **179**, 284, **408**

tulip fire, **171**, 245

tulips (*Tulipa*), 161, 218, 234, **243**, **405**, **406**, **410**

tumors, 433

twig girdlers, **131**, 282

twig pruners, **131**, 282
two-lined chestnut borer, **134**, **144**
two-spotted spider mites, **286**, 288

Ulmus, **392**, **398**
The Urban Farmer Store, 425

Vaccinium, 93, 237, 427
variety, 433
Varoa mites, 287
vascular, 433
vectors, 433
vegetables, 433. *See also* fruits; *specific varieties*
verticillium wilt, **18**, **46**, 244, 252, **335**, **348**
viburnums, 334, 337, 347, 350, 357, 358, 368, 397
vine maple, **26**
Viola, 62, **63**, **216**, 361
viruses
    defined, 433
    flowers damaged, **68**, **71**
    leaves damaged, **23**, **42**, **60**, 337, **346**, 359
    overview and functions, 307–308
    solutions, 309–312
    stems damaged, **399**
Vitis, 111, **120**, 227, 353, 357, 378, 387

walnut blight, **196**, 301, **412**
walnuts, 199, 280, **380**, **412**, **414**
wasps, 113, 263–264, 267, **381**
water management
    drip-trickle systems, 230
    excessive, **21**, **32**, **91**, **114**, **204**, 232, **336**, 339, 374, 381, 415

fungi and, 246, 253
insufficient (*See* drought)
irregular, **59**, **147**, **177**, **185**, 231–232, **396**, **407**, 409
transplant shock and, 231
watermelons, **400**
weak forks, 146, 228
weather problems, **205**
weed-eater damage, 133, **143**, 226, 331
weeding, 221
weevils
    black vine, **181**
    carrot, **180**
    flowers damaged, **76**, **92**, 363
    identification of, 262, **263**
    leaves damaged, **49**, **51**, 351
    nut, **199**, **413**
    root, **20**
    seed, **199**, **413**
    solutions, 267, 276–277, 282–284
    strawberry bud, **92**, **375**
    strawberry root, **181**
    sweet potato, **180**
    white pine, **150**
western red cedar, **27**, **348**
Westgro Sales, Inc. and Agrico Sales, Ltd., 425
white clover, 418
whiteflies, **50**, 215, 219, 265–266, 267, **351**
white-fringed beetle larvae, **180**, 284
white grubs, **197**, 284
white maggots, **198**, 282
white mold
    fruits damaged, **103**, 378
    solutions for air-borne varieties, 244–252
    solutions for soil-borne varieties, 252–254

stems damaged, **19**, **142**, **152**
white pine weevils, **150**, 282
willows, 355
wilt. *See also* fusarium wilt
    cucurbit bacterial, **120**, 306, **386**
    defined, 433
    ethylene and, 224
    flowers wilted or rotten, 82–85, 369–370
    leaves wilted, limp, or droopy, **15–20**, **44–46**, 347–349
    plant wilted, **15–20**, 334–335
    verticillium, **18**, **46**, 244, 252, **335**, 348
wind damage, 146, 228
winter chill, **90**, 234, **371**, **373**
winter desiccation, **33**, 233, 339
wireworms, **179**, **181**, **197**, 284, **407**
witches' broom, **149**, 309, 399, 433
woodpeckers, **144**, **398**
woolly aphids, **140**, **158**, 267

Xanthomonas campestris, 427
xylem, 126, 433

yarrow, **63**, 217, 269, **364**
yellowjackets, **113**, **264**, 267, **381**
yellows, 77, 78, **80**, **186**, 261, 306, 433
yews, 359

Zea mays. See corn
zelkova, **391**
zinnias, **335**
zoysia grass (*Zoysia*), 418
zucchini, 93, **363**
zygotes, 433